D0983451

The German Aces Speak

The German Aces Speak

World War II Through the Eyes
of Four of the Luftwaffe's Most
Important Commanders

Colin D. Heaton and Anne-Marie Lewis

ZENITH PRESS

Quarto is the authority on a wide range of topics.

Quarto educates, entertains and enriches the lives of our readers—enthusiasts and lovers of hands-on living.

www.quartoknows.com

© 2011 Quarto Publishing Group USA Inc.
Text © 2011 Colin D. Heaton and Anne-Marie Lewis

First published in 2011 by Zenith Press, an imprint of Quarto Publishing Group USA Inc., 400 First Avenue North, Suite 300, Minneapolis, MN 55401 USA. Telephone: (612) 344-8100 Fax: (612) 344-8692

quartoknows.com
Visit our blogs at quartoknows.com

Zenith Press titles are also available at discounts in bulk quantity for industrial or sales-promotional use. For details write to Special Sales Manager at Quarto Publishing Group USA Inc., 400 First Avenue North, Suite 300, Minneapolis, MN 55401 USA.

ISBN-13: 978-0-7603-4115-5

10 9 8 7 6 5

Digital edition published in 2011

eISBN: 978-1-610597-48-7

Library of Congress Cataloging-in-Publication Data

Heaton, Colin D.
The German aces speak : World War II through the eyes of four of the Luftwaffe's most important commanders / Colin D. Heaton and Anne-Marie Lewis.
   p. cm.
Includes bibliographical references and index.
ISBN 978-0-7603-4115-5 (hb w/ jkt)
   1. World War, 1939-1945—Aerial operations, German. 2. Germany. Luftwaffe—Officers—Biography. 3. Fighter pilots—Germany—Biography. 4. Fighter pilots—Germany—Interviews. 5. Fighter plane combat—Psychological aspects. 6. World War, 1939–1945—Personal narratives, German. I. Lewis, Anne-Marie. II. Title.
   D787.H3216 2011
   940.54'49430922—dc23
                              2011018239

Design Manager: Brenda C. Canales
Designer: Helena Shimizu

All photographs are from the author's collection unless noted otherwise.
On the cover: Messerschmitt 109 G-6, circa February/March 1944, Bundesarchiv, Bild 101I-662-6659-37, *photo: Hebenstreit*; portraits, left to right: Falck, *Courtesy of Lubomir Copjan*; Galland, Adolf Galland; Krupinski, *Author's collection*; Neumann, *Eduard Neumann*
On the back cover: (top) Messerschmitt Me-109s in flight over Germany, late July 1944. *Bundesarchiv,Bild 101I-676-7974-13, photo: Keiner.* (Bottom) Pilot in the open cockpit of a Messerschmitt Me-109. *Bundesarchiv, Bild 101I-607-1846-02A, photo:Väth*

Printed in the United States of America

Certain proceeds from the sale of this book will support the Wounded Warrior Project and the Volksbund Deutsche Kriegsgräberfürsorge e.V.

This book is dedicated to the memories of those airmen mentioned within these pages who have now left us, especially Col. Raymond F. Toliver, USAF, who started me on this path.

Contents

Foreword

Jon Guttman

WHEN MY PATH FIRST CROSSED COLIN HEATON'S in the 1990s, I was editing for *Military History and World War II* magazines, both of which published interviews from veterans. Until I came along, the veterans interviewed were primarily American, but from my own previous ramblings, I contributed a few changes of pace, such as a Persian who volunteered for the French air service and flew bombers during World War I, a Japanese artillery officer from the Guadalcanal campaign, and an Italian fighter pilot who had seen action over North Africa and Malta. To those unique examples, Colin turned up with a veritable omnibus of firsthand accounts that he'd managed to amass from meeting some of the most prominent, famous, and notorious warriors who served the Third Reich.

My job was to edit Colin's manuscripts, which were as "raw" as they should have been, into a readable style for our subscribers. In the process, I occasionally had to tone down questions that often reflected the interviewer's awe at being able to converse with "legendary" characters such as Adolf Galland, Hajo Herrmann, and Erich Hartmann, making them more down to earth. He got to see the re-edits, and often so did a lot of the interviewees. Eventually that led to my tagging along on two of Colin's trips to World War II veterans' reunions in Europe and meeting some of his Luftwaffe acquaintances myself.

I have to admit that I was rather impressed with the *flieger* I met. Allowing for the environment in which they were raised, and the indoctrination that attended their education at every turn during the Third Reich, they were intelligent and professional—and expected as much from the journalists who interviewed them. This included an insistence on getting the story straight, as they remembered it, that could be as exacting as any stylebook. One particularly intense experience involved the publication of Colin's interview with former bomber and *Wilde Sau* night-fighting mastermind Hajo Herrmann, who upon checking the first edit I sent him, found a lot of items that Colin misinterpreted or misconstrued, or were simply in need of expounding. After a series of transatlantic phone calls and faxes, the article that finally appeared in *World War II* was considerably different from the original manuscript, but our readers found it as fascinating as Herr Herrmann found it satisfactory!

In the course of publishing his stories in magazines, Colin polished his style and kept on recording the memories of a generation of warriors who are now vanishing rapidly. This first volume of *Voices of World War II* shows the fruit of his experience while essentially leaving the words of the airmen as originally voiced—edited with a far lighter touch than they had been, so as to be left fundamentally unrefined and "as is" for posterity. This is as it should be, for these are men who must, for better or worse, be judged on their own merits. And taken apart from the cause to which they were committed—the folly and evil of which so many of them came to recognize before it was over—the reader will find merits aplenty in these old soldiers of the sky.

Brigadier General Robin Olds, USAF (Ret.)

As a fighter pilot in two wars, I suppose I have the unique distinction in the minds of many of being one of the first combat pilots to fly fighters from the piston engine to the jet age. However, this would be untrue. It was the German pilots of the Luftwaffe who broke that barrier. I have had the pleasure of knowing a few German pilots from World War II, most notably the late Adolf Galland, a man I respected and admired for many reasons.

Galland and a handful of selected young Germans took to the skies to serve their nation, not a political agenda. Most of these men were never involved in politics, and none that I knew even supported the political ideology of their nation or its leadership. That being said, I think that the time has come to place these men, as one must place all warriors, into the proper perspective. They were men serving their nation and doing their job. Nothing less.

What I did experience firsthand was the caliber of these pilots. You had to be sharp, and on your game, or you would be killed. Colin Heaton's expert interviewing methods have brought these stories and these men back to life. The hardships they endured as pilots I can readily comprehend, as those are universal. However, what is beyond my experience, thank God, was their struggle against their own leadership at the same time they were fighting a war of national survival.

Colin has become great friends with many of us over the years, and his focus upon even the smallest detail comes through. However, what is perhaps the most important factor is that his works, in particular this book, illustrate the humanity and chivalry felt by my enemies toward their opponents, something that sometimes gets lost in the postwar rhetoric.

This book is truly a testament to good men doing a tough job. Even though they were my enemies, I can still call them my brothers. I hold no ill will against the Germans I fought, just the opposite. I admired their skill, and feared their effectiveness, and after the war I enjoyed their company. I hope that the rest of the world can also allow these pilots, these men, to be accepted as national heroes in their own country. They should be proud of their dedication to Germany. I am proud to have fought against such worthy adversaries, who were good men.

Oberleutnant Kurt Schulze
3. (F) 11, I/KG.2, III/JG.5

The German Aces Speak is again one of Colin Heaton's factual and revealing books. It brings me back to my time in service with the *Luftwaffe* from 1939–1945, and then to the many hours of pleasurable discussion I often had with the late *Generalleutnant* Adolf Galland after the war. Galland was an outstanding officer and gentleman, and a friend.

Galland and the others mentioned in Colin's new book served their country with everything they had, and in very hard times, and often with very little assistance or understanding from *Reichsmarschall* Hermann Wilhelm Göring, who commanded the Luftwaffe, and was second in command only to Adolf Hitler.

In World War I, Göring was the last commander of the legendary Richthofen squadron, and he received the highest decoration, the *Pour le Mérite*. However, in World War II he made many mistakes, costing many German lives.

Colin Heaton gives the readers a chance to look behind the still prevailing opinions in Germany against the German soldiers, honorable men who served their nation during World War II, even though our fortunes had changed. They were men of conscience, feeling, courage, morals, and honor.

After Stalingrad we fought a losing battle, but even worse, we fought our own leadership, which was not in touch with reality, and did not properly support our military in the very war that our leaders had started.

Our thanks should go out to all fair-minded historians like Colin who are writing in the United States, Canada, and the United Kingdom and treating us with a fair consideration. They have helped us to overcome the treatment we received after the war, and are still enduring in Germany today.

This reminds me of when, twenty-five years ago, approximately two thousand American enthusiasts paid twenty dollars each to see and listen to Adolf Galland, Günther Rall, Walter Krupinski, and others at a symposium. They took part in a seminar in Long Beach, California, which was sponsored by Virginia Bader.

Adolf Galland was impressed with the friendly reception and the high number of participants. He then mentioned that if a similar seminar had been held in Germany, there may have been perhaps a hundred or so persons who would have come, but they would all have been outside protesting.

This book shows what our men had to say, in their own words, about their experiences. They had no agenda, and they had nothing to protect. They just wanted the truth to be told, in full, to ensure that history would see all of us as honorable German airmen who served our nation, as would any man in time of war.

Thank you Colin and Anne for your book, which gives the readers a chance to find out how some of our most famous aces lived and survived an unforgettable time in their lives.

Acknowledgments

THIS FIRST BOOK IN THE SERIES ON AVIATORS would not have been possible without the immense interest and assistance of the following persons who over the last twenty-five years gave their time and expertise, in essence creating a final legacy to the men of the air: Trevor Constable, Adolf Galland, Erich Hartmann, Walter Krupinski, Dietrich Hrabak, Johannes Steinhoff, Heinz Marquardt, Hermann Graf, Hannes Trautloft, Eduard Neumann, Günther Rall, Hajo Herrmann, Werner Schrör, Hans-Ekkehard Bob, Helmut Lipfert, Gerhard Schöpfel, Georg-Peter Eder, Robert S. Johnson, Francis S. Gabreski, Adolf Borchers, Arno Abendroth, Raymond F. Toliver, Edward R. "Buddy" Haydon, Brig. Gen. Robin Olds, USAF, Ulrich Steinhilper, Adolf Glunz, Adolf Borchers, Wolfgang Späte, Kurt Bühligen, Lt. Col. Robert Schmidt, USAF, Dietrich Peltz, William Reid, Cy Stapleton, Erich Rudorffer, and many others. Thanks also to my agent, Gayle Wurst of Princeton International Agency for the Arts.

Greatest thanks to historian, author, and editor for Weider History Group, Jon Guttman, who edited and proofread the final draft. I hold him in the highest esteem. I also asked him to write one of the forewords, as he is the world's foremost expert on this subject. I have learned much from him, and I owe him much. Thanks to Kurt Schulze, former Luftwaffe bomber and fighter pilot, for his many years of support, contacts with aces, and a fine proofread.

Introduction

OVER THE LAST QUARTER CENTURY of interviewing veterans from all conflicts, this collection of interviews with the Luftwaffe pilots tended to be the most enjoyable endeavor. Having come to know these men in varying degrees, and becoming friends with most of them, it seemed only appropriate to publish these full interviews in a single collection as a series of books.

Readers who are familiar with such publications as *Aviation History*, *World War II, and Military History* may remember the abridged versions of some of these interviews, as they were published by Cowles History Group, later Primedia Publications, and more recently the Weider History Group. This book (and the others to follow) provides the unabridged, full-length interviews, complete with greater details and additional photographs.

We hope that these interviews, as they are presented, will enlighten and entertain the readers, as well as enhance the study of aviation history, and World War II in general. It has been a great privilege to have been afforded the opportunity to meet and get to know these fine gentlemen. Despite the regime for which they fought (and had little choice in doing so), I found them very friendly, respectful, and to a man, they each despised the war, and wished it had never occurred.

The Third Reich's fighter pilots destroyed some 70,000 enemy aircraft during the war, with approximately 45,000 destroyed on the Eastern Front. For example, JG.52 alone is credited with more than 10,000 enemy planes shot down. Of these Luftwaffe aces, 103 pilots scored more than 100 victories, while of this number, 15 pilots scored more than 200, and with two men, Erich Hartmann and Gerhard Barkhorn, shooting down 352 and 301 aircraft, respectively.

During the war, the Luftwaffe lost a total of 150,000 personnel killed, wounded, or missing; 70,000 of these were pilots, with

1

more than 20,000 being fighter pilots. The last reliable date for posted losses, according to Dr. Alfred Price, and reliably checked against the German archives, posted the following losses: 44,056 aircrewmen were killed or missing, with 28,200 wounded and 27,610 taken prisoner, or also reported missing. However, what is known is that by May 8, 1945, there were only approximately 2,400 Luftwaffe fighter pilots still alive and accounted for. Many, such as Erich Hartmann, Hans "Assi" Hahn, Hermann Graf, and Hajo Herrmann, spent long years in the Soviet gulag system in what was an illegal postwar confinement.

It has been estimated that the German military lost 3,800,000 personnel killed in total, along with 635,000 civilians. By comparison, Great Britain only lost 65,000 civilians killed by German bombings, with 430,000 military personnel dead. The Soviet Union lost at least 25,000,000 civilians and as many as 6,000,000 military dead (not including the 25,000,000 people Soviet premier Josef Stalin may have killed before the war even began), with the United States losing just over a quarter of a million military lives.

The war in the east versus the war in the west has been sorely unappreciated by the Western Allied nations. Without a doubt, the air war between the Soviet Union and Germany was the largest theater of aerial conflict, and involved far more men and aircraft. The same was true for the ground war, which pitted the two greatest military nations on earth in a life and death struggle, where there was little if any quarter asked, and hardly ever given. It was on this front that the air war, unlike in the west, virtually discarded the accepted rules of chivalrous warfare. Sadly, this was true on both sides, as two great opponents were locked in the ultimate example of total warfare for national survival. However, the Germans in the air hardly wavered from their concepts of chivalry and fair play, unless provoked. This is not in dispute.

It should be mentioned that, in spite of wartime and even postwar propaganda, there is not a single case of a German pilot intentionally shooting a parachuting enemy on any front. Of course, accidents will happen in warfare, especially aerial combat. The Soviets, however, did not adhere to the rules of warfare as mandated by the existing Geneva Convention of 1929. In fact, killing enemy pilots, regardless of the situation, was expected. Stalin himself stated that he would neither sign nor abide by the 1929 Geneva Convention, although he did state that he would follow the rules of conflict as outlined in the Hague Convention, as previously revised in 1907.

The readers will perhaps be interested to see the thoughts of these men. True, it is hindsight, and therefore reflective. However, it is also in their own words, and their own experiences, seasoned by time and aged to maturity. They were the best people to discuss the war from their perspective, as opposed to historians writing about them in the third person. Writing about a man flying and fighting is not the same as the fighter pilot telling his own story.

The information gathered from all of these interviews is cross-referenced with the available sources, and even other interviewed subjects. This method serves several purposes, such as verification of data based upon memory, and historical accuracy to present the facts, even if in contradiction to the testimony, in order to provide a more accurate account of the events in question.

These pages will come to life as some of Germany's bravest and best pilots tell their stories about the war, their battles, lives, and perhaps most important, how they felt about their leadership under the National Socialist German Workers Party, or NSDAP (Nazi Party). None of these men interviewed were card-carrying National Socialists. In fact, they adhered to the long held tradition of *Überparteilichkeit*, or "above party affiliation." These were men who were serving their nation in the cockpits of aircraft. Their job was to fight and, if possible, destroy the enemies of their nation. They were no different than the pilots of other nations.

Setting propaganda and postwar myopia aside, the Luftwaffe pilots were not only brave men defending their country from obliteration; they were men of honor who still fought by and believed in a code of chivalry, reminiscent of the First World War, when enemy pilots often saluted each other in battle, and wounded enemies were allowed to escape to fight another day.

Historian Telford Taylor blamed much of Nazi Germany's woes upon the generals, whom he blamed collectively for not being more proactive in serving their nation and resisting the Nazi Party.

Taylor stated: "What the officers' corps needed and lacked were the leadership and moral discipline to protect the German name and their own tradition against the degradation with which the Third Reich had threatened both ever since its birth. Instead, for reasons which we have traced, the generals chose to become, themselves, a pillar of the Third Reich. Now the terrible consequences of that choice lay before them."[1]

That being said, it will be clear to the readers that the men chronicled here were made of more solid fiber. Obviously, for the most part, World War II was a completely different environment from the previous global conflict. Totalitarian regimes, the mass murders of civilians and violations of international laws of conflict, and the sheer numbers of men and women involved in the war in the air and on the ground, created an entirely new mindset regarding war.

Killing became easier, and dehumanization of one's opponent through propaganda and racial and ethnic bigotry became the norm for all nations, Allied and Axis alike. The Luftwaffe men, for the most part, were above all of the polemic and prejudice, even when inundated from their youth by the evil propaganda spewed by Propaganda Minister Dr. Josef Göbbels, the incoherent ranting of Adolf Hitler, and the illogical and the inhuman policies of both *Reichsführer-SS* Heinrich Himmler, and *Reichsmarschall* Hermann Wilhelm Göring. Certainly, no one can look into the heart of every man, yet one tends to get a feel for the essence of who a man is when spending many hours, or even days with him.

Some of these men returned to military life after the war, rising to higher rank, as exemplified by *Generalleutnant* Günther Rall, *Generalmajor* Hannes Trautloft, *Generalleutnant* Walter Krupinski, *Generalleutnant* Johannes Steinhoff, *Generalmajor* Dietrich Hrabak, and *Oberst* Erich Hartmann. Others chose a different path in civilian life, most engaging in business and industry. They had made their mark on history, and simply wanted to live quiet lives, each in his own way.

All of these men spent various amounts of time as prisoners of war when the hostilities ceased. Some were held by the British and Americans, until their discharge papers were processed within one to three years after the war. Others, such as Erich Hartmann, Hermann Graf, and Hajo Herrmann, would spend a decade in the Soviet gulag system, stripped of their rank and removed from the protection of both the Geneva Convention and the International Red Cross, in an illegal confinement that has still yet to be properly addressed. It should be also noted that an estimated seven hundred thousand German POWs were held in violation of Geneva 1929, and used as forced labor by the Western Allies. No one's hands were completely clean.

All of these men endured their own kind of hell, an existence that most of us could never imagine. Americans held by the Japanese in World War II, in North Korea or China, or in the Hanoi Hilton and the jungles of Vietnam by the Viet Cong, can attest to the brutality and hardships endured over several years of captivity. They know all too well the pain and fear of being held by a ruthless enemy who follows no rules but his own. It is perhaps these men, our own heroes who were mostly aviators, who were wounded and tortured, who will best appreciate the stories within these pages.

Freedom is the most cherished ideal we as human beings have. Losing it is the greatest tragedy. Anne and I hope that the readers of this book will look beyond the politics of the day, and the postwar propaganda, and see these men for who they really were. They were Germans fighting to save their nation and their populations from destruction. Some of these men suffered multiple wounds and injuries, with Johannes Steinhoff, Günther Rall, Georg-Peter Eder, and Walter Krupinski being some of the best examples of men who were extremely lucky to have lived through the war. Eder, being the prime example, was wounded over a dozen times, while Steinhoff was also wounded on several occasions and burned alive.

Some of the men interviewed for this series over the years were groundbreakers. Some, like Hajo Herrmann, Hannes Trautloft, Eduard Neumann, Herbert Ihlefeld, and Adolf Galland, were veterans before World War II began, as members of the famous Condor Legion that fought in support of *Generalissimo* Francisco Franco during the Spanish Civil War. These men brought their hands-on experience in effective tactics home to provide the Luftwaffe with a competent and well-qualified cadre of combat leaders.

Wolfgang Falck, who became known as the "Father of the Night Fighters," ushered in a new form of warfare, specializing in nocturnal and limited visibility aerial combat, which was a revolutionary development in World War II, although commonplace in today's high-tech world.

Likewise, Hajo Herrmann, using the low-tech method of night fighting with single-seat fighters and no advanced radars, carved his name into history flying both bombers and fighters. He had become a national hero for sinking more than seventy thousand tons of Allied shipping before he created his famous "*Wilde Sau*" (Wild Boar) tactics in July 1943. Later, he became one of Germany's most successful criminal defense attorneys, handling high-profile cases well into his nineties.

Adolf Galland and Dietrich Peltz became the youngest generals of the war, each commanding the fighter and bomber forces, respectively. Their abilities in combat, their competence in logistics, planning, and intelligence, as well as their abilities to inspire the unwavering loyalty of their subordinates, also created an ongoing love-hate relationship with their higher ups. Galland's interview includes a prime example of superiors—whose egos exceeded their capabilities—making their subordinates pay for their own shortcomings.

The methods, tactics, and technologies the airmen employed, elements that were produced through wartime necessity, ushered in a revolution of scientific knowledge and better tactics. Both the German and British airman during the night war received an ever-continuing series of technological gadgets, with each side working to counter the other's latest threat with an even more effective instrument. This created the first true technological arms race, which also continues to this day. Today's military and civil aviation worlds are the direct descendants of these efforts by the first practitioners of instrument and radar-guided flying in limited visibility.

Some of these pilots made history in very different ways. Krupinski, Eder, Steinhoff, Rall, Herrmann, Galland, and other select German and Austrian flyers became the first jet pilots in history, with a few becoming aces in the Messerschmitt Me-262. In fact, many of these men were in great demand by the Allies on both sides after the war, due to their expertise, technological and combat experience.

Wolf Falck, Hajo Herrmann, and others pushed electronic warfare, tactics, and technology to their limits, forcing their British counterparts into a war of financial and intellectual attrition. Today, many everyday military and civilian techniques, tactics, and devices, such as the microwave oven, radar detectors, airborne combat controllers, pressurized cockpits, electronic jamming and scrambling devices, as well as emission detection and control systems, to name a few, are a direct result of the "wizard's war" between the RAF and the Luftwaffe.

Readers may see many connections between these men as they tell their stories. Most of them knew each other to some degree, often flying in the same units at various times. Others became acquainted with each other after the war and shared their experiences. All were lucky to have survived.

Perhaps the greatest tribute to their branch of service was the creation of the Gemeinschaft der Jagdflieger, which shortly after its creation became an international organization. This "Community of Fighter Pilots" opened its doors to the pilots of all nations, including the Allies, in order to further the fraternity of aerial warriors and embrace their enemies, setting all history and politics aside.

The Gemeinschaft even opened its doors to some of us who were historians, interested in the German airmen's stories, with an invitation to become honorary members. It was this acceptance that launched the careers of many of us. When I was there with Walter Krupinski, then the acting Traditionsreferent, he simply told me: "Colin, I want you to join the Gemeinschaft, you know most of the guys. This will allow you greater contacts for your research." And so started my career.

We hope that readers find these first-person narratives informative and entertaining, and that they create a continued interest in the study of aerial warfare in World War II. Although the men interviewed for this book have all passed away, their contributions to history and their legacy to aviation is undeniable. I wish they were still with us to see these full interviews, edited for this series of books, come to life. Their friendships were priceless, and the assistance was also invaluable.

— Colin D. Heaton and Anne-Marie Lewis

German Military Ranks, Medals, and Service

CORRESPONDING GERMAN AND
ALLIED AIR FORCE RANKS

German	American	British
Generalfeldmarschall	General of the Army/ Air Force (five star)	Air Marshal of the Royal Air Force
Generaloberst	General (four star)	Air Chief Marshal
General der Flieger	Lieutenant General (three star)	Air Marshal
Generalleutnant	Major General (two star)	Air Vice Marshal
Generalmajor	Brigadier General (one star)	Air Commodore
Oberst	Colonel	Group Captain
Oberstleutnant	Lieutenant Colonel	Wing Commander
Major	Major	Squadron Leader
Hauptmann	Captain	Flight Lieutenant
Oberleutnant	First Lieutenant	Flying Officer
Leutnant	Second Lieutenant*	Pilot Officer
Sonderführer	Warrant Officer	Warrant Officer
Hauptfeldwebel	Sergeant Major	Flight Sergeant

* This is usually the lowest rank for pilots in the U.S. military. There were exceptions, when enlisted pilots flew, but it was rare.

9

German	American	British
Oberfeldwebel	First Sergeant	Chief Technician
Stabsfeldwebel	Sergeant First Class	Sergeant*
Feldwebel	Staff Sergeant	Junior Technician
Unterfeldwebel	Sergeant† Technician	Senior Aircraftman
Unteroffizier	Corporal	Senior Aircraftman
Privat	Private	Leading Aircraftman

LUFTWAFFE TABLE OF ORGANIZATION

Office or Formation	Rank of Commander
Oberbefehlshaber der Luftwaffe (Supreme Air Force Commander)	Reichsmarschall
Chef des Generalstabes der Luftwaffe (Chief of Air Staff)	General der Flieger or Generaloberst
Fliegerkorps (Air Corps)	General der Flieger or Generalleutnant
Fliegerdivision (Air Division)	General der Flieger, Generalleutnant, or Generalmajor
Geschwader (Wing)	Generalmajor, Oberst, Oberstleutnant, or Major, with title of Kommandeur
Gruppe (Group)	Oberstleutnant, Major, or Hauptmann (in rare cases), with title of Kommandeur

This table is an operational matrix that was not engraved in stone. Adolf Galland was a *generalleutnant*, the equivalent of an American

---

* Usually the lowest rank for a pilot in the RAF. There were exceptions.

† This was typically the lowest rank of a German pilot in training. Given the one year of flight training and then advanced training, the average enlisted pilot would be a *feldwebel* or higher.

major general, who led a *geschwader* (wing) he named which never rose above *gruppe* (group) strength, and hardly ever functioned above the *staffel* (squadron) level. Many times an officer with great ability, but not holding the rank, was placed in a command far above his pay grade. The best example was Wolfgang Falck, appointed a *kommodore* while only a *hauptmann* on June 26, 1940, a position usually reserved for an *oberst* or above. Combat attrition and the rapid redeployment of units and personnel issues also factored into the equation as well.

This table remained more or less as stated above from 1939–1943, with few exceptions until 1942, when even more junior officers took higher levels of command responsibility. By 1944, this rank requirement was even lower in some cases.

ORDER OF THE IRON CROSS AND KNIGHT'S CROSS

The Iron Cross and its subsequent levels (listed below from lowest to highest) were not just awarded for battlefield valor. Leadership and other military contributions in a battlefield environment were also factors. The Iron Cross was progressive—you had to earn the lower award before achieving the next—although simultaneous awards of two levels did occur.

Iron Cross Second Class
Iron Cross First Class
Knight's Cross (Approximately 7,500 awarded.)
Knight's Cross with Oak Leaves (Only 860 awarded.)
Knight's Cross with Oak Leaves and Swords (Only
    159 awarded.)
Knight's Cross with Oak Leaves, Swords, and Diamonds
    (Only 27 awarded, 10 to Luftwaffe pilots, 9 to fighter
    pilots; the one exception was Stuka pilot *Oberst*
    Hans-Ulrich Rüdel.)
Knight's Cross with Golden Oak Leaves, Swords, and
    Diamonds (Only awarded to *Oberst* Hans-Ulrich Rüdel.)
Grand Cross of the Iron Cross (Only awarded to
    Reichsmarschall Hermann Wilhelm Göring.)

The criteria for the various awards were subjective, and for pilots the requirements for the higher awards, starting at the Oak Leaves, became more stringent as the war progressed. Scoring forty victories on the Channel coast between 1940 and 1941 would often secure a pilot the Knight's Cross in most cases, while seventy kills would almost guarantee the Oak Leaves, with one hundred securing the Swords, and so on. However, after the invasion of the Soviet Union, with some pilots scoring forty victories or more in a month, and even a few rare exceptions shooting down that many in a good week, Hitler raised the bar.

Some may find it strange that pilots such as Günther Rall, who scored 275 victories, and Gerhard Barkhorn, who shot down 301 adversaries, did not receive the award of the Diamonds, whereas Erich Hartmann (352 victories) and Hermann Graf (212), for example, were awarded them. Likewise, Adolf Galland had 104 victories, and he received the Diamonds, along with Werner Mölders, with 114 (14 in Spain), while the others who scored in the 200 victory range received at least the Swords, but most did not receive the Diamonds.[1]

Walter Nowotny with 258 victories held the Diamonds after scoring his 250th. However, these Diamonds awards for less than 200 kills were made before 1942, after the war had greatly expanded. Remember that Erich Rudorffer scored 222, Rall 275, Otto Kittel 267, and Barkhorn 301, and yet they never received the Diamonds, although Barkhorn was recommended, but the war ended before they could be conferred.

It is important to consider how these pilots evaluated their enemies based on their individual experiences. The war in the east was a different type of battleground than in Western Europe and North Africa. Most of the Luftwaffe victories were achieved over the Eastern Front, although several pilots—such as Josef Priller, Egon Mayer, Joachim Müncheberg, Heinz-Wolfgang Schnauffer (night fighter kills; Diamonds holder), Helmut Lent (night fighter kills; Diamonds holder), Hans-Joachim Marseille (7 in France and 151 in North Africa; Diamonds holder), and Adolf Galland (all on the Western Front)—scored more than 100 in the west.

There were many reasons for this disparity. One was the fact that, once Stalin ordered all major factories, including munitions, tank, and aircraft production facilities, moved east beyond the Ural Mountains, they benefited from the lack of a German long-range bombing program. The Soviets could build aircraft and train pilots without interruption, and with the American Lend-Lease program supplying upwards of 80 percent of the USSR's wartime matériel until 1944, and the Germans only able to attack the transatlantic shipping convoys arriving at Archangel and Murmansk, the war had irretrievably turned against them by August 1943.

Soviet aircraft production continued unabated throughout the war, while German industry suffered punishment from RAF night bombing raids starting in early 1940, and later "round the clock" bombing, as the United States Army Air Forces joined in with precision daylight bombing in November 1942.

The first few months saw the Americans striking French and Belgian targets, in effect getting "on the job experience" before driving deeper into heavily defended German territory. However, the Americans would not effectively engage deep into Germany and occupied Europe proper with any great effect or in great numbers until after January 1944, when the North American P-51 Mustang became the USAAF's premier long-range fighter.

The Mustangs were able to escort the heavy bombers from their bases in the United Kingdom and Italy, all the way into the heart of Germany, and still take on the Luftwaffe over its own airspace. The Eighth Air Force even launched several shuttle missions from its British bases to the Soviet Union, starting on June 21, 1944, in which P-51s of the 4th Fighter Group under Col. Donald Blakeslee landed in the USSR, where they would be refueled, rearmed, and flown back to the United Kingdom as a return escort force.

The research and the interviews presented here show the progression of the war from the halcyon days of blitzkrieg in 1939–1941, until the final days of the Third Reich, through the eyes of the men who fought from the cockpits of these aircraft. Without men such as these, World War II would have probably been over much sooner, and it might be argued that their competence and skill prolonged the agony and attrition of all nations involved. Even so, they should not be condemned for serving their nation. In fact, given the peculiar circumstances of their national leadership, they should be commended for maintaining their professionalism and humanity, when all around them was madness.

Most of Germany's greatest and highest scoring pilots spent most (if not all) of their careers on the Eastern Front, which was, by all measure, a much larger war in both scope and depth than the war in the west. The Soviets had been receiving Lend-Lease aid since 1940, as did Great Britain. However, thousands of aircraft, tanks, food, and millions of rounds of ammunition did support the Soviet war effort through the maritime convoy operations to Murmansk and Archangel.

This assistance provided enough support to keep Stalin's people in the fight until they could increase their own domestic production capability. By 1943, the Red Army and the various Soviet air arms were well staffed, well stocked, and had largely recovered from the initial German invasion of 1941, as well as the prewar purges of Stalin against his own people, especially the military, which he had destroyed from within.

Most of the men included in this book fought a long war, from the Channel coast in France to the steppes of Russia, from the Arctic Circle to the Sahara Desert of North Africa. The Germans, much like the Soviet and Japanese pilots of World War II (and unlike their American or British counterparts), did not fly a specific number of missions and then rotate back home, or receive a long period of "downtime," participating in bond drives or instructing in a training facility. The Luftwaffe pilots flew until they were killed or too severely wounded to fly, or until defeat ended their careers. It was a long, hard war for them, without a doubt. Unlike their Allied opponents, there was not an endless supply of well-trained replacement pilots.

It may seem unusual that the German, Soviet, and British ranks had large numbers of enlisted pilots, but this was true of every air force in World War II (including the Imperial Japanese naval air squadrons), with the exception of the United States, where the vast majority (perhaps 95 percent or more) were commissioned officers. In fact, it is estimated that less than 12 percent of all German fighter pilots had more than the equivalent of an American high-school education, while perhaps over 50 percent of American pilots had at least a university level baccalaureate degree, with another 40 percent having at least two years of university or college education, usually as a mandatory requirement to fly.

Another important factor in evaluating the German fighter pilots (which would include all Luftwaffe aviators) was that rank was based upon merit, as opposed to higher education or political connections. For example, Hermann Graf, the son of a blacksmith, had no formal education beyond the equivalent of an American high-school diploma, but eventually rose to the rank of colonel, wearing Germany's highest decorations for valor, including the Diamonds. If nothing else, Nazi Germany was the perfect environment for individual success, a meritocracy free of class distinctions, enabling personal and professional advancement through bravery, skill, intellect, and personal service to the Reich.

Perhaps the most important thing to take away from this book is not simply the personal narratives of combat pilots. What we hope to show is that these men, while no doubt fighting for an evil regime, were not participants in those horrific events that forever damaged the image of the German military.

These were men who lived by a code, and fought a war of attrition against overwhelming odds and enemy numbers. They were gentlemen, true professionals at their craft, who proved their character during and after the war. It should be noted that not a single German combat pilot was ever charged with a war crime under the Hague and Geneva Conventions. The same cannot be said for their national leadership.

A small piece of history that is often overlooked is the fact that there was open dissent within the ranks of the German military regarding their superiors, and how they handled the war, which they in fact had started. One shining example was when Waffen SS *Obergruppenführer* Wilhelm Bittrich openly criticized SS chief and *Reichsführer* Heinrich Himmler to a group of fifteen senior SS officers and Nazi Party officials, regarding his disdain for Himmler's open policy (at least among the SS) of killing civilians.

Supporting him was another traditional soldier, *SS Gruppenführer* Felix Steiner. They may have been exceptions to the accepted rule, but they did no doubt voice their opinions. The story of *Oberst* Claus von Stauffenberg and the July 20, 1944, bomb plot is perhaps the best-known act of dissent, which is mentioned in the volume by Galland and Falck.

It is also very important to remember that subjects living in a totalitarian police state do not enjoy the same rights and freedoms, including the option of dissent with their government, as those persons living in democracies and representative republics. In the free nations, dissent is a basic right. In Nazi Germany, it was considered deadly subversion.

The same situation regarding rebellion occurred within the Luftwaffe, although on a more placid scale, culminating in the "Fighters' Revolt" of January 1945, which is discussed in detail by four of the surviving participants within this book series: Adolf Galland, Hannes Trautloft, Johannes Steinhoff, and Eduard Neumann. The senior Luftwaffe leaders had become so disillusioned with their leadership in general, and Göring in particular, that they even voted to select the *Reichsmarschall's* successor after the planned coup was over.

Many of the German fighter group and squadron commanders were disgruntled with the war, although for the most part they kept their opinions to and among themselves. National Socialist Germany was not the place to stand out and be noticed as a "dissenter," especially in the waning days of a losing war. There were men, however, who were willing to address the problems as they saw them. They were very target specific in their grievances, nearly all of which were directed at their leader, *Reichsmarschall* Göring.

By 1944, Göring had lost faith with his fighter force, and was very vocal in his displeasure. Likewise, Hitler had lost faith in Göring, who had mismanaged funds, misallocated resources, made promises to Hitler and the German people that he could not keep, and allowed Hitler, who had only the most rudimentary layman's knowledge of aerial warfare, to interfere, relocate units, deplete manpower, and strip antiaircraft defenses on a whim.

Göring rarely stood up to Hitler's childlike manipulation of these assets. Given the fact that Hitler had to approve any and all budget expenditures, to include new aircraft designs and developments,

Göring should have been more assertive. It is fortunate for the world that both men were less than brilliant in the prosecution of the war. Another factor that limited Germany's effectiveness in prosecuting the war was Hitler's method of government. With dozens of departments, all led by Nazi Party members who had their own agendas and ambitions, this created an atmosphere of mistrust and open competition among the various overlords. This ad hoc manner of national rule served Hitler's purposes; departments and organizations being at odds with each other reduced the possibility of a unified front challenging his ultimate authority. He forced his minions to worry more about currying his favor than plotting collectively for his usurpation.

The Luftwaffe was no different, with rivalries and turf wars the order of the day. When Galland was appointed as general of the fighters in November 1941, upon the death of his good friend and predecessor, *Oberst* Werner Mölders, he had no idea just how difficult his position would be. Galland, the young, handsome, and successful fighter ace, was relegated to the role of clerk and manager, a position he hated. In his own words, he preferred "fighting in the air than dealing with the upper echelons of the Third Reich on a daily basis."

At least in Galland's mind, fighting the enemy in the air was a fair fight, a clean war. The political battleground of Berlin was a different matter altogether, where dissent and obverse opinions, no matter how well formulated, logical, and properly presented, smacked of rebellion. The concentration camps were full of people and their collective families who had dissented in some manner. The Gestapo made few distinctions between presumed guilt or innocence when they crashed through doors in the middle of the night.

The pressure of dealing with Göring and Hitler eventually took the lives of many good men. In November 1941, *Generalfeldmarschall* Ernst Udet, who had emerged as Germany's highest-scoring ace to survive World War I with sixty-two victories, and like Göring, a *Pour le Mérite* recipient, chose death at his own hand over having to serve his unrelenting masters.[2]

It was Udet's funeral that brought Werner Mölders in from the Eastern Front, a journey that cost him his life in a flying accident, resulting in Galland succeeding him as general of the fighters. Another senior Luftwaffe officer to die by his own hand rather than handle the pressure and indifference of his superiors was *Generaloberst* Hans Jeschonnek, whose long-running battles with Göring proved too much to handle.

The men presented in this book all had their demons. The life and death struggle of aerial combat is an alien world to those who have not experienced it. In some cases, their demons emanated from their close proximity of the inhuman specimens that ran their country, and were responsible for millions of deaths. When reading these memoirs, we must remember that Göring was not just an original member of the National Socialist German Workers Party and the commander in chief of the Luftwaffe. He was also a chief architect of the Holocaust, even surpassing Himmler with his attention to detail, until relinquishing those responsibilities as the war began and progressed.

We historians may analyze data, collect sources, interview subjects, and chronicle the events, but the actual adrenaline-pumping, heart-pounding, and gut-wrenching exposure to death in the air on a daily basis remains the exclusive domain of those who have experienced it and survived. This was what separated the pilots from their leadership, men in power who could not comprehend the air war in the modern age, and even Göring was lost with his inability to understand what his pilots needed, and expected.

Perhaps the one common denominator that these men shared, gathered from the many years of interviews, was the fact that not one of them thought that he had done anything extraordinary. In fact, every man personally interviewed would have been pleased if there had never been a war. They would have been content to simply continue the natural course of their personal and professional lives and raise their families.

As a result of the war, most of these men lost most of everything they held dear. Galland lost two of his three brothers, Paul and Wilhelm, both successful and decorated fighter pilots, and Krupinski lost a brother in the U-boat service. Günther Rall's wife, Hertha, lost four babies during bombings.

Perhaps the most important revelation regarding the legacy of the Luftwaffe pilots is not their stellar records, but what their enemies thought about them during and especially after the war. Many of the Luftwaffe pilots became close friends with their former adversaries, such as Galland befriending RAF aces Johnny Johnson, Robert Stanford-Tuck, and Sir Douglas Bader (who was a guest of Galland's after being shot down in France), just to name a few.

Galland even had fond words for Capt. James Finnegan, the American Republic P-47D Thunderbolt pilot who was the last enemy to shoot down the general of the fighters in his Me-262, wounding him in the process in April 1945. There are dozens of similar stories among the aces, who proved that their war was not a political one, and no hard feelings were held after the guns fell silent.

This book is perhaps the last time these men's voices will be heard in their entirety. It is only fitting that they be brought together in a compilation work, as single volumes in a series. As they lived and fought as friends, it seemed only fitting that they should all be immortalized together as well.

Ironically, what started as a young high-school student's questions at an aviation symposium in 1978, to both American and German pilots speaking at the event, eventually developed into a three-decade-long love of the history and lives of these great men. It is my fervent hope that the tragic history of Nazi Germany, and all of its horrors, will one day be placed in proper perspective, and the proper guilt and responsibility be applied. Not every German was a Nazi, and not every member of the NSDAP was a killer.

Once, when I was a house guest of Günther Rall's in Schwäbisch Hall, he said: "Remember that we Germans will always carry the blame for what happened, and we must in some way bear a little responsibility. We have no excuse for being naïve. However, we would have been lost men had we not fought for our country."

Likewise, when I stayed with Wolfgang Falck at his lovely home in Saint Ulrich in Tirol, Austria, he said something that I found worth noting: "People are creatures of habit, and for the most part, we do not always think for ourselves. I would hope that our history shows just how foolish that entire method is."

I was just fortunate enough to have been allowed into their world, become their friend, and sit back and listen as they relived their lives during both war and peace. These men started my career, long before I had one, and for that I owe them a great debt. My greatest hope is that perhaps one day their own countrymen will understand, forgive and embrace their legacy as true heroes, even if the regime they fought for was notorious in its actions. Heroes do not choose their wars, or their governments; they just serve their nations, and these men served in an extraordinary capacity, against insurmountable odds. We should all remember that fact.

— Colin D. Heaton

The Count

Walter Krupinski
197 victories, Knight's Cross with Oak Leaves
German Cross in Gold, Wound Badge in Gold
(November 11, 1920–October 7, 2000)

GENERALLEUTNANT WALTER KRUPINSKI WAS one of those men destined to always tempt fate. Beginning his flight training on October 15, 1939, he flew fighters with distinction throughout World War II, serving in Germany's most prestigious units and training, and flying with some of the world's greatest pilots, such as Adolf Galland, Otto Kittel, Dietrich Hrabak, Erich Rudorffer, Gerhard Barkhorn, and Erich Hartmann. His friends and colleagues called him "Krupi" and "Count Punski" out of affection.

Krupinski's leadership style was similar to that of his most prominent commanding officer, Dietrich Hrabak, who was also much like the great Werner Mölders, as both men were held in high esteem by all who knew them. Krupinski's fatherly approach and genuine concern for the welfare of his pilots, as well as his respect for captured enemy pilots, illustrated his humanity in a world where savagery was the order of the day. He became a teacher to many pilots, the most notable being the future "Ace of Aces" Erich Hartmann, who learned well from "Krupi" and other experts in JG.52.

By the time Krupinski was awarded the *Ritterkreuz* (Knight's Cross) on October 29, 1942, he had been credited with shooting down 53 Allied aircraft. His final score of 197 could have been much higher, but he never claimed a probable victory or argued over a disputed claim, always giving the victory to the other man. Krupinski probably gave away more than 30 potential victories in that manner. To him, a victory was just not that important. He flew more than 1,100 combat missions, entered combat more than 600 times, became one of the first jet pilots, and survived many incredible events, which he related in the course of his many interviews.

His chivalrous attitude and Prussian birth earned him the nickname "*Graf* (Count) Punski," a name that lingered in the reunion halls and among his friends until his death in October 2000, when I last spent time with him in Strasbourg, France (with Heinz Ewald, Hajo Herrmann, Wolfgang Falck, Günther Rall, Eduard Neumann, Gerhard Schöpfel, and many others), along with my great friend, fellow author, and historian Jon Guttman.

After the war, Krupinski worked closely with Organization Gehlen (the West German Secret Service, named for and operated by the wartime and postwar intelligence general Reinhard Gehlen), and also with the American Central Intelligence Agency—work that he declined to discuss in detail, honoring his oaths of secrecy. He joined the West German air force, worked with the United States and Royal Air Forces, assisted in the early foundations of the emerging North Atlantic Treaty Organization (NATO), and later functioned as a coordinator and leader in the new *Bundesluftwaffe*.

Walter and his wife lived in modest retirement at their home in Neunkirchen, Germany. Krupinski had often assisted me in contacting many of Germany's aces for interviews, and he himself agreed to be interviewed many times, the last being in 1999. What follows are his experiences during the war and his reflections about his life, in his own words. An abridged version of this interview was published in *Military History* in June 1998.[1]

Walter Krupinski

My name is Walter Krupinski, and I was born on November 11, 1920, in a little town called Donnau in East Prussia, which is now under the jurisdiction of the Russian government, but I lived in

Braunsberg, which is currently under the Polish government. I recently visited Braunsberg, where the family had lived from 1933 to 1945, and found that it has changed little since I was last there. In fact, I found my old home and even the old sewing machine my mother had used when I was a child. It was very strange as well as very familiar, almost comforting.

When I was born, my father was in military service. He had been in the First World War, as were all the able-bodied men, and later as the war ended, he was called upon to serve again. At that time, starting in 1918, he was fighting against the Communist groups trying to take control of Germany after the war, and the first large riots started in Berlin, as well as the navy revolt that occurred in Kiel and other places.

He served in the army during World War I and after—until 1923 or 1924. He finally left the army and became a government employee. He soon joined the army again before the outbreak of World War II, but he was discharged after the 1939 Polish campaign ended, as a first lieutenant. Later during the war my father became a government employee once again, but as the war progressed he was enlisted as a member of the *Volksturm* [civilians conscripted in defense of Germany in the closing days of the war] as the Soviets entered Germany proper, from January to May 1945.

I had two younger brothers, Paul and Günther. Paul and I were born on the same date, but two years apart. Paul joined the *Kriegsmarine* and entered the *Unterseeboot* [submarine] service, where he met his fate. He was killed when his boat, *U-771*, was sunk off the Norwegian coast, and only the bodies of Paul and a noncommissioned officer were found on the shore. [*U-771* went down with all hands in Andfjord after being torpedoed by the British submarine HMS *Venturer* on November 11, 1944.] They were buried at the military cemetery in Narvik, Norway. My youngest brother, Günther, was born in 1932, and he fled Prussia to the west with my mother in January 1945, during the Soviet advance. He died of cancer in 1970.

My education was the same as most of the others in the Luftwaffe, and the military in general: primary school and then *Gymnasium*—similar to an American high school but a little more advanced—studying the basic curriculum. I passed the *Abitur*, which is the final exit examination, in 1938, and decided to join the military. I had thought about joining the navy. I always liked ships and the sea, having read many books and high adventure novels, such as the works of Robert Louis Stevenson and Daniel Defoe. I also liked Herman Melville and the like.

What is probably very interesting is that I never really had any interest in flying. In fact, I attempted to become a naval officer like my friends Johannes Steinhoff and Dietrich Hrabak, as I always liked the sea.[2] However, when I finally was admitted into the navy, they transferred me to the Luftwaffe. I did not apply for it. It seemed as if fate threw us all [Steinhoff and Hrabak] together for most of our lives, even far beyond the war.

I started flight training as a new Luftwaffe pilot candidate, training in September 1939, just as the Polish campaign started, at the Officers Cadet School at Berlin-Gatow, later transferring to Vienna-Schwechat, which was the Fighter Weapons School. So I missed the first battles of the war. It all started with classroom instruction, aerodynamics—the basics, really. Then, after a couple of months in the classroom, we were introduced to the Heinkel He-51 biplane trainer, in which we learned the basics of takeoffs and landings, or touch and goes, as well as proper aerial maneuvers with an instructor. When we were considered competent we soloed, and I just took to it quickly.

The instructors looked at us, assessed our strengths and weaknesses, and somehow made suggestions as to who would transition into fighters, bombers, or dive bombers. They did allow us to apply for what type of aircraft we wanted to fly, and I learned that the bomber and reconnaissance programs were much longer than the fighter program, due to the extra requirements for long-range navigation, and more detailed instrument rating requirements.

Well, I knew that if I went into fighters, I would get to the front more quickly. I also thought about the survival ratings between fighter and bomber pilots, and figured I would have a better chance in a small, fast plane, as opposed to a larger, slower target. One of my American friends I made after the war called it the "big sky theory," which really is nonsense, but it made me feel good.

It was after six months or so of training, mostly on the He-51 and Arado types, that we actually trained on the Messerschmitt Me-109, which as you know was actually the primary fighter throughout the war, with around thirty-five thousand being built. I know this has been said many times, but I think it is very important to say here. The Me-109 was a fine fighter when it was in its element. That element was higher altitude, and in a diving battle, but it was a good dogfighter, with good weapons, with the 7.92mm machine guns and the 20mm centrally mounted cannon. Just a few hits from those would bring down almost anything. It also had what we called "short legs," and therefore did not have the range necessary to be a great fighter for long missions.

The tricky part about flying the 109 was the takeoff and landing. Now, this is true of any aircraft, but in the 109 you had to really stand on the rudder until you achieved airspeed, otherwise you could pull a ground loop. This was due to the torque of the engine on the propeller. Once you mastered that, you were fine. However, landing was just as hazardous.

The 109 was the first German monoplane fighter with a retractable landing gear, developed in 1935. The plane was better with each variant produced, but they all had the same Achilles' heel; the landing gear undercarriage was very narrow. Many pilots cracked up landing the 109, and this happened quite often after we transferred from the grass fields in the Soviet Union to hard surface airstrips in the defense of the Reich. It was sometimes quite embarrassing, and I should know. I cracked up a couple of 109s on landing myself during my career.

The gear struts were mounted centrally under the fuselage at the wing root. This was good for weight displacement and allowing for more fuel and weapons to be introduced later. It also helped the fighter to have a great roll rate, very important in combat. However, that narrow landing gear caused a lot of problems for many trainees, and many fighters were cracked up on the landing during training.

The other problem with the 109 in combat was the fact that it was liquid cooled, meaning the radiator was vulnerable to damage, which if hit, would cause a coolant leak and the engine overheating. This was an experience that I and most fighter pilots are very familiar with. Most of us Luftwaffe pilots who were forced to bail out or crash-land did so with this very problem being the reason.

I must admit that I liked the [Focke-Wulf] Fw-190 for the reason that it had an air-cooled radial engine, and it was also a great heavy weapons platform, it was faster, more maneuverable and better for engaging bombers and ground attack than the 109, in my opinion. The Fw-190 could also take more structural damage than a 109. However, most of us fell in love with the 109, because once you mastered the airplane, it was a very reliable fighter.

Then, getting back to the training, after achieving competence in the fighter, we trained on instrument flying, enemy aircraft identification, emergency procedures, formation flying, gunnery skills such as deflection shooting, and learned about our own particular aircraft, including minor maintenance. In Russia that was to become very important, as we never really had a solid supply line after 1943. Our mechanics were always worked to death, so knowing more about your own aircraft and doing minor things helped everyone.

Shortly after completing the year-long training process, I was transferred to the Channel coast and, in late October 1940, assigned to JG.52 [*Jagdgeschwader*, or fighter wing, 52], where Günther Rall, Dieter Hrabak, Johannes Steinhoff, Gerhard Barkhorn (who transferred to JG.2 *Richthofen* and then returned to JG.52, as Hrabak alternated between JG.52 and 54), and others were starting their careers, later becoming *Experten*, which was a term usually used for those with one hundred or more kills.

By the time I got involved in the war, the Battle of Britain was just about over, which was in November 1940. I flew only thirty missions over the United Kingdom, and I was involved in a few dogfights with [Supermarine] Spitfires and [Hawker] Hurricanes, but scored no victories. I was a slow starter, as I was suffering from bad shooting, and I was very anxious since I was afraid of being shot down over the English Channel and having to swim home! I was then commissioned as a *leutnant* in 6/JG.52 [6 *Staffel*, or squadron, of JG.52] in February 1941.

I served at the Channel front until the late spring of 1941, when JG.52 was transferred east. We flew from Ostende in Belgium to Suwalki in East Prussia, and we had been staging there ten days prior to Operation Barbarossa [the invasion of the Soviet Union on June 22, 1941]. The war started for us at Suwalki, where we took off to perform ground attack missions against the Red air force air fields. During these missions, there was not much air-to-air combat. We mostly strafed air fields, at least in my squadron, destroying aircraft on the ground. We did not get credits for victories against those. I was also quite surprised that there was not much antiaircraft fire, hardly any at all during that time. I was certain that, given the response, we had caught them completely by surprise. However, I also believed that we were to be the target of an advanced Soviet attack, as their aircraft were all staged in forward areas, in what appeared to be preparation for offensive operations. I flew a lot with Gerd Barkhorn, and usually Heinz Ewald was his wingman, but later he usually flew with me, and then later Erich Hartmann flew as my wingman quite often until he became a *staffelkapitän*.

In 1942, I was transferred to the replacement group of JG.52; then to 6th *Staffel*, attached to II *Gruppe* [II/JG.52] in southern Russia. This was where I also flew with Rall, Steinhoff, Herbert Ihlefeld, Willi Batz, and Hrabak for a while.[3] Later, I became *staffelkapitän* for 7th *Staffel* of III/JG.52 during the transfer to Romania with Erich Hartmann, Hermann Graf, Heinz Ewald, Helmut Lipfert, and others, guarding the Ploesti oil fields and refinery, bridges, and that sort of thing from the American long-range bombers from North Africa, and later I went to Italy for a short time until the spring of 1944. I must say I like southern Europe more than Russia.[4] I still go there for vacations to warm my bones.

The Russian winter! It's famous, you know, and all of the horror stories are true. We could not fly many times due to heavy snow and bad weather, and when we could fly it was hard to know how to get back unless you flew totally on instruments, and landings were quite often more hazardous than combat. Engines would not start due to the oil freezing, incredible. Many planes cracked up as well.

Naturally, I was there with Steinhoff [176 victories], Oblesser [127], Graf [212], Ihlefeld [132], Grasser [103,] Grislawski [133], Rall [275], Hrabak [125], Barkhorn [301], Batz [237], Ewald [84], Düttmann [152], and many others who became well-known names.[5] Later, when Helmut Lipfert [203] and Erich Hartmann [352] joined, we were quite a crew.[6] We all had the same experience, but not just during that winter. Every winter in Russia was miserable, but we were better prepared for the winters after the experience of 1941–1942.

Like most German pilots, I liked the 109 more than any other fighter I flew during the war, probably due to the familiarity I had with it. I think that we make that collective statement due to the ease of flying, the comfortable fit of the cockpit, and the instrument layout. Everything was within easy reach, and we also had a good weapons system, and the Revi gunsight was a very nice piece of equipment. It was not a true computer gunsight, but it was reflective, with a yellow ball and a targeting sight with range estimation.

If you knew your weapons, you could estimate the range to your target, and then fire. The best of the deflection shooters, like Nowotny, Rall, Marseille and others, used this sight to good effect.[7] I preferred to close as fast as I could, and then fire from no more than two hundred meters, the closer the better. That way, no bullets or shells go stray, you conserve ammunition, and every round makes an impact. Even better, you are close enough to assess the damage to the aircraft. This was what I taught Hartmann, and Grislawski had him for a while also, so he had good on-the-job training.

However, there were some drawbacks to closing in close and getting the kill. Whenever Hartmann was forced down, it was always by flying debris from his victories. He was never shot down by enemy fighters; he was downed by his victims. I also had a similar experience once, against a Yak in the area of the Crimean peninsula, when I closed in after shooting down his wingman. I hit this fellow with a full cannon shot, perhaps five shells that ripped into the fuel tank. The fighter blew up, and pieces of the fighter cracked my canopy, put large holes in my right wing surface, and the right ailerons hardly worked.

In 1941, we really did not have a lot of air combat, not when compared to later in the war, but this increased in 1942. After Rall crashed in November 1941, while we were fighting in the Caucasus, the front seemed to go to sleep a little. We heard reports from the north front that there was hardly any activity. Then, after February 1942, the war picked up pace.

I can tell you that from the reports we received up and down the front, the northern sector stayed pretty static. The central sector had more action, but was pretty stable, with air activity being constant, steady. However, in the southern sector, where we were, the war just exploded. It was as if Stalin had taken a personal hatred against JG.52, and sent every plane and pilot he had against us.

We had just lost Rall, and we did not even believe that he would ever come back, and Steinhoff had taken over some of his duties. In fact, I was with Macky on this mission when he shot down three planes in less than one minute. Absolutely incredible, as I was about two hundred meters behind him, covering his tail, and I had yet to score any kills on this mission. Macky chased two Yaks and fired into one, and that fighter simply disintegrated, and the other broke right, but Macky made a deflection shot that nailed him solid, and he also went down.

Then out of nowhere another Yak flew past me, at great speed, and was going to get Steinhoff, who was still turning hard right, reversing course, which brought his 109 head-on into the Yak as he pulled up. I saw both the Yak and 109 fire, but the Yak took the worst of it, shuddered, stalled, and Macky flew past and above the Yak. They were so close I thought they would collide.

My fighter just happened to pull alongside the left wing of the Yak, Macky's third kill, and being only forty or so feet away, very close, I could clearly see the pilot. He was beating against the canopy, trying to open it as smoke began filling the cockpit, and flames began to erupt from the cowling. The front of the Yak had been shredded by Macky's 20mm cannon fire.

The Yak's canopy must have been jammed shut from the 109's guns, as I could see shell strikes all over the bevel, where the canopy frame meets the fuselage. The plane started burning even more from the engine, the fuel line apparently feeding the flames. I saw the terror in this man's face, and I was even screaming into my oxygen mask for him to get out, which was silly. There was no way he could hear me, so I made the hand gesture for him to get out.

Macky pulled alongside him on his right and saw as well what was happening. I heard Macky over my radio, "Jesus Christ, Punski, I hope he can get out," and I could feel Macky's emotions. The man in that plane had no surface control, the elevators were gone, and the rudder was just hanging on. He could do nothing but ride out this flaming torch until it crashed, killing him, or he burned to death slowly, or the smoke killed him. He could not bail out, and we were at high altitude, perhaps eight thousand feet or so, I think, and I knew he would not survive a crash landing. Macky knew this also.

"Punski, go away, I will catch you," he told me. I knew what he was going to do. It was a clear violation of our ethics to kill a disabled opponent, one who was fairly beaten. But this was not murder. Macky was performing a mercy killing. That pilot was going to burn to death, slowly. Before I pulled away, I saw him slip in just behind the Yak. Then the Soviet pilot, who must have known what was going to happen, just relaxed, and gestured with a wave and nodded his head. He knew what was going to happen, and this was simply his way of saying "thank you."

I rolled away and called the men to form up on me, as all of them were watching this spectacle. As I reversed course, I could not help but look over, as did Ewald, and the Yak had apparently already exploded. There was nothing but a large evaporating ball of black dust and flame. The minimal pieces of the wreckage rained down like confetti. Some missions stand out more than others, for many reasons, but this is the most vivid image I ever took away from the war, other than Macky's crash on April 18, 1945. I felt a cold chill come over me. I think that this was perhaps the sobering moment, that time in your career where the reality of death is most vivid, and could only be more so if it were happening to you.

Once we all landed, I walked over to my superior officer and good friend, Macky Steinhoff, who just stood there, leaning against his fighter, his hand on the fuselage. I swear I think he was crying. I know he was. He knew that killing and shooting down aircraft was our job. But this mission really shook him up. He always tried to shoot the plane, not the pilot. That was just his way, he was a true knight in every sense of the word. Eder was the same way. They were cut from the same cloth.

Macky Steinhoff would not talk to anyone beyond discussing war business for several days after that event. I do not think it ever left him, and beyond that day in the Caucasus, we never spoke of it again. The only thing he said was: "If I am ever in that situation, please do the same. I would not want to burn alive trapped in my fighter." I assured him that would never happen, but I gave him my word anyway. How ironic, almost three years later to the day, he would be trapped in a burning fighter, and there was nothing any of us could do to help him.

For us, 1942 was a busy year, and this was when we first encountered Spitfires in the Caucasus, which happened later that year. I had seen them in France earlier in the war, but not in Russia. We knew that the Allies were supplying the Soviets with tanks, trucks, aircraft, and all kinds of things, but this was a new development. We had heard reports of Spitfires and Hurricanes being engaged, and even a few shot down, but none of us had been that lucky. Well, in August 1942 I came across a few, and these pilots were not your average Russian. These fellows knew their business. There were also some American-made twin-engine bombers that the Soviets used with great effect, and we also encountered these on occasion.

We had been flying nonstop throughout 1942, scoring a lot of victories, and losing a lot of good men. The Sixth Army had entered Stalingrad on the Volga in September, and the Eleventh Army was taking care of the Crimea.[8] We had been stopped at Moscow the previous December, but our superiors assured us that this was only a minor setback. That fall, Hermann Graf dominated the air over Stalingrad in his Messerschmitt Me-109. In thirty days, he shot down sixty-two Soviet aircraft, and I witnessed a few of these kills. One of those missions was a dogfight that Ewald and I had with an expert Russian pilot and his wingman, when I was with JG.52, which lasted for about fifteen minutes, which was rare for a Red Army pilot.

After his tally reached 172, Graf was awarded the Diamonds to the Knight's Cross [on September 16, 1942]. One of only nine fighter pilots to receive this enviable decoration, and one of only four pilots having that award for reaching 200 kills, I believe, and he did so in the course of more than 830 missions. It must be remembered that Graf scored 200 of his kills in only thirteen months of combat. That was quite astounding.

Those next two victories were hardly worth it. I was over enemy territory, I could not roll or bank very well, and the cold subzero wind was blasting me inside my cockpit. I decided that it was time to leave, and I managed to touch down on my grass strip. Actually, I glided in with a whirling propeller, since the engine died due to a lack of fuel. I had apparently been damaged in my main fuel cell, as I was losing fuel, although my fuel gauge never registered I was losing fuel at all.[9]

I had just become commanding officer of 7th *Staffel* of III/JG.52 [7.III/JG.52] when in March 1943, I first met Erich Hartmann. He had been with JG.52 since about October with Paule Rossmann and had been groomed by him and Alfred Grislawski, as well as, later, Dieter Hrabak, who took over from Hubertus von Bonin. He was such a child! So young, and that was when I gave him the nickname of "*Bubi*," or boy, and it stuck with him for the rest of his life.

He remembered me from about six months earlier, when I had a memorable crash landing in a burning Me-109 at Maikop. He had just arrived and was assigned to III/JG.52 under [Hubertus] von Bonin, although we did not formally meet. I was shot all up after a sortie against the Soviets, a very difficult mission, and I was blinded by smoke and slightly wounded.[10] Later we heard the early reports that Hartmann had a bad habit of breaking formation, and losing his aircraft with little to show for the efforts. He learned eventually, after being grounded a couple of times.

Regarding this mission, we had flown eight of our Me-109s to look for a group of [Ilyushin] Il-2 *Shturmovik* bombers, and we found over a dozen of them with a like number of fighter escorts, mostly Yaks. These fighter pilots were not the usual suspects, and their markings indicated a Red Banner unit. These were the fighter units that contained the best and brightest Soviet pilots, real hot shots who knew how to fly and fight. They looked for a fight, unlike the average enemy pilot.

The Yak was also a fighter that you could not underestimate. It had great speed, could outdive us, outclimb us, and was just as good, if not better, in a turning fight. Unlike their brothers in the more traditional units, these men wanted to fight. Once you engaged, you had to keep your head. The Red Banner fighters would dogfight with you, and then ram you if they could once they were out of ammunition. I saw this happen on more than one occasion. It happened to me once, while I was flying with Dieter Hrabak as the element leader. [11]

One of our guys called out "enemy aircraft" at nine o'clock low. We had the altitude advantage, about two thousand meters in fact, so I banked over and told my wingman, who I believe was Heinz Ewald, to follow me. I went into a shallow dive, pulled up and closed in quickly on the trailing Il-2, and when I was perhaps three hundred meters away I fired. I continued firing as I closed the distance, short bursts, cannon only.

The rear gunner was hit; I knew this as glass flew everywhere, it just exploded. Almost immediately afterward, the engine started smoking, so I continued on. I stepped on the left rudder and drifted into a really good firing position to engage another bomber. I scored some good hits on him and the aircraft's engine exploded, the range was only one hundred meters, so I kicked more rudder to avoid a collision. The engine fire turned to black smoke and he dropped out of formation.

Ewald called out more "Indians" and we attacked, as they were below us, two Il-2 *Shturmoviks*. Ewald managed to shoot one down, and another pilot got the second, both using the standard method: close in and hit the oil cooler. This was really the only way to shoot down one of these airplanes. I had once wasted an entire inventory of ammunition, to include all of the ammunition in my 20mm cannon into just one *Shturmovik* to bring it down. These planes were built like tanks, and could withstand all but the heaviest 88mm and larger AA fire.

I was once able to inspect a crash-landed Il-2 and I studied it closely, all of us did. We located the bomber's Achilles' heel. The radiator coolant system was centrally located, and if you could come up from below and attack, that was the place to aim for. I taught Hartmann this, as well as many others as I mentioned before.[12]

I flew into a formation of eight Il-2s, and I followed them right through our flak screen. Now this was not the brightest thing to do, but I really wanted to get a couple of kills. Suddenly, one of the enemy bombers took a direct flak hit, and the entire plane was thrown up about a hundred feet straight up, above the others. It was still flying, streaming smoke. Never one to pass up an opportunity,

I pulled the nose up and finished him off. Then I kicked left rudder and fired into the cockpit of the nearest Il-2. He started smoking and went down, both men bailing out.

I then knew I had enough ammunition for a third pass, when suddenly my fighter was hit by flak. I felt the engine dismount from the brackets forward of the firewall. Shrapnel had torn dozens of holes in the right wing. The canopy was blown off and smoke was coming into the cockpit. I smelled burning oil, and then decided to bail out. I looked up and released my straps to climb out, but when I looked up, I saw the ground. I was upside down and did not know it, so I moved the stick all the way to the left, but the plane would not respond. I looked at the altimeter, which had disappeared, as the instrument panel was gone.

Well, as I could see soldiers clearly on the ground, bailing out was not an option, and landing upside down was definitely not my first choice. As if by divine intervention, my 109 was rocked again by flak, which luckily righted the plane. I looked ahead, saw an open field, and then decided not to trust the landing gear. I plowed right into a smooth landing, perhaps the smoothest forced landing I ever had. I got out, walked away as my plane started to burn furiously. Three of my friends flew overhead and I waved that I was fine.

Once I had a similar situation, not too long after this event. We were flying a mission to support a Stuka strike, and the flight in was very uneventful. I had flown perhaps almost a dozen flights with no action at all, so I guess I was becoming complacent. Then we saw a flight of over twenty Il-2s and a like number of escort fighters, which woke me up. I heard Ewald call them out over the radio. We had, I think, seventeen Me-109s, the Gustav models, in this flight. We divided into two sections; the first flight attacked the fighters to keep them busy, while I led the flight to hit the bombers.

The bomber formation was slightly below us at our two o'clock, while the fighters were about five thousand feet higher. I called the attack, kicked the right rudder, and threw the stick hard right. I rolled over and glanced behind me, and saw my seven comrades following me. I remember that Rall had just returned to flight status again, but he was not on this mission, and neither was Hrabak. Graf was, and he had two kills, I think. I had two new pilots who were on their first war patrol, and that made me a little nervous. I also wished that Hartmann was with us, but he was not up there that day either.

I began closing on the bombers, and they definitely saw us. They seemed to try and take evasive action, but at the speed we had in closing on them, it was no use. I closed in on one, about the third from the right, and fired into him. I saw the cannon shells strike, but having little effect other than shattering a glass pane where the pilot sat in the cockpit. The plane was not smoking, but it did go straight down. I did not bother to see if it crashed, as I was rather busy. I heard "*Horrido!*" and knew someone had scored a kill.

I pulled up and then hauled back hard on the stick, kicked left rudder, and banked left to come around again. I immediately came up on the right rear seven o'clock position on another Il-2 and fired. He started smoking and lost altitude in a shallow dive, and then he started burning, leaving a thick black smoke trail. I knew I had enough ammunition for another attack and I was undamaged. I called out my status and learned that all of my flight were undamaged, and six kills were confirmed.

After hitting the second bomber, which I knew was a confirmed kill, I flew through the formation, losing altitude to gather airspeed, and then I pulled into a climb again. My wingman, the ever-present Ewald, called in a kill of his own, which I saw. As I pulled the nose up, I banked right in a shallow turn and could see four bombers going down and only three parachutes.

I also saw a Messerschmitt going down trailing smoke, followed by four Yaks, Red Banner boys that were followed in their dive by a single 109. I saw from the markings that it was Barkhorn firing, and one of the bombers just exploded and then careened into another Il-2, and both fell in flames. Then he pulled up to avoid the falling wreckage and almost collided with another Il-2. He would have clipped it with his wing if he had not rolled over to the right in his climb. His wingman killed that one, and the fourth and last one turned into me. I thought, "Damn, two kills for Gerd, maybe I can get this guy."

Then I felt the "whump whump whump" as my fighter was hit. I looked at the instruments, and all seemed fine, although I then noticed a rather large hole in the left side of my canopy. Had I banked left instead of right, the force of banking would have placed my head right where the cannon shell had penetrated. That was the wake-up call I needed. The shell had continued and went through the left corner of my windscreen, so I now had the slipstream pouring in on me.

My wingman, Ewald, chopped his throttle and slid in behind my enemy, who was trying to kill me. He shot him down, which was his second kill, but then he radioed that he was also hit. Then I saw a Yak flash past me from above, and I tried to pull the nose up to shoot him down, but I was near stalling, so I rolled upside down and pulled the stick back. I decided to dive away and gather speed, allowing me to pull up and then have a better look.

Well, this one guy stayed with me through the maneuver, which was a reverse split-S by the time I was finished. I rolled upside right and level, gained more altitude, and then saw another Il-2 headed east, so I fire walled the throttle and closed the distance. I looked behind me and I was clear on my tail, and Ewald was smoking.

Again I had the bumpy aftereffect of enemy rounds hitting my fighter, and my wingman called out the problem: another Yak had caught me while it was in the dive, shooting me up pretty good. I radioed back that I was well aware of the problem, because I had a burning smell in my cockpit, but saw no flames or smoke.

Then out of nowhere, I heard a call sign, and a *"Horrido!"* I think it was Heinz Sachsenberg, who was also another outstanding fighter pilot. He joined the battle and made two kills in a row, and the irony of it was that he was not even assigned to fly on that mission. He was in the process of ferrying a repaired 109 from another unit, where the pilot had landed it after a fight a few weeks ago. He just happened to hear the fight over the radio, and decided to join in.

I decided that it was time to break off and go home. I heard over the radio that my comrades had called out nine kills, one loss to us, which must have been the 109 I saw going down. That was a bad feeling, because we all knew that nothing good could come of being captured by the Soviets. I found out it was one of the new men whose name I cannot remember. The other new pilot claimed a probable, but definitely damaged an Il-2, which was later confirmed as a kill by ground troops.

Barkhorn had also fired on the same bomber, which was the last one I saw and wanted to get, but when the new pilot fired and then finished it off, Gerd gave him the kill. That was the kind of guy he was. My fuel warning light was on, and I was losing fuel, as Ewald said he saw the vapor trail from my fuselage and wing. That sober reality was probably more influential in keeping me aware of my fuel than anything else. However, these Red Banner boys were not interested in breaking contact.[13]

Soon there were only the two of us and eight Yaks, all turning ever tighter to try and get an advantage. I did not see the other German fighters. I later learned that they had climbed for higher altitude, as another fighter group was being vectored in to pick up the very formation we were attacking. Again I felt this "whump whump" and noticed another good-sized hole in my left wing.

Ewald flew past me, and his fighter was scored with what appeared to be dozens of bullet holes. Then a pain flashed through my leg; an exploding shell had hit the fuselage, and a piece of the hot metal struck me in the thigh. I was bleeding, but it was not life threatening. I called that I was headed home, so I let the *Shturmovik* go, as I was still at least twenty to thirty minutes flying time from my base and low on fuel. I still had my wingman, and that was always the way I defined a successful mission. Even if you shot down a few airplanes, if you lost your wingman, the mission was a partial failure.

Well, I noticed that my fuel gauge was still dropping fast, so I assumed I was losing even more fuel. Soon I saw my air field loom into view. We had a standing rule: the aircraft that were the most badly damaged were to land adjacent to the landing strip. This was so that the air field would not be choked with debris, thus preventing undamaged fighters from landing. If the landing gear locked down, you could use the auxiliary strip. If they did not lock down, we were to belly into the field adjacent to the auxiliary airstrip.

The fighters in good shape would land first, and taxi off if possible. Then we damaged fighters, with solid gear down and locked, would set down. I tried to lower my landing gear, but something was wrong. Ewald told me that the entire undercarriage was shot full of holes, and the smoke I smelled was a small fire, as one of my tires was slowly burning up in the wheel well. Rather than bail out, which I hated, I wanted to save the fighter. I was really too low to safely bail out anyway. The thought of that fire touching off my streaming fuel and blowing me up, or turning me into a flying torch, preyed upon me.

Without my gear able to come down, I came in to land, engine switched off, fuel off, belly riding across the grass strip, taking two bounces and slamming into a pile of bombs that had been placed at the edge of this field, and I scraped right through all of it. I was lucky that my plane was not on fire and the bombs had no fuses. That event was written about by Raymond Toliver and Trevor Constable in Erich's biography, *The Blond Knight of Germany*.[14]

The reason I mention this is because this was the first day I met Erich Hartmann, which was October 1942. He had just arrived at the unit, and I was assigned as his temporary section leader. So, the first time Hartmann sees me is when I am climbing out of that shot-up fighter, stepping over a scattered collection of bombs, bleeding from a minor leg wound, my flying jacket also with tears in it from the cannon shot through the canopy as the glass shattered.

Many months later, when we were together on a more permanent basis, I assigned Hartmann to serve as my wingman many times, and also with Gerd Barkhorn. Before this, I was informed by Rossmann that Hartmann was hardheaded, so watch him, but he also said that he was a naturally gifted pilot. He was just rash and impetuous. Under Alfred Grislawski, he was given his first opportunity for a victory when we met a single Soviet fighter, which was also in October 1942.

He was a typical fighter pilot. Young, impetuous, and easily excited when he thought of getting a kill. We called it "the fever," and we all had it at some point early in our careers, but Erich had it really bad. He took a lot of foolish chances early on that he would never repeat after he gained some maturity and experience. On more than one occasion he gave full throttle to chase a kill, only to get into trouble. Dieter Hrabak was also a little concerned, as was Hubertus von Bonin. Erich was placed on probation a couple of times, and he had to work with the mechanics and ground crews as punishment.

He also got hit by flak a few times, which I always called the "great equalizer," since antiaircraft did not distinguish between friend or foe, but that dealing with it was part of the average day's work. Hartmann was a good student, and I taught him combat aerial gunnery, primarily deflection shooting in a turn, which was very difficult in a banking maneuver, after I had experience myself. He was already a good gunner, and he picked up on it easily. He finally completed the war as the top fighter ace. The great thing about Erich was that he never allowed his success to go to his head, and he always remained a very humble and friendly young man.

Erich had already been reprimanded earlier for breaking formation and chasing fighters, getting damaged and crashing his plane with nothing to show for it. [Authors' note: Prior to Krupinski's assignment to command 7.III/JG.52, Hartmann had, in fact, taken part in a team effort in downing a *Shturmovik* of the 7th Soviet Guards Attack Aviation Regiment on November 5, 1942.] As he followed his already burning victim down, the *Shturmovik* exploded, damaging Hartmann's Me-109G and forcing him to make a belly landing. This was properly credited to him as his first victory, as a means of encouraging the new man in the squadron.

Erich was a slow starter, only having two kills by the end of the year, and he was never a high-scoring pilot in missions, or even in the daily reports when compared to many others. However, he was a steady scorer once he found his rhythm and gained more confidence. His first solo victory, scored while flying as my wingman, was over a [Mikoyan-Gurevich] MiG-1 on January 27, 1943.[15] I think this was his third victory.

Erich was a great shot at long distances, unlike me. I preferred to get in close and shoot, and many times I brought pieces of the enemy aircraft home with me. Erich later adopted the same tactic, and he was always successful and was never wounded or shot down by an enemy fighter pilot. He did get forced down once from debris, after scoring a kill against an Il-2 in August 1943, when he was first captured, but he managed to slip away pretending to be wounded, almost getting shot by a German sentry after a couple of days on the run.

What was really amazing to me was that his mechanic, Heinz Mertens, whom I knew pretty well, loved that guy. When he heard that Erich was down in enemy territory, he grabbed a rifle, map, and rucksack and—without any orders, or even informing anyone at all, which was a serious court-martial offense—headed out on foot, east toward the front to try and find him.

That was foolish for a number of reasons, but he and Erich had a special relationship. This special bond between a pilot and his chief mechanic cannot be underestimated. I do not know of a single fighter pilot, especially a successful one, who would hate to have to choose between his wife and his chief. The wife may not have liked the decision he made. It was that man who kept you in the air, and kept you alive as much as a good wingman.

I remember that on May 25, 1943, when Erich shot down a [Lavochkin-Gudkov] LaG-5, and as he pulled up to avoid the explosion and debris, he collided with another LaG, probably the wingman of his victim. It was a horrible crash and he was also credited for the second kill, but somehow, despite the clear damage that we could all see, he managed to bring his 109 back to base. That was excellent airmanship for certain. We then went back up for a second mission later that day, and Erich climbed into a new Me-109. Mertens had not had a chance to change the oil and run a check on the engine, especially the manifold pressure and rpms.

Erich believed that it was fine, as it was a brand-new aircraft with less than ninety hours on it. Mertens, who turned out to be something of a soothsayer, I guess, shook his head and said he was opposed to it, that he wanted to check the fighter out. Well, Erich dismissed his superstition and took off anyway, but within ten minutes of the mission, he turned back, stating that there was an engine problem. Hrabak was there when he came back, and asked what the problem was. Erich told him, and Hrabak decided to take the plane up himself. He had just retracted the landing gear when a loud bang was heard, and smoke began pouring from the exhaust manifold. I did not see this, but learned about it upon my return.

Hrabak banked back toward the air field, lowered the gear, and eased into a landing, and climbed out as the 109 was still rolling. Mertens and his team checked out the plane, and found that a crack in a piston had created a stress point. The piston head, under pressure, had blown apart, sending shrapnel into the engine and oil crankcase, which in turn started a domino effect. The fighter was covered with oil all underneath, and a piece of metal had cracked the windscreen as it was blown up through the cowling.

Hrabak asked Hartmann how he knew there was a problem, since when Hrabak took off, he could feel nothing wrong, and the instruments did not indicate any problems. "It just felt wrong," was Erich's response. He had that gift. He could tell if there was a problem with a plane long before the warning indicators informed him of a problem, and this saved his life on numerous occasions, of that I am sure.

I had returned from the mission, and Hartmann and Mertens were sitting, drinking some warm beer. That was when I found out about the entire event. Apparently, from that point forward, Hartmann had Mertens check out and run the engine on every fighter he flew before every mission. He trusted his instincts and he trusted Mertens. That is what I mean by the special relationship.

During Operation Citadel, the Battle of Kursk in 1943, we were flying as an entire unit supporting the Immelmann Wing [*Sturzkampfgeschwader* 2, or StG.2]. This was the famous *Stukageschwader* with Hans-Ulrich Rüdel. They had just started changing from a traditional dive bombing unit into a tank destroyer unit. We had three groups up, staggered at different altitudes, providing layered top cover as the Stukas killed tanks. I have to say, just watching this over a period of a couple of days, I was quite happy to stay up in my fighter. The life expectancy of a Stuka crew was not very good, flying slow and low right into the face of massive enemy forces. They were perhaps the bravest men I ever saw.

From July 4 to 9, 1943, near Orel, I think, we had some of the greatest dogfights I ever experienced outside of the Caucasus. These were fights that drained every drop of sweat and emotion from you. In three missions during this time, Erich scored seven kills, probably his best one-day total. I think that in one engagement, there must have been over two hundred German and five hundred enemy fighters, all chasing, firing, and killing each other.

On this day, [July 5, 1943] I scored eleven kills in four missions, bringing my total up to ninety *Luftsiege* (victories) at that time. But

I was not unique. On this first mission, everywhere you looked there was a plane going down streaming smoke, or exploding, and a thin wisp of smoke, or a fire where a plane had crashed. Parachutes were easy to see, and this is interesting, since most of my contacts were at altitudes below five hundred to one thousand feet, which is very low to exit an aircraft. Incidentally, by the next month, Erich was at the one-hundred-victory mark, and had been assigned as *staffelkapitän* for 9/JG.52. He had come a long way in a short time, and was over his "fever."

I have to mention this first fight I was in with my guys on July 5 in more detail. I was following Barkhorn and the others, when someone called out enemy fighters at six o'clock high. That meant that we had enemy above and behind us, which is the worst position to be in as they can dive on you, gathering airspeed, hit you and then break away before you can react. The two elements broke, one right and high, which was Barkhorn's group with Hartmann and I, numbering some fifteen planes, and the other went left and around. We were going to turn into them head-on.

The reason for this was that one element would climb into the enemy, engage and scatter them to break up the attack. The other group, led I think by Hrabak with Rall, who had returned to us, and others, also numbering fifteen fighters, was to catch the enemy who flew past us, and then swing onto their tails. Then we, the climbing element, would check to make sure that there was not another high cover of Soviet fighters protecting the group diving. If there was, we would engage. If not, we would fly top cover as the lower echelon took care of its business.

Well, Hartmann was on my wing, and we had another enemy group with top cover, which Barkhorn called out over the radio. This alerted all of us that there were more enemies above. We continued the climb, and they winged over to get us, and I sighted one Yak at long range, although the distance was closing fast. I fired and he blew up, then I fired on another right next to him, and he passed by me smoking.

The lower enemy flight were LaGs and the top flight were Yaks, but they all had red noses and cowlings. This meant they were a Guards unit. These were the guys to fear and respect . . . and there were over sixty of them. I had just shot down two, and Hartmann, Barkhorn, Ewald, Rall, Graf, and Hrabak were all calling in "*Horrido!*" so I assumed they were pretty angry with us.

Well, I called over to Hartmann that we were in a real good fight, and this was when he scored the first three of his seven kills that day. I was still pulling up into the enemy at an angle of perhaps seventy degrees when I had another Yak in my sight. I fired a quick burst, and I saw the plane start smoking, and the propeller stopped, then he flew past me, right past my left wing, and just over Hartmann, who was at my seven o'clock, and then he hit the ground. You must understand that all of this happened in the space of about six seconds or less. That was how fast moving this fight was.

We heard calls of "*Horrido!*" several more times, and then two voices stating, "I am going in," or "I am down," or "bailing out," and the sky was filled with aircraft, both ours and the enemy. One of the men called out that he had been rammed, and I saw a Yak on the tail of a 109, chewing off the rudder, and then both aircraft spun into the ground. There were, of course, no survivors from either plane. I thought about just how crazy that Soviet pilot was. He had already shot the 109 up and it was smoking, and he still did that. This was incredible to me, but I had seen such things before.

I had scored my third confirmed kill, and one damaged, when I fired upon another Yak, but I then ran out of ammunition. Barkhorn said he had him, and shot him down for me. Hartmann called in three, two confirmed and a probable. That last unconfirmed kill would be confirmed by ground forces the next day, and there was also a Stuka crew who witnessed the kill.

We finished up the fight that only lasted about ten minutes, I think, and then I made a radio call check on who was still with me, and who went down. I then radioed to our flight leader, Hrabak, I believe, on his channel. After that, after we landed, the base was pretty quiet. We were exhausted, and it was only the first of four missions, and it was only around 8:00 a.m.

We took off within the hour, after the fighters were refueled and rearmed. This would take us on the second sector patrol and support mission if needed. July 5, 1943, was a very busy day, and for us it had just started. We flew with external belly tanks, which added another hour of flight if we controlled the fuel mixture and did not fly at low altitude, or at high speed, or drop the tanks when engaged.

Within twenty minutes or so, we came across a flight of bombers, a few American-made [Douglas] Bostons and Il-2 types. There were no fighters that we could see, but that did not mean they were not there. One thing that we did know, which really astounded us, was that many Soviet aircraft did not carry radios. I know that by taking them out, and reducing weight, you could extend your range. However, given the great numbers of aircraft, and the scope of the fighting, I could not even imagine going into combat without communications.

I managed to take my *Schwarm* of four planes into a nine o'clock position attack profile, where there would not be much lead on the targets. I heard the other leaders also calling their targets, as there were thirty of us, and a like number of the bombers. Barkhorn took his flight top high, while Steinhoff remained low, and we in the center took the bombers. The lower flight with Steinhoff would take care of those that dropped altitude and tried to escape. We cut through the formation, firing, and I had two bombers smoking and dropping towards the ground. Ewald fired, and his exploded, and then he hit another, but I could not see what happened to that one.

We flew into them firing and then passed under them at full throttle and then pulled up over the bombers, climbing to evade their defensive fire, and also banking over to see what the enemy formation looked like, and which aircraft were remaining. I saw that out of about thirty or so bombers, six or so seemed to be missing, and dark smoke trails followed their path down. I had five kills so far in the two missions, but I was not finished.

I banked back, and Ewald, knowing me well, also banked with me, and the rest followed. Hartmann called in "fighters," and I continued to attack. I shot down another Il-2 and continued firing into a Boston, I believe. That bomber began to smoke and the crew bailed out. The Il-2 just kept flying, dropping altitude, and I winged over and finished him off. That was seven for the day so far.

I called out that I was out of ammunition, but the rest of the men were still good, and Hartmann had called out two fighters he'd shot down, but no bomber kills so far. The strange thing was I never even saw the enemy fighters up to that time. Ewald had two kills for sure, and Steinhoff apparently picked up two kills on the low echelon. Barkhorn, who had, I think, scored three kills like me on the first mission that day, chalked up five on this one.

Then I saw something amazing. Steinhoff was climbing, chasing a Yak-9, and I saw the white smoke of his fuel injector kicking in. He must have wanted that guy. The Yak-9 was pulling away, since the Me-109G was not as good in the climb, but Steinhoff then fired, and the cannon shells streaked into the fuselage. The plane began to stall, and the canopy flew back. Well, the pilot of Steinhoff's third kill, his plane still climbing slowly, climbed up on the seat and jumped, leaping out.

Steinhoff's wingman was perhaps one hundred feet behind at five o'clock low of him, and also climbing. This Soviet pilot, upon leaving his plane, fell back quickly. I was banking left and looking over the wing straight down, and I saw this pilot's body actually get clipped by the propeller and then strike the windscreen of the 109, which shattered, and then bounce over the fighter and tumble away.

The German pilot, whom I did not know and cannot remember, called in that he was blinded and wounded. I would have assumed that his fighter was uncontrollable, so he set it down on the battlefield. Unfortunately for him we were over enemy lines, and I do not know whatever happened to him. It would seem that Steinhoff's victory finally got his revenge.

We all turned back to base as another group rotated in, relieving us. We went back, again refueled, rearmed, and ate a quick meal, and then took off within two hours for the third mission. We had lost only two fighters, and claimed eleven kills on the first mission and fourteen on the second, for twenty-five kills in total. We did not have long to wait to engage the enemy on this third mission, because they were over our lines.

This was almost exclusively a fighter formation and these guys were headed to our bases, which was not that unusual. Strafing and dropping the odd bomb may not have done much in the way of material damage, but it certainly kept you on your toes, and awake if you were on downtime. They usually targeted our fuel depots if they could not get to our fighters. Well, these guys were all headed straight for our field, and we just carved into them. I shot down two so quickly, there is really nothing to say about them. They passed right in front of me, so I led them, squeezed the cannon, then machine guns, and two went down, one right after the other. I then kicked left rudder and whipped in behind another dozen of these guys.

Well, they knew that Ewald, Hartmann, and I were there. The rest were behind us, and Barkhorn had found a medium bomber group he was going after. Steinhoff called out *"Horrido!"* twice, and I did the same. I was then on the tail of this Yak, so I fired quickly, and then did not wait to see what else happened, and then fired into another that went past, and after rolling over and maneuvering into another attack from low and behind the same fighters, I saw they were gone. There were others, and all of us were very busy. I fired into a total of six aircraft on this mission, but only managed to get three kills confirmed.

Hartmann again had two kills, along with Steinhoff, and this time Barkhorn only managed to confirm one, I think, with Ewald claiming five damaged, but only one kill to be confirmed, and this took about a week to do, if memory serves. The last mission of the day was also eventful, but not very interesting. I did manage to confirm three kills, easy victories, and nothing great to report. Hartmann also finished up, and had a claim of eleven kills also, but not all would be confirmed.

I claimed eleven kills for the day, with another seven enemy aircraft as probables, since they were badly damaged. My kills were easy to confirm, but the rest remained unaccounted for. It is possible that another pilot finished off one of mine, and vice versa, as unless you see fire, a parachute or smoke, you may not know that a fighter was hit by either of your fellows, or even friendly fire. That night, due to our great success, we really did have a few drinks, until about 10:00 p.m. That was when we all had to get rest, since the next day, and indeed the next few days, were going to be very busy for us.

Like most of us, Erich did not have much respect for our enemies, mostly due to the primitive method of their technology. We often examined the crashed remains and looked at MiGs, Yaks, LaGs, and other aircraft. They often did not use any modern aiming or gunsight technology. It is true that many of the planes we found actually had hand-painted circles on the windscreen, which formed an estimated aiming point. But you must remember that the Americans and British were also sending their own aircraft to help the Soviets, such as the P-40, P-39, Spitfire, Hurricane, and medium bombers.

Now these western aircraft did have modern sights, and good ones. The Soviets often cannibalized these planes if they were damaged and mounted the sights on their own planes. Also, the Soviets duplicated these sights and began producing them, as well as, I am certain, captured examples of our Revi. What you could get away with in fighting the enemy in 1941 to mid-1942 was a foolish thing to do in later 1943 and 1944, up until the war was over. Russian pilots were getting better, their technology and fighters were very good, and you would not find more courageous and skilled pilots than those within those elite units. These men were fearless and well trained.

We were quite a unit, JG.52 scoring more than eleven thousand victories during the war, and all of us were, and still are, good friends.[16] We lose members every few years, so the circle of friends grows smaller. The greatest joy I have is when we get together, and despite what you may think, we do not really discuss the war so much. We talk about our children, grandchildren, and how well we are doing, and remember those of us who had passed away since the last time we were together. The *treffen* (reunions) are always great.

During the war, I bailed out four times, crashed a few times, and was wounded seven times in all, but two of those were superficial wounds. I was awarded the *Verwundetabzeichen* [wound badge] in black, silver, and gold. I don't recall the exact number of belly landings, since my flight log and Knight's Cross with Oak Leaves were all taken by an American GI when I became a prisoner at the end of the war. I would guess the number of landing crashes I walked away from to be between ten and twelve, and not all combat related. I would like the readers as a favor to me, please let the world know about that logbook. If it ever turns up, I would like to give it to my grandsons one day.

Regarding [belly landings], this is a good one. I had taken a flak hit, and lost coolant and engine power. I did not have any fire or smoke. I saw the lines and being at ten thousand feet or so, I just glided in. I saw the ground coming up, and as I had surface controls, such as elevators, aileron, and rudder, it was like flying a heavy glider. Since we all trained in gliders, dead stick landings were not difficult for us. However, the Me-109 makes a very heavy glider.

The coolant had leaked into the cockpit somehow, probably from the blast after the flak hit in the radiator and fuel cell, and I could smell it, and the fuel line was also ruptured, so the last fifteen minutes of flying was dead stick, I just went into the glide slope and chose the best open terrain I could find.

[After I made my landing] a German soldier started waving his arms and yelling at me. I opened the canopy and could hear him. He was saying, "You are in a minefield, do not get out!" Well, I was thinking that if I were in a minefield, the last place I wanted to be was in the middle of it, so why would I not want to get out?

Then, as I climbed out of the cockpit, I began doubting my own intelligence, since the left wing I was standing on began to dip toward the ground. I knew that if it struck a mine, the remaining fuel in my 109 would ignite, and I could smell the fuel leaking from somewhere, and if that did not kill me, the shrapnel from the mine would blow through the wing and get me. So, I said to hell with it, and I just carefully walked the remaining thirty meters or so to the edge of the minefield, and then I was safe.

The German soldiers shook their heads and had a look of complete disbelief, saluted me, and one of them said that it "was the most insane thing he ever saw." I told him that I just decided that rather than wait, since I assumed there would have been a map of the minefield as it was ours, I would walk out and take my chances. His response was, "No, sir, I was referring to why you chose to land in a minefield in the first place." What do you say to that?

I am often asked what battles stand out the most, and that is too much to remember, as I flew more than 1,100 missions, and I mentioned July 5, 1943, when I shot down eleven planes in four missions in a single day. This one Soviet pilot I engaged was a damned good one, not the usual guy you ran into.[17] This fellow had some skill. His problem was that he was flying an older, slightly inferior aircraft, a Yak-1, which could turn very well at low altitude, and could out-turn the 109, and it had good firepower also, and a strong engine. The problem was that the early Yaks did not have a good self-sealing fuel tank, and it was vulnerable that way. The later Yak-9 was a totally different and very dangerous aircraft when in the right hands.

Soviet pilots, for the most part, were not as well trained or gifted as the British and Americans I flew against, at least early in the war, although there were a few exceptions. All of us Luftwaffe pilots ran into these exceptions, great pilots, at some point in time. They did not seem to have the stomach or the skill to maintain a solid dogfight. I do not think it was cowardice, because they would ram you if they had the chance. I just think it was the lack of good tactical training, and the inability to think for themselves, relying upon their flight or element leaders to make decisions. If you could locate the flight leader and shoot him down, the rest of the average units just lost heart, since they had no leadership.

I even saw Soviet pilots right on the tail of our aircraft, firing all their weapons from within a hundred meters, and never scoring any critical hits. I just assumed it was due to bad gunnery, or a lack of training. I had a guy on me, and I was done for certain, and I could see his shells passing by me, left and right, but only a few hits. I managed to get him instead. This was actually due to most of their aircraft not having proper gunsights as I mentioned, which were really important for deflection shooting, but when they were right on our tail, I think it may have been a problem of inexperience. This was at least true until 1943.

Once you shot down a flight leader, the rest usually scattered, and when they lost unit integrity they were usually easy to shoot down when you worked as a team. In a fight they usually broke off after engaging and headed home after a couple of minutes if they could not bounce you or get an advantage. These extraordinary pilots I mentioned were usually found in the Red Banner units, the cream of the crop for the Soviets. We also knew that there were Free French volunteers flying with the Red air force also.

Once you saw these fighters, usually later model Yaks, LaGs, MiGs, and some American P-39 Airacobras, with their distinctive red paint on the fuselage, you were probably going to get into a real brawl. These were the encounters that made you sweat and rely upon your training and the teamwork of your fellow pilots. You rarely had a second chance to make a bad mistake against these pilots.

There are many missions that do stand out in my mind. I had one encounter over the Ukraine, before Stalingrad anyway, and we were in a formation of perhaps thirty Messerschmitts, and with a fighter-bomber group of Focke-Wulf 190s, which were going to attack ground targets and strafe a nearby air field. We were flying top cover, and we had been in the air for perhaps half an hour when someone called out enemy aircraft. Passing by and under us was a flight of more than sixty Soviet fighters, to include all types. I believe that this was the first time I scored a kill over an American fighter, a P-39.

The Soviets really loved that aircraft, and it was apparently good as a ground attack aircraft, but I sat in one, and I knew that it was not a fighter I wanted to be in if a dogfight broke out. However, it had great armor plating and self-sealing fuel cells, which were lifesavers.[18] The engine mounted in the rear meant they could load up four heavy cannons, two in the nose and also in the wings, so this plane had a lot of firepower, more than ours. [The original configuration of the P-39 had one 37mm cannon in prop hub, two machine guns in nose and two or four machine guns in wings. Some Soviets modified the armaments, increasing the weapons for ground attack operations].

We broke up the group, and three *Schwärme* of fighters peeled over left and we gathered airspeed. The enemy was about two thousand meters below us, on our nine o'clock low position headed northwest, as we were headed east. They were headed for the ground attack aircraft that we were there to protect. I assumed they did not see us, but as a precaution, Hrabak had two flights stay up as top cover, just to make sure that the attacking fighters were not being drawn into a trap. I later found that his decision was most prudent.

I was leading the other three fighters of my *Schwarm*, and we closed the distance quickly. I closed in on a group of Yaks from their seven o'clock high, and sighted in on one. I fired and saw my shells rip the left wing off, and it spun in, no parachute. I was closing too fast to make another shot so I flew through their formation, and then pulled up, converting my dive into airspeed to reach higher altitude while pulling out. My wingman called out his kill, and the other two called them out also. I banked right and looked over the side, and saw four fighters falling and two parachutes to confirm the kills.

The second *Schwarm* had also scored kills, and one of the pilots took out three Yaks in a single pass, but then we heard Hrabak's voice over the radio. This was a trap, and the LaGs up top were coming in on us. Hrabak then ordered his remaining flights to catch the new ambushers from the rear. I had completed a full turn, counted all my men, and saw what happened next.

This Yak closed in on an Fw-190, firing with everything, and the German fighter started smoking and fire erupted all over the engine cowling. The pilot pulled up and reached probably one thousand meters altitude and bailed out. His parachute opened, and I was thinking that he would have more problems waiting for him on the ground than just bailing out of a damaged fighter. The Yak pilot that shot him down then pulled around and climbed, and headed straight for the German pilot in the parachute.

I saw the cannon shells from the Yak strike the parachute, shredding it. The poor man fell to his death, I am certain. That moment, which was perhaps the angriest I had ever been in my life, caused me to break Hrabak's cardinal rule, "Fly with your head and not the muscles," as I broke from my flight and increased the throttle, streaking down to get the Yak. I wanted to kill that guy. I closed in on him and he saw me on his five o'clock. I figured he would break left or right, so I chopped my throttle, another violation of Hrabak's rule: "Fighter combat should be engaged from altitude and at full power to achieve altitude after the attack." Well, that rule was out the window, but this guy was mine.

The Russian was a smart guy. He also chopped his throttle, thinking I would overshoot. I was still going faster than he was, but I dropped the nose and bled off airspeed, and lowered the flaps as I pulled up. I lost airspeed rapidly. He was drifting into my gunsight, and I squeezed off a three-second cannon burst, as he was only fifty feet in front. The Yak shuddered and pieces flew off, striking my 109, but no damage as far as I could tell.

I then pulled alongside this guy. He knew he was over friendly terrain, and had no problems if he landed or bailed out. He looked over his left wing at me, and I looked at him. Just then he blew up. The explosion rocked my fighter severely. My wingman at that time had followed me and finished the Yak off. I gave him the kill. I had a habit of doing that. Besides, we did not share kills as in the American or British air forces.

When we landed, Hrabak called me into his office after reading the *Abschuss*. He chewed me out and read me what you would call the riot act. I knew he did that for the benefit of the other pilots outside, who could hear everything. I thought he was going to ground me. Then Hubertus von Bonin came in, and he told me what he thought about my actions.

Then, after that was all over, Hrabak placed his hand on my shoulder. "Walter, I would have done the same, after what he did to that Focke-Wulf pilot, but I would have told my flight what I was doing, and not gone alone. I saw what happened, and I understand. But never allow your emotions to dictate your actions. Cemeteries are full of pilots who did what you did, and I prefer having you around. Besides, the other new fellows may learn bad habits from you, such as landing in minefields."

I learned from that ass chewing, and I never again allowed my emotions to override my common sense. Hrabak was a great leader. He knew how to get the best from his men, and I learned much about leadership from him, which I tried to pass on to others when I became a section leader.

Another mission I should mention was earlier in the war, about 1941, when I came across fifteen to twenty [Polikarpov I-16] *Ratas*, during which my aircraft was hit by a large air-to-ground rocket of some kind. It must have been a dud, as there was no great damage, no explosion, but I felt the entire aircraft shake violently. This was when the *Ratas* were attacking ground targets, and one *Rata* turned on me, shot the rocket at me and hit me. I did not even know they carried them. That was an unbelievable situation. I managed to recover control of my 109, and then roll over in a chase.

I then closed on one *Rata* and it was an easy kill, less than a dozen rounds of machine gun ammunition. He caught fire and went right in. I then pulled up, kicked the right rudder, and got a great deflection shot on another, and he flew right into my cannon shells and broke apart. I then pushed the stick down and dropped the nose, and saw another *Rata* about four hundred meters away, so I increased the throttle and closed in.

This guy saw me and he cut power, trying to make me overshoot, but I also chopped the throttle, and I drifted closer to him, stepping on the left rudder, going into a yaw. This turned out to be fortunate, because at that time two more Soviet fighters, Yaks, flew past me. They had been on my tail and I never even knew it. They overshot me. I then fired into the *Rata* that slowed down, he burned and fell away. The pilot took to his parachute.

The two Yaks that had overshot flew ahead of me and one rolled right and the other left. My wingman killed the right Yak, and I then managed to kick the left rudder and damage the left Yak. He was smoking but still in good shape. I was on empty and the fuel light was staring at me, and I was out of ammo anyway, so I guess he got away. I did not claim him, as I never claimed a damaged fighter. I did report this in the *Abschuss*, but I believe another pilot finished him off. I always gave the other pilots the kills if they finished off one of my cripples. Gerd Barkhorn, like most of us, did the same. We never argued about a kill.

Speaking of Barkhorn, I must say that I saw him in a fight that still makes me sweat to this day. If I remember correctly, the entire unit was in the air. This was, I think, in September 1943, and we were in the south. There were about forty of us escorting a Stuka flight of about fifteen aircraft against Soviet ground targets. We were to fly top cover while the dive bombers followed the medium bombers.

The Heinkels [He-111 bombers] were to soften up the targets, and the Stukas would dive in and pick off vehicles, troops in the open, whatever they could find. We soon became involved in a twisting, turning, and vicious fight. More than fifty or so enemy fighters, which included Yaks, MiGs, LaGs, you name it, dropped from out of the sun. Their red paint and bold emblems identified them as a Red Banner bunch.

I was less interested in scoring a large number of kills as I was in making sure my flight stayed together. I saw three 109s smoking, but I also saw perhaps a dozen enemy aircraft smoking and burning. As I pulled up and rolled over to my left to look down, I saw this 109 turning with these three Yaks. They were flying in what we would call a lose *Kette* formation of three ships, when the right Yak exploded. The concussion rocked my fighter, then the lead Yak started burning, and then the left Yak rolled over and the pilot bailed out. The right Yak was turning to get on me when my wingman fired on him, getting hits, which forced him away in an inverted dive. Unfortunately for him, we were at so low an altitude by that time that he nosed straight into the ground.

I did a dive to get in there and cover this 109's tail, in case he had unwanted visitors. These three Yaks had gone for the Stukas, and the pilot, which turned out to be Barkhorn, had attacked the three fighters alone. This was at fairly low altitude, less than a thousand meters, and he had rolled over after shooting the first one, managed a deflection shot on the second, and barrel rolled over again into a great kill position on the last fighter, pulling up as I came down.

Another Yak was on his tail, which I was able to shoot down, and I pulled up next to him. He just looked over and held up three fingers. I tapped my head as if to say he was insane. We do that today to other drivers on the autobahn, also. He was a fantastic fellow as well. This was absolutely incredible airmanship. If I remember correctly, his 109 never even had a serious bullet hole in it from an enemy fighter on this mission, with one exception to a round that struck his windshield from the rear gunner of an Il-2 he shot down.

I would also have to say that my victories in the narrow Caucasus passes were memorable, as was my victory over an LaG-5 at Stalingrad, where the Russian lost more than a third of his left wing and was burning like hell. About fifteen Luftwaffe pilots saw that, including Johannes Steinhoff, who was my commanding officer in the *staffel* at that time, as well as Graf, Hrabak, Wiese, and Rall. That LaG was still spinning slowly at low level and I watched him go in, twirling like a leaf, slowly fluttering down to the ground. He burned like a candle. He crashed but did not explode, just burned.

I never really had the opportunity to meet too many of the big people in the German government. I did, of course, meet Adolf Hitler, when I was with Hartmann, Gerd Barkhorn, and Johannes Wiese, but I never met Hermann Göring face to face, though I saw him once. That was when I became a lieutenant at the ceremony in Berlin on January 31, 1941, along with several hundred other cadets. He was a very big man, I can say.

How I met Hitler, although only once, is a good story, when I was awarded the *Eichenlaub* [Oak Leaves] to the *Ritterkreuz* [Krupinski's score at that time was 177]. *Bubi* Hartmann and I had partied heavily the night before and were still drunk as hell, despite the fact that we were to receive our awards from *der Führer*.

My head felt like a cement block: too much champagne and cognac. It is never a good idea to mix those two under any circumstances. Then, in the corridor, Erich saw Hitler's hat on top of the coatrack, and he put it on. The hat was too large for Erich, and it fell over his eyes. He made some joke about Hitler having a big head for such a small man. We heard someone behind us, and it was Hitler's Luftwaffe adjutant *oberst* Nicolaus von Below. He was not amused at all, and told us that if we were finished clowning around, we had an audience with *der Führer*.

Barkhorn, who had previously received the Knight's Cross on August 23, 1942, as an *oberleutnant* with 59 victories, knew him [Hitler] from before, because he was also decorated by Hitler with the Oak Leaves on January 1, 1943, with 120 victories. I always thought that he and Rall, and maybe even others, should have also received the Diamonds, such as Nowotny had who scored 258 kills, and [Otto] Kittel, who had 268 or so [no Diamonds awarded].

Well, I was getting the Oak Leaves along with Hartmann and Johannes Wiese on March 4, 1944, and Barkhorn was getting the Swords after scoring 250. In over 1,100 combat missions, he was shot down nine times, bailed out once, and was wounded twice. The first injury took him out of combat for about four months, and the final injury took him out for the rest of the war. His last crash I saw, but more about that later.

I am certain that if Barkhorn had not been out for those four months, and then placed into an administrative job, he would have been the top ace, and Erich always thought this. The only exception may have been Marseille, who had 158 by 1942, after only a year and a half in combat. Then again, Rall was out for six months after his crash in the Caucasus, which was a grim day for us. I thought he was dead for sure, as I was with Hrabak on a top cover flight as we heard the radio call. Rall could also have been the top ace if not for the broken spine. Who knows?

All of us at the *Reichschancellery* had received our orders sending us to Berlin two days before to get our medals, which is probably the award date that the record reflects, unless I am mistaken. Such award records are dated from when the approval was given, not when the medal was received. We were also all JG.52 men and caught the same transport plane, then the train into Germany.

Barkhorn wanted to see [his wife] Christl, and Hartmann longed to see his lovely Ursula. I made the comment that it was great to be back on the ground, since pouring champagne in a Ju-52 was quite difficult. That was when I suggested he just pass the bottle around, and abandon the tin cup. Erich never talked about the war, only in briefings or debriefings, but he always spoke about his Uschi.

Hartmann was making some funny comments about Hitler, mimicking him as giving a speech at Nuremberg, and he tried to stand still without falling over. I was in not much better shape, and he knocked me down by accident, but I caught myself against the wall. Barkhorn had a hangover and I may have been too drunk, but I thought I could actually see his head expanding and contracting. Perhaps it was just my vision being blurry. Wiese was sober, as he did not drink during this time. He had been ill with some stomach problem.

We only started to sober up as von Below called the room to attention, and Hitler, after walking into the room, started handing us the awards, although I felt that I would throw up. He handed us our medals in their presentation boxes, shook our hands and congratulated us individually. He gave a short speech about how we were holding the Bolshevik beast at bay, and how the Western Allies were still trying to take Italy, but were not brave enough to cross the English Channel. Then he began describing his plan for his "*Panzerfestung*" [armor, or tank fortress] which was a way to immunize the army divisions against enemy tank attacks. This was part of his greater Fortress Europe plan, and he gave his prophecies as to how we were going to push the Communists back in the east.

Erich looked at me, looking at his Oak Leaves, and then at Barkhorn, who had taken off his Knight's Cross with Oak Leaves to fasten the new Oak Leaves and Swords to it, who also looked at me. Wiese was ahead of us and he turned around also, and as we walked out of the room to have lunch, Hartmann whispered, "Do you really think that he believes all that rubbish?"

I just shrugged my shoulders and said, "I would think so."

Barkhorn said, "Sure, he believes it, and that's the problem."

Then we sat down at the table. The waiters brought out the meal, and Hitler had a spinach salad with some kind of fruit and a glass of water. They had several bottles of wine, and finally Wiese had a glass. I figured "hair of the dog," and I had some and passed the bottle to Erich. I have to say the meal was pretty good. The wine was not bad either, a Riesling, I think.

I had heard that he did not eat meat, did not smoke, and did not drink alcohol. Hell, I did all of those things, and in a momentary lapse of mind, after I finished the meal of sausage, bread, and carrot salad, I took out my cigarette case. Erich looked at me, and he gave me this look, and shook his head. I then remembered hearing about Hitler hating smoke, and carefully placed my case away. Hitler did not miss it. He never looked up from his plate and said, "Krupinski, that is a disgusting habit, you should think about quitting that." Wiese, Barkhorn, and Hartmann all tried not to laugh, and I felt like a reprimanded child.

As soon as Hitler finished his meal, the casual chatter turned into a more serious discussion. Part of his plan was to dig very deep and intricate tank traps all along the frontier using forced workers. These would slow down the Soviet advance and allow our tanks, infantry, and Stukas to hit them. He also began talking about the new wonder weapons, such as the rockets and new jet technology. I had no idea that before the war was over, I would become involved with this project.

He asked us about Lemberg, where we had come from and where our brave soldiers were fighting against those Russian tanks and [the men] were dying terribly. He told us about the war in Russia, and you had the feeling that you were listening to a complete madman. I thought he was a raving lunatic, and by the time the meeting was over, Hartmann and I needed another drink, and Barkhorn kept saying, "I told you so."

Erich always had a strange feeling about Hitler, and he did not trust him. Erich had a very good feeling about people, almost psychic, I guess you could say, just like with aircraft. I learned to trust his instincts. He had these same instincts as a pilot. Hartmann was a very gifted young pilot, and a very sensitive man, very quiet, unless you knew him, but a great person.

Flying with men like him, Rall, Hrabak, Steinhoff, Ewald, Grasser, and the others was a great experience. You felt safe in that kind of company. Erich and I had a good relationship from the day we met, as I was assigned to be his mentor when he arrived in the unit. I felt bad for him when we learned he was sent to Siberia after the war, along with Graf and others.[19]

When I transferred back to the Western Front in the spring of 1944, I was assigned as *Gruppenkommandeur* of II/JG.11 and promoted to *hauptmann*. This was not long after receiving the Oak Leaves, when many Russian Front experts were sent to fight against the American four-engine bombers. By that time it was a very different war from 1940. I did that for a while with JG.5 and JG.11, including during *Bodenplatte*, when I commanded III/JG.26 from early October 1944 to March 25, 1945. I had been wounded again, this time by my own flak, and went to the recovery hospital where Steinhoff found me.

Fighting against the American bombers and fighter escorts was often much worse than fighting in Russia. I never came across a bad American fighter pilot, just a few that were unlucky. Attacking the bombers, the big ones like the [Boeing] B-17 and [Consolidated] B-24, was difficult. It was bad enough just because of the defensive fire, and the old-timers such as Walther Dahl, who was good at shooting down bombers and many others, said that it was much worse now that American fighters and sometimes RAF aircraft were always escorting them.

I even met with Herbert Rollwage, the best bomber killer, who told me that 1944 was a different war from 1943, and with 44 heavy bomber kills out of his almost 100 victories—just as Eder had 36 bomber kills of his 78 or so. I listened to these men, like Toni Hackl, who also had 32 bomber kills out of his total of 192. They were the experts, I was the novice.

These meetings were very important. Even my old friend Steinhoff, who transferred from the east, was shot down on his first mission attacking bombers. "Damn, *Graf*, I must have turned into an idiot or something," he told me during a brief meeting shortly after my joining JG.26, while he was in Italy with JG.77. Such was the difference in the two fronts, they were just different wars.

The B-17s and B-24 Liberators were difficult to engage due to their potent .50-caliber defensive fire, and the American fighters made it even harder to get close, since they outnumbered us somewhere around ten to one on the average until later in 1944, when it often felt more like fifty to one. I found this all very frustrating, and had to change the way I thought about things.

I had been flying the Fw-190D model, which was a great departure from the 109, and even very different from the earlier 190A series. First, the early Focke-Wulfs were air-cooled radial engines. However, the "Dora" was like the 109, liquid cooled, only it used the BMW liquid-cooled engine that was in use on the Junkers Ju-88 medium bombers, just the next generation of design. This meant higher altitude and a faster aircraft with a more powerful engine. We were as fast as the P-51D, but still did not have the range of the American fighter, though we had great firepower.

I had a meeting with Georg-Peter Eder, who was one of the men who developed the frontal attack method of hitting the B-17s. He was a wealth of knowledge, but he also had been wounded fourteen times and was shot down a total of seventeen times, the last fifteen crashes and wounds being from doing this kind of work. He was absolutely fearless for sure, but I also kind of thought him to be a little mad. He taught me his method, but try as I did I could never really master that. It was a gift that I simply did not possess.

We were losing experienced experts all the time—we were just overwhelmed. Allied fighters and bombers attacked our air bases day and night, as well as bombing the cities. American long-range Mustangs, and then later, the other Allied fighters flying from French and Belgian bases, really gave us hell. Exhaustion was also a factor, since we could never get enough replacement pilots, and the newer pilots just did not have the experience to survive long under such conditions.

Galland was really upset about this, and he demanded that Göring reverse his order to turn out more pilots faster. He knew that half-trained fliers would be killed in larger numbers than veteran pilots. In addition, Galland had been very resistant to Operation *Bodenplatte* of January 1, 1945, and he predicted the result as it was planned. He was furious with Göring for not consulting him in the planning, and having him draft a proper, and perhaps better, plan. This was one of the many situations that led to the Fighters' Revolt. Galland cared very much about us all. As our commanding general of the fighters, he was not opposed to going up against those whom he saw as making bad decisions.

That was one of the things we admired about him. Yes, I think it was his ego to some degree, but then again, I would not want to fly in combat with a pilot who did not have a healthy ego, and a good sense of self-respect. Call us a little narcissistic perhaps, but if you don't have that kind of arrogance in the cockpit, you will die. That is what makes you aggressive, and active aggression is most of what is needed to achieve victory over your opponent.

Even Hartmann, as mild mannered, quiet, and polite as he was, would become a raving madman in battle. I do not mean that he would go crazy and scream over the radio. No, not that, but what did happen was he had a complete personality change; he became deadly, serious, and, as history shows, quite successful. This was also Galland, although "Dolfo" was a much more gregarious person than Hartmann, or the rest of us, for that matter.

Regarding Galland, you must understand that back in those days, it was considered very unhealthy to be noticed as someone who openly disagreed with Nazi policy. I had heard rumors that the Gestapo tapped his telephones and bugged his office. They also followed him around to take down the names of anyone he spoke with. Later, after the war, Galland confirmed this. He told me that Reinhard Gehlen personally told him of a conversation that he had with Göring, where the *Reichsmarschall* told him to "get something solid on Galland, because I cannot court-martial a Diamonds holder without something that Hitler and the German people will believe."

You must also remember that this was around the same time that *Admiral* Wilhelm Canaris was arrested for treason, making Gehlen the top intelligence man. We also knew that Gordon Gollob had been ordered to get "the dirt" on Galland, such as the accusations that Galland had been living with a girlfriend, while not married for a couple of years. He was also accused of working in the black market, since his mess halls had always been stocked with the best food, all of which was strictly rationed, and required government approval for purchase in government stores. Even generals had to have ration cards.

I knew, as did we all, that following the Fighters' Revolt, Göring had issued arrest warrants for Galland and [Günther] Lützow. He wanted them court-martialed, and he wanted Lützow executed, Steinhoff banished, everything. This was very frightening, and showed just how panic stricken Göring had become. I remember getting the message read to us that came from Berlin, directly from Göring himself, stating that Galland was fired and that Gollob was his replacement.

I think that the information I learned, and the rumors I had heard during the war, which were later confirmed, made me feel as if I had wasted my life, and that my country, and the rest of Europe, had been destroyed for no logical reason. I really did become an active pacifist after all of that, despite remaining in the military. I hated the thought of war, and when the Yugoslavia problem exploded recently, I could only think of how stupid we humans must be. We have learned nothing from our great collective failures.

By late 1944 through early 1945, after I had been wounded several times, I was trying to finish the war out at our fighter recreation center, which was a medical recovery spa of sorts at Bad Wiessee in Tegernsee. This was when Steinhoff and Galland stepped up to some of us on April 1, 1945. Steinhoff asked me, "*Graf* . . . how would you like to fly the 262?" Well, he did not have to ask twice. I was well aware of the "Turbo," as we called it. I had even seen photographs, but had not seen one in flight yet. I was very excited. I knew that I wanted to be a part of this program.

The very next morning, I jumped into the cockpit of a Messerschmitt 262 and flew my first test flight after a short familiarization period. I described all of that in a long paper I wrote for our *Jägerblatt, The Fighter News*, of February–March 1987. My last sentence was this: "*Es war der Beginn eines neuen Zeitalters der Luftfahrtgeschichte*" (It was the beginning of a new epoch in aviation history).[20]

I was only distraught over the fact that we did not have this plane sooner. Steinhoff had told me about the jet a few months earlier, after he had taken over JG.7 for a short time. He loved the jet, and he explained the delicate nature of the engines, the problematic takeoff and landing characteristics, but also the great advantages of the 262.

Galland was using Steinhoff as his recruiting officer, and they had collected some of the best in the business. They also got Barkhorn and tried to get Hartmann, but Erich still had a soft spot for JG.52. His decision to remain with this unit would prove very costly. As you know, he spent over ten years in Soviet prison camps after the war, after the Americans handed them over to the Red Army in May 1945. I would not see him again until the late 1950s, and he was never the same man afterward.

I joined *Jagdverband* 44, Galland's "squadron of experts" at Munich-Riem, and then we moved to Salzburg in Austria, then Aibling-Heilbronn, and then back to Munich, and so on. What was interesting about the squadron was that, with only perhaps four or five exceptions, every pilot wore the Knight's Cross or a higher version of the Iron Cross. Also, we were the only squadron in history that was led into combat by the equivalent of an American three-star general. How many squadrons have a sergeant flying wingman to a full colonel, let alone a general?

We were rank heavy, and that tended to raise eyebrows among the upper echelons in Berlin. Galland did not care. Almost every pilot in the unit was either an escapee from a hospital, pending some form of military reprimand or discipline, or had been in trouble in some fashion. One great example was Erich Hohagen, who had also been taken from the hospital. He was in the room two doors down from me at Bad Wiessee, and had been badly wounded again. He needed a little help walking, but could sit in the cockpit just fine. Galland also wanted Walter Schuck and Heinrich Ehrler, who were both Swords holders and flying with JG.7 and had both already scored victories in the jet under Nowotny's command before his death, then flying under Eder and then Steinhoff.

I still do not know how Galland and Steinhoff managed this, but I suppose when two officers enter wearing those high decorations, and who are both well-known heroes, very few low-ranking medical officers are going to rub them the wrong way. Galland had that way about him: cigar in his mouth, that smile, and his very persuasive way of speaking. I can say that, no matter how angry he was I never heard him raise his voice. He just stared into a person, made his point, and never waivered. He even did this with his boss, the "Fat One."

We had some spectacular missions, especially when we received the R4M air-to-air rockets for our jets. My introduction to the unit was interesting. JV.44 had some success the previous day, when on April 8 Steinhoff shot down a Liberator, and Ernst Fährmann shot down two B-17 Flying Fortresses.[21] Steinhoff had come over from JG.7, along with a few of the others, and they had already used the rockets with success even before we were a formed group. Having that experience in the unit was invaluable.[22]

The first time I saw them work was, I think, on April 5, 1945, as the unit shot down five heavy bombers.[23] I had recently been made adjutant of the unit, meaning paperwork, which I hated. There was quite a large number of enemy escort fighters around, so that tended to keep you busy in the cockpit. There was no way we were going to dogfight with these Mustangs, Thunderbolts, and Lightnings. We had to just come in fast, hit them (bombers) very hard, and then get away very quickly. Once we were at least four to five miles away, we could turn back and line up another target. The one great advantage that we had in the 262 over the 109 or 190 was our approach and climbing speed. This was both a positive and a negative thing.

Our speed allowed us, as I said before, to attack rapidly and then leave. That speed gave the enemy gunners on the bombers much less reaction time to sight in, lead us, and get a solid killing burst. Our speed also allowed us to approach from underneath, closing the gap quickly, and if you had the rockets that gave you a great advantage, as you could fire the R4Ms from outside the effective range of the .50-caliber machine guns. The rockets also gave you a better chance of a hit, as they spread out, like a shotgun. This allowed us to pull away before we could be fired upon in many cases. However, the rockets also increased drag, thus slowing us down from our 100-mile-per-hour speed advantage over the Mustangs when flying "clean jets" to a 70- to 75-mile-per-hour advantage.

The Mustangs and other Allied fighters would have to drop from very high altitude, convert that into increased airspeed, and then hope to close in on one of us, and even get a good deflection shot. This was the most common way our jets were shot down, other than being shot trying to take off or land, when we were very vulnerable. We had no maneuverability or speed until about two to three minutes after takeoff. That is a lot of time when you have the enemy on your tail.

The only great downside to having the jet was the loss of maneuverability; we could not turn as tight as the other fighters, so speed was our life insurance. The other problem with such a fast attacking and closing speed was that, just as the enemy gunners had little time to lead you for a kill, you had much less time to pick out a target. You had to be right the first time, and if you did not have rockets, you had to adjust your shooting to compensate for the much slower targets. In this case there was very little deflection shooting. You closed in quickly, fired a quick burst, and then you left.

The 30mm cannons were incredible weapons. It took only a half dozen or so to bring down a heavy bomber if you hit it in the wing root, which weakened the structural integrity of the aircraft, and also housed fuel cells. Just one explosive shell could bring down a fighter. When thinking back about those days, I never really had much fear in flying the jet, even against such large numbers of enemies. Well, that was until I decided to land once after a mission. The one thing you had to be aware of was the fact that the Allied fighter pilots would use two methods of getting you once you broke off combat.

The one method they would use was going to our air fields and shooting them up. They knew where we were, it was no great secret. These guys would hang around and try to catch us landing, hoping for an easy kill. This was why we had Fw-190s or Me-109s that would fly cover for us to protect our landings. The other problem you had was that, after you broke contact, and were usually out of ammunition and low on fuel, the enemy fighters would be following a few miles behind you. On a good day, you probably had about ten to fifteen minutes to approach, extend your gear, hoping it would work, land, and get out of the cockpit. Many times we jumped out of our jets to have the shadows of enemy fighters pass overhead as they strafed us.

My first couple of missions after joining JV.44 were uneventful, but on April 16, the squadron took off, armed with the R4M rockets mounted in racks under the wings. We were radio vectored by ground radar to the formation of [Martin B-26] Marauders, which were twin-engine American medium bombers. Galland took the lead as always and we followed, flying in a *kette* formation, also known as a "V" formation, which was the same type of formation flown in the old days before World War II and the invention of the *Schwarm*, or "finger four" formation.

Galland flew into the bombers, but nothing seemed to happen. Galland, who was leading our flight, flew past the formation without firing, but he turned around and then fired his salvo of rockets at a group of B-26 bombers. In moments, one disintegrated and another was falling—the tail had been blown away, and both parts were fluttering down through the light clouds. I fired my rockets and had some near hits, and damaged a couple of the bombers, but the smoke from Galland's two kills obscured the sky in front of me. Seeing the result of those rockets hit was incredible, a fantastic sight, really.[24]

After this attack, we flew off a few hundred yards so as not to hit any debris or get jumped by enemy fighters, and then attacked again using our four 30mm cannons. I damaged a couple of bombers but scored no kills that day and Galland had the only confirmed victories. I had a rocket misfire myself, and only a few of my rockets fired and did not do their job well. Galland pulled around and fired again. Later, he admitted that he had failed to take the safety off the rockets, and he did not even think about using his cannons.

On the second approach was when he had fired, and during that mission, he brought down two bombers. I lined one up and then fired my cannons on the second pass. I heard some thumps and hits in my jet, but nothing major. I could not believe just how effective those rockets could be. It was like firing a shotgun into a flock of geese, really. Galland had some .50-caliber bullets that struck his fighter and it had to go in for repair after we landed.

The next day [April 17] I took off with Galland, Steinhoff, Grunberg, and others, and I attacked a B-17 formation targeting Munich. We scored hits, and one of our pilots collided with a B-17, which I think was Eduard Schallmoser, taking it down, and I managed to hit another B-17 myself, but it did not go down. I did not see this collision between Schallmoser and the bomber, but Steinhoff radioed this information to us.[25]

We had many such missions, but we also ran into American fighters. Mustangs were a constant problem, and they would always follow us home, hoping for an easy kill. Taking off and landing, as I have said, were the most tense moments for a 262 pilot, as the plane built up speed slowly, and you could stall out easily if you pushed the throttles forward too quickly, which caused a flameout. This happened several times with pilots, and we finally learned how to throttle up slowly without killing ourselves.

I flamed out once when I was in transition training. I was used to pushing the throttle full open rapidly to increase takeoff power. This was a great error in the jet. I know that many of the pilots who were killed flying the jet probably died due to stalling out this way. The 262 was a very heavy aircraft when compared to the 109 and 190, and at low speed I would equate it to flying a brick.

On the day Steinhoff crashed, his flight of six jets was commanded by Galland. Other pilots that day, including me, were Heinz

Wuebke; Gerd Barkhorn, then with three hundred victories; "the Rammer" Eduard Schallmoser [so named for his penchant for ramming his jet into enemy bombers once his ammunition ran out]; Ernst Fährmann; Klaus Neumann; and Heinz Bär, who had sixteen kills in the jet. We were all either taking off for a bomber-intercept mission, or preparing to go on the second mission on the morning of April 18, 1945.

The reason Steinhoff crashed was that the previous day we had an American bombing raid on our field, and there were still a few potholes in the grass strip, bomb fragments scattered about, and although the men were trying to patch them up as well as possible, some remained filled with water and were sometimes hard to see. There had not been much damage inflicted upon the planes or the fuel depot, although one of the barracks took a hit and had some damage. I think it was also at this time I heard that my old friend Heinz Ewald had been awarded the Knight's Cross, which would have been one of the last awarded, being April 1945.[26] He deserved it a long time ago, not so much for his victories, but because he was a damned good and loyal wingman.

Like the rest of us, Steinhoff was loaded up with fuel and rockets, and his left wheel dug into a crater that had not been properly repaired after the latest American raid on our base. His left tire blew out, which caused him to yaw, and he almost careened into me as a result, as I was on his wing. His left engine then flamed out [possibly due to hitting the crater, throwing his hand forward on the throttle too fast, thus blowing the engine] and his jet went into a left skid, crossing my path. I thought we were both going to collide. I was certain of it.

I had enough airspeed to pull back on the stick and I lifted up, just clearing his jet and avoiding the collision, even though his jet bounced up into the air, almost hitting me, and again banged against the ground, ripping the undercarriage away, which I did not see. Once I was up and began raising my landing gear, I looked back as I banked slightly, and I saw the crunch of the impact and the explosion. The shock wave was felt even as I climbed away. I just knew Macky was dead. There was no way in my mind that he could have survived, and I was feeling very bad at that point.

There was Macky Steinhoff, trapped in this wreckage, the burning fuel exploding the rockets and 30mm ammunition around him. But he managed to crawl out, on fire, rolling on the ground.[27] They got him to the hospital and he somehow survived. I did not see that part after the crash as it happened, but everyone heard about it.

We were informed of his condition when we returned from the mission. He was the best friend any of us had, and a true patriot and leader. All of us felt that we were only a thread away from a similar fate after that accident, as well as the later loss of Günther Lützow [who went missing on April 24], and others too numerous to list. Steinhoff suffered for many years with many surgeries after the war, but his strength of character and determination to survive pulled him through. I give his wife Ursula a lot of credit, as she was his strength during those tough years.

Bär actually shot down two Thunderbolts on the mission that day, and he said that he would gladly give them back if he could trade them for Macky. Normally, we would celebrate victories, but no one felt like saying or celebrating anything. I would have to say that Steinhoff's crash dropped our morale, and Lützow's failure to return from a mission the following week plummeted our morale even further. Then Galland being wounded a few days later, and Barkhorn being injured and out of the war, pretty much closed the door on JV.44.

Our problem was that not all the jets were ready for flights. We were short on parts, fuel, even ammunition, or sometimes small technical problems happened. I flew one 262 that did not have a working fuel gauge or altimeter, as an example. Another one I flew actually had the complete instrument panel, but none of the wires were hooked up! One of our mechanics was also an electrician, and he managed to get a wiring diagram for the jet and repaired it.

Although I scored 197 victories in the war, I was only able to confirm two of them in the 262, with a third bomber claimed as a probable. This was on the April 16 mission with Galland, Steinhoff, Lützow, Bär, Barkhorn, Schallmoser, and I think Fährmann. There are probably many pilots who damaged enemy bombers that later crashed, but without verification on the ground or in the air, these were not counted. The fighting against the American fighter escorts and bombers was the worst, since they were excellent fliers and had so much top-rated equipment. I did damage a few other aircraft, all bombers. That was interesting. Galland once told us that if we did not have holes in our planes upon returning, then we must not have been doing our jobs.

I need to say something about some of the pilots in JV.44. [Gottfried] Fährmann [4 kills in the jet] keeps coming to mind, along with Schallmoser, who was successful, but he was also a rammer, bringing his bombers down by crashing into them sometimes. These guys were just a different cut of the cloth. Günther Lützow was another great man. While not a great ace in the jet, he was an outstanding leader, and a very brave man for many reasons.

We all knew about he and Galland, along with others having argued with Göring, and Galland being removed as general of the fighters. Lützow, who had the Oak Leaves and Swords, was a very serious, quiet, and dependable leader. He was also a Condor Legion veteran like Galland. I did not know him as well as I would have liked. He went missing on a mission, and I do not know if it was ever learned what happened to him. That was very sad. And then of course we had "Macky" Steinhoff, who was more dead than alive.

The morning before we lost Lützow, Galland informed us of the situation with Göring. Apparently Hitler had fired him and relieved him of his command. Finally, Galland said, after all these years, and the lives lost, Hitler finally made a logical decision, but too little too late. He had been replaced by *Generaloberst* Robert *Ritter* von Greim, whom we all respected very much.[28]

Georg Eder was also a great pilot, and a really interesting fellow, and he had great success in the 262 also.[29] He flew mostly on the Western Front during the war, and was a holder of the Oak Leaves. He was famous, along with Egon Mayer, as they were the guys who figured out that the head-on attack was the best method of hitting the heavy bombers in piston-powered aircraft.

However, this was only successful if you could do it very quickly, since the closing speed was fast, perhaps 700 miles per hour, giving perhaps a split second to fire into your target. The great benefit was that it greatly reduced the amount of defensive fire they received during the attack. Eder and Mayer were very good, and

I saw Eder shoot down a few bombers in JG.7, and even hitting some fighters.

At the end of the war, the unit was disbanded. Galland had been badly wounded by a fighter and crashed his 262, but we did not have near as many losses as say, JG.7. However, we were also a smaller unit, and did not operate as a unit as long. Some of the JG.7 pilots were recruited by Steinhoff, such as Köster, Lützow, Grunberg, Fährmann, Hohagen, and a few others. These men brought great jet experience with them when Steinhoff brought them in. I still do not know how he and Galland managed to accomplish this, since both of them had fallen from grace with both Göring and Hitler. Steinhoff once said that "if you looked a gift horse in the mouth, it was often missing teeth."

As the war ended, and the fighters were being destroyed, I was captured when the unit surrendered after blowing up the last of our jets, when the Americans were practically rolling onto the air field with tanks, infantry, everything. An American intelligence officer found us and took us via Heidelberg to the U.S. Army Air Forces/Royal Air Force interrogation camp in England.

Well, after four weeks of answering questions, I was being transported to Cherbourg, I believe, when I was attacked by a French soldier with a rifle. He struck me in the head from behind, knocking me unconscious. I later found myself in the hospital in Munich with American guards. After all of the interrogations, I ended up with the Americans, but while I was in custody I was robbed of my *Ritterkreuz* and *Eichenlaub* and my flight logbook, as mentioned earlier. Our decorations, especially the Knight's Cross, were highly prized by our captors. It was a difficult time, but my contact with the American military and the U.S. Army Air Forces officers prepared me for a new career later in the 1950s, until I retired in the 1970s.

After the war the unemployment rate was high for former officers of the military in Germany. Finding work after a career as a professional officer was not easy, especially since anyone who owned a business did so with the local Allied military commander's authorization. Professional officers were considered the elite of the

National Socialist Party, and any connection to us could have been economically unwise.

It was not until much later that this attitude changed, and people began to realize that, if anything, it was the professional officer corps who remained nonpolitical for the most part. We had no agenda except to defend our country from attack, right or wrong. There is no difference between us and any officer corps in any nation. All would defend their homeland and families, regardless of the political leadership in control of their country.

It was not long, however, before I started working for the U.S. Intelligence services under the umbrella of Organization Gehlen, the military and foreign intelligence service branch of the *Abwehr*, formed by *General* Reinhard Gehlen during the war. Gehlen was one of the *Abwehr's* chief intelligence officers, who later replaced Canaris as head of the organization [after Canaris was dismissed for his suspected role in the July 20, 1944, assassination attempt against Hitler and subsequently put to death at the Flossenburg concentration camp in 1945]. Gehlen's work and the examples he set were responsible for the creation of many postwar intelligence networks, including the GSG-9 [the famous German counterterrorist/intelligence service].

Gehlen died in 1979, but his work in collecting intelligence on the Red Army, and his ability to collate intelligence on every aspect of Soviet military operations, proved invaluable to the NATO Allies during the Cold War. Their understanding of the Soviet mindset, order of battle, political aims—all of that probably prevented another European, if not world, conflict. Gehlen believed that knowledge was power, and in this case he was proven correct. I learned quite a bit working with him, among many others, about intelligence and counterintelligence. I cannot discuss my work with any of these groups, as it is all still highly classified and I took an oath of silence.

I then worked for *Amt Blank*, which was the beginning of our Defense Ministry under Theodor Blank, West Germany's first postwar minister of defense during the Konrad Adenauer administration. There was a lot going on, not the least of which were the long-running discussions with the Soviet Union regarding the return of our men held there. This was a complete violation of the Geneva Convention, which stated clearly that all prisoners must be repatriated after the ending of a conflict. The Soviets had reclassified our men as "criminals" and not soldiers, and they had also refused to follow Geneva during the war.

During this entire process, until they were finally released in December 1955, I thought of my friends who were held in a Siberian hell. I thought of Erich often, as well as Hermann Graf and Gerd Barkhorn, and I did stay in sporadic contact with Uschi [Ursula, Hartmann's wife] and his family every so often. All of the wives and families wrote tens of thousands of letters to Konrad Adenauer and [Vyacheslav] Molotov, demanding their men be returned.

Stalin did state that his nation would observe the existing Hague Convention during the war, but not Geneva. The USSR never signed the 1929 agreement. We knew the reason for this was the fact that in Geneva of 1929, there was a special provision that stated a neutral power had the authority to inspect prisoner of war camps, check on the conditions of prisoners, ensure they were humanely treated and received proper care, and so on. Stalin was very paranoid about outsiders, and he was not going to allow any third party to interrupt his massive slave labor program. I suppose he had killed so many Ukrainians and others before the war, he needed the extra manpower.

I was approached by some officers in the 1950s who mentioned that we were forming the *Bundesluftwaffe*, which I already knew from my work with intelligence, but they did not know that. I was easily recruited, as there were many of the former Luftwaffe experts already there. I went for refresher flight training in the United Kingdom as CO [commanding officer] of *Jagdbombergeschwader* [fighter-bomber wing] 33. I was trained on the latest fighter types of the day, including the Lockheed F-104 Starfighter. I really liked that plane, as did Rall, but Steinhoff, Hartmann, and others were much less enthusiastic.

I was then later commanding officer of German training in the United States, German 3rd Air Division, chief of staff for the Second Allied Tactical Air Force, and afterward I was appointed as director of flying safety for the armed forces. I retired as commander of the Tactical Air Command in 1976. It had been a long career. Those were a lot of different hats, as you would say. I worked closely with many of the important political personalities of the time, such as Robert McNamara, who was secretary of defense under President [John F.] Kennedy.

My wife and I have only one daughter, who is married to an air force officer, a lieutenant colonel but not a pilot. I have two grandsons who attended the University of Munich. I have been the *Traditionsreferent* for the *Gemeinschaft der Jagdflieger* for many years, helping organize the reunions every year with my friends, men such as Galland, Wolf Falck, Rall, Hrabak, Edu Neumann, Ewald, Steinhoff, and Toni Weiler, just to name a few.

I am relaxing in my old age, and come to America and Britain sometimes to attend gatherings and meet old friends and make new ones. It may sound contrary to logic, but I have many friends who were once enemies. I have been very fortunate to have met and become friends with American, British, French, Belgian, and even some Free Polish fighter pilots. It is good that we were able to place that terrible war behind us, and embrace living.

I once met this Russian pilot, and after some discussion, I learned that he had been one of my victories in the Caucasus in 1942. I had shot down two of his comrades and then shot him down. He was the only survivor, and when he landed he was taken prisoner by our ground forces.

He then survived being placed in a camp until he was liberated by his fellow Russians at the end of the war. He told me that he had a very bad time in the gulags afterward, since Stalin did not recognize Soviet prisoners, just collaborators who surrendered, so he spent a few years alongside some German prisoners.

I also met his wife and his son, and learned this former enemy pilot was also a grandfather. I was very happy that he was alive, and I told him so. He thanked me for not killing him. I explained to him that regardless of our two nations' recent histories, I never took a fight personally (except that one time when an enemy pilot strafed the Focke-Wulf pilot, but I did not mention that to him). It was my job. Anything else would have been unprofessional, and clouds your judgment. He agreed, and we drank a lot.

I am not alone in thinking like this. Most of us former Luftwaffe types have good friendships with our American, British, and even some Russian opponents. It was good to see that the war did not last after the fighting had stopped. Politics, or perhaps the failure of politics, creates wars, and young men pay the price for that. I do not know of a single pilot from any country who does not wish there had been no war. It was not a fun occupation.

I am often asked many questions during these gatherings. I think that there is a kind of mystique surrounding us, especially from the younger generations in America, but not in Germany. Most young people know nothing of us, and they have little interest. Given our history, I cannot say that I blame them. We will be forever tied to the monsters who ran our country into the ground, killed millions, and ruined the great culture and prestige of Germany. It will take many years to remove that stain. I am also asked for advice, and I have some. Don't trust dictators or madmen!

General of the Fighters

Adolf Galland
104 victories; Knight's Cross with Oak Leaves,
Swords, and Diamonds;
Spanish Cross in Gold with Diamonds;
German Cross in Gold
(March 19, 1912–February 9, 1996)

WHEN HISTORIANS SPEAK OF PILOTS and the history of air
combat, certain names invariably come up sooner or later–
Manfred von Richthofen, Edward Mannock, René Fonck, Erich
Hartmann, Aleksandr Pokryshkin, Johnny Johnson, Dick Bong . . .
and Adolf Galland. Galland was the youngest general grade officer
of either side in World War II, and at age twenty-nine he was more
competent in aerial combat, strategy, and tactics than many of the
experts nearly twice his age.

Galland fought a hard battle against his superiors on the ground,
which made the danger in the air inviting, almost welcome. Adolf
Hitler and Luftwaffe chief Hermann Göring, who were always
trying to find fault and place the blame on others for their own
failures, began pointing fingers at the fighter pilots as the war turned
against them. Was it not the fighter pilots who failed to stop the
death and destruction delivered by Allied bombers? Was it not
the fighter pilots who demanded more of the resources and new
technology, yet produced the least results? Göring betrayed his pilots

and publicly denounced them as cowards, provoking the Fighters' Revolt in January 1945.

Galland, well known and admired by his enemies across the English Channel as an honorable and chivalrous foe, had found an enemy he could not vanquish: his own leadership. The consummate warrior was constantly engaged in heated battle with absolutist politicians, intellectual inferiors, and demagogues, who considered honor and chivalry a weakness and unnecessary in the modern age of warfare.

Galland eventually returned to where he had risen, the cockpit of a fighter plane, but as a lieutenant general leading a squadron. As a fighter pilot he was credited with 104 aerial victories, of which eight were scored flying the Messerschmitt Me-262 jet. It is suggested that anyone wishing to read Galland's complete autobiography, see *The First and the Last*, in multiple reprints. It is considered perhaps the best first-person publication on the Luftwaffe ever written, and done so from a man who was there as a major figure from the first day to the last.

Galland survived the political intrigues and combat of both the Spanish Civil War and World War II, only to find himself in postwar South America working for Argentine dictator Juan Perón, who at least appreciated his expert knowledge and relied upon his honesty. A holder of the Knight's Cross with Oak Leaves, Swords, and Diamonds, as well as the Spanish Cross in Gold with Diamonds, Galland died in 1996 at the age of eighty-three.

Galland granted this series of interviews, the last taking place in 1994. A greatly abbreviated version was published in *World War II* magazine in January 1997.[1] Additionally, many thanks go to his widow, Heidi Galland, for assisting in the final stages of these interviews, long after the process began. Great thanks also to the late Jeffrey L. Ethell, who gave me much of his first-person data collected from Galland going back to the 1970s. Jeff was one of a kind, as was Galland.

Adolf Galland

I was born in Westerholt, a small village in Westphalia on March 19, 1912. I was the second son, Fritz being the oldest, then myself,

Wilhelm, and Paul. My father was an administrator of private lands and properties, and he was very fair, but harsh. We had the best mother in the world, and during the war, she used to pray for fog to cover our bases so we could not fly. Two of my three brothers served as pilots, Wilhelm and Paul. Paul was the youngest and the first to die in combat, shot down and killed in 1942, and Wilhelm was killed a year later. Paul had seventeen victories, and Wilhelm had fifty-four and the Knight's Cross. My brother Fritz was an attorney.

Right from the beginning, as a boy, my greatest interest had always been flying. I started building models of aircraft when I was twelve years old, and when I was sixteen I flew in gliders. Over the course of the next three years I became a successful glider pilot, with my entire purpose being to study and become a commercial airline pilot.

However, my father was not very enthusiastic about this idea at all. This was my dream since 1925, and he had no understanding of my dream. He was a very practical man, and looked at things in simple terms. These were very interesting times, especially during the 1930s; Europe was undergoing great changes. Germany was again a great power, although still rising and recovering from the terrible times after the First World War.

After one year of training as a commercial pilot, I was strongly "invited" to join the "black air force" (the clandestine air force Germany was training prior to Adolf Hitler's rise to power). This was in the remarkable year of 1933, and I already had my first pilot's license. My coinciding training as a fighter pilot helped immensely with the commercial pilot's courses, but by 1937 I had already become a volunteer in the Condor Legion.

This was where I met and started the great friendships with men such as Günther Lützow, Werner Mölders, Eduard Neumann, Herbert Ihlefeld, Wolfram von Richthofen, and many others. Many of the pilots had trained in Russia, such as Wolfgang Falck, and there were a lot of very experienced pilots going to Spain. This was where we would learn the modern methods of air combat, and this experience would serve us quite well in the next war to come.

This activity was liked very much by all of the young fighter pilots. I did have a small problem after a crash in a Focke-Wulf

Fw-44 biplane in 1935 while in training, and a colleague, future Luftwaffe ace Dieter Hrabak, had one the following week due to bad weather. I had modified the plane beyond normal limits, which was a great violation, and I lost control and slammed into the ground.

Well, everyone thought I was dead, and I was in a coma for three days with severe injuries. My parents came and stayed with me until I came out of it. I had very serious skull fractures, a broken nose, which never looked the same again, and I was partially blinded in my left eye from glass fragments, so I still had to pass the physical. For many years after this crash, I could still on occasion pick small glass fragments out of the eye. To this day I still have some of the glass in my eye.

My CO (commanding officer), *Major* Rheitel, a flier from the First World War, assisted me in my goal to return to flying. So, I continued to fly, but a year later I crashed an Arado Ar-68 and again went into the hospital, where they pulled my old file stating that I was grounded. Well, with many days in the hospital, and knowing I would be banned from flying, I again memorized every letter and number in every possible sequence on the eye chart for my next examination.

We left for Spain with the Union Travel Society, ostensibly bound for Genoa on a tramp steamer. After twelve days we arrived in El Ferrol, Spain, on May 7, 1937. I had been to Spain before with Lufthansa and looked forward to returning. In our group of men, there were many future aces and leaders fighting for Francisco Franco's Nationalists, such as Hannes Trautloft, Wilhelm Balthasar, Günther Lützow, Herbert Ihlefeld, Hubertus von Bonin, Eduard Neumann, the famous World War I ace Eduard *Ritter* ["knight," or "sir" in Britain] von Schleich, and Hajo Herrmann, who was a bomber pilot and flew Junkers Ju-52s.[2] I became a squadron leader in the Legion Fighter Group, and we were equipped with Heinkel He-51 biplanes. Lützow commanded a squadron of the new Messerschmitt Bf-109s, and I envied him.

We were briefed on the political and military situations in the country at that time. The entire nation was being torn apart by civil war, with Francisco Franco starting a revolt with the military in Spanish Morocco, and finally being airlifted by our transports into Spain proper. His other forces were also brought in from other areas, including the Canary Islands, allowing him to establish a strong headquarters element, consolidate his forces, and plan his operations against the Communists.

The need for air support, at the tactical, strategic, and logistics levels, were why we were there. Hitler had offered his assistance, obviously expecting Franco's support later, when Hitler continued with his great plans in Europe. He was, as history shows, going to be badly disappointed.

Generalleutnant Hugo Sperrle was a no-nonsense leader without anything resembling a sense of humor, and he was the overall commander of the air contingent of the legion. We also had Wolfram von Richthofen, who was a transportation and logistics master. I came to know him quite well, as not only the great airman and genius thinker, but also as a very humane man, and we developed a great professional, if perhaps not personal, friendship until his death just after World War II.[3]

I must admit that Richthofen, who was first cousin to the famous Manfred from the Great War, was a genius on every level. He would later manage to coordinate and command some of the greatest air support missions in history, often with very little to work with, and against great odds. The one thing that I admired about him, and perhaps this sort of rubbed off on me, was that he was not a Nazi supporter, as he was of the old regime, where nobility and duty superceded politics. He was well known to have openly disagreed with illogical orders. I know personally that he argued with Göring about the feasibility of supplying Stalingrad in November 1942 through January 1943 with the required tonnage of supplies, to include food, weapons, and munitions. I was there.

However, the events in Spain, while not completely unknown to some of us, were not exactly what we expected. Most of the men sitting in the room had never heard of Franco or the political problems going on in the country until they were recruited. We learned that there was a massive Communist support network supplying the Republican movement.

This support primarily came from the Soviet Union in the form of weapons and aircraft, but there were other and more covert support networks. While the other European governments, and even America, did not openly support the anti-Franco faction, there were international sympathizers who volunteered to fight against the Nationalists and even arm and fight with the Republican Loyalists. Italy did join us in the fight.

The Condor Legion's strength in Spain when I arrived was only four squadrons each of fighters and bombers and a reconnaissance squadron. We had four heavy and two light AA batteries and signal units, but we never exceeded around 5,600 men. Hugo Sperrle was the first CO of the legion in Spain, and he personally led a flight of bombers against ships at Cartagena. He was an old Great War pilot and he believed in leading by example.[4]

My first engagement in Spain was Brunete, where we sent every plane we had against the Republican forces in July 1937. This battle was very important for a variety of reasons. First, it was a full-scale coordinated military engagement, with infantry ground attacks supported by artillery and of course our air support. We had all of the available intelligence on the enemy movements and locations, and acquired a pretty good picture of their capabilities, including their available air assets. One of the main objectives was to hit their air fields with bombers, followed up with a group of fighters to strike in a follow-up raid, thereby eliminating their air assets on the ground.

While these missions were being flown, other fighter squadrons would work in two groups; one group commanded by me would engage and strafe and bomb the enemy troops on the ground, while the other group commanded by Lützow would fly air cover and keep enemy fighters and bombers away from us.

This took great planning, and I learned a lot about operational planning from this and subsequent operations. I had been experimenting with a few of our technicians on new weapons in order to be more effective. I thought about using petroleum-based munitions, and that was how I came about developing what would later become known as naphtha weapons.

These makeshift bombs were oil and fuel drums filled with old engine oil, black powder, petrol, and a combination of mothballs and other organic materials, such as, in some cases, soap shavings. We experimented with everything. We finally hit upon the right combinations. Once the barrel was dropped, it would be ignited by a firing pin striking the primer, which in some cases was only a shotgun shell, grenade, or any other ignition system.

The initial impact and percussion would blow the powder, igniting the petrol, which would blow, igniting the oil, which would spread out over a large area and burn. This was several years before the Allies used them, especially the Americans who would devise these weapons, although their versions were to prove to be far more efficient.

The Madrid front was totally controlled by the Communists, equipped with modern fighters, such as the Russian Polikarpov I-16 *Ratas*. We bombed and strafed and engaged Loyalist fighters while our artillery pounded their ground positions. Finally we won, and Franco's forces were saved from a disastrous defeat.

We also performed dive bombing missions with our new weapons, which were effective in both tactical as well as in psychological terms, and that was one of the ways we created new tactics in ground support. After the victory, I was awarded the Spanish Cross in Gold with Diamonds by Franco, which was only awarded twelve times in Spanish history.

We had also developed what later became the *Schwarm* formation while flying in combat. This was what the British called the "finger four" formation later. The *Schwarm* was a combination of two *Rotte*, or two fighters, into a formation of four fighters. This gave us a great tactical advantage in many ways. For one, it gave us more eyes to scan the sky, and it provided security. If one *Rotte* attacked, the second pair could provide rear security, as if having two extra wingmen. It also helped us to confirm victories, as we had to have at least one eyewitness, unless you had ground confirmation, or later in World War II, gun camera film. Later our enemies adopted this tactic as well.

I stayed in Spain until my orders came up. Some of the men were either leaving or getting ready to return home, and our replacements came in to be briefed by us old hands. This was when I first met Werner Mölders, and this has been written about me by others, but it is a good story to tell again. When I first met him I was not very impressed. He was Catholic, did not drink much, if at all, did not smoke, and I was Protestant, less inhibited, and although this did not have any bearing upon our relationship, these qualities made him a far more serious and introspective person.

He did not have the typical fighter pilot's personality, which for the most part is a devil-may-care approach to life, and jovial, with few exceptions. Mölders was a very quiet, serious, and analytical officer. He was more like Lützow in his demeanor, which was not a bad thing. Lützow had already proven himself as a competent combat pilot and leader. This new man standing in front of me, taking over my command, was an unknown factor. I left Spain feeling a little uneasy, but that would soon change.

After the Second World War started, Werner Mölders and I were the first fighter leaders of the new age, along with Wolf Falck, and Mölders and I were later appointed as wing kommodores. Mölders very much liked having that distinction from the beginning. The promotion meant more time behind a desk and in meetings.

As for myself, I was unhappy because I only wanted to be a fighter pilot, and just fly and fight. I was never really into the concept of flying a desk. That was not my nature, ever. However, that was the order and we had to follow it. Mölders took to it naturally, as he was a far more analytical creature than I was. He was a very detail-oriented person, but this was not to say that he was not a deadly pilot. He was one of the best.

My first combat in the new war started almost from the first day in 1939. I flew in Poland in the Henschel Hs-123, performing ground attack missions and proving the dive bombing concept I had worked out in Spain. This continued until October 1, 1939.[5] That was when I won the Iron Cross Second Class. Then I was assigned as adjutant to Jagdgeschwader (fighter wing) 27 (JG.27) under Oberst Max Ibel, a former World War I fighter pilot, which I did not like very much, as it did not allow for much combat flying. Ibel had not grounded me, as he was an old fighter and knew that when it was in the blood, a true fighter pilot would risk court-martial to be in the air. He just turned a blind eye, and as long as we came back successful, he said nothing.

I did get away every now and then for a quick mission, and this was during the French invasion in 1940. I finally got my first kills in this war on May 12, 1940, near Liège, when Gustav Rödel and I went on a mission. Rödel called out an enemy fighter, and then we saw four, all Belgian flown Hawker Hurricanes, which he saw on his left wing, as my vision was obscured. I was flying on his right, and we had about two thousand feet altitude advantage, flying at about eleven thousand feet. Then Rödel called out two others, then more, for a total of eight enemy planes.

We banked left and increased our airspeed in the dive. We closed very quickly, but the enemy pilots saw us, and I fired a burst that scattered them, and then they also went into a dive. One broke right while the others continued down to get away. I took the single fellow, closed in, and fired a quick burst. There was nothing great about the experience, as my second burst ripped the tail off, tearing away the rudder. He just spun into the ground as the wings fell away. I then chased another one that tried to evade into the clouds, but I fired, estimating where he would be. I then saw him climb, break from cover, and then he rolled over and went straight into the ground.[6]

Rödel lost his two in the clouds after shooting one up, and we were low on fuel anyway so we returned to the air field. As we headed back, we dropped low and could see my first kill burning on the ground. I do not think the pilot managed to get out and he probably died. I then thought about that, about how that could have easily been me, or my wingman. That is when the reality of your business comes to you.

I shot down two Hawker Hurricanes on two later missions that day, but only one was confirmed. I had about a dozen victories by the end of the French campaign, which ended in June 1940. Next was the Battle of Britain, of course! That was a tough fight, where I was assigned to JG.26 *Schlageter*. I became the *gruppenkomman- deur* of III/JG.26 as a captain, and shot down two fighters in my first mission with them. It was in JG.26 where I formed my best relationships with my pilots. I flew with Gerd Schöpfel, Eduard *Ritter* von Schleich,[7] Joachim Müncheberg, and Josef Priller, just to name a few. These were all outstanding men and great fighter pilots. All received the Knight's Cross or higher awards for valor.

We had started the painting of Mickey Mouse on our planes in Spain, from the *Steamboat Willy* film, and when I painted it on my Me-109E in JG.26, it was holding a hatchet and smoking a cigar, which I loved. I always carried my cigars and became famous for them. I even had a humidor that was kept in my quarters where I kept them fresh, which I picked up in Spain. I think I had the only cigar lighter-equipped fighter in the Luftwaffe, plus a holder for it if I went on oxygen. It created quite a controversy, and the journalists were keen to focus upon that. But after the war I had to give cigars up on doctor's orders.

Flying combat in the Me-109E at that time over the English Channel, let alone over Britain, was a very dangerous thing. By the time we reached the British coast, we had perhaps thirty minutes of flying time, and less than twenty minutes if flying near London. This time decreased dramatically if you engaged in combat, which forced you to use more fuel. The British were almost always waiting to engage us as we crossed Dover or other areas along the coastline. When we carried the auxiliary drop tanks, we could sometimes extend that time an additional half hour. This really came in handy when we were later detailed as bomber escorts, which I hated.

I was promoted to *major* on July 18, 1940, and received the *Ritterkreuz* (Knight's Cross) from Göring on August 22, 1940, for my seventeenth victory. I then succeeded *Major* Gotthard Handrick as *kommodore* of JG.26, and received the Oak Leaves from Hitler on September 25 for my fortieth victory. On November 1, 1940, I scored my fiftieth kill and was promoted to *oberstleutnant*. In December I became an *oberst*.

As the *kommodore* of JG.26, and I would have to say that this was the best part of my career as a fighter pilot, I was able to really work with my men. The unit was very strong, with great personalities and successful pilots. By the time we fought in Russia, the

Luftwaffe was the best-trained and battle-tested air force in the world, in my opinion. Fighting the British had tested us and honed our skills. The rest of the year was simply an occasional patrol, with a few engagements, mostly intercepting British fighters coming over France.

I have been asked about this innovation regarding the head shield. It is true that I insisted that the Messerschmitt company build the fighters, and all later fighter types by all the firms, to include the steel plate behind the pilot's head. This came about because my mechanic, caring for my safety, took it upon himself to weld an inch-thick plate of steel to the canopy roof behind my head. I was unaware of this new device, and the next time I jumped into my Me-109 and closed the canopy, I leaned back to get my feet into the rudder pedals, and this heavy guillotine came down on the back of my head.

I felt as if I had been hit in the head with a club. I could not really focus for a minute, the pain was so intense. I swore under my breath that I would court-martial my mechanic when I landed. However, the irony of this was that after the battle, where I shot down two fighters, a Spitfire and I think a Hurricane, I had received some damage myself.

Upon lifting the canopy, my mechanic looked at me. I was still furious and told him so. Then he had me look at the back of the steel plate. That plate had stopped a heavy shell from decapitating me. Had it not been there, I would have been killed. I remember thinking suddenly that he had saved my life. I gave him a bottle of champagne, some money, and a three-day pass.

On May 11, 1941, I received what was perhaps the strangest telephone call in my life from Göring. I took the phone from my operator, and he was yelling out an incredible order. I was to take off with every aircraft and shoot down an Me-110 that was headed out over the North Sea. I asked him to repeat the order, as I was certain I misunderstood. "It's Rudolf Hess! He is going to England, find him and shoot him down!"

Needless to say I was stunned, and I asked if they had a coordinate, flight plan, or something. Göring said he had no idea, that every unit was on the alert and we were to find him. This was the ultimate needle in a haystack, not to mention a great shock. When I tried to ask how long the aircraft had been in the air and from where it took off, he hung up on me. Talk about an impossible order! I did not have the data needed to accomplish that mission. If I knew how long he had been gone, I could have estimated where he may be, given the distance he could fly, estimate the speed, and if he had an auxiliary tank, that would also be good to know.

I ordered the alarm siren sounded and took a squadron up, and we broke up into three flights, headed north and northeast, but found nothing. Gerhard Schöpfel led one flight, and we divided up the zone into three grids, with three groups fanning out. We stayed in radio contact, which we normally never did when over the Channel, due to trying to keep the British unaware of our activities. That day they were probably quite entertained.

We finally turned back when the fuel ran low. I heard later, of course, that Hess was in British custody. You cannot imagine how stunning this news was to me personally, and this incident was the subject of great discussion. Gerd Schöpfel later asked me if I thought " . . . Hess knows something about this war that we do not?"[8] I often thought about this question during the war, especially as we began losing.

Every fighter pilot dreads the thought of being shot down. We do not dwell upon it, since to do so can make you ineffective. But it does happen, and it happened to me more than once. This first time was on June 21, 1940, when JG.26 was stationed at Pas de Calais. We had attacked some Bristol Blenheim bombers and I shot down two, which were my sixty-eighth and sixty-ninth kills, I believe, but some Supermarine Spitfires were on me and they shot my plane up.

I lost coolant and the engine began to overheat. I pulled up and cut power to make my enemies overshoot, and I extended flaps to further slow me down, and then I kicked the rudder hard to yaw right. One Spitfire flew past and I snapped a quick shot, and scored some good hits. But his wingman got me again, and this time the engine oil light went on.

Some smoke began entering the cockpit; I lost power and threw the throttle full open to get more power to get out of there. I radioed my plight and headed for the deck. I did not think about bailing out, as I still lost engine revolutions and altitude. I was not at a very high altitude, perhaps only three thousand feet, and dropping quickly. I checked to see if I was being followed and it seemed clear. One of my squadron mates radioed I had no enemies on my six o'clock, so I felt better. I looked for a clear place to set down. Given the uneven terrain I did not lower the landing gear. I had seen planes that had tried this, and the results were less than perfect.

I had to belly-land in a large field, where I was picked up and I went on another mission after lunch. The fighter was salvaged, repaired, and later flew again. On this mission, I engaged a group of Spitfires and shot down number seventy, but I did something very stupid. I was following the burning Spitfire down when I was bounced by another one and shot up badly. My plane was on fire, and I was wounded. I saw blood splatter in the cockpit against the inside of the canopy. I did not know how badly I was wounded, and had even less time to think about it.

Smoke filled the cockpit, and flames were visible just under the inside of the firewall, under the control panel. I had lost rudder and aileron control. All the glass had been shattered, the canopy cracked, and the throttle had been shot away. The joystick where my hand had been had lost about two inches of height from a round that struck it. I could hear the wind whistling through the broken canopy Plexiglas. I was pretty well screwed up on all counts.

I tried to bail out, but the canopy was jammed shut from enemy bullets. So I tried to stand in the cockpit, forcing the canopy open with my back as the plane screamed toward earth. I could not understand why I was having so much trouble. I had forgotten to unstrap myself from the seat straps. I did so quickly while cursing myself.

I did [make some progress and heard] the metal give way, and more glass from the canopy shattered, which the slipstream blew into me. If not for my flight goggles, I think I may have been blinded. My head felt as if I had been hit with a hammer, and my right arm was very painful from the bullet that had passed through the skin before it struck the joystick.

The canopy gave way even more, and I was very cognizant of the fact that I was still losing altitude. I finally opened it, the canopy breaking free of its hinges and blowing away, and I almost cleared the 109 when my parachute harness on my back became entangled on the radio aerial just behind the cockpit. I fought it with everything I had as the fighter rolled over, inverted, and I could see the ground quite clearly.

Many things go through your mind during a time like this. I remember thinking about my mother, some paperwork I had not finished, including a few promotions and recommendations for awards for a few of my pilots. I also thought about a date I had with a special lady, which I was certain I was not going to make. Almost everything that had nothing to do with my situation was in my head for some reason.

I finally decided to relax and accept death.[9] It was actually a very peaceful decision. There was not any stress or regret, just peace. As the slipstream continued to beat me against the fighter, which was now nose down and had rolled over again so I could see the sky, I had accepted death until I finally broke free, my parachute opening just before I hit the ground. I was bleeding from my head and arm, plus I had damaged my ankle on landing. I was taken to safety by some Frenchmen, who could just as easily have finished me off. They placed me in their horse-drawn cart and carried me to a nearby aid station. I was very grateful and I paid them for the taxi ride.

After being shot down twice in one day I was worried that my wounds, and the loss of two expensive fighters, might ground me for a long time—that was my greatest concern, not to mention I had lost two airplanes and only had three kills that day to show for it. Those fears proved to be unfounded. After a few weeks of recuperation, I was awarded the German Cross in Gold and the first Wound Badge. I was also told that I was going to be the permanent *kommandeur* of the III *Gruppe* of JG.26.

It was just a few weeks later, on August 13, when we launched *Adler Tag* (Eagle Day), which was to be the single largest offensive against the British air bases and fighter units up to that time. Göring had planned this in conjunction with others, who were not in my opinion the best and brightest at tactical operations. The planning was a failure from the beginning.[10]

In addition, his intelligence was flawed. We were informed that the RAF fighter strength was somewhere in the neighborhood of only three hundred or so fighters. This was truly an erroneous assumption, as later I believe the actual number of enemy fighters was more like five hundred to six hundred or so.[11] I do have to say that, in Göring's defense, he did target Fighter Command at the bases and wanted to destroy their aircraft on the ground. This was a sound method; he just chose to go about it in a strange way, in my opinion.

The problem was that at no point in time were the fighter leaders called in to assist in the planning. Göring had planned a series of bombing missions against the aircraft industrial complexes, five waves in fact, which was reasonable. Under the assumption that [there were] only three hundred fighters, he thought that perhaps a third would be destroyed on the ground, another third in the air, and the lack of pilots, as well as the following missions afterward, would completely eliminate RAF Fighter Command. The plan on the surface was good. It only fell apart when you took it apart piece by piece.

However, in one example, he decided to send all of the available Stuka units into the battle as well. Now, this was quite stupid in my opinion for a variety of reasons. The most important reason was that the dive bombers were strictly ground support weapons, flying artillery, so to speak, which could only function with success when we had complete air superiority. This meant we had to have fighter control of the operational airspace. The same was true of the medium bombers. Sending these aircraft into battle improperly, especially in daylight, was suicide. Later, the Americans would learn this lesson, as did the British. We were sort of slow to realize this.

Göring decided that both medium and dive bomber groups would be escorted by Me-110s. Again, this was a stupid thing to do, since the Me-110 could not fight the Hurricanes and Spitfires. In addition, they often needed our Me-109s to escort them, since they were easy targets. When we did have single-engine fighters available for escort, we were pinned with ridiculous rules, making us stay with the bombers. We were actually ordered to not engage the enemy fighters for fear of leaving them vulnerable. Well, logically, by not engaging the enemy fighters we were all vulnerable, so I ordered my flight leaders to follow my plan, not Göring's.

Adler Tag proved to be the greatest and first defeat the Luftwaffe would sustain during the war. We lost only around ninety aircraft and aircrews. What we lost, in fact, was the initiative and focus necessary for future success. I knew that there was no way we were going to defeat the RAF with our limited-range fighters, let alone invade Britain successfully for an occupation. But then again, no one was asking my opinion. Good men on both sides were lost for nothing more than Göring's arrogance and Hitler's ambitions.

The next month [September 3, 1940], Göring had decided to change the operational tactic. He then decided that, rather than focus upon the RAF air fields and industry, he wanted to bomb London, as a response to the British bombing Berlin in August [August 25–26, 1940]. Hitler was extremely enthusiastic about this new plan also, and from that point the war changed. This was when Wolf Falck's ideas became all the more important.[12]

This decision to bomb London and other cities was to be perhaps the greatest mistake Göring would make during the war. The immediate impact was upon the fighters, as we were then strapped to the bombers as never before, not even allowed to engage enemy fighters. We were supposed to be used defensively, and only fire at the enemy who came in to attack the bombers.

This was insanity, and everyone knew it. Bombing London and other cities, at the expense of hitting air fields and factories, would not help us win the war. I knew this. No nation up to that time had ever been bombed into surrender, but only forced to submit after being conquered. This was basic history. In mid-September, Hitler planned his launching date for Operation Sealion. This, of course, never happened, as our losses had become so high. The rest of 1940 would be very uneventful, as we had both exhausted each other.[13]

What followed was the famous Blitz against England, with all of the major cities being bombed. Most of this was later conducted at night, since bomber losses really increased during daylight operations. We were also losing fighters, not just due to the contact with the RAF fighters, but we were stretching the range on our Me-109s.

Many fighter pilots landed without fuel along the beaches of France. During these missions, London was the primary target. Of course, the British paid us back, and they did so for the rest of the war.

During my time with JG.26, I had the great opportunity to spend time and fly with men who would become my greatest friends for many years. Gerhard Schöpfel flew as my wingman on several missions and was an excellent pilot, good humored. Gustav Rödel was also an outstanding man. Both were with me when we had a great dogfight with a Spitfire formation on August 9, 1941, in which Wing Commander Douglas Bader was shot down.[14]

One of his artificial legs was left in the Spitfire when he bailed out, and the other was smashed after he landed in his parachute. He had been shot up and then collided with one of my fighters. Both men survived. We knew about him [Bader], as he was quite famous as a pilot and the only legless fighter ace in the Royal Air Force. He was something of a celebrity.

We all felt bad for this courageous man, so I made a request through the International Red Cross, with Göring's approval, of course, and the British were offered safe passage for the plane to drop his replacement artificial legs. Well, they dropped them, but only after they bombed my air base.

Bader was fitted with the new prosthetics and sent to a prison camp. He had asked if he may be able to fly in one of our Me-109s, and I told him that such a request, while I would wish to grant it, would not be possible. Then he just asked if he could sit in the cockpit of one, so I placed him in my fighter. He familiarized himself with the controls quickly, and remarked at how well laid out and logical the instrument panel was.

He was a typical British officer. This is not a bad thing, but he was pretty concerned with the rank of the man who shot him down. I knew what that meant, so we found one of the young officers who had confirmed a kill on the mission and presented him to Bader, who seemed quite relieved that he was not downed by an enlisted man.[15]

After the war he was knighted as Sir Douglas Bader, which I think he richly deserved, and we remained friends until his death a few years ago. He was an extraordinary man and a worthy opponent, and I liked him very much. He and RAF ace Robert Stanford-Tuck became good friends of mine until they both died. They were both extraordinary men.

I became *general der jagdflieger* after Ernst Udet had committed suicide on November 17, 1941, and after Werner Mölders was coming back from Russia for the funeral. His Heinkel He-111 struck some telephone wires during bad weather at night, and he was killed in the crash.[16] At the time of his death, he was acting as general of fighters, holding the rank of *oberst* (colonel) with 114 kills. After the funeral of both men, Göring called me aside and made me Mölders's successor, even though I was still only an *oberst*. This was possible in the German military, but not so in [the American] armed forces.

Gerhard Schöpfel became *kommodore* of my JG.26 and was promoted to *major*, and I went to Berlin. I had already been awarded the Swords to the Knight's Cross, and upon my arrival on January 28, 1942, I saw Hitler several times, and on the third time he awarded me the *Brillanten* (Diamonds) after shooting down a total of ninety-four enemy aircraft. I was the second recipient, as my friend Mölders was the first. Hitler and I had a long chat along with some other military men who had also been decorated with various orders of the Knight's Cross.

Hitler had a certain fascination with the air war. Having been a ground soldier in the First World War, he had very little knowledge of air warfare, although he had a keen interest in learning from those who were experienced in it. Almost every time I was with him, outside of a private meeting on matters of a more serious nature, he always asked me, or asked a group of us pilots, about the enemy aircraft, their fighting capabilities, and the quality of their aircraft. I could tell that he was very concerned about maintaining a technological advantage against the Allies.

However, by the time I became very familiar with him on a regular basis, his interests lay elsewhere. This was particularly true after we invaded the Soviet Union in June 1941. By 1943, after Stalingrad and the loss of North Africa, Hitler became far more concerned with the Eastern Front.

As far as the Western Front, he did become more obsessed with shooting down American and British bombers. He was of the same opinion as Göring, that the German people, suffering under the weight of all these air raids, needed to see enemy aircraft shot down on the ground. I could understand the need for the preservation of national morale, but I could not understand the obsession with this method, and Göring once even told Propaganda Minister Dr. Josef Göbbels that he should work on moving some crashed aircraft around as a type of wandering public curiosity, so people all over Germany could see the wreckage. I could not believe what I was hearing, with the limited resources and the growing problems on all fronts. He wanted to stage these shows for the public!

Remember that this was in 1943, and given the problems we were having, I could think of a far better way to utilize our men and material, let alone our other assets. I think that this discussion, along with many other ideas regarding propaganda, simply showed that, despite the publicly accepted perception, just how much Hitler, Göring, and the other top Nazis feared a revolt and losing their power. However, there were many events that occurred long before this, which would both assist, but also harm me where Göring was concerned.

One of the most memorable events was in January 1942.[17] I was called into a meeting with Göring, among many others, and there was a problem for which I was being consulted. We had three ships that needed to return to Germany, and this was not an easy issue. The British Royal Navy controlled the seas, especially the North Sea and the English Channel, and the Royal Air Force controlled the skies for the most part. This was largely due to our Luftwaffe being sent en masse to the Soviet Union for and after Operation Barbarossa, as well as our commitments to North Africa.

I looked at the problem and saw the charts. I knew that the only way to get the ships through safely was to present a superior overlapping air umbrella to our enemy. However, we did not have the numbers. This forced me to improvise accordingly. Göring called me into a meeting and said I had to be there the next day.

When I arrived at this meeting, almost every branch of the military was represented, and included navy admirals Erich Raeder,

Wilhelm Canaris, Karl Dönitz, and their staff officers. From the Luftwaffe there was myself, Göring, *Generalfeldmarschall* Erhard Milch, and *Generalleutnant* Dietrich Peltz, and from the signals branch, *Generalleutnant* Wolfgang Martini.[18]

I had my best officers join me after this major meeting, which lasted almost seven hours. The navy was concerned about losing the ships, and it was stated to me by Göring, personally, that Hitler himself wanted to know the plans by the next day. You must understand that planning a major combined naval and air operation is not like planning a football match. Just the logistics alone, regarding fuel, ammunition, pilot assignments and availability, and serviceable aircraft available, were a nightmare, so I gave that responsibility primarily to some outstanding officers on the Channel front, as well as subsequent leaders.

These were mainly Josef Priller, Gerd Schöpfel, and others. At that time we only had two day fighter units stationed there, which were JG.26 and JG.2, but I also contacted the night fighters and informed Wolf Falck of what was about to happen. I did this by secure telephone, as radio transmissions were not the most secure method. I then went to France and met with them all, and after that meeting we had a plan.

I informed Göring that all was in order. I was then given the responsibility and authority to launch the operation in conjunction with Raeder, and I commanded the fighter cover for the famous Channel Dash by the battle cruisers *Scharnhorst*, *Gneisenau*, and the heavy cruiser *Prinz Eugen* in February 1942. I had thought about it for two days and had little sleep, and even discussed the problems I expected with a few of my staff officers and their respective pilots, and then I organized a rotation of various fighter wings to fly top cover for the ships, an air umbrella to protect them from British air attacks.

I also had to coordinate the flak units along the coast, create the communications table, confirm fuel allotments, ammunition, everything. I did not want to lose my men and fighters to our own antiaircraft fire, so organizing that was a major issue as well. In this capacity I spoke with Josef Kammhuber, who had managed to organize the flak units to work in conjunction with Wolf Falck's night fighters.[19]

It was primarily the responsibility of JG.2 and JG.26, each of which rotated a squadron from the time the ships entered the English Channel, flying with drop tanks. I had at least thirty fighters in the air at any one time over the ships, and each group was replaced by a new formation before they left their station. We also had twin-engine Me-110 fighters just to keep any British bombers away.

This mission lasted for an entire day, as we had to make certain that the pilots could protect the ships from enemy bombers. The British came and they made a good show of it. We managed to keep the ships from receiving any real damage from the air. There was some damage from mines, however, but the Luftwaffe fighters shot down many British planes, and not a single major hit was made on the warships from the air.

That was a great success story that made me proud, and I was called to Berlin where Hitler, Göring, Josef Göbbels, and the entire General Staff, along with Wilhelm Keitel and Alfred Jodl, were present. Göbbels saw this as a chance to create a massive propaganda program, while all the others just congratulated each other. I found it all sort of unnecessary and just another job that had to be done. I saw the value of giving the German people good news, but Göbbels, although a master of manipulation, was, in my mind, not a very honorable character, and I detested him personally.

I had also been handling a request from Wolfgang Falck, who we all called "Father of the Night Fighters." I had many discussions with my old friend regarding the night fighters. In 1940, Falck's airfield in Denmark was under constant British night bombing, ever since they had decided that daylight bombing was not a great idea. This was after the two disastrous RAF bomber missions to Wilhelmshaven in December 1940. Falck came to the conclusion that he had taken enough punishment. He devised a plan, flew a few missions of his own, and then decided to write an operational feasibility study. Göring had approved his concept in theory, and Falck had Udet assist him in proving it.[20] This was done long before I was ever general of the fighters.

By the time I was involved, after my appointment in November 1941, I was then briefed on the night fighter development. Göring had allowed me to read the initial report that Falck had sent to Berlin.[21] I must admit that I was initially opposed to the concept, simply due to the fact that I thought that logistically it would drain away assets and pilots from the day fighter force. I possibly have many flaws, but I was always able to admit when I was wrong. I eventually saw the potential of Falck's idea, and then I assisted him with bringing Kammhuber around. I knew that the method had its merits, and I discussed this with Göring who was already aware of it. I have to admit he was very enthusiastic, and even Hitler nodded his approval.[22]

Despite this, I was a victim of my own success, and I was once again placed in a desk job, and later in 1942 I was promoted to *generalleutnant* when I was thirty and a half years old, based mostly I believe on my competence, but I was still unhappy about it. I would have rather continued flying. There were many positives and negatives to holding this position. I had the authority to arrange things and oversee all of the technical deployments, new equipment, weapons, and even enhance the training program to some degree. The bad part was that I also had only two people to really answer to, Hitler and Göring, and on occasion, Erhard Milch.

Not even Milch challenged my decisions, although I had to send all of my ideas and plans up the chain of command through him. He did ask questions, but he knew when he was out of his depth. This was especially true after *Generaloberst* Hans Jeschonnek committed suicide, and Milch really became the primary liaison between the Luftwaffe and Göring, who in turn, of course, answered to Hitler.

Milch was not a bad sort, but he was a bureaucrat who loved the political intrigues that I could not tolerate. He had been perhaps the most instrumental person in creating the Luftwaffe as early as 1934, and it was his blueprint from which the air arm was created.[23] I had many meetings with Milch, and not all of these were on good terms, I can assure you. But I know that he respected my opinions, and he truly listened to my ideas. He was a very intelligent man, and a very dedicated member of the [Nazi] Party. He had been very instrumental in the early days of the Reich in supporting Hitler and the party with obtaining funds and securing the political support of the main business and factory owners.[24]

As time went on, despite my ability to work with Milch, this arrangement proved to be a very uncomfortable situation. Göring was always trying to stay in Hitler's good graces, and this was often at the expense of the fighter arm. Göring was never able to accept personal responsibility, which was his greatest character flaw, and we lost all respect for him.[25] He was always looking into any topic that he could bring to Hitler's attention, anything that would take Hitler's mind off of Göring's problems. It was like he was trying to start fires for Hitler to see, so that he would not take notice of his own home burning down.

This became an interesting development when I was informed that the Gestapo were investigating certain German pilots for possibly being Jewish. This was brought to me by Johannes Steinhoff in person, and we had to see Milch about this. I did not know for sure, but there were rumors that Milch was Jewish.[26] This may explain why he wanted to help these brave men who had shown such courage and been successful. Milch managed somehow to get Göring to convince Heinrich Himmler to abandon the witch hunt.[27]

Well, being in this position, it was a big responsibility, and you could never get what you needed. Our fighter force was small, and we received no understanding from Göring. I was not alone in this. I received reports, complaints, and requests from all of the senior fighter leaders from all over Europe and Africa. This included everything from fuel, ammunition, and better maps to inquiries on new weapons, access to new and upgraded aircraft, even requests for replacement pilots.

Göring was a great sportsman at heart. One of his great enjoyments was to have the pilots on leave, or just on layover for business, stay at his great estate at Karinhall. He had his own game preserve, with all manner of wild game. We really enjoyed the hunting at his estate and lodge at Rominten, and I had these excellent Belgian shotguns I used for birds. Göring also kept a small arsenal of hunting weapons, every caliber and model, for any type of game. The times I spent there, when we were on good terms, were in fact some of the best days in my life, or at least during the early years of the war.

To be fair, Göring was a great hero in the First World War, receiving the *Pour le Mérite* and flying with the great aces Oswald Boelcke, Ernst Udet, Manfred von Richthofen, and he later commanded the Flying Circus after Richthofen's death. However, after speaking with some of the pilots he flew with, they did not think much of him as far as being a leader, or even a good tactician. Losses in the unit rose under his command as their success dwindled, and he had a tendency to blame others for his errors. I was to learn that this characteristic was not to change.

Following his being wounded in the *Putsch* of 1923, he became addicted to morphine. I never knew much about drug addiction, and I never knew Göring before his problem with drugs started. I only knew him afterward. Early in the war he was quite enthusiastic, charismatic, and energetic. This began to change in 1943, right after Stalingrad, and he really changed after we lost North Africa and Sicily. This was the time where he began to place blame on everyone except himself, and it started a very miserable period in my life.

Udet told me about this collective opinion of Göring when Mölders and I had recently been decorated with the Oak Leaves and Swords, as he knew Göring during the Great War. Theo Osterkamp also knew him, and he did not have a high opinion of him either, but in true gentlemanly fashion, "Uncle Theo," as we called him, would never say anything directly prejudicial against Göring or anyone. The same opinion of Göring was held by Eduard von Schleich and Robert von Greim. They could not stand him either.

This opinion of Göring was not to change in my war. I was actually not that surprised when he allowed Falck to start his unit, as Göring always liked new ideas and audacious leaders. I could only assume that if the night fighters were successful, it would be one more great idea that he would claim was his own and present it as such to Hitler. He did that sort of thing. Later I was proven to be correct, and I made certain that Hitler knew where the genius really originated.

Yes, Göring had many problems, but he was basically an intelligent man, although not creative, and well educated from the aristocracy. However, he had many weak points in his life, and he was always under pressure from Hitler, yet he never contradicted him or corrected him on any critical point. That was where he made his greatest mistakes.

This weakness in the face of Hitler increased as the war dragged on, along with his drug addiction, until he was nothing. As far as our Luftwaffe was concerned, he was even less and should have been replaced. I cannot think of a single fighter leader who knew him who had a positive opinion of him.[28] Of course, we now know long after the war that he was also involved in the terrible activities regarding the Jews and others. He was also a major policy maker regarding the occupied territories, and he made many great mistakes.[29]

I can say with confidence that Göring had his troubles. He could not really understand the nature of modern warfare—the increased speeds of aircraft, the evolving tactical and even strategic situation—and he was always calling me for advice on even the simplest of matters. Once I gave him the solutions to his problems, he would take these ideas to Hitler as his own, and I was even told that he was telling Hitler that he had to give me instruction on these very matters. This was to make Hitler confident in him. After Stalingrad, where Göring lost much of his credibility, I found myself being drained of my knowledge, and also being blamed for the shortcomings of the fighter force. I could almost understand Jeschonnek and Udet taking their respective courses.[30]

In 1942, Göring sent me on an inspection tour of all Luftwaffe units. I went to Russia, Ukraine, France, Holland, Denmark, Norway, North Africa, and the Balkans. I inspected the men and aircraft, and this was as much a fact-finding mission and checkup on the morale of the men as anything else. I surprised my old friend Edu Neumann, who was at that time *kommodore* of JG.27 in Libya. He knew I was coming, but not when.

I had read the many reports and heard several pilots talk about this young fellow named Hans-Joachim Marseille. Steinhoff had fired him when he was his commanding officer in France the year before, and I heard that a few senior officers had their various opinions of him. There was even the rumor that an army general wanted him court-martialed, due to something involving his wife and daughter. I really did not want to know any more about that, as I was no angel myself.

Marseille was much like my lost friend Helmut Wick, who died in 1940, as both were very rebellious, and just wanted to fly. Marseille was not much of a stickler for the rules. He was hardly, if ever, seen in a proper uniform, and Neumann even told me that if it were not for his great success as a fighter pilot, he would have fired him also, mainly for being undisciplined.

Steinhoff told me stories of some of his exploits that made me laugh until I cried, such as the time Marseille stole his staff car, picked up several girls, and was so drunk he had the local mayor's daughter drive him back to the base, in Steinhoff's car. He was supposed to fly that morning, so naturally he was in no condition to fly even if he were sober. He was exhausted from his time with the girls.

Once, Marseille had gone into town to collect some of the enlisted men who were late returning to the base. These were mechanics and ground staff. He was also late returning with these men. Another officer was sent to find him and the missing enlisted men. The report, as I understood it, was that Marseille was drunk and had managed to fall out of a young lady's window. I believe it was the same girl who was involved in the driving incident, but I am not certain.

I met Marseille for the second time in the desert during my visit to the North African front. I had first met him when he received the Oak Leaves. I arrived in a Ju-52 and had to go to the latrine. Marseille and I met and we spoke, and I also met others in the unit. I congratulated him on the award of the Swords as he was going to Berlin to receive them. I was the person, as general of the fighters, who recommended him to Göring for the Diamonds award, after Neumann sent me the unit report, and after his seventeen victories in a single day in Libya. I found him very boyish and free spirited, but not completely immature, do not get me wrong, but he really marched to his own drum. He never even mastered the salute properly, but he was a very gifted pilot. I have to admit, he was not shy at all about his lifestyle. He played his banned American jazz music so loudly that I was sure the British could hear it in Egypt.

Marseille would have never had a great career in the Luftwaffe, or rose to great rank, but he could have cared less. He just wanted to fly, and he looked at the war as a great sporting event. He also had a great hunting instinct, but this was tempered by a deep sense of chivalry. He was known to have notified the British that one of their pilots was down and wounded, after he scored the kill. He did not believe that a man should die on the ground if he survived combat. That was the kind of man he was, and Neumann told me about that event during my visit. I read the after action report about the whole affair. Göring even mentioned to me how gallant he must be to do such a thing, and then he banned anyone from doing it again.

I had also heard the reports from some of those senior officers who were less than pleased with Marseille's lack of conformity to regulations, especially regarding his friend Matthias. He was a black South African, actually Marseille's self-appointed assistant. He cooked, cleaned, and did almost everything except work on his aircraft. Marseille taught him how to play chess and speak fairly good German, and his servant taught him better English.

This fellow Mathias bartended the unit parties and did Marseille's laundry. They were obviously great friends. I suppose you could probably understand that, during those days, and with the rules and racial codes we were expected to live by, such a friendship would have been impossible anywhere else except in the war zone, especially in Europe. That fact is an unfortunate legacy we Germans will always live with. However, Marseille broke all the rules, and did so with a smile. He lived his life as if he was immortal.

Neumann once told me that he had to ground Marseille for violating the strict rules of engagement. Basically, it boiled down to the fact that he would not inform his wingmen that he was going into an attack, and he always attacked violently, often without support, and often at reduced speeds, sometimes nearly colliding with his enemies, and simply doing things that would have washed him out of flight school. Yet he was magnificent, and I personally recommended him for the Diamonds. Unfortunately, he was killed before he could receive them.

Upon my return to Berlin, the ongoing feud between the bombers and the fighters was at full rage. I once again had to demand to speak with Milch, or Göring, I did not care who, but someone had to listen. The one sympathetic ear came from Jeschonnek, who understood my position, and even understood that I was correct. Even Kammhuber agreed, but Hitler wanted bombers built over fighters.[31]

I told them all that such a decision would be foolish, since we were getting heavier British night raids, and I also mentioned the fact that the Americans would be over soon enough in large numbers, and they would need to be addressed. I felt all alone, and Göring did absolutely nothing to assist me, but everything to hinder my progress, and then blame me when things fell apart due to his interference, or mismanagement. I have to say that, despite our differences, even Peltz agreed with me that more fighters were needed, not bombers.[32]

Several weeks after I left Libya, still on my European tour during the first week of October 1942, I received the message that Marseille had been killed.[33] This was a great blow to his unit. Marseille may have not been the perfect officer, but he was the perfect fighter pilot, scoring 158 victories, with seventeen confirmed in one day. Neumann has far more detail on him, but it felt like a personal loss to me. I really wished that I had known him better. The end of 1942 was proving to be a bad year all around.

In January 1943, after the Soviets had finally encircled the Sixth Army, we had another meeting with Göring. This time he again promised Hitler that the Stalingrad situation would be handled by air transport and supply. Soviet fighters and flak were taking a heavy toll on his Ju-52s, and they had placed artillery on the air fields. I actually had a meeting with both he and Dietrich Peltz about this in Berlin.

Peltz told him that the bomber arm could perhaps assist in neutralizing the artillery issue, but that fighters were needed to protect them. I told him that we did not have enough aircraft to cover the entire front from the Baltic and Leningrad area all the way to the Crimea and Black Sea, unless we pulled every fighter unit from either Norway, France on the Channel coast, or from North Africa.

The reports had come in that the situation was getting worse. Replacements were needed, wounded and dead extracted, supplies, food and munitions delivered, and even winter clothing and medical supplies were in great need. There had even been unconfirmed reports of cannibalism on the part of the Russians against German dead and wounded when captured. I do not know if any of these conditions actually existed, but I can assume that there must have been some truth to the rumors. This could have just been propaganda for all I know.

Even then the weather was not always cooperating with us, grounding our aircraft often for days at a time. It became so cold, lubricants and oils froze. Men became ineffective, and cold-weather injuries were the greatest cause of our military debilitation. Richthofen even mentioned the difficulties of getting the required matériel sent by rail and road to air fields, and even if that happened, he simply did not have the fuel, and there was never enough daylight to ensure safe winter landing operations, which were impossible at night.

Göring had promised Hitler something he could not deliver, and Richthofen knew it, and he even said so, stating that the *Reichsmarschall* was condemning a quarter million men to death. That much matériel support, given the situation at that time, was unrealistic, and simply could not be done. I saw Richthofen move some plates away off the table, and he took his ink pen to the starched white tablecloth.

He began doing complicated mathematical equations, algebra, calculus, everything, and even drew a chart, maps, and scales, then jotted down the numbers of everything, as well as kilometers to be flown, numbers of sorties, kilograms of fuel, the maximum load per aircraft, the numbers of the aircraft required, serviceable aircraft, previous and projected losses, as well as the estimated length of time the Sixth Army had to live with its current inventory of supplies.

Göring, who was always currying favor with Hitler, just waved his hand and said to Richthofen, "You will make it so; you have always done so in the past." Such was the way Göring saw the realities of the world at that time. Just like me, Richthofen was a victim of his own success. He had managed to brilliantly organize the transport service during the *Blitzkrieg* and the invasion of the Balkans, as well as the mission in Crete. He was a genius, and like so many others, Göring drained his talent and took the credit for himself, and placed the blame for his own errors upon others.

Tragically, as the reality set in, I remember that at the end of that meeting Richthofen told Göring: "*Herr Reichsmarschall,* how will we tell the families of a quarter of a million men that their loved ones did not have to die? Will you write the letters to these people explaining this disaster? Will the *Führer*?" Göring went white, and for the first time since I had known him, but not the last, he was completely speechless. He actually turned his back on Richthofen and walked out of the room without saying a word. Once the door closed, Richthofen said to me: "Adolf, we just lost an entire army. This is the future for Germany, you can believe it."

Previously, Richthofen had a private meeting with Hitler and *Generalfeldmarschall* Erich von Manstein, and both generals actually told Hitler in late November [1942] that a breakout must be affected, or the Sixth Army would be lost. Hitler would have none of it. After this discussion, Richthofen called me for another meeting along with Dietrich Peltz, Erhard Milch, and others in December 1942, wanting to know the status of the fighter units in the region. He asked if there could be enough fighter escorts for the transport aircraft, which would have to fly around the clock every day, seven days a week, just to get two-thirds of the matériel required for the German troops in Stalingrad. This meeting would be repeated in June 1943, during Operation Citadel, with similar results.[34]

Our leadership killed our brave men, and we all knew what was going to happen. No one else wanted to state it openly, but Richthofen did. Richthofen was just a very conscientious and refined gentleman. In February 1943, after [Friedrich] von Paulus had surrendered what was left of his army, Hitler verbally accused Göring of incompetence, accusing him of not being able to keep his word in supplying the Sixth Army. He also railed against Manstein, claiming that the Fourth Panzer Army was not properly motivated enough to support Paulus. He also attacked our Romanian allies, claiming that they were cowards, given the ease of their destruction in the field, and that they were incapable of bearing arms in support of National Socialism.

Of course, Hitler accused Paulus of treason. Hitler had promoted him to field marshal in January 1943 just before he surrendered, knowing that no German field marshal had ever surrendered or been captured. Hitler blamed everyone except himself for the greatest disaster to ever befall a German force in the field. Naturally, Göring was cut of the same cloth. He was not going to take any responsibility for promising what he could not deliver. The second week of February 1943, there was a general officers meeting in Berlin at the Air Ministry, and I was there, and Göring immediately attacked Richthofen in front of all the others present, claiming that he had in fact made the promises that he could not keep.

Richthofen, to his credit, showed his temper for the only time I had ever known him, and he fired back at our boss. He reminded Göring of the conversation they had a month earlier, what had been said, and who had said what. Richthofen also reminded him of who was in that previous meeting, as some of us were in the same room on this particular occasion. Göring called him "insane" and said that Richthofen was "losing his mind, as no such meeting ever occurred."

I knew at that moment, as did Peltz and the others, that Göring was not to be trusted. I had no idea that his ego and warped character would later fall upon me and the fighters. I suppose I should have anticipated that. I know that this was the point where Hitler lost faith in him. Due to this event, as well as previous meetings and becoming familiar with many within the hierarchy, I concluded that Hitler's inner circle was nothing more than a comedy of errors in several acts.[35]

However, regarding Richthofen, I had no idea that I would come to know this officer so well, and work closely with him in the years to come after we first met in Spain. His sense of integrity, professional bearing, and sense of duty to the nation, as well as his loyalty to his men, was legendary, and his men loved him back. He was a very special man indeed.

It must be understood that, even as general of the fighters, I could only make the final recommendations to Göring through Milch, based upon the reports and requirements from the field leaders. Göring had the authority to approve moderate allocations of matériel and men, but Hitler always had the final say. If Hitler did not like an idea, the idea died right there.

Soon, by early 1943, around March I believe, I was getting questions from Hitler directly, and neither Milch nor Göring were even involved. I found it comical that Hitler called upon me many times to ask the same questions that Göring had posed to me, for which I had given him answers. I knew that Hitler completely understood that Göring was taking credit for my work, and he even said so once, although not directly. From this point, I knew that Hitler had lost almost all of his faith in Göring. He even openly suggested, although without stating clearly, that he could not rely upon him for accurate information, thus his wanting corroboration. This was a very serious indictment against Göring, who was effectively the second in command under Hitler until April 1945.

I had again been summoned by Göring, along with a few other fighter leaders to his estate at Karinhall. We often went there to hunt boar, deer, and talk about the war. These were supposed to be relaxing times. However, on this occasion Göring had a different agenda. After we had a heavy lunch, he walked us through to admire his new art collection, which he claimed he had purchased throughout Europe. I did not learn the truth about his acquisitions until long after the war, but he was very proud of his personal collections of old masters, and even some of the supposedly banned artworks.[36] Then a question was asked about a discussion Hitler and I had some weeks before, and I was honest, and told him what Hitler and I had discussed.

This infuriated Göring when he found out that Hitler had come to me, and he blamed me to my face for Hitler's losing confidence in him, which he equated with losing faith in the Luftwaffe. This was the same problem facing Hans Jeschonnek, the chief of staff. Hitler would confide in him, bypassing Göring in many cases, knowing that Jeschonnek would never lie to him, and he would always place the nation and the service above himself. Göring hated him for this also, which finally led to Jeschonnek committing suicide, just like Udet.[37] In fact, I remember later that after his funeral, Edu Neumann made a comment to me that "we had better stop allowing our senior generals to carry side arms. They seem to have a lot of accidents with them."

Göring would never separate himself from the service in these discussions. I told him that I did not feel that it was my place to tell the *Führer* that I could not answer his questions until he explained the situation to him, the *Reichsmarschall.* Göring and I had a very uneasy relationship to say the least, especially from that point. But it became much worse. I disagreed with him on most of his suggestions and orders.

This was when we had a meeting, and the basis for this conference with the other leaders was Göring's concerns over our losses in Russia up to that point, and the forthcoming loss of North Africa, as well as the fact that Stalingrad had been lost. I had long made up my mind that I would not take the route of Udet and Jeschonnek, not on his account.

By early 1943, Göring had openly blamed the fighter and transport pilots for Stalingrad, actually accusing them of not having the proper fighting spirit, and not believing in the National Socialist ideals of our perfect Aryan race, all that rubbish. I found this an incredible statement to make, and I could not imagine how it could get any worse. I would be proven wrong on that a year later, but I remember that I was there with Joachim Müncheberg, just before he was killed over Tunisia upon his return, along with Lützow, Trautloft, Neumann, Peltz, and others. This was a meeting regarding the problems with our Luftwaffe protecting the Afrika Korps, given the British and American advances through Libya.

Göring always started his meetings with a long-winded sermon, usually touting our technical superiority, our victories, and then continuing into the latest problems we were facing. This was when he stopped taking credit for, or even mentioning the successes, and then began applying blame for our defeats. He then clearly accused the Luftwaffe fighters of lying about their victories and not earning the medals they had been awarded. He even for the first time mentioned cowardice under fire, which was an execution offense, and he demanded the names of pilots who had shirked their duties. There was actually no record of anything like that existing, and I told him so. He said that I could not lie and hide the truth forever. I was stunned.

I have been accused of being a little hotheaded in my time, and I must admit that when I felt I was being wronged, or my men were being incorrectly accused, I took personal offense. However, I was a mild and meek creature when it came to Lützow. This man was a fearless fighter and a great ace, and a demanding yet fair leader who never asked his men to do anything he had not already done. He would also be the first to fly a new aircraft, just in case there were any problems.

Lützow hated Göring, and I think he was the person who coined his nickname "the Fat One," and I think that Göring knew this, and he hated him back. I think it was more jealousy on Göring's part; he was envious of us younger pilots, getting the glory that he felt should be his. I remember a conversation I had with Lützow, Trautloft, Neumann, Falck, and others in the fighter fraternity, when I called our so-called leadership court jesters.[38]

During the first part of the meeting, which seemed more of a lecture, Göring even mentioned Lützow's unit by name [JG.3 *Udet*], claiming that many of the pilots had fled in the face of the enemy on the Eastern Front. Lützow, who was sitting right next to me on the left, had been fuming the entire time, about twenty minutes, I think. Finally, as Göring was still speaking, Lützow pounded his fist on the table, and it so frightened Trautloft—who was commanding JG.54 [*Grünherz*] at that time, I think, and who was sitting on my right—that he jumped, as did I.

Having had enough, Lützow then stood, leaning over the table, and raised his voice to Göring who was still talking, and totally interrupting him, said something to the effect: "Your incompetence and living in the old days will not change the facts, *Herr Reichsmarschall!* Wise men know their limits, but you obviously have not yet received that education. Well, I am here to tell you that the only cowards I can see are the old men in Berlin giving orders, but not taking the risks, and you are the greatest example! If you wish to change our circumstances, I would suggest that you allow those of us who are leaders lead, and stay out of our way!" The room was completely silent.

I had never seen Göring speechless since the meeting with Richthofen, and the silence that followed Lützow's outburst lasted almost half a minute. Göring's face turned white from the shock of being challenged by anyone. Then his face turned red, then almost purple with rage, and he then began screaming at Lützow, telling him that he was a hair away from being shot for insubordination. Lützow fired back, "Then I will take my complaint to the *Führer*, who may be more inclined to listen to reason and facts, rather than relying upon gossip and ridiculous innuendo, *Herr* Göring!" This last statement was important, because he never even addressed Göring by his rank. I grabbed his arm and looked at Trautloft and Peltz, who were both ashen faced. I think that all of us at that moment saw a great pilot and hero commit suicide.

However, in a move that surprised us all, Göring suddenly calmed down a bit, and then he looked at me, and asked me if I shared Lützow's views. I told him that I did indeed, and I felt that I should take it one step further.

I then told Göring, in a calm voice, that Lützow was simply voicing the opinions of almost all the frustrated leaders who had seen Soviet air power increases, while our numbers dropped due to combat attrition and lack of replacements. I also told him that it was universally unfair to accuse brave men who risked their lives every day, and achieved remarkable results, of cowardice. I also told him that the position he had taken would do more to undermine morale than superior enemy numbers.

This was when Göring decided to change tactics, and he began saying that these accusations came from Hitler, and that he was the one who demanded answers. I knew this was a lie, because unknown to Göring, I had just met with Hitler a few days before, where he actually praised the fighter pilots and was very impressed with their record. He had even discussed some of the men being recommended for high decorations, asking my opinion for confirmation. This was when I challenged Göring on that very subject, and told him that I had spoken to Hitler about this very matter, and he was of a very different opinion. Caught in the lie, Göring then accused me of falsifying reports and hiding deficiencies from him.

This was the last straw for me. I then stood, unhooked my Knight's Cross, Oak Leaves, Swords, and Diamonds, and threw them onto the heavy oak table. I then took off my Wound Badge and Iron Cross, along with the Spanish Cross in Gold with Diamonds, and they went on the table also.

I then told him in front of the assembled men that I would not wear those due to my being "unworthy" along with my men, and then something else happened that is not told very often, and I have not seen in any of the books I have read. Trautloft, Müncheberg, and Lützow also took off their medals from around their necks and placed them on the table. The bomber boys, such as Peltz and the others, just sat in stunned silence. This was not the last time we would have such an encounter with Göring.

I then moved my chair back and turned to leave the meeting, with my fighter leaders following me. Göring yelled at us, stating that we had not been dismissed. Then, as if the situation were not bad enough, Lützow shot back: "Then I would suggest you tell the *Führer* that his cowards walked out. You can't shoot us all," and then we left. Once the door closed behind us, I will tell you that I was sweating heavily, as were Trautloft and Müncheberg. We were all thinking that we had just terminated our careers, if not our lives.

Unbelievably, Lützow was calm and unmoved by the whole event. I was certain that we were going to be shot, but nothing happened. Hitler found out about it, and we never heard anything further about it from Göring. My medals were sent to my office a few days later, but I did not wear them for about six months. That was my protest. Unfortunately, this would not be the last time I had a major argument with him, and again some of the same persons would be involved, along with a couple of others in January 1945, when I was fired.

Shortly after [the argument with Göring], when Hitler called me into a meeting in late May 1943, regarding the collapse of North Africa, he asked me where my medals were. I told him of the event, and he asked me questions. He then told me that he had heard about the event from Göring, as well as Peltz. He even stated that Peltz's version coincided with mine, but that was all he said. He never commented upon Göring's version of events. He knew who was right and who was wrong, and he told me not to worry, that he had everything in hand. He also mentioned Müncheberg's death, of which I was unaware, which was a heavy blow to all of us. He was much loved in the fighter force, a real original personality, a perfect gentleman. He was also my friend, and I did not have that many to begin with.

The rest of 1943 was tense, as we began to suffer setbacks in Africa and in the east. Sicily was lost, and the Allies were in Italy. The Soviets had halted the advance at Kursk and Orel. The Caucasus was in chaos. Things were falling apart. Again there were meetings, and again Göring had his moments, but the great problem was the large numbers of American bombers attacking us by day, and the British striking us at night.

I also had a meeting with *Oberst* Hajo Herrmann, the first of many, and we were discussing the merits of his *Wilde Sau* method. I had already discussed this with Falck, who would take whatever additional support he could get. I was initially opposed to the program, primarily due to the wear and tear on engines, airframes, and of course the fact that we did not even have enough pilots to handle the American daylight raids.

Milch called me in for a meeting, where he and I discussed Herrmann's thoughts. In addition, Göring was very excited, but then again he was always excited about any new idea or concept. Milch agreed to examine the program, but he was also less than enthusiastic. Then, just before July, I met with Hitler again, about many subjects, and he raised the question of the *Wilde Sau* program. I gave him my reservations, but I also told him that I thought that it should at least be given a try, and settle the issue after the first few missions.

Well, Hitler and Göring approved the operations, and even Jeschonnek was enthusiastic. I decided to let Wolf Falck come onboard also, with his experience, and have a vote on this issue. The end result was that after his initial flights, Herrmann was made *kommodore* of JG.300, his personal creation, and I have to admit they had some success, more than I would have imagined.

Our fighters were taking out large numbers of bombers, including the night fighters against the RAF. One day in August 1943, the fighters shot down sixty-four bombers over Schweinfurt alone. But in 1944, things began to change drastically. I was called to a meeting where I met with Ferdinand Porsche, Albert Speer, Kurt Tank, Willi Messerschmitt, and others once again. The purpose was to discuss the new innovations in our fighter aircraft designs, the armaments industry in general, which was why Albert Speer was there.

I had first met Speer briefly earlier in August 1943, and again in November 1943, and this was also around the time I first met Professor Ferdinand Porsche, when I reported to Göring about American fighters that had been shot down near Aachen.[39] Hitler had previously called me on the phone and asked if this were true, and I confirmed the fact that American fighters had in fact entered German airspace. Göring was getting ready to board his train when he turned to me in a very heated voice, asking, "Why in the hell did you tell Hitler about the American planes?" That was when I told him that we could expect even deeper penetrations as they escorted their heavy bombers. Göring had previously promised that no Allied plane would fly over Berlin. I was assuming he was not counting RAF Bomber Command.

By this time, Berlin was already a regular bombing target by both the British and American air forces. It was only a matter of time before their fighters followed all the way.[40] In this meeting, which I attended with Speer, and only two months after Jeschonnek killed himself, Göring actually ordered me to publicly state "that American fighters had not been shot down over Aachen."[41]

Well, I found this order incredible, and I told him he should go see for himself, that I could not issue such a statement. He repeated the order, but it did not happen. I believe this was when I knew that he had lost touch with all reality. Later, my meetings with him would be very cool and impersonal, merely to discuss the problems regarding shortages of almost everything needed to fight the war.

A year later, Göring exploded over the issue of not having fuel, claiming that we were sabotaging the fuel depots ourselves to not have to fly and fight. He also claimed that the fighter pilots had lost their zeal and aggressiveness, and that was why we had so few fighters in the air. Seeing his ability to go insane in an instant and throw out unsubstantiated accusations was quite unsettling. I informed him that we had fewer fighters in the air due to our heavy losses, and the simple fact that we could not replace dead pilots as fast as the infantry could replace soldiers.[42]

In the previous August 1944 meeting, Speer and I had discussed the critical fuel shortages experienced by the military all over Europe. Speer had just met with Hitler and Göring the previous month, and he was also working on increasing fighter production, and I had previously given him the recommendation that the Me-109 be phased out, and only Fw-190D and the later models be produced as far as conventional aircraft. I also told him, following my first test flight in the Me-262 jet at Rechlin, that this was the fighter we needed to focus upon. This was also the subject of discussion in 1943.[43]

However, as the world knows, Hitler had other ideas. Göring knew the reality, and he was very excited by the 262, and told me personally that he would see to it we received the new fighter. He read the reports on how and why it was a better fighter. It was not just the faster speed and heavier armament, it was also able to operate on much cheaper and readily available fuel and did not require the high-octane fuel that the conventional fighters did. Speer also mentioned that, in order to appease Hitler, he would increase construction on the Arado and Heinkel jet models as bombers, allowing us to have the 262 as a fighter.

This was when the Americans began using the P-51 Mustang as a long-range fighter escort, and this saw our fighters now having to engage enemy fighters, and being lucky just to try and get to the bombers. This was a complete reversal of what we had experienced during the Battle of Britain, where we were ordered to escort heavy two-engine Me-110s and bombers to attack Britain. The Me-110s were also thrown into the attacks against American bombers, which was all very well, unless they had escort fighters.

Our losses rose on escort missions for the Me-110s, when we were not allowed to fly free of that problem, what we called a *Freie Jagd*, for "free hunting," and this was where we had our greatest successes. Now the Americans were on escort duty and were very good at it. In March 1944 they hit Berlin with fighters overhead.[44] We had already lost many of our best pilots against the Americans, who were highly trained and had great fighters.

Speer and I again met with Hitler, and Speer tried to get him to rescind the order to have the two thousand new fighters just built sent to the Western Front. I agreed, and I explained to Hitler that, given the tactical situation, lack of fuel, few highly qualified and experienced pilots, that the best we could do would be to use these aircraft as a protective force at our critical industries, especially the petroleum and aircraft locations. Speer even gave him the data, which normally Hitler would examine in great detail.

One of Speer's best arguments was the dire need for copper, manganese, aluminum, cobalt, and iron ore, among other metals for war matériel.[45] This was especially needed for aircraft and anything with engine generators. I explained to Hitler that if we sent these new fighters with young pilots against the Americans, we would lose them rapidly. I also explained that each American bomber shot down cost us at least one fighter, and half the time the pilot was lost as well.[46]

The great problem was that we were losing pilots faster than we could replace them, and this was not an accident. My friend General [James H.] Doolittle had devised the plan to force our fighters into the air to be killed, and we played right into his hands.[47] There was nothing else to do. Our losses were staggering over the next few months.[48] That was when I decided to focus our fighters inside Germany proper, and defend the installations that seemed to be the Allied targets of choice.

I knew from experience, after the Battle of Britain, and seeing the RAF ability, that if these fighter pilots had shorter distances to travel, they could concentrate on a smaller operational area, and focus upon attacking the enemy bombers over or near targets, that several things would happen. First, our men shot down would be able to be back in the air more quickly. Second, the larger numbers of German fighters in a more concentrated area would provide more opportunities to attack enemy bombers. Third, it would save on fuel. Hitler waved his hand and said he had heard enough. He had absolutely no interest in discussing anything that would have made him change his mind.

Speer and I did our best to persuade him. It was like talking to a deaf man. I explained the situation to Hitler, and also gave him proven statistics, but he went mad. He then stated that he would order the halt to all fighter aircraft production, the fighter arm was to be disbanded, and those industries were to be then focused upon building flak guns. He firmly believed that flak guns alone would keep Germany safe. I could not believe it. Speer reassured him that we had plenty of flak guns, but we did not have the munitions for them.

It was during this meeting that Göring brought up the possibility of strafing enemy pilots as they bailed out, and he asked me my thoughts on that subject. I told him in no uncertain terms that I would never issue that order, and I would court-martial any man who I could prove did such a thing. I also invoked the Geneva Convention, explaining that such a method was illegal.

Göring seemed less interested in the laws of warfare, and as I learned much later after the war, I understood why. He was more concerned with the image of the chivalrous fighter pilot being tarnished, so he did not really push the issue further. He also told yet another story of his days in the Great War flying with Boelcke and Richthofen, and how chivalry was only seen in the air. Enemies respected each other. I agreed with him. The killing of parachuting airmen was then dropped.

[Speer] told me that I should not worry about the fighter production, that he would work around Hitler. He actually managed to do this, as we still managed to get out jets, which allowed me to create my *Jagdverband* 44 in 1945.

I have to say that he was a brave man for doing so, and I told him that I would help him in any way I could, but that I was not on the dinner list with Hitler and Göring during those days, so I would be limited in what I could accomplish. I know that later in the war, Hitler gave the orders to Speer to destroy cities, bridges, buildings, anything that the Allies could have used. He refused. He actually went to many *gauleiter* and military commanders, and convinced them not to destroy Europe. General Dietrich von Choltitz in Paris was one of them. He refused to destroy the city, and to that end I give him great credit.

Hitler was an interesting study. I spent many months and years around him, speaking with him and having meetings, but I don't think anyone ever really knew Adolf Hitler. I was not very impressed with him, to be honest. The first time I met him was after Spain, when we were summoned to the *Reichschancellery* in 1938.

There was Hitler, short, gray faced and not very strong, a weak handshake, and he spoke with a crisp language. He did not allow us to smoke, nor did he offer us anything to drink, nothing like that. This impression was only strengthened every year that I knew him, as his mistakes mounted and cost German lives, the mistakes that Göring should have brought to his attention. Other officers did, and they were relieved for their honesty, but at least they did the right thing and voiced their objections. For Göring to willingly follow along was a terrible situation for me personally.

Hitler was truly a strange person in the fact that his personality could change instantly. One moment he could be laughing at a joke, or happily discussing his latest great plan. Then, someone could say something that contradicted him, perhaps even challenged his accepted wisdom on a subject, and he could fly into a rage. I saw this on so many occasions, so I knew that he was an unstable person. His drug addiction was probably the most important factor in his character flaws, but I think that even before this he was an egomaniac.

However, to give him credit, he had a photographic memory, he forgot nothing, and read everything. Every afternoon he had the world's newspapers in German translation scattered about. He wanted to see what the rest of the world was saying about him, as he was such an egomaniac, but nothing like Göring. I remember the story that when *Time* made him "Man of the Year," he thought that he had won over the Americans, and even the British. However, like Hitler, Göring was in a class of his own. He even painted his fingernails, quite disgusting, if you ask me.

I met most of the major personalities. Göbbels was definitely a strange person, following Hitler's every word, acting as a marionette. He was always trying to further himself into Hitler's graces. Heinrich Himmler was also a very interesting person. To know that this unassuming man had so much power was quite frightening. Himmler did not strike me as being a very intelligent person in any manner. In meetings, he always waited until the end before saying anything. He seldom had a logical suggestion. Once he even proposed that the SS take over the Me-262 project, which I said was absolutely insane, and did say so in so many words. He also had the ability to make you feel very nervous, as if he were looking for a way to find fault with you.

Martin Bormann, in my opinion, if I removed Göring from the list, was the most obnoxious person in the hierarchy. Bormann was the silent one, always listening at meetings, often taking notes, and making his list of enemies. Speer told me about this list, a tactic he learned from Reinhard Heydrich, whom I never met but everyone knew of. Bormann's direct front man was Gerhard Klopfer, whom I met on one occasion, and another person to be wary of.[49]

Being that I was not a political person, with no interest in such things, I was the outsider in most of the meetings. Even Keitel and Jodl were fervent Nazis, and like Göbbels, followed Hitler's whims like lapdogs. Unlike Göbbels, who was actually an intelligent man, if spineless, these two never struck me as being very intelligent, and I was not very impressed with their inconsistent method of issuing orders from Berlin to the military. They were on the same level as Göring in that regard.

Göring was the other problem. Sure, if Hitler cared, he could have replaced him, but who would take Göring's place and stand up to Hitler, to do what was right? People were not lining up for the job. Hitler, although intelligent in many areas, was unable to think in three dimensions, and he had a very poor understanding when it came to the Luftwaffe, just as with the U-boat service, or even the navy in general. He was strictly a landsman. He could not comprehend that which he was not personally familiar with, and his great detriment was that he always thought he knew better than the experts he should have relied upon.

I still had to convince Hitler to continue the flow of jets to JG.7 and other units. The men flying them needed more familiarity before committing them to combat, and the jet never really went through the type of peacetime evolution of refinement through research and development as it should have. The greatest problems were the engines, which were very delicate, and often flamed out on takeoff. Even worse, we had reports of flameouts and burned-out engines in flight.

This was not a comforting thought for pilots expecting to go into battle outnumbered fifty to one on a very good day. The unit at Achmer had been doing great things since July 1944 under Werner Thierfelder, proving the value of the jet in combat.[50] This success allowed us to push the issue to Hitler again, building upon that success once we began to get more 262s in the field.

Before all of this occurred, I had been telling Milch, Göring, and Hitler for a year, since my first flight in a Me-262 in May 1943 at Lechfeld, that only Focke-Wulf Fw-190 fighter production should continue in conventional aircraft, specifically the "Dora" model and later variants, and to discontinue the Me-109, which was outdated, and to focus on building a massive jet fighter force.[51]

This was discussed in the meeting in August 1944, where Milch decided that Speer's production program should produce four thousand fighters per month. I agreed, but I suggested that one thousand should be jets. Milch was unimpressed with my suggestion, telling me that Hitler did not think we needed the 262 at that time. I was stunned. I could not believe Hitler would throw away the one potential advantage of regaining air superiority, after years of his complaining about the Allied bombing raids.[52]

I had a talk with Speer behind Milch's back, and he promised me that he would speak with Professor Messerschmitt about getting us some pure jet fighters, while still making a few bomber versions for Hitler. Speer knew the situation. He also knew that the Arado and Heinkel companies were building jets as potential bombers, and this gave me hope.

Speer was a smart fellow, and he knew that the war was lost, as did I, and much sooner than later unless massive changes were made. Like most clear-headed people late in the war, he also knew that negotiating a peace from a position of strength was preferable to accepting defeat while powerless. Speer even once said that, given the alternative, having Americans and British with our technology was far preferable to the Soviets.[53]

On May 22, 1943, before my first flight in the Me-262, I was in Lechfeld for a preview of the jet, which was fantastic, a totally new development. This was 1943, and I was there with Professor

Willy Messerschmitt, Milch, Hitler, and other engineers responsible for the development. I spoke with Fritz Wendel and Horst Geyer, and after my first flight I discussed my opinion of the jet, which at that time was a tail-dragging model, in my book *The First and the Last*, and this has become a very well-known story. I knew that this aircraft was not just our last hope in the air war. I could see the future of aviation for the next century right in front of me. I had felt its power, and it was quite intoxicating.

The fighter was almost ready for mass production even at that time, and Hitler wanted to see a demonstration. When the 262 was brought out for his viewing at Insterburg, I was standing there next to Hitler, who was very impressed, despite the first fighter having engine flameout on takeoff. The second jet lifted off and performed marvelously. Hitler asked the professor: "Is this aircraft able to carry bombs?"

Messerschmitt said, "Yes, my *Führer*, it can carry for sure a 250-kilogram bomb, perhaps two of them." In typical Hitler fashion, he said: "Well, nobody thought of this! This is the *Blitz* [lightning] bomber I have been requesting for years. No one thought of this. I order that this 262 be used exclusively as a *Blitz* bomber, and you, Messerschmitt, have to make all the necessary preparations to make this feasible." I felt my heart sink at that moment.[54]

This was really the beginning of the misuse of the 262, as five bomber wings were supposed to be equipped with the jet, with Wolfgang Schenck and Werner Baumbach being given the order to oversee this activity. In June 1944, KG.51 was converted to Me-262 training as a jet bomber unit. These bomber pilots had no fighter experience, such as combat flying or shooting, which is why so many of them were shot down. They could only escape by outrunning the fighters in pursuit. This was the greatest mistake surrounding the 262, in my opinion, and I believe the 262 could have been made operational as a fighter at least a year and a half earlier, and built in large enough numbers so that it could have changed the air war.

Despite all of Göring's faults, I must say that he did support me in the position that the 262 should be specifically built as a fighter. I had his support by the time of my meeting with him in May 1944, after he had come to his senses regarding just how deep American fighters were entering German airspace.[55]

Not even he could dismiss the swarms of Mustangs and Lightnings flying overhead. Having the jet as a fighter was critical, and despite Hitler's bomber order, fighter testing was still allowed. It would most certainly not have changed the final outcome of the war, for we had already lost completely, but it would have probably delayed the end, since the Normandy invasion on June 6, 1944, would probably not have taken place, at least not successfully if the 262 had been operational and in large numbers. This could have been possible, since *Kommando* Thierfelder had been receiving the jets at Achmer since April.[56]

I certainly think that just three hundred jets flown daily by the best fighter pilots, even at a 10 percent loss, with a like replacement ratio, would have had a major impact on the course of the air war. This would have, of course, prolonged the war, so perhaps Hitler's misuse of this aircraft was not such a bad thing after all.

After Thierfelder was killed in July, I was looking for the right type of pilot, someone daring and successful who could lead by example of his courage and determination, and [Walter] Nowotny had all of these qualities. He was young, successful, energetic, intellectually gifted, and very brave.[57] According to his fellow pilots in his old unit, JG.54, and his CO, Trautloft, he was absolutely fearless in battle. Thierfelder's death, despite the unit's initial successes, endangered the program. I had to find a replacement immediately, although Horst Geyer took over operational command for a while. However, in order to get Hitler interested in considering the fighter option, I needed a named hero, someone successful and highly decorated, liked by Hitler, and one he recognized and hopefully admired.

With the Diamonds and over 250 victories, Nowotny was the right man for the job, and I liked him very much personally.[58] More important was the fact that Hitler liked him very much also. He reminded me very much of Hans-Joachim Marseille, only more mature. I saw to it that he was promoted to *major*, and he was only twenty-four years old, but more than qualified to be a *geschwaderkommodore*.

Nowotny had been reassigned in February 1944 as a fighter instructor for JG.101 in France for a while following his being wounded, as Trautloft had ordered him into a rest period after his magnificent career in Russia.[59] He had become perhaps too brave, or reckless, depending upon to whom you spoke. The one thing about Trautloft was that he really cared about his men, and Walter was one of his favorites.[60]

Being an Austrian, good looking, and well spoken, he was one of Hitler's favorite pilots. Perhaps only [Hans-Ulrich] Rüdel, [Hermann] Graf, and [Erich] Hartmann were held in equal esteem. In fact, although I was not there, I was informed that Hitler had initially ordered "Nowi," as we called him, off flight status. He and I discussed this briefly on the last day of his life.[61]

Like other Diamonds holders who had flown into legend, Hitler had this idea that he needed to preserve these men as shining examples of National Socialism. Nowi was much like me, apolitical and only wanting to fly, but had been banned. Hermann Graf also received the same order not to fly after he was given the Diamonds, as did Rüdel and others. Hartmann also received the order not to fly, and he told Hitler that if receiving the Diamonds meant not flying, he could keep them. Hitler finally gave in to him.

I was ordered to stand-down also, after being promoted to general of the fighters in 1941, but I was able to get around that problem. By late 1944 until the end of the war, Hitler stopped issuing those orders, except in Rüdel's case, after he received the Golden Oak Leaves, Swords, and Diamonds in January 1945 or so.[62] Rüdel just turned a deaf ear and continued flying, losing a leg in the process.

I received a telephone call from Hitler within a week of placing Nowotny in command of the test unit at Achmer, which was in September.[63] It seemed that Hitler was giving the jet fighter idea another lease on life, since his favorite Austrian fighter pilot next to Graf was in command. I knew that this situation had to be a success for Hitler to take his hands off the project, and I felt completely confident in my choice.

There were several other men who flew in the jet unit, which was called *Kommando Nowotny*, and which after Nowotny's death was redesignated JG.7. Men such as Erich Rudorffer,

Theodor Weissenberger, Franz Schall, Johannes Steinhoff, Georg-Peter Eder, Heinrich Ehrler, and many others, all of them great aces, rapidly adapted. Eder already had a few bomber kills adding to his impressive score.[64] I also think he was shot down more than any other pilot. I also think he was the most wounded pilot in the Luftwaffe.

[JG.7's] record was fairly good. It had around fifty jets, with perhaps thirty operational at any given time, despite a few always being grounded with technical problems, and they had shot down a few bombers, and losses had actually been minimal, with most of these losses being in July, as men learned to fly the jet.[65]

I think most of these noncombat losses were due to engine failures. Operational survival was good as long as top cover was flown by conventional aircraft to protect the jets on takeoffs and landings. American fighters would hang around to try and catch them at those weak moments, which I was to learn firsthand in a few months. The big problem that was growing was that the Allies would target, bomb, and strafe the air fields, hoping to destroy the jets on the ground.

I allowed Nowotny to choose his pilots, and basically run the unit as he saw fit. He had requested his support fighters to come from his old unit, and Trautloft had my permission to send III/JG.54 to Achmer. It had transitioned from the Me-109 to the Fw-190D. This was a much better aircraft for engaging the enemy heavy bombers, and in the hands of a good pilot, could tackle the Mustangs and Spitfires.

[III/JG.54's] mission was to engage enemy fighters and protect the jets from being ambushed on takeoff and landing, directly engaging the enemy fighters who made a habit of doing just that. Many times we would have American or British fighters flying around the air bases to ambush the jets returning from a mission, or strafe them on the ground.

I arrived on that evening [November 7, 1944] to inspect the unit and write a report, plus I spoke with Nowotny that previous evening, and he was going to give me his pilots' reports concerning their actions for the previous three weeks. The next day [November 8] a flight of American bombers was reported heading our way, and the air raid warning went up. Nowotny smiled and ordered the jets warmed up, and so the unit took off, about six jets, if I remember correctly, in the first wave, then another.[66]

Nowotny wanted to take off, and had to use a spare aircraft, if I recall, but I could be mistaken. The Fw-190Ds remaining on the ground were waiting on the runway to take off and cover their return, while an additional flight was already airborne, engaging the Allied fighters escorting the bombers, which were sure to follow the jets back to base. I was in the operations shack with [Luftwaffe chief of staff] *Generaloberst* Günther Korten and Eder, and we all stepped outside, where we monitored the radio transmissions over the loud-speaker and could get an idea of what was happening.

Several bombers were called out as shot down. Schall called one, and Nowi called out one, then another, and finally a third kill. Then Nowotny radioed that he was approaching and had damage. The flight leader on the ground, Hans Dortenmann, who had landed after engaging for rearmament, was ready to take off again, and requested permission to take off to assist, but Nowotny said no, to wait. The defensive antiaircraft battery opened fire on a few Mustangs that approached the field, but they were chased away, from what I could understand, and the jets were coming in.

One Me-262 had been shot down [Schall's jet, and he bailed out], and Nowotny reported one bomber kill [which was believed to be a Consolidated B-24, but records show was a Boeing B-17], possibly a Mustang kill [which fits with the known losses for the day], and hits on another bomber over Dummer Lake, which was a B-17. He was returning and he reported one of his engines was damaged. He was flying on the right engine alone, which he reported to be on fire, which made him vulnerable.[67] I knew he was in trouble. Schall had already bailed out, but this was unknown to us at that time.

I was outside with Eder, Korten, and other pilots, including Karl "Quax" Schnörrer, Nowi's best friend and wingman for many years, and the ground crew personnel to watch his approach to the field, when an enemy fighter, clearly a Mustang, pulled away not far from us. I remember being surprised because rather than coming in from altitude, this Mustang was low. Eder called out some Tempests as well, which I did not see. I heard the sound of a jet engine, and we saw this 262 coming down through the light clouds at low altitude, rolling slightly, then inverted, and we could not see much as the forest obscured our view, but then came the sound of it hitting the ground.[68]

The Mustang I saw pulled up and away and around the treeline, so I lost sight of it, but I remember the markings on the nose. I later learned [after speaking with Jeffrey Ethell in 1982] that it was the same fighter unit that American ace Charles Yeager belonged to, which turned out to be the 357th Fighter Group. We had very good intelligence on enemy air force units, and the information gathered from crashed aircraft and captured pilots also gave us great information. There were two other Mustangs that approached from altitude, perhaps a kilometer or so further away. The explosion of the jet rocked the air, and only a column of black smoke rose from behind the trees.[69]

We all jumped in a car and took off and reached the wreckage, and it was Nowotny's plane. After sifting through the wreckage, the only salvageable things found were his left hand and pieces of his Knight's Cross, Oak Leaves, Swords, and Diamonds decoration. He had simply disintegrated. The hole in the ground was about four meters deep and the area for about a hundred meters all around was on fire and smoking. I remember the smell of the jet fuel being quite heavy in the air. We heard by radio that Schall was alive. Eder was standing next to me as we looked through the wreckage, and I promoted him on the spot to take over command of the unit. He just looked at me and said, "Yes, sir," and then turned away.[70]

Losing Nowotny was a great blow, but we had suffered so many by that time, it was almost expected. Hitler, from what I understand, was upset about his loss, but I don't think he really said anything about it to me. I was mostly concerned that Hitler might have perceived this as a failure, and killed the entire fighter program.

Well, that did not happen, and the remains of that unit went to form JG.7, commanded by our friend Johannes Steinhoff who replaced Eder as *kommodore* for a while.[71] Later, Steinhoff recruited other great aces to command the various groups, and then he joined me in JV.44 and was my recruiting officer for that unit, going to the hospitals, training units, wherever he knew a pilot may be who perhaps might need a job.

Steinhoff managed to collect some of our best pilots, although not all of them. This was a direct result of my last meetings with Hitler in January 1945, and with Göring in December 1944, before the meeting that I was not invited to in January, where I was fired by a telephone call, and those officers who supported me were likewise in a lot of trouble.

Basically, it was the same old problem we were having with Göring, and the fact that he was blaming us, the fighter pilots, for the bombings and the losing of the war. All of the senior *kommodores* brought their grievances to me, and we chose a spokesman to represent them. I sat on the panel and arranged for the meeting with Göring, as he did not want me in his presence. He even told me so in December.

This first meeting of December 1944 was to be of great importance, and it had taken two months to arrange. The leaders decided to meet at Trautloft's place near Lake Wannsee, about an hour or so driving time from my office, where Steinhoff and Trautloft had already arrived. Edu Neumann was on his way from Italy as well, and Lützow had called me and said that he was already there.

It was agreed that these leaders should meet without my being present, since I already met with Göring, as this would provide me some cover and protection should things go terribly wrong. I learned later what had happened in this meeting amongst the leaders themselves before the official meeting with Göring the next day.[72] I would not be at that meeting either, and that was Göring's demand. I wanted to be there, but it was probably best that I was not, and I understood.

The men gathered at the hangar in Schönwald. The men had their meeting with Göring, which Steinhoff said was an exercise in futility. He just did not have a real comprehension of the war, what was possible, and what was not. Afterward, Steinhoff told me about the event. I felt sorry for him. I should have been the one taking the abuse, not the pilots alone in front of Göring. When Göring continued his inspection the tension seemed to grow, but thankfully, Steinhoff did not have to endure it for too long.

Once this inspection and meeting was over I joined all the men, and we had a long conversation. I believe it may have been

Lützow who made the recommendation about trying to get the SS on our side against Göring. He knew one of the high-ranking SS generals who was not a fan of our national leadership. In fact, he even believed that he was a conspirator in the bomb plot who had gone undetected. If anyone had a vested interest in Germany not losing the war, and avoiding captivity, it was definitely Himmler and the SS.[73]

I warned them all that this was dangerous business, and I would not be able to help them, given the fact that Himmler and I did not like each other at all. You must understand that when it came to a Luftwaffe general, even a Diamonds holder, I could not challenge the *Reichsführer* and hope to win. No one could, and the last thing we needed was a visit from the Gestapo. The men understood, for it was far too risky to go that route.

The next major meetings were in January. The first of these was during the first week, just after [Operation] *Bodenplatte*. Steinhoff, Trautloft, and Lützow had somehow managed a meeting in Berlin. This proved an interesting development, and at the end of it all, the SS general in question left the very real impression that I was not going to be a problem much longer.

Getting back to *Bodenplatte*, I was completely against this operation, although I was only informed of the basics, not all of the details. Afterward, when it was finished, and I read the reports, I had to admit I lost a little control. At that time I was still general of the fighters, and I should have been at the very least informed of all the details, if not actually involved in the planning. However, given the plan as it was, I would have ruled it unfeasible, and tried to kill the idea as it stood. Göring knew how I felt about it, as I did not try to hide it.

I was informed by him [Felix Steiner] through my men that they had been tapping my phone and recording my calls, gathering whatever evidence they thought they could use to get rid of me. I guess I should have been flattered. In most cases, the SS did not need any evidence to get someone. He just disappeared. I owed Steiner a great debt for that information, although I already had my suspicions.

I suppose that my opposition to the SS taking over the Luftwaffe, or at the very least the jet program, had ruffled a few feathers. I had also been recorded discussing many of the problems with various leaders regarding our industry, operations, and the like. I would imagine that lack of National Socialist spirit was coming through too much. You must also understand that ever since the July 20 plot, life in Germany had changed forever. Everyone was under suspicion. That was not the time to stand out as someone who challenged authority. I even heard that Himmler tapped Göring's phone, but I do not know if that is true. I would not be surprised if this were the case. Göring was probably tapping Himmler also.[74] Speer told me his phones were tapped for certain.

The Fighters' Revolt was the last straw for Göring, and the men also spoke with *Generaloberst* Robert *Ritter* von Greim.[75] He was a gentleman of the old school, the senior fighter pilot next to Göring in Germany, and the man we hoped would replace our boss. Greim understood the real world; he was no fool. Although he was not a fervent National Socialist, he did have many positive political connections, and he was one of the few senior Luftwaffe officers who were held in high regard by Hitler, Himmler, and even Göring. He really wanted to help, and in fact he did succeed Göring as the Luftwaffe chief in April 1945, when Göring was dismissed by Hitler.

Lützow was the spokesman as always; he was a great leader and a true knight, a gentleman. He was also a very serious person, and in all the years that I knew him I can probably count the number of times I ever saw him laugh on one hand. However, Lützow was a cold pilot, very unemotional, even on the radio in combat he was the calmest person I ever knew, even in a fight. It was as if he never exhibited any emotion except anger, and ironically, this was usually directed at Göring, and never the enemy. He was never angry in combat, and he never hated his enemies.

The meeting that is today called the Fighters' Revolt almost occurred by accident, and there were actually two meetings. This final meeting also ended my career, as well as the careers of many others. The fact that others and I were still alive afterward still puzzles me to some degree, because I was not even present at that meeting, but I was being constantly informed. I have to say that for all his faults, it was Hitler who actually saved my life, and possibly that of Lützow as well.

When all the men present were approached by Göring, he [Lützow] told Göring that if he interrupted, which he always did so that he could show his importance, nothing would get accomplished. Lützow, Neumann, Steinhoff, Trautloft, and others and I, had voiced our grievances many times, but since I was not invited to this meeting, Hannes Trautloft, along with Lützow, kept me informed as to their recommending that Göring step down for the good of the service.

Basically, the meeting started with Lützow providing a proper picture of the war, our condition, the enemy situation, and all of these kinds of details. He even gathered a folder containing all the statistics I had compiled and given to Trautloft, who was inspector of day fighters. It was a very thick and impressive folder, containing the names of every lost pilot, wounded pilot, dead pilot, aircraft losses, their units, the reasons for the damage or destruction, fuel availability, allotments for fuel and ammunition, replacement pilots, enemy aircraft destroyed, victories per round fired, enemy action and aircraft reports, everything you could imagine.

The purpose of the meeting was to make certain that Göring understood without question our condition. It was also stated by Lützow that it had come to our attention that Hitler was not being given the proper data from the front, which we supplied to Göring. The greatest problem besides losing pilots and aircraft was the lack of fuel and oil. Our refineries, depots, and even the rail traffic transporting these critical items were primary targets for Allied raids.[76]

As Lützow, Neumann, [*Oberst* Günther *Freiherr*] von Maltzahn, Rödel, [Hans-Heinrich] von Brüstelin, and Steinhoff were in the first part of the meeting, Trautloft was in the hallway on the phone with me. He would enter when called in, carrying the bulky dossier, and give his report. He could clearly hear what was going on, and he was giving me the actual dialogue as he heard it. I was on the other end of the line in my office, listening to his commentary, and I could not believe what I was hearing. I could even hear Lützow and Göring myself through the phone as their voices rose during the argument, even with the door closed.

Much of what started this heated argument was the inaccurate information Hitler had been receiving, either from Milch or Göring, but I knew that Milch also sent his reports through either Göring or [Nicolaus] von Below, Hitler's Luftwaffe adjutant, often directly to von Below to make sure Hitler received them. Not even Milch trusted Göring, and for good reason. Göring had done many of the same things with Milch, who was a Hitler favorite, and Göring would halt or edit information that made himself look bad, incompetent, or perhaps even foolish. The fates of Udet and Jeschonnek were still fresh in many minds, including mine. I am certain that these events were vivid in Milch's mind as well.

Whenever Hitler called, or just happen to speak to me about certain facts, I was often stunned at the questions or comments. Often I was completely unaware of what he was talking about, and when he said, "the *Reichsmarschall* stated that . . . ," or something to that effect, and I almost always knew it was rubbish, and I told him so. I never told him that Göring had been the source of the unreliable information, or that I even told him anything. I just let Hitler think he was informing me of new information, which was actually the case more often than not.

I also set Hitler straight on many of the inaccuracies as related by Göring to him; the majority of this information was the exaggerated strengths of the fighter or bomber forces on the various fronts, so that Hitler would feel that he still had a great air arm. Land generals also did the same inflations regarding their forces. Hitler listened intently and hung on every word, making his usual mental notes. I knew that he was taking stock of all my data, and by the look on his face, he was not pleased.

I could tell quite easily that Hitler knew he was being misled by some of his senior generals and field marshals. I think this was why he had little difficulty calling in field grade leaders and asking them specific questions, knowing that these officers would not lie to him. They had no reason to, but their bosses certainly did. They did this to reduce the level of their own personal responsibility, as a measure of self-preservation. Failure at the top was not a very healthy way of serving Germany back in those days. There were a few exceptions, such as von Manstein, [Heinz] Guderian, [Günther] von

Kluge, [Wolfram] von Richthofen, [Hasso] von Manteuffel, [Wilhelm *Ritter*] von Leeb, and others. They were men who always gave the real situation, and for most of them it cost them their careers.

It was this very situation, this meeting being conducted, where I suppose the chickens came to roost, when Lützow had a long list of Göring's well-documented lies and direct misrepresentations to Hitler. Göring, caught in the open, went completely mad, and I could clearly hear this on the phone without Trautloft saying anything. Göring told Lützow to take his dossier of lies away, and he would speak to Hitler about it. That was when Trautloft told me what happened next. Steinhoff stood, addressed Göring, and told him that he had his own folder from his time as commodore of both JG.77 in Italy, and more recently, JG.7.[77]

Steinhoff proceeded to point out several major flaws in the original reports given through the chain of command, which were supposed to go through Milch to both Göring and then Hitler. Steinhoff had proof in Göring's own hand that he had changed facts and figures, and had failed to provide von Below with the proper information to submit to Hitler. Göring stated that this was a serious offense, and Steinhoff stated, "Yes, and this is why you should step down for the good of the service," which was the same argument Lützow had made. I could hear the shouting so loudly, I felt as if I were in the room.[78]

Göring told Steinhoff that his endless muttering was meaningless, that he knew the truth. Steinhoff argued that he was wrong, and could be proven to be wrong. The fact that Göring did not court-martial us, or even kill us, meant that Hitler probably had already had enough of Göring, and even he knew that it would leak out and look very bad if so many highly decorated and successful pilots were to just disappear, let alone stand public trial.

I was under no illusions. Later Hitler allowed me to form JV.44 as a way of saying "thank you" for past service, and if I died, then I fell for the nation in battle and I was no longer a problem. Same with Trautloft, Lützow, Steinhoff, and even poor Edu Neumann, who was only there at my request.

You must understand that after the July bomb plot that failed to kill Hitler, the level of paranoia emanating from Berlin was so heavy one could feel it. The Gestapo made many visits to front commands, even rear commands. I had more than one visit from these fellows, who were hoping to ferret out dissent. They were still executing people who were believed to be involved with [Claus] von Stauffenberg.

Now, Göring had his own plot against us. We were not violent; we simply wanted steady, competent, and consistent leadership, which he did not, and could not, provide. Well, Göring knew that the fighters did not respect him. He did not have their loyalty, and we knew that we could not count on Berlin doing anything to help us, so we were alone. At least it was now out in the open, with no pretenses.

Well, at the end of that meeting I was fired as general of the fighters, Steinhoff was banished from Germany and sent back to Italy, and Göring told Lützow that he was going to be shot for high treason, and that he would see to it personally. All of this Trautloft told me on the phone. Apparently, Göring's final comment as the men left was his stating that he would "have Galland shot first to set the example."

I heard this all through the phone, and can say that hearing that did not make me feel very comfortable. Well, at the very least I was out of a job, and as I hung up the phone with Trautloft, I was not sure if I even had a future. My family had lost two of four sons already. That was a high price to pay. I was not sure if my mother was ready to lose a third. Speer called me, and then he visited, and he informed me that he had a special relationship with certain persons in the SS who thought a lot of me. In fact, Speer went to see Hitler on my behalf, and I was assigned an SS bodyguard, just in case Göring tried anything.

I should mention why Felix Steiner thought a lot of me. When he was in Russia, his unit was in a very horrid battle against Soviet tanks and troops, heavily outnumbered. Three Luftwaffe fighter pilots, low on fuel, still stayed to strafe and attack the enemy, buying him time to get his reserve force and additional tanks into the battle. The three pilots saved a lot of his men from death, or worse.

He later sent the unit commander and me thank-you letters, and wanted to recommend these pilots for decorations for bravery.

Even his men on the ground could see that they were taking heavy hits from enemy ground fire, but they stayed. Only one of these pilots survived, and that man was Assi Hahn. Hahn received the Oak Leaves to his Knight's Cross, and Steiner was repaying me for his life and the lives of his men. He was truly an honorable man, and I know that it was he who kept us informed, and somewhat protected, although he never made any mention of it.

My replacement was Gordon Gollob, and he was not well liked across the board. Although he was a good pilot, very brave, and with the Diamonds, he had no character. Gollob was also well known for being a great National Socialist, even from the early days. However, he was still not Göring's first choice. Hajo Herrmann was also being considered, and he would have been a better selection, despite his career of being a bomber pilot. Herrmann was a very brave and accomplished leader, and I think he would have been a better choice. He also supported me with the Me-262 program.

When I was released as general of the fighters, Göring was still preparing a coup against me, which I also learned from Trautloft and a couple of others who thought well of me. He had been in Milch's office and overheard the telephone call when Milch was speaking with Dieter Peltz. Trautloft and I had a wonderful working relationship, and I also had a reasonably decent relationship with Milch, and in his defense he called Lützow and informed him of the events when he could not reach me.

Later, I was called into to meet with Hitler, without Göring being informed or invited, and informed that Göring had issued a warrant for my arrest on charges ranging from dereliction of duty, conspiracy, incompetence, to insubordination. He stopped short of treason, which would have been too hard for anyone to swallow, which Hitler said to me himself. The other charges were just as difficult to believe as well, but make no mistake, I was in great danger, especially with the shadow of the July 20 bomb plot still very much alive, and Himmler seeing my removal as a way to gain control over the jet program. Hitler did not trust Göring not to try arranging an "accident" of some sort to get rid of me. Hence the bodyguard.

Later, perhaps a week afterward, Göring ordered me to Karinhall again and formally fired me, and said that he had rescinded the arrest order due to my service to the nation. I knew better, as I had heard from Milch and Speer, even Kammhuber, that Hitler himself had dismissed the charges, even before I met with Hitler, who told Göring he "was mad for even trying such a thing."

That was when, during our private meeting, Hitler said that he would let me do what I wanted. Of course, Göring was unaware that I knew all of this information. It was actually amusing to have him try and make me think he changed his own mind. Well, then, I was dismissed and stripped of my professional duties as general of the fighters. He never had any idea that Hitler and I discussed him and this particular situation.

Also, regarding the warrant and dismissal, Peltz did not know that I already knew, or that Trautloft overheard and told me, or that Lützow had already been informed by me, that when Hitler learned of this, he ordered Göring to stop the actions against me. I told no one until after the war about that private meeting with Hitler. Then Hitler ordered my replacement [Gollob] to be posted immediately, but he kept his word and still allowed me to form my own 262 unit, basically allowing me to keep my rank but reducing my responsibilities.

I think that if Göring had not failed Hitler so many times, and had maintained his respect in Hitler's eyes, I would have been killed. Problems had a tendency to just disappear in Germany at that time. I find it quite ironic that the very man who is so despised today, and was the creator of so much suffering, was the very man who saved my life.

If I were to name the men I knew and respected, that would be a long list. Of all the names you could mention, I think perhaps the greatest leader was still Mölders. All the rest still living are still very good friends of mine, but we are old men now, and life is not as fast as it was in the cockpit. However, as their leader, I also made many mistakes. I could have done better. I was young and inexperienced with life, I guess.

It is very easy to look back retrospectively and criticize yourself. However, at that time it was very difficult. My situation was that I had to fight with Milch, Göring, and Hitler in order to accomplish what they wished, but without their support, if that makes any sense. Göring was a thorn in my side, and Hitler simply destroyed our country, and many of the others functioned without any regard for the welfare of others.

I was happy again, although I knew the war was lost. I was then able to choose all the pilots I could find who would join me, with Steinhoff's assistance, and almost all had the Knight's Cross or higher decorations. It was our badge. This was the beginning of March 1945, when I created *Jagdverband* 44.

I made Steinhoff my recruiting officer, and he traveled to all of the major bases, picking up pilots who wanted to once again feel a sense of adventure. The first confirmed victory over a fighter for JV.44 was on April 4, 1945, when Eduard Schallmoser miscalculated an attack and crashed into the tail of a P-38. This was perhaps not the best of beginnings, but it at least showed we had determination.

We had most of the greats, like Gerd Barkhorn, Walter Krupinski, Johannes Steinhoff, Heinz Bär, Erich Hohagen, Günther Lützow, Wilhelm Herget, and others. I tried to get Erich Hartmann, but he wanted to stay with JG.52. That decision would prove very costly for him at the end of the war. We were finally stationed at Munich-Reim, and on March 31 flew the first of several missions, and later we were very successful using the R4M rockets, which we fired at bomber formations. During my first attack with rockets, Krupinski was on my wing, and we witnessed the power in these rockets. I remember that I shot down two Martin B-26 Marauders.

By the middle of April we were very hard pressed to receive fuel, and even ammunition was hard to come by. Our supplies were not coming, and there was a great bureaucracy strangling our operations. On April 10, I was again summoned to see Göring, this time at the Obersalzberg, and to my astonishment, he greeted me as if we were old friends. There was none of the arrogance and pompous, critical attitude I had known for almost five years.

During our conversation, my boss explained, almost as if an apology, that I had been right all along. When he dismissed me and shook my hand, I think he wanted to say he was sorry, but not even at that point of contrition could he summon the words. The last time I saw him, he simply said, "Good luck." I guessed that the arrest warrant was still a dead issue by that time.

Then, on April 23, I received a telegram that Göring had been dismissed by Hitler, and even charges of treason were given as the cause. I called the men together and told them, and I also told them that von Greim was the new Luftwaffe commander. If this had been in 1942 or 1943, there would have been great parties thrown. But at that time, as the war was crashing down around us, it made little difference. At least I knew now that I had an even more free hand with my fighter pilots.[79] My greatest concern, ironically, was for Macky Steinhoff.

Barkhorn, Schallmoser, Fährmann, Klaus Neumann, Krupinski, and I were taking off on a mission shortly after our base had been attacked, with several of us trying to catch a B-17 formation on April 18. Steinhoff's 262 hit a crater made from a bomb. His jet lifted into the air but without sufficient takeoff speed, then he nosed in and exploded. The fire exploded the rockets and ammunition as the kerosene-based fuel engulfed him. He managed to stagger out, a human torch, and I cried, because I knew he was a dead man. Even though my gear was already up, I could look back and see the smoke.

We returned to base after the mission to find him in the hospital, more dead than alive. The fact that he even survived is the most incredible thing, and I am glad he did, for he is one of my closest friends today. That crash was April 18, and soon after Lützow failed to return from a mission, which was April 24, if memory serves. For years after the war I hoped that he would turn up, perhaps long held by the Allies, or wounded and recovering in anonymity. Very sad.

On April 25, with no sign of Lützow, I called my men around and told them the war was lost. I knew that I was not providing them with anything that they did not already know. What I did tell them was that with the war lost, I would fly only with volunteers who wished to continue. I would not issue an order that may see them killed at this late day in the war. No one stepped aside, much to their credit.

On my last mission, which was the very next day, I was shot down by a [Republic P-47D] Thunderbolt as we took off to intercept a bomber force. The fighter was flown by a man named

James Finnegan, whom I met some years later, and we became friends. We were intercepting bombers near Neuberg. I was leading a flight, and we were approaching almost head-on to them. I switched off the safety on the cannon, but forgot to release the safety for the rockets, yet again. I am not sure where my head was. I guess I was just thinking about too many things, and not focused on the mission.

On this mission I saw Schallmoser, who was famous for ramming enemy fighters, fly past me, his "White 5" too close for comfort, and I led the group head-on. As a result of my ignorance my rockets did not fire, but I poured 30mm cannon shells into one bomber, which blew up in spectacular fashion and then fell in flames, and I flew right through the formation, hitting another. I could not tell if that bomber was finished off, so I banked around for another run, all the while my jet was receiving numerous hits from the bombers' defensive fire.

When large .50-caliber bullets strike your fuselage it makes a very interesting sound, unlike cannon fire or small-caliber .303-inch British bullets. It packs a heavy punch, and when several hit you, it shakes the aircraft. Once I felt I was out of range of the bombers' defensive fire, I tried to climb slightly and bank around for another pass, but my right engine began flickering and sputtering, then it caught again.

Suddenly my instrument panel disintegrated, my canopy was shattered, and my right knee was struck by a bullet that grazed me. I was losing power and in great pain. My right engine suddenly started losing thrust rapidly, and then died. I thought about parachuting out but realized that might be dangerous, as some of our pilots had been strafed upon exiting their jets.[80]

I was also at a high rate of speed, perhaps five hundred miles an hour after I dropped the nose, then my airspeed bled off. I thought at the time, and for some years afterward, that it was one of the Mustangs that shot me, as I saw a few on escort duty. Later I learned it was Finnegan in a P-47. I had previously radioed for [Leutnant Heinz] Sachsenberg to get his fighters in the air. He was an outstanding and very reliable fighter pilot, and we trusted him with our lives.[81]

I flew for the deck and headed for this field at the air base, which was also under attack. I cut the power to my good engine as I leveled out, and since I still had aileron and rudder control, stabilized my jet into a level attitude and thumped across the field on the engines. My gear would not come down, and later I found that my nosewheel had been flattened and smoke was pouring from my plane. The first thought I had was of Steinhoff, and remembering what had happened to him. I also knew that it was not beyond reason and experience for pilots to strafe a downed jet, or the pilot, and I did not want to be sitting in it or even be anywhere around it.

I opened the canopy and climbed out to get away, in case it should explode, only to find aircraft dropping bombs and firing rockets at me. Well, our mission netted five victories total, and none of the pilots were killed, but Schallmoser rammed another bomber, parachuted out, and he actually landed in his mother's garden at his home near Munich, bruised, but not severely injured. His mother even fixed him a nice meal and he took a hot bath, smelling better than the rest of us when he returned the next day.

From that point forward Bär took operational command, and before the month was out every unit in Germany with jets began bringing them to us at Reim air field, near Munich. I was sent to the hospital, but I discharged myself, walking with a cane, and relocated to Tegernsee, where I still had telephone contact with Bär. There was a rumor that we were the only unit to have the jet fuel! For such a long time I had been begging for planes.

Now that the war was almost over I had more planes than men to fly them, around seventy jets or so, and even fuel, which we used to destroy our wonderful fighters. We had lost some of our friends, such as Lützow, Steinhoff, and even the iron man Barkhorn, who almost had his neck broken after being shot down, as his canopy slammed forward on his neck when he crashed. Our little band grew very small, very quickly.

Well, I ordered the remaining aircraft flown to Innsbruck, where Hans-Ekkehard Bob was located. I had sent Wilhelm Herget with Hugo Kessler in a [Fieseler Fi-156] *Storch* to get a message to General [Dwight D.] Eisenhower, arranging a special surrender for JV.44. Herget was bringing back the message to Bär, but his plane was shot down. Herget was all right, just tossed around a bit, but the message never made it.

Well, hearing nothing from Herget I surrendered the unit, blew up the jets, and the Americans took me into custody. I was then sent to the RAF base at Tangmere, where I was interrogated and held until my release over a year later. Günther Rall was also there, along with Rüdel and others, all of those they thought could serve the American and British cause after the war. I guess that even at that time they were concerned about their Soviet ally.

I would have been concerned as well, and said so. I was able to once again see Bader, who came by after he was repatriated, and he wished me well. I also met many of the top American and British officers, who knew of me. I guess the natural curiosity and camaraderie of fliers brought that about.

After the war I was invited by Juan Perón to go to Argentina. He wanted German experts to build his air force, and I was asked to come along with others. I went and established a training and operations school, developed their tactical training program, and was able to fly again in some of the new designs purchased by Argentina, most of which were a few British and French models. They were bright young boys, willing to learn and quick to grasp the essentials of air combat.

I really loved that period. It was one of the happiest of my life. Kurt Tank (designer of the Focke-Wulf 190 series of fighters) came, as did others, and he was the one who convinced President Perón to bring me over. I did that until 1955, when I returned to Germany and entered the business world, consulting and getting my life together. As you probably know, the Argentine air forces were still using much of my strategy and tactical doctrine as late as the Falklands War, with great effect. Yes, they lost the war, but they had the best success in the air.

My life afterward has been interesting. I still flew my private plane for a number of years and enjoyed going to America and Britain, meeting my old enemies who became my good friends. Among these was Jimmy Doolittle, a great American and a great airman. I respected him very much. It was really a great shame that he and I commanded the two groups that were trying to kill each other. Others are Johnnie Johnson and Robert [Stanford] Tuck, as well as Douglas Bader, who all became very good friends. He [Bader] was knighted after the war for his remarkable service and, I think, as a flier and leader, he deserved it. We lost many fine young men, on all sides, and this is something that has always stayed with me. It is a reminder that, although we may do our duty, and perhaps do it well, there is always a cost. That may be an emotional or physical expense, but you cannot walk away from it without some regret. I worked my business, and my faithful old friend Gerd Schöpfel stayed with me. We still get together on occasion and have a drink to the men we lost. I think the world of Gerd and his family. As the years pass, there are fewer of us.

I have two children—a son, Andreas-Hubertus, whom we call Andrus, combining the two names, and Alexandra, my daughter, two years younger than her brother and a very sweet girl. Both are from my first marriage. Andreas-Hubertus just recently married and is studying to become a lawyer, while Alexandra goes to school and studies languages. They are the sunshine of my life.

Mentor to Many

Eduard Neumann,
15 victories; Iron Cross, Second and First Class;
Spanish Cross; German Cross in Gold
(June 5, 1911–August 9, 2004)

THE LUFTWAFFE WAS THE MOST POTENT FORCE in Europe until the emergence of American air power during the Second World War. As a result of excellent engineering and aircraft designs, spearheaded by the Messerschmitt Bf (later and most often designated Me) 109, the German fighter pilots carved through their enemies and assured the rapid ground victories during the halcyon days of *Blitzkrieg*.

When Hitler decided to aid his Fascist ally Francisco Franco during the Spanish Civil War, the premier group he sent was the famous Condor Legion. Many of Germany's future leading aces and exceptional combat leaders took their long and detailed peacetime training, and honed those skills in aerial combat over Spain. New tactics were developed, and the men involved in this dress rehearsal for the world war to come would prove critical in the period after the days of early victory.

Eduard Neumann was one of the young Luftwaffe officers sent to Spain. Along with such men as Adolf Galland, Hajo Herrmann, Hannes Trautloft, Werner Mölders, Herbert Ihlefeld, Wilhelm Balthasar, Günther Lützow, and others, "Edu" Neumann adopted and later pioneered his own unique brand of leadership. His style and personal touch would see him become the teacher to many great pilots, and the mentor of a few, the most notable being a young and completely unmilitary-like fighter ace destined to become a legend: Hans-Joachim Marseille, the "Star of Africa."

Neumann, with his modest score of thirteen aerial victories, does not stand out as one of history's great aces. In analyzing his record as a commanding officer, however, his legacy is secure due to his ability to instruct and lead by impeccable example. Neumann would not only serve in two wars and fly combat in both Europe and North Africa, he would also be one of the senior fighter leaders to join his colleagues in the Fighters' Revolt of January 1945, in which they confronted *Reichsmarschall* Hermann Wilhelm Göring regarding his incompetence.

For years the Luftwaffe's supreme commander had made disastrous decisions that had cost millions of lives, misled the German nation, and even Hitler, with false prophecies and reports, and displayed utter indifference to the loss of thousands of young pilots. Göring then resorted to blaming the very instrument of Germany's early success of cowardice and incompetence. Neumann was fortunate that Hitler would not allow Göring to retaliate against the brave men who had challenged him. A large part of the *Führer's* reluctance to punish the mutineers was the fact that he had also lost faith in his second in command, and for good reason.

After a series of interviews over more than two decades, Neumann's life, experiences, and the many notable personalities with whom he interacted come to life. His straightforward manner and remarkable attention to detail fill many of the gaps in the historical literature of the Luftwaffe. His personal interactions with both the very top and bottom levels of the Luftwaffe command structure gave him many perspectives from the mechanics to the aces; he understood their concerns and motivations, and he knew how to get the best from his men. Eduard Neumann, the father figure to some of Germany's greatest combat aces, passed away after a long illness on August 9, 2004, at age ninety-three.

Eduard Neumann

I was born in June 1911 in the area that was once called Bukovina, but this was during the days of the old Austro-Hungarian Empire.

My parents passed away when I was young, so my sister and I were raised by my grandmother when we moved to Germany. This was in 1919 or 1920, I believe. I was always pushed by my grandmother to do well in school. "Education is the future," she would say, and she always made sure I did my schoolwork. The same for my sister, in fact. Education was the only path to success, and I tried to learn as much as I could.

When I was still a teenager I was in school, working in mechanical engineering. I had a knack for mathematics and I liked school very much. I also played sports, and football was my favorite. I then joined a youth glider club, and after a year or so I also then applied for powered flight school. I had entertained the idea, much like many young men, of being a commercial pilot. I passed the written examinations and started training in the Fieseler [Fi.5], which was the standard training aircraft back in the early 1930s. This was in Cottbus and later in Schleissheim, and I graduated a fighter pilot in 1935.

My first unit was the new Richthofen wing with Wolf Falck, later redesignated JG.2 in 1935. I was a young *leutnant* and probably had more spirit than experience, and more bravery than common sense, but that is the same with most fighter pilots. That is until you get involved in a shooting war, then that tends to change very quickly. In around August 1937, I went to Spain as part of the Condor Legion. There were many new and old friends there already, such as Galland, Trautloft, Mölders, Balthasar, Herrmann, Lützow, and many others. We were a very close group, the fighter squadron in particular.

I only scored two confirmed victories in Spain, where I spent a year, and I was awarded the Spanish Cross with Swords in Gold, and this was very special to me, and a rare award. Galland and Mölders also received this from Franco, but they had Diamonds. Spain was a marvelous period for me personally, although I was shocked at the complete poverty in the larger cities. I was able to meet and work with many of the men who would become the future leaders of the Luftwaffe in the Second World War.

The war from the air was nothing like it was on the ground. The war had stripped everything from the countryside, destroyed farmland, most animals had been stolen by troops from both sides, schools and hospitals were even destroyed. I would not see such images again until after Germany lost the war. The ground war was brutal, just horrific.

The Communists and Nationalists really went at each other, and it was horrible. And as always happens in a war, the civilians, especially the children, suffered. You could see them on occasion wandering the streets. Orphans, starving and begging for food. That is perhaps the greatest memory and tragedy that I took away from Spain.

When I arrived back in Germany in 1938, I was assigned to JG.26 in Düsseldorf, where I was the *Gruppenkommandeur* for IV [IV/ JG.26] *Gruppe* until 1940, when the unit had moved to France. This was in support of our operations after the French campaign, when everyone thought we would be invading Britain. Personally I did not see that happening, but I kept that thought to myself. I shot down my first aircraft of this war, a [Bristol] Blenheim on July 20, 1940. This was right after the Battle of Britain had started.

I was then transferred, as a new *gruppenkommandeur*, to I/JG.27, which was also already on the English Channel under the command of [*Oberstleutnant*] Max Ibel until [*Major* Bernhard] Woldenga took over later in the year. I was replacing *Major* Helmut Riegel, who had been shot down. This was interesting, as I was only an *oberleutnant* at this time. Fighting the British was a very serious business, as they were a dedicated and very professional group of young men. One thing I learned very quickly was to never underestimate them. I was also very surprised at just how efficient and marvelous the Spitfire fighter was. It was so maneuverable and agile.

This fighter was a real threat, and we all knew that in the hands of a decent pilot it was a fighter that could get you. I think what saved many of us from being shot down was not the abilities of our Me-109, which was the E model at that time in 1940, but our experience and hard training. This E, or Emil, was an upgrade from the early C and D model, with a more powerful engine. I liked having the 20mm canon and 7.92 cowling-mounted machine guns. It gave a good punch.

However, I never did like the limited visibility that our canopy afforded us. This would not be corrected until the later G models arrived in late 1942 and 1943. That was when I managed to get them anyway; I know that Galland was very instrumental in having that design changed. In fact, it was called the "Galland Hood" throughout the Luftwaffe. I also know that such a small change saved many German pilots' lives by increasing side visibility.

We had certain limitations placed against us, both technically and operationally, from our high command, such as our limited range once we crossed the coast. If we fought over the Channel proper, then all was reasonably well. However, if we had to fly to England, especially London or slightly further, we had less than twenty minutes of flying time, and a lot less than that if we were involved in a dogfight. This became less of a worry when we had the long-range drop tanks, but then you really wanted to get rid of that thing when you tangled with Spitfires and Hurricanes.

I would have to say that the worst mission any true free-spirited fighter pilot can fly is a bomber escort mission, unless it is a ground attack mission, which has its own list of problems. I understand that these escort missions were critical to protecting our bombers from fighter attacks. However, as a fighter pilot, your greatest wish is to engage your opposite number, a test of skill, nerves, and endurance, man against man, and fighter against fighter. It may sound like a game, but that was the way I think most of us approached the war. It kept us sane.

I flew several escort missions with the boys, escorting He-111, Ju-88, and Me-110 fighter-bombers. I always had a small chuckle about escorting the Me-110s, since these were Göring's personal pet aircraft. He touted them as being the new air superiority fighters, which was laughable. This factor alone showed how out of touch with reality he actually was. The twin-engine fighters were easy kills for the British fighter pilots. However, they did perform very well in the ground attack and night fighter roles, as demonstrated later by Wolf Falck.

I got involved in one dogfight that I will always remember. I did not get the kill, but I did not get killed either, which was even more important. We had flown a mission to pick up a group of inbound bombers returning from a raid, as the fighter escorts were also returning low on fuel. This was our way to protect incoming flights, by having a group airborne as top cover. One of the men called out enemy planes, and I looked left and dipped my wing. Sure enough, there were three Spitfires trailing the bombers and closing the gap. There were four of us, so I felt pretty confident that we could get the kills and make it back to Calais.

Well, we were about two thousand meters above the enemy fighters, and I knew that they saw us. They immediately pulled up to greet us as we winged over into the dive. I focused upon one Spitfire and had him in my gunsight. He was less than three hundred meters away and closing when I pulled the trigger for my cannon. Nothing happened, and we passed each other. I had forgotten to take off the damned safety catch! I felt three or four thumps in my fighter. I knew I had been hit, but as I pulled up and banked right to get on his tail, I looked at my instruments. Fuel, engine, oil, all were good, so no problem. I had no control surface damage, and no discernable coolant leak. The coolant was the Achilles' heel of our Messerschmitts.

As I completed the turn and saw my intended victim, one of his wingmen was on me. One of my wingmen called out over the radio that he had him, and I cut power and kicked left rudder, throwing the stick right, going into a skid. The Spitfire passed right by me, within three or four meters of my right wing. I looked over and saw the pilot, who was looking right back at me. I could not believe it, but he actually waved to me, and without thinking, perhaps because I was so mesmerized by the event, I just waved right back at him!

His fighter was trailing smoke and glycol, so I knew he was not going to make it home. I stayed with him for about a minute, and I saw him open the canopy and the small hinged door that allowed entry into the cockpit. Then he rolled the fighter over slightly, reduced his airspeed, leaped from the fighter, and then passed by underneath me. I called the bail out over the radio, and my wingman had his first confirmed victory. I do not recall who that was, but he was later killed in Russia. The other two fighters were also shot down, but not by me. Being the idiot that I was I should have had the kill, but I made the most common novice's mistake.

When I landed I yawed to the right and almost made a complete circle. I then rolled to a stop at the end of the grass field. The fighter was leaning to the right and the wing was dipped, and I climbed out. My chief mechanic came to me and said that he was concerned, as they had heard the battle, as it was on the radio in the radio shack. I walked around the fighter with my mechanic, and we saw something that was interesting.

Apparently, the thumps I had heard were the British .303-caliber bullets hitting my undercarriage. The right tire had been shot flat, hence the awkward landing. Then, as we looked at the tire it was smoking, and then caught fire. Some men came running with the fire extinguisher and pumped water on the fire. Had that tire caught fire up inside the wheel well while I was flying, it could have set the entire aircraft ablaze, and that would have been bad for me, especially at low altitude and unable to bail out.

After the Battle of Britain the war became pretty quiet for us. There were a few patrols flown over the Channel, but the British had pretty much stopped, as they concentrated on night bombing for the majority of their missions. Every now and then we would be called upon to scramble, as photographic reconnaissance aircraft would be detected, but we were never able to catch them.

[Major] Wolfgang Schellmann then became our kommodore. The unit then moved to the Balkans, where we supported the invasion of Yugoslavia that April of 1941, but that did not last long. We took the country quickly, and then my unit [I/JG.27] moved to Libya, near Al Gazala on April 18. I was awarded the German Cross in Gold the next year on May 11, 1942.

The other groups were still in the Balkans and III/JG.27 was in Sicily. My group would be sent to Sicily for a short time, but we returned in short order. Not too much we could do against Malta. We would be the only fighter group in all of North Africa for almost a year, until 1942. We pilots flew across Greece, then to Sicily, and then to Africa. Most of our men and matériel came by ship, with most of our supplies flown by Ju-52s from Crete. We managed to relocate and get established in short order, and within a month we were flying missions.

I was an *oberleutnant* at that time, but then promoted to *hauptmann* the same day as receiving the German Cross in Gold by Woldenga, who returned as *kommodore* and also received the German Cross in Gold in May 1942. I was then placed as the *gruppenkommandeur* in June 1942 as a *hauptmann*, as the fighting was very furious at this time, and in June I was promoted to *major* and appointed as the *geschwaderkommodore* for JG.27. The unit would have more than three thousand kills by the end of the war. It was a really nice unit to be in.

I did not really like the job, to be honest, as it took me away from flying. I was able to get away on a mission every now and then, but the demand for field reports every day, and then the filing of all of my pilots' after action reports took up most of my time. I think I spent most of my time on the telephone and radio just trying to get my fuel and ammunition allocations.

Supply was a great problem in the desert. Often we did not even have enough glycol to use for the fighters. Just getting a steady fresh water supply was often a problem. The British would bomb the truck convoys, and the Royal Navy did a good job of intercepting many of the supply ships coming from Sicily and southern France. The Royal Air Force flying out of Egypt and Malta kept the pressure on. Even after we secured Crete that May of 1941, we still had problems.

I would have to say that the highlight of my experience there was getting to know the many interesting personalities. Of course, the most famous is Hans-Joachim Marseille.[1] He was a great pilot and a wonderfully humorous person when he first arrived, but sometimes he was more trouble than he was worth. I had Steinhoff's report in his service record, and despite his seven victories in France, he had lost a few aircraft in obtaining those kills, if memory serves. He also had a problem with superior authority and adhering to regulations. This was especially true when it came to his haircut.[2] In January 1941, Steinhoff had him transferred to JG.27 at Döberitz near Berlin.

Well, Marseille soon had a real problem with his immediate superiors, especially his *staffelkapitän*, *Hauptmann* Gerhard Homuth. Homuth took an immediate dislike to him, and he grounded Marseille from a mission. Well, Marseille, being a hotheaded sort, took off and then he strafed the ground close to Homuth's tent, and he was very lucky not to have been court-martialed for that stupid stunt.

Homuth continued to have problems with Marseille. He wrote a report stating that he was "undisciplined in the air, as well as on the ground, and displayed nothing resembling proper airmanship in combat." These are the kind of words that can kill a career, but Marseille had no intention of being a career military pilot. He could have cared less. Nevertheless, Homuth did not want to fly with him.

Marseille was not openly disrespectful to his superiors, so do not think that. However, his approach to military discipline was quite relaxed to say the least, despite his father being a general. Once *generalmajor* [Stefan] Fröhlich visited the unit, and as the officers and men snapped to attention and saluted, Marseille walked by and simply waved at him and said, "Hello there, *Generalmajor*, nice to see you again." You see they knew each other, but not that well.

Needless to say that Fröhlich, although he thought a lot of Marseille, had a chat with me shortly afterward about the lack of discipline in my unit. He reminded me that just because we were in the desert, far removed from the civilization of Europe, we did not have to go native. I had to agree with Fröhlich, but he also knew Marseille. You would have just expected more from him, especially being an officer with men under his command.

But all he cared about was flying, nothing else, and he clearly stated that he did not want rank and the command responsibility that went with it. Sometimes his unorthodox methods in the air combat got him into trouble, and even worse, his wingmen often found themselves in trouble due to his violating the basic rules of combat. Yes, he was successful, but often reckless in his zeal for getting the kills.

Often he would see an enemy flight and then just take off, without alerting anyone. He would just plow into them, guns blazing, often outnumbered ten to one, but he somehow always shot down or damaged enough of the enemy to get away intact. I think that it was his audacity that took his enemies by surprise.

* * *

When speaking of Marseille, I must mention just how much of an anomaly he was. This was a great German hero, often in the newsreels, who cavorted with movie stars and celebrities, and chased women just as effectively as he did enemy aircraft. I recall after his first visit with Hitler, Marseille returned and said that he "thought the *Führer* was a rather odd sort." The bad thing was that he said this in front of three generals, with his Negro aide Matthias laughing with him.

Marseille had a way of flouting his personal celebrity and ignoring what was then the accepted rules of conduct, and this also applied to the racial laws. Although I and many of my friends thought they were ridiculous, they were nonetheless the laws, and Matthias drew many looks from visiting superiors and dignitaries, and Marseille was the subject of much debate amongst officers who visited our various bases. I really think that if not for his success and the aura of celebrity that surrounded him, he would have been sent back to Germany and disciplined many times over.

I remember that when he arrived in Africa he was shy, until you came to know him. I can also state that, despite his unmilitary methods, the lack of military discipline, he was in contrast a very disciplined pilot. He was absolutely focused upon his task, like no one else I ever knew. I think that his ability to focus so intently upon his victims was the reason for his success, but it was also almost his demise on several occasions.

His wingmen often complained that flying his wing was like catching fish with their bare hands blindfolded. He was unpredictable, spontaneous, aggressive, and almost reckless. How he managed to survive so many engagements still astounds me. I think the lack of women was what helped him focus and hone his skills and sharpen instincts. This was what Steinhoff always thought.

Marseille was also a great renegade. You must understand the times in which we lived in the 1930s and throughout the war. Certain books, art, films, and even music were banned. Marseille did not follow any of these regulations, and when he arrived he brought a phonograph player with him and a box of records he had purchased in France. He loved the American jazz and swing music, which was at the top of the prohibited list, as it was deemed "black" and "degenerate" music and therefore forbidden material under the Nazis.

I must admit that I was also partially at fault, as I allowed my pilots to indulge their interests in their off time. You never knew when a mission may be a man's last, and I never personally held any prejudice towards people, music, culture, what have you. Many of the pilots would be in their tents listening to the banned music, drinking the occasional and very rare beer or bottle of wine, just relaxing, and having a great time with Matthias, the bartender.

These were the times that built up a unit's camaraderie, and this bonding period was crucial for a flying unit. Once Marseille was sent a bottle of champagne from the wife of an army general after his fiftieth victory I think, and without going into great speculation, let me just say that there were various rumors about that relationship. Marseille, as a true gentleman, never discussed his personal life. That was good for him, as there may have been more than a few jealous husbands with high rank who would have paid us a visit, and that was the kind of trouble no one needed, especially me. I was well aware of the headaches Steinhoff had dealt with.

Marseille's success was nothing short of meteoric, really. If I remember correctly, he had fifty kills and the Knight's Cross by February 1942, then seventy-five kills and the Oak Leaves and the Swords by June, with a hundred kills. September 1, 1942, was when he shot down seventeen fighters in three missions. Upon landing, his armorer's report stated that he had used just twenty cannon shells and sixty rounds of machine gun ammunition in downing nine aircraft on one mission, which was remarkable.

However, despite his success, I could see he was becoming physically exhausted. Endless hours of flying, an erratic diet, difficulty in obtaining fresh water, sandfleas, flies, the heat, and also the cold at night made North Africa a very inhospitable place. Mental and physical exhaustion were to be expected in any theater of the war, and we always had the fear of malaria.

This exhaustion happened to every pilot after a period of time, but Marseille would fly every possible mission, volunteer for multiple missions in a day, tearing himself down. I had to ground him after he broke his arm, which was the result of a crash landing after a battle where he was shot up once. This gave him a break, until he borrowed an Italian fighter and cracked it up. I never gave him authorization to fly; he just jumped in it and took off, broken arm and all.

I always had a fondness for him, almost as if he were a stepchild. Despite his rank, he was only twenty years old or so, and the older enlisted men also took care of him, and his mechanics felt very proud to be serving under him. Whenever Marseille received a cache of wine, champagne, or anything, he would gather his wingmen and ground crew first, and celebrate with them. He really did not understand the concept of fraternization; or if he did he did not care.

I remember once when he came back from Berlin, and shortly afterward Galland came to visit us on his inspection tour. Galland had been present when Marseille received the Oak Leaves and Swords, and he told me that Göring really liked him a lot, and that he and Marseille seemed to get along fine. Göring made a comment that "Germany could use a lot more like him," and then he inquired as to the rumors of Marseille's romantic dalliances. Apparently an army colonel filed a complaint that his wife had been seeing a young fighter pilot with a French name, and he wanted details. Göring knew who he was talking about, and what the situation was, and he killed the inquisition.

Even Hitler thought a lot of Marseille. I know that when he received the Oak Leaves, Hitler asked him about his thoughts regarding the British pilots and their aircraft, among many other things. I heard all of this secondhand, but I know it to be true. Marseille apparently told Hitler, in his usual nonchalant fashion, that we needed to hire the fellows who were handling the British supply and transport lines. They were better at their jobs than we were.

I also know that when Hitler presented him with the Swords sometime later, he had a special chat with Marseille, about what only he and Hitler would know. As they emerged from the room after their private conversation, Galland told me he overheard Hitler say to Marseille that he wanted him to be safe, that Germany would need fine young men like him when the war was over. Marseille responded within Galland's earshot, quite prophetically, that he did not think most of the men he served with, himself included, would outlive the war. That is a very strange prediction, as Marseille would be dead within a few weeks afterward, and he would never see his twenty-fourth birthday.

However, Marseille had said some very unflattering things about Hitler and the Nazi Party that seemed not to have been very well received. I know this because several officers, including Galland and [*Oberst* Nicolaus] von Below, overheard it all. If I remember correctly, one of the staff officers, perhaps von Below himself, asked him if he had considered joining the party, being a national hero and all. Marseille said something to the effect that "if he saw a party worth joining, he would consider it, but there would have to be some very attractive ladies present." You must remember that he said this with a straight face. I can only imagine how well that was taken. Galland was laughing uncontrollably as he told me the story, and I have to admit, I laughed also. Yes, Marseille was one in a million.

However, that was his humor and he was completely apolitical. Ironically, just when Galland left us after his inspection tour, someone had painted a sign on the latrine door that stated it was the resting place of the general of the fighters, or something to that effect. I knew it was Marseille. He and Gustav Rödel were the practical jokers in the group.[3] What was also humorous was that Rödel flew a 109 marked with a yellow "4" and Marseille was "14," and some of the men made the joke that if the British wanted revenge against one or the other, they may become confused.

Part of Marseille's success was his growing self-discipline. He would practice flying maneuvers whenever possible, logging a lot of air time. He would push a new aircraft to its limits, and then learn from each flight. I would have to say that there were two Marseilles; the jovial, happy-go-lucky, irreverent Bohemian, and the serious, studious, and very lethal pilot. It was as if once he was in the aircraft his personality changed, completely opposite from when he was on the ground.

However, when he was informed that his younger sister [Inge] had died in Vienna, possibly murdered, his character changed forever. I saw this change, and I was concerned that he may grow more reckless, lose focus, and become a liability to himself or others. I think that tragedy was what created the Marseille of legend, to be honest. He just became a far more determined, serious, and less jovial man from that point forward.

He soon stopped drinking alcohol for a while, which was good for him, due to the fact that it dehydrated a person, and in the desert that was an easy thing to occur. Marseille would go over every downed or captured enemy fighter he could, like all pilots, learning about them, studying their strengths and weaknesses. He knew all of the blind spots, and when he was in close fighting, he would get within ten meters of an enemy, preferring the low six o'clock position, which hid him from view of his victim. Often, if he could not close, he was a master of the deflection shot; at long range he was perhaps the best aerial killer.

He also used to stare into the sun, getting his eyes used to the brightness so that he could train his mind to locate enemies before anyone else. This was the same as what [Oswald] Boelcke did in the First World War. However, unlike Boelcke, Marseille was not a good leader, not in the military sense. He was not a great role model for other pilots, especially new ones while in the air, as he was undisciplined in formation flying. I would say he was very lucky, but also skilled. Almost everyone tried to catch some of the Marseille magic.

He once told me that his method of shooting did not require using the Revi gunsight in shooting. He found it too involved. He would fly into the enemy, close in, shoot a few rounds, killing or crippling an aircraft, and then find another victim. Once those that had been severely damaged had crashed, he would look for those he had damaged that were still flying, and unless they were finished off by his fellow pilots, he would finish them off himself. He also had a way of computing where an aircraft would be, and often his pilots would see him fire from impossible angles, often into empty sky, only to have an enemy fighter fly into the stream of shells.

For long-range shots he preferred to use the 20mm cannon, and after the first round fired he would adjust his point of aim if on a deflection shot, but he seldom ever needed to adjust his aim. He was that good. I do not think he ever used more than five or six cannon shots to bring down a fighter, and probably around fifteen or so machine gun rounds per kill as well. I know that Trevor Constable, and even Hans Ring had those records at some point. This was also well known in Berlin. He was quite remarkable.

Once, I read a report about an action over Libya where Marseille managed to shoot down two fighters with the same burst of cannon and MG fire. Both fighters were in a tight left turn, with Marseille above them at the eight o'clock high position. He then rolled his Me-109 over, inverted, fired, completed the barrel roll, and then pulled up as both fighters fell away burning.

To make this even more remarkable, he then chopped power, lowered his flaps, and allowed two other Hurricanes to pass by him, one above and another below. He lifted the nose, fired, down the Hurricane went, and he rolled over, fired, and the fourth victim went down. When he landed, he still had half of his ammunition load. Incredible.

He would also exercise—running, situps, pushups, that sort of thing. He developed incredible abdominal muscles, which were very important for handling the G-forces one experienced in combat. He was able to hold tight turns that blacked out most other pilots. This was how he was so able to kill his enemies in a turning fight; no one was going to turn into him for an easy kill. When he flew combat, he would often attack alone or take a single wingman with him. One may say that he was greedy and did not want to share the kills, but that was just his way. He liked to fight without having to worry about shooting at one of his own men.

He was possibly the best deflection shot who ever flew a fighter. His mind was almost like a modern computer, I would have to say, and he was gifted with supernormal eyesight. He could gauge any angle, relative airspeed of his own fighter, as well as that of his enemy, and knew just how much lead to pull to ensure a kill with the least amount of ammunition. He always aimed for the engine when possible. When he was once asked, I think by Galland, why, he said that he preferred to have the pilots captured. He liked speaking with them. It was that simple. He did not see any reason to kill a man if it could be avoided.

That was the humanity within the man, and as a pseudo father or big brother figure to him, I was proud that he had not allowed the war or his personal misfortune to reduce his integrity. I have always believed that war may be necessary on occasion, and we men must fight. However, at no time do I believe that we must be barbaric. Gentlemanly conduct, at least among the Luftwaffe pilots, and especially in my unit, was expected, and unforgivable if violated. We honored our enemy dead as if they were our own, and we buried them with full military honors befitting a fallen soldier. I know the British pilots did the same with our dead. That was what separated us from animals.

On more than one occasion I saw Matthias actually help Marseille out of the cockpit, as he was sometimes completely exhausted from flying multiple missions. This was especially true after we received the newer F model of the Messerschmitt. Marseille would fly as much as possible, not only in combat but in practice. Matthias would help him keep his gear sorted out, prepare him a meal, set up his washing basin, and put him to bed, just as one would a child.

Marseille would never allow anyone, regardless of rank, to say anything bad about his friend, black or not. Marseille was far ahead of his time in this respect, I think. He could not condone prejudice in any form. He hated no one that I am aware of, not even his enemies. He was just a man who I wished had lived out the war. It would be good to have sat with him in later years and speak with him. He was just that kind of man, perhaps born in the wrong century.

Despite his brash nature and lack of discipline, he had a deep sense of fair play. He once even took great care to make sure a wounded enemy pilot that he had shot down, and fell into our hands, was taken to the nearest field hospital, escorting him personally in the vehicle. Marseille remained with the man, even waiting outside, until the attending medical doctor assured him that the British pilot would be fine after surgery.

Marseille then made sure that a Red Cross prisoner of war card was properly completed, so that the man would be accounted for by his family. He even had a photo taken with the pilot. I do not know what ever happened to it, and I wish I knew that pilot's name, but I think he was actually an Australian. There were many Commonwealth fliers in the area.

Marseille did all of this because he knew the man was married with a small child, and he did not want a dead father on his hands, and he thought it important that the pilot's family know he was all right. He even made sure that a photo of the man with his wife and child was salvaged from the wreckage, and placed into his pocket. This was an event that occurred before his famous flyover, dropping that note near El Alamein. The British already knew him and his "Yellow 14" Me-109 as a chivalrous opponent, as well as an enemy to be feared. This may have saved him when he did the note dropping flight over a British air base near El Alamein.

This event almost forced me to ground Marseille. I had on occasion chewed him out for various things, but nothing really serious. That day he was late returning from the second mission. He had shot down a Hurricane and saw that the pilot was wounded, but alive. I received the radio call that, since he had the fuel, he was taking a detour. I had no idea where in the hell he was going, and he ordered his flight to head back to base and not to follow him.

He then flew on his own and wrote a note while in the air. He had written the coordinates of the downed pilot, and as he flew over the enemy air field, dropped it out of the aircraft. This must have been difficult, because the Me-109 had what we called the "coffin lid" canopy. You had to open it by unlocking the secure latch inside the cockpit, open it, and then Marseille had to keep the slipstream from ripping it off as he dropped the note. While doing this he still had to maintain joystick control, lower flaps, maintain airspeed and attitude.

When he landed I asked him what he did. He did not know that we had already received, or rather intercepted a British transmission describing the event. They even mentioned his aircraft marking, the yellow 14 on the fuselage, and the rudder, which had over a hundred victory markings on it. He had passed by the enemy air field at less than fifty meters altitude, and was lucky that they did not shoot him down with ground fire. They even knew his name, which was not very surprising given the newsreels and newspapers where he was often featured.

Both sides, theirs and ours, read each other's propaganda and newspapers when they were available. The British knew exactly who he was. However, they were very appreciative of his gesture. That was Marseille. Yes, he was a killer, but he was also a knight, a very chivalrous man. He did not see any need for a man to die once he had been vanquished, and most of us felt that way. At first, I chewed his ass for ordering his flight to return to base as he flew on to drop his message, and I told him not to do it again. Never fly without a wingman, and he should have known better.

But then I had to change hats, and shift from being his commanding officer to being a human. I told him that I personally appreciated the gesture, and that the British did as well. Even in war there should not be a dehumanization of anyone, but I made him promise not to risk his life and aircraft again. He agreed, but then he said, "Yes, sir, but if I were shot down, I would like to think that my unit and family would know what had happened. I just wondered about that man, if he had a wife or children. I just did not want him to die in the desert."

The professional officer in me completely understood where he was coming from. This was a good example to set for the rest of the unit. I even thought that there was a good propaganda piece in that, but I suppose it was not meant to be. Once Göring found out about that stunt, he issued the ban on such actions in the future. I heard this from Galland personally.

As I recall, I think it may have been [Werner] Schrör, Rödel, Homuth, and Marseille in one *Schwarm*, among others, that had taken off on an escort mission. We had a *Stukageschwader* making a ground strike, and our fighters were to fly escort. Most pilots hated this assignment, because it forced them to fly slow and weave to stay with the dive bombers, but Marseille enjoyed them, and he saw these missions as opportunities. Marseille knew the slow flying dive bombers were favorite easy targets of the enemy fighter pilots, and he saw them as bait. True to form, the British fighters went after the Stukas.[4]

Contrary to standard battle doctrine, which we had developed in Spain and used during the early years of the war, Marseille would often not climb for higher altitude and then dive out of the sun, using that altitude to gather greater speed, make the attack, and get away and prepare for another attack. Most pilots would use their altitude as security, and after their attack, return to a higher altitude.

But not Marseille. He would often wait until the enemy came in close, and then he would cut power to the engine, lower his flaps, and kick the rudder, getting on the tail of an enemy plane. He sometimes liked attacking from underneath, in the blind spot, where he could hit one, two, or three fighters rapidly before the others even knew he was there, then slip away and prepare for another attack. He would do this, often at stall speed, and then after shooting, give full throttle, retract flaps, adjust trim, and repeat the same method. Incredible, and lucky, but then he had the nerves and the skill to accomplish that task. Pilots of lesser ability would have just killed themselves.

Despite his liking to get very close to his enemies, he was, in fact, perhaps the best deflection shot in the Luftwaffe. He was so good he often fired from beyond the accepted maximum effective range of the 20mm cannons, the shells arcing over and down ahead of the enemy plane. Often he used only two or three rounds per cannon to achieve a kill. Werner Schrör told me of one event he witnessed, an incredible event. Marseille had fired three times, for three deflection shots, as he gave lead to a flight of six Hurricanes. He scored three kills.

I think his success was due to the fact that his methods were so unorthodox that no one expected it. It was dangerous flying, especially at low altitude. He also had a very great ability to lure an enemy pilot on his tail, dangerously close sometimes. The enemy pilots must have thought they had a novice, an easy kill, until Marseille cut all power, dropped the nose forward, stood on a rudder, and slid to a stop, basically stalling in midair.

As his enemy passed by at a greater speed, he would almost instinctively know where the plane would be. He would snap a quick shot into empty space, and the enemy fighter would fly into his projectiles. He did this on a regular basis, and I think that some pilots who tried to emulate him killed themselves doing this.

Marseille would always look for a fight. I once saw him fly right into a Lufbery, where there were sixteen P-40s, and he shot down six, damaged two others, and the rest ran from the fight.[5] I was unfortunately on the ground the day he scored his seventeen kills on

September 1, 1942, but I can imagine what happened based upon his previous experiences.

I know that he landed, rearmed, and refueled, and had eight kills on that first sortie. They were scored in about ten minutes, where again he entered the Lufbery and had success. He used less than one hundred rounds of machine gun ammunition and half his cannon shells. We know this because the armorer's report had to be filed after every mission, or at the very least at the end of a day's flying. The weapons were then cleaned and ammunition reloaded. This was a very remarkable accomplishment.

Marseille was also a celebrity among our Italian allies. He had saved more than a few Italian pilots involved in air combat from the enemy. Mussolini even called him to Rome to award him the Italian Gold Medal for Bravery, which was a rare distinction to be sure.[6] He made friends easily, and sometimes we had Italian pilots over, and since Marseille did not speak Italian, and most of the Italians did not speak German, they spoke in either English or French, as Marseille was competent in both languages. He would play his jazz records and remove himself from the war for a while.

I once sent him home on leave for a couple of weeks. He was exhausted, and becoming more of a danger than an asset. He was very reluctant to leave, fearing that someone may take Matthias away, as he knew that he was his only protector. Marseille called him the "best friend and bartender one could wish for," since Matthias handled all of the pilot gatherings, even cooking meals.

I promised him that I would look after his servant, although Marseille never treated him as such, but as an equal. I think that this open friendship on such a scale was one of his [Marseille's] problems with the senior officers who visited on occasion, with exception to Galland, Rommel, and [Wolfram von] Richthofen, among others. Marseille left the unit on his enforced vacation and we continued on.

I heard a report that Marseille had once again started his pursuit of women, even bedding a few film stars. I also heard that Leni Riefenstahl was one of them, but I do not know if this was true or not. I would not doubt it. He was a very good-looking and smooth-talking young man who had women all over Europe. I cannot even begin to describe the amount of fan mail he received, especially after he was featured in *Signal*.[7]

I have it on decent authority that Marseille became somewhat aware of the Holocaust, which is a subject that we do not like to discuss, even today. Hell, I was even unaware of it until after the war, but there were rumors. Marseille had spoken with a couple of his pilots about rumors he had heard from our Italian allies; in fact, Homuth mentioned this to me, as well as conversations he overheard from when he was in Berlin.

As I said, I was unaware of this, as were all the other pilots. There was a great deal of secrecy regarding this, which is understandable. This is still a very sensitive subject, as people may imagine. Later, when Marseille had received the Oak Leaves and Swords, our supreme theater commander, *Generalfeldmarschall* Erwin Rommel, came by the unit the second week of September, I believe, and congratulated the *geschwader* for its service, and Marseille personally for his success, and also for being the youngest *hauptmann* in the Luftwaffe at age twenty-two. He would never see twenty-three.

Well, Marseille had been nominated to receive the Diamonds to the Knight's Cross on September 2, which was approved by Hitler, for the seventeen kills on September 1. That was when Rommel placed a phone call to me as he wanted to speak with Marseille.[8] Rommel was going to Berlin, and they were to see Hitler together as Marseille received the award.

Well, I know that Marseille declined the offer, as well as the Diamonds. I do not know for certain what Marseille had learned about the Jewish situation. I had heard that he had Jewish relatives on his mother's side, but this was rumor, so I cannot say that this is in fact accurate. In learning more after the war, and knowing after the fact as to what Rommel in fact knew, and his knowledge of the July 20, 1944, plot, I would assume that there was not a lot of transparency regarding this issue.

I do know that Marseille had overheard comments about his best friend Matthias, and the fact that he was black, and that many senior non-Luftwaffe officers had discussed resolving this problem.

It was bad propaganda, in their opinions, to have one of Germany's greatest heroes cavorting with a black man. I personally never cared, it meant nothing to me, since this was not an unnatural friendship at all, and this was also well known. Matthias was a loyal servant to Jochen.

When he returned that August, Marseille was eager to get back into the scoring. He had a brand new Me-109G that was waiting for him, and even the rudder had been painted by Matthias displaying his victories. The Knight's Cross with Oak Leaves and Swords was also painted at the top of the rudder, just above the victory bars on this particular aircraft. In fact, he had a stack of love letters from women that filled almost three full mailbags that he had to respond to. His first night back he signed dozens of Hoffmann photograph cards sent to him by admirers.

This was the aircraft he flew on September 1, 1942, when he took off on his most legendary mission. I did not fly that day, but it was a good thing that we had the men in the air that we did. The after action reports were almost unbelievable. The flight took off early that morning escorting the Stukas, and he shot down three P-40s. After that mission he shot down six Spitfires. He then flew two more missions and added eight more fighters, Hurricanes I believe, to his score for seventeen that day. Two days later I promoted him to *hauptmann*.

The second mission was a Ju-88 escort, but they did not make the rendezvous, as they were attacked by a full squadron of P-40s. This had never been accomplished before. In fact, scoring five or six in a day, let lone a single mission, was great news for a pilot. That day *Generalfeldmarschall* Albert Kesselring had arrived on an inspection of the unit, and he was there to hear the reports of Marseille's triumph.[9]

Marseille flew a couple of days later, if memory serves, and managed a couple of more kills. He did not fly on the day [September 5] that his best friend next to Matthias, Hans "Fifi" Stahlschmidt, was shot down and killed.[10] Marseille felt bad as this fine young man flew in his place that day, due to his having an ear and nose infection. He felt a deep sense of guilt over that.

It was not a normal thing for German fighter pilots, or any soldier, to show emotion or any kind of weakness, but I saw Marseille break down. I think it was the combination of months of relentless combat, his sister's death, and his friends being lost, that finally got to him. Sadly for his family, his father, *Generalmajor* Siegfried Marseille, was killed in 1944, by partisans, I believe.

We had just received the new G model of the 109s, which Marseille test-flew, and despite the heavier weapons, he did not like it as much as the F model. He liked the fact that the F was a more agile and streamlined machine, and he even wrote a report with his observations, stating that in his opinion we should simply place the newer engines in the F model airframes. However, the loss of agility and slightly slower rate of climb when fully loaded did not impress him. He did like the additional armored cockpit and new canopy, as did I.

Marseille died on September 30, 1942, after an escort mission.[11] The pilots who were with him, who I think were Schrör, Rödel, and Homuth, filed their reports, and all agreed that his engine caught fire.[12] We had the radio on in fact, and I heard the transmissions. Jochen called out he was going to have to bail out, that he had smoke in the cockpit. Some of his wingmen confirmed this, saying that when he opened the canopy the black smoke poured out.

According to the reports, they could not even see Marseille until the canopy flew off and he inverted the aircraft. They had convinced him to stay with the fighter until he crossed German lines. He waited until the all clear was given, and he dropped out, and that was when the 109 nosed down. The tail struck him solid, right across the back left side of his torso, probably killing him instantly.

His friends watched in horror as his body fell out of sight until it struck the ground near Sidi Abdul Rahman. He never even opened the parachute. When I heard this I felt very sad. I was used to losing men; that was war. But Marseille was special, like a small boy playing war. He never took it too seriously, and his smile, which was less evident as time progressed, was infectious when present.

His loss was a very serious morale issue for the unit, and we held a ceremony for him in Derna. Marseille had this mythical quality about him. He could not be killed, despite crash-landing fighters or returning with dozens of holes in his fighter. It was as if a plug had been pulled and the lights went out. The person who took it the hardest was Matthias. I felt very sorry for him, as his only friend was now dead. He above all others was completely alone.

Well, Hitler awarded him [Marseille] the Diamonds posthumously, which seemed only fitting. As I remember, after the funeral service that we held on October 2, which was where his grave was located, that was perhaps the last time I saw Matthias. He just wandered away and disappeared. I do not recall whatever happened to him.

When we heard that American forces had landed in Algeria and Morocco in November, we knew that we were going to lose Africa.[13] The British and Commonwealth air forces outnumbered us greatly. We had probably three hundred operational fighters with all the Luftwaffe fighter units, and they had perhaps a thousand fighters available to them, and this did not include the American aircraft that began flying against us from the west. We were simply over-whelmed, until we were forced into Tunisia, where we spent the last four months of our time in Africa. The surrender of German and Italian forces there was in May 1943, and it cost us around two hundred thousand or more men. I was already gone by that time.

In April 1943, I was assigned to Galland's staff as a recently promoted *oberstleutnant*, and Gustav Rödel took over JG.27 as *kommodore*. I was later promoted to *oberst* in 1944 while commanding the Luftwaffe fighter units in Italy, where I had a lot of direct contact with *Generalfeldmarschall* Albert Kesselring, the German commander in chief of our forces in the country. That was a very interesting time, and I had Steinhoff under me in Italy until he was sent to take over JG.77.

I also operated a gunnery school; well, rather I commanded a school that taught many refresher courses, including tactics and aerial gunnery. We had many pilots coming in who had flown on the Russian front, but we were fighting the British and Americans, and this is important due to the fact that we had to deal with the American heavy bombers that flew over us into Germany and back. Fighting this threat was a very different war than in the east. Steinhoff was transferred and he was shot down upon his return to the west, and he made a note of how much he did not know, and he was very valuable to us as a leader.

Our instructors gave shooting instruction to new pilots fresh from the schools who were recently assigned to the units in Italy. One of these was Hajo Herrmann, who was starting his night fighter group in 1943.[14] Being a bomber pilot, and very successful, he and other such pilots did not receive gunnery training, so we were able to assist. We also had many classes on formation attacks against heavy bombers, as well as protecting various flights in those attacks against enemy fighters. We were almost always outnumbered in the air, and we had many attacks against our air fields.

Much has been said about the Fighter's Revolt against Göring, of which I was a participant. It must be understood that we were not simply a collection of disgruntled fighter unit leaders who wanted miraculous changes. We were a group of men who had been fighting, seeing the bad decisions made by Göring and Hitler, and the growing problems regarding all abandonment of logic and a failure to see the reality of the war. I had several discussions with Galland about this very subject. The very first thing that we agreed must happen was that Göring be replaced as commander in chief of the Luftwaffe. This was not negotiable. He had to go.

We then had to decide upon which officer was going to replace him. This had to be someone Hitler would approve of, and someone all the branches of the Luftwaffe could respect. Many names were tossed around, but Galland decided upon asking Eduard von Schleich, who was a hero and *Pour le Mérite* holder from the First World War. He was not only a great pilot in his day, but he was also someone Hitler listened to and even more important, respected highly. I knew him to be an honest man and a decent person.

However, despite Schleich being the great man that he was, I thought that Robert von Greim, also a *Pour le Mérite* holder, would be the best choice. I explained this to Galland, who listened. I agreed that Schleich was a great choice, with all the qualities that we could want. Despite this, Greim was more involved in the inner circle, and he was usually involved in many of the high-level meetings to which Schleich was not, and Greim was also an even greater opponent of Göring.

He [Greim] had openly said many times in public, and in front of Hitler and Göring himself, that Göring had things wrong. This was demonstrated in an especially heated meeting just after we lost Stalingrad, in which Galland was present, and he told me about it. Ironically, it would in fact be Greim who was given command of the Luftwaffe in the final days of the war, when Hitler threw Göring out of the party and ordered his arrest for treason.

Greim was fearless and Hitler did not impress him very much, and Göring even less so. I once even heard him say that Himmler was a poor excuse of a man, and that Hitler's faith in him was misguided. He said that any average schoolboy with above-average intelligence could do his job, just not with as much enthusiasm. Greim was the one for me, but Galland said "No," because he did not want anyone who was deeply involved in Berlin politics.

Galland thought it would be better to have someone who was not considered a reliable Berlin man, although he thought the world of Greim, as did we all. [Günther] Lützow, Gustav Rödel, [Günther] "Henri" von Maltzahn, and [Hannes] Trautloft also thought Schleich would be the best choice, although Steinhoff and [Herbert] Ihlefeld sided with me. We voted just to be fair, and Schleich won. He would be the one who would be approached. I figured anyone had to be better than Göring.

We spent the evening before with Trautloft at his place, discussing the next day's events, and then we discussed the fact that Galland would not be there. It was uniformly agreed upon that it would have been perhaps better if he were absent, given the hatred the two men [Galland and Göring] held for each other. I was brought along as another senior leader, one that Göring actually seemed to get along with. He also had respect for Trautloft, and this was another reason why he was there, as well as being the inspector of day fighters. Ihlefeld was also held in high esteem, hence his presence. All of us were men Galland knew he could trust. In those days that was life and death.

We entered the room and took our seats. Göring walked in and we stood, then he motioned to us to take our seats again. As I recall, we were supposed to update him on our current strengths in aircraft and pilots, and the combat condition of the units across Europe. I handed Trautloft the information for the Italian front, and Steinhoff handed him the folder on the jet unit at Achmer, JG.7. Boiling this down, Lützow started off as the spokesperson. I liked him very much, and I had known him since flight school and Spain, but I was a little concerned that he should be the one representing the fighters in this particular meeting. He had a temper when it came to Göring; he really hated him, and he never kept it a secret.

Lützow started by telling our boss that if he interrupted, we would accomplish nothing. I think we were about ten minutes or less into the meeting when Göring interrupted him, asking some silly question. Lützow, not missing a beat, did not even respond, but kept on giving him the details and grievances. Again, Göring interrupted him, and Lützow then stood up and told him that he was once again failing to understand the reality of the situation.

During this time, Trautloft was outside on the phone with Galland, although Göring did not know this. I think he thought he was bringing in more files, which he did to make a good impression. As inspector of day fighters, Trautloft was expected to have data from every fighter unit, on every front.

Göring then allowed him to speak, and Lützow then completed his lecture with telling Göring that it would be for the good of the service if he stepped down as our leader. Well, Göring went silent for a few seconds, and then he flew into a rage, screaming at Lützow, who screamed back, each shouting over the other. Göring raised his marshal's baton and said that he would hear no more about this nonsense.

Göring then looked at Steinhoff, and asked him in an elevated voice if he felt the same way. Steinhoff responded that yes, he felt that Göring should step down for many reasons, and then Trautloft entered, also voicing his opinion, agreeing. They looked at me as did Göring, and I was on the spot. But I knew what must be said, and I also agreed. Göring then asked who they thought could do a better job, and Lützow replied something to the effect, "anyone not blinded by power who understands what our situation is, unlike you, *Herr* Göring."

Well, that was it, and Göring yelled back at him, "Just who in the hell do you think you are Lützow?"

That was when Steinhoff spoke up and said: "He is our senior spokesman, *Herr Reichsmarschall*, although I wanted the job, since *Generalleutnant* Galland cannot be here. It would be the best for the service if you stepped down."

Then Lützow said something like, "Yes, at least we could regain some honor and credibility!" I knew at that point things were going to get much worse. I looked at Trautloft who seemed in shock. Ihlefeld stood up, cleared his throat and said that we were accomplishing nothing, and we should leave.

Göring again exploded in a violent rage that I had rarely witnessed in my life by anyone. He was actually dripping sweat and foaming at the mouth, his eyes bulged out of his head, the veins on his neck were pulsating. He said something like: "Steinhoff, your career is over, and so is Galland's; that coward would not even face me! And you, Lützow, I am going to have you shot!"

Trautloft then looked at Steinhoff, and we all looked at Lützow, who did not even flinch. He [Lützow] yelled back: "I will wait and see what the *Führer* says, as your judgment has not been sound for some time, and everyone in Germany knows it. This is finished." Then he said a few other things that I cannot remember.

We all looked at each other again and stood up and began to leave, with Göring screaming even louder, telling both Lützow and Steinhoff as we left that they would both be shot, and then he screamed again that we would all be court-martialed. He then yelled that he would have "that traitor Galland shot first to set the example." Göring had completely lost his mind, and we had all just witnessed him having a nervous breakdown.[15]

Trautloft walked over to the desk in the hallway where he had been speaking with Galland periodically, and when we went back into the meeting, he had left the telephone off the cradle. Galland heard most of it, and Trautloft quickly filled him in on what happened. Once Hannes hung up the phone, I asked him what Galland's thoughts were. He said, "Adolf thinks we should save time as he did."

Well, I naturally asked him what he meant. [Trautloft said,] "Get measured for our coffins now. He did his before Christmas." I was not certain if he was using gallows humor or if he was serious, but he did not smile.

All of us were sweating in the corridor, except Lützow, who muttered something like: "That damned fat bastard. I wonder how long he will last sitting on his fat ass as we lose a war he and Hitler started." I was stunned that he said openly what we were all thinking. The corridor was full of officers who heard the explosive conversations.

Needless to say, the rest of that day was spent wondering about our futures. We already knew that the Gestapo had been recording the telephone calls, and we were well aware that after the Stauffenberg plot, and the resulting backlash against hundreds if not thousands of people, that we were not exactly in the best position to be antagonizing the second most powerful man in the Reich. However, sometimes we must follow our conscience, and I did, as did the others.

I later had a long talk with Galland about those events. He was under the impression that soon would be the time for scapegoating. Göring was never one to take personal responsibility for his own shortcomings. This was very well known throughout the Luftwaffe. I suppose the same could be said of almost all of the higher leaders in the Reich at that time. It was just much simpler to apply blame, punish the accused, and then move on to the next debacle. Göring was also a great disappointment when it came to ideas and concepts. He would only approve of something if he thought it would work and if he could take the credit for it. He was a truly disturbed individual.

Well, Göring followed through with his threats for the most part. Gordon Gollob replaced Galland as general of the fighters, and Steinhoff and Lützow were banished, but later joined Galland and many others when he created his JV.44 with the Me-262 jets. I went back to Italy and was able to watch the Allies continuously move up the country. The various groups of JG.77 and JG.27 were scattered around, as the Defense of the Reich order had been issued in 1944, and then revised in February 1945, which I think is correct. I know JG.27's groups were scattered all over the place. Our surrender was anticlimactic.

After the war I started an engineering company, nothing fantastic, but it was a good way to use my time. I also kept flying later when that was allowed, and I flew with Galland, Gerd Schöpfel, and some of the others in private airplanes. As you may know, old habits die hard indeed. In 1989, many of us JG.27 survivors were able to place a proper grave marker for Marseille, and the Egyptian government was very accommodating.[16]

They respected our intentions. I was also honored by being appointed rector of the Free University in Berlin for a time. That was an interesting experience. After an event-filled life I retired to Munich many years ago with my wife, and I like the Bavarian way of life. I am now an old man, and I like going to the reunions and seeing my old friends, who grow fewer every year, it seems. I often think of those days, long ago, and what would life have been like for us all if the war had never happened. Would we have ever met? Would most of us become pilots? There are many "what ifs" in a life.

When I think of those days during the war, I cannot help but remember the excitement of battle and the feeling of loss as fewer and fewer friends and comrades returned. I must say that I regret the war ever happened. There was so much loss and suffering. I know that hoping mankind would be able to eliminate mutual destruction is an impossible dream, but we must have some hope for the future.

The war brought me into contact with what were perhaps the most interesting people I had ever met, some being great personalities, some less so. I felt honored to have served with them, and I am proud to have those who remain around me later in life. I also look at our young people, and I have a good feeling that they will never have to suffer through what my generation did. I would wish only happiness and success to them.

Father of the Night Fighters

Wolfgang Falck
8 victories; Knight's Cross
(August 19, 1910–March 13, 2007)

WOLFGANG FALCK WAS ONE OF THOSE MEN who simply fell into history as if by accident. As a young pilot, and a natural leader, he was a thinking man. He was very similar to other young Germans in his position, where his skills and intellect combined in a wartime environment to create a very formidable adversary. Falck was to bring his creative genius to the forefront when he devised the concept of night fighting.

Falck was on the ground floor during the creation of the Luftwaffe, and from the mid-1930s until the end of the war, he was intricately involved in the planning, policy making, and logistics of defending Germany from 1940 onward. His contributions to history, aviation, and even technology and tactics will long outlive him. He was a living legend during the war, with the ability to speak his mind openly with the likes of Hermann Göring, Adolf Hitler, and senior generals and field marshals, just as easily as with an aircraft mechanic. When asked a question, he always gave a forthright answer, politics be damned.

Falck was a very good-natured man, even during the war. He deeply cared about his pilots, as well as the millions of civilians depending upon him and his night fighters to reduce, if not eliminate, the nocturnal air raids that destroyed their cities. Falck was duty bound to serve his nation, but he was also wise enough to know his own limitations, which were few.

An intellectually gifted and deeply focused officer, Falck's photographic memory and logistical genius were overshadowed by the politically corrupt and intellectually bankrupt leaders of his nation. Like his boss and great friend Adolf Galland, Falck did not suffer fools easily. Like Galland, he also had the tendency to irritate his superiors by using logic to refute their arguments, as demonstrated in this interview.

Falck was a major organizer and featured member at all of the annual reunions of the fighter pilots. He finally retired to his lovely home at the foot of his beloved mountains in Saint Ulrich, Tirol, Austria, where he passed away in 2007. The "Happy Falcon" will be missed.

Wolfgang Falck

I was born August 19, 1910, in Berlin, so I am a dirty old man! My family came from West Prussia in Danzig, which is now Gdansk, Poland. My mother, Berta, was from Bremen and she married my father, Hans, who was from Prussia, as the family was from West Prussia, and he was a pastor.

One interesting fact was that my grandmother was Catholic, yet she married a Lutheran, and the family was so from then onward. My oldest sister, Ilsa, was born there on February 7, 1898. My other sister, Irmgard, was born on July 19, 1904. They both married officers and had children, but they have both been deceased for many years. It should be said that I was the only boy born to the family, as all my cousins were girls also.

I was only four years old when the Great War started, but I do remember many things. My father and even my mother were very much involved with the soldiers, especially those who came back wounded. She was very caring in that way. I remember the families always receiving the notifications that their sons, brothers, husbands, or such, were dead or missing. Also, during the war there were many times where we did not have enough to eat, but somehow my parents made do. This did not get better after the war either.

After the First World War, times were very hard; inflation was outrageous, no work, it was terrible. I barely remember, but there was a lot of talk and many problems about Communists possibly taking over the country, just as had happened in Russia. There was a lot of fear, I would say. I recall many years of people waiting in great long lines trying to buy food, and there was not a lot to buy or eat.

I remember my mother taking my hand as we waited for hours once, and a fight broke out in front of the only grocer in the town that was still selling anything. People were willing to even kill and steal for food.[1] A couple of hundred children in my district were sent away to Latvia in a program for a few weeks. This actually left a great impression on me, as I made great friends there. I later returned a few times.

I remember as a young man when Adolf Hitler was doing his campaigns, and his speeches would be played over the radio. He seemed to be the person who could save Germany from ourselves and the outside dangers. Well, of course we were wrong, but hindsight is always much more clear. I also remember as a young boy hearing about the *Putsch*, and how the National Socialists and Hitler tried to take over the government. As a boy these things did not really interest me, but these events were to play a great role in my life, and in the future of Germany later.

When the National Socialists came to power, suddenly there were jobs, industry increased, building of homes and cities were undertaken, the armaments industry created millions of jobs, and of course the resurgence of the military improved life as well. What we know today about the concentration camps and such during the war was unknown to most of us, even those of us in high military positions. I think this was probably because the leadership knew that the average German, and without doubt the average German officer, would have not been in agreement with those practices. I know that I would not have been, so keeping it quiet and only spoken about amongst themselves makes sense, I suppose.

That does not excuse what happened, but it should be mentioned that the situation with the camps during the war was not a well-known, collective operation. These terrible events were undertaken by men who abused their power in the name of the German people, and this led to our destruction and had nothing to do with the true soldiers, the professionals. We as Germans will always have that era around our necks.

From 1917 to 1931, I was educated in the *Realgymnasium* at Berlin-Treptow and I passed the *Abitur*. That was the point where you either went to a university or learned a trade. I became a member of a flying group; some of us students who, under the watchful eye and control of a teacher, built and flew models of gliders.

After I finished my education I had decided to join the navy. It just seemed to be a great adventure for me. Unfortunately, or fortunately, depending upon your perspective, I was eventually transferred to the army. Ironically my uncle was an *oberst* and a veteran of the First World War. He commanded the 7th Hirschberger Battalion, so I applied. I then began the track to becoming an infantry officer.

Since we were living in Berlin, I visited all of the airshows in the area, including airports where I admired and studied the different types of aircraft. I was like most young boys all over the world. I was terribly fascinated by aviation, aircraft, and pilots. I had decided that even at that young age I wanted to be a pilot. I read everything I could get about pilots and air combat. I could not get enough of it. It just seemed to be the best choice for me, but the chances were few and far between. I had an interview once where I was asked about aviation, and I replied that I did have an interest. I think that started the ball rolling that would change my life.

This was due to the fact that the Versailles Treaty limited Germany to a 100,000-man army, the navy was allowed only 15,000 men, and U-boats and the air force were both totally banned. This was called the *Reichswehr*, and each year the army took about 225 volunteers as cadets to be educated as officers. Thousands applied each year and it was considered great luck if you were accepted.

My unit, the 2nd Rifle Battalion, 7th Infantry Regiment "Hirschberg-Silesia," decided to take me as one of the five men accepted each year. Since the German government decided to establish its own air force, the Ministry of Defense selected thirty young men each year, previously enlisted by the regiments to receive the education necessary to become pilots.

This arrangement would go on in secret for one year, and the camouflage was excellent. Then, in 1933, Hitler and the National Socialists took the government, and in 1935, Hitler abandoned Versailles, and openly stated that Germany had a military and was rebuilding. You must understand that this was a very good time to be a German, and we were a proud nation again. We felt that we now had a future, but I do not think that the great majority of us could have ever predicted what that future would eventually be.[2]

I was so lucky to be one of the thirty who were later selected, so on April 1, 1931, to March 1932, I was at the *Deutsche Verkehrsfliegerschule* [German Commercial Flight School] in Schleissheim, near Munich, where I finished advanced training. We were "civilian" students of the school, where we were officially trained as the pilots of the airliners. This was all before Hitler brought everything out in the open.

After the one-year training period, twenty were sent back to their regiments. Then ten men from Schleissheim were selected to spend about half a year in Lipetsk, Russia. The trip took twenty-four hours by train, with our destination being just south of Moscow, where we were to be trained as fighter pilots. This was a very interesting time, as Germany and the Soviet Union had agreements for trade and training. There were thousands of Germans there, including those men who were learning tank warfare, and additional specialty schools. We even toured the sights, and I was able to see Lenin in his tomb, which I thought was quite interesting.

At that time there existed a top secret arrangement, combining the Treaties of Rapallo and Berlin between the *Reichswehr* and the Red Army, and Germany was allowed to operate this school away from the eyes of the Western governments.[3] There was also a camp farther to the north for making and training with chemical weapons, with another training camp close to the Ural Mountains for tanks. At this time Germany was not even allowed tanks or U-boats! This was how I spent the summer of 1932, from April to September in Russia. It was like a holiday with flying thrown in.

We all had a great time, and we also got to know the Russian girls very well. I really liked this part of my time there, and I had a steady girlfriend, a wonderful girl. However, we had to be careful, as all of these girls would have loved to marry any foreigner just to leave Russia, which was still a very impoverished country. It is still pretty primitive even today, I suppose. I can also say that we ate better than the average Russian, as most of our supplies came in from Germany, or were purchased in Russia, which meant that our money was more available than their rubles.

The time there was really exciting, and it was very interesting the first time I had an in-flight failure. I collided with one of my fellow pilots during an air combat exercise. He had turned into me, and I had an immediate engine problem, as I heard and felt a bang in the engine, and the cowling blew away. Well, I still had power and landed. I was severely chastised for not bailing out, as the plane was in bad shape. I thought I had done the right thing, but I was told in no uncertain terms that aircraft were more easily replaced than pilots.

That period was a wonderful time for me and for the "black air force." This was despite the fact that we did have deaths in training, which was expected in any flying regimen. I had an interesting situation when Soviet Marshal [Mikhail N.] Tukhachevsky arrived for an inspection. Later he would be killed by Stalin in the Great Purge, along with many of that nation's best and brightest leaders.[4]

On October 1, 1932, I rejoined my regiment, yet no one but the regimental commanding officer knew that I was a qualified fighter pilot. Now, to be a recruit was a hard time for me, but then I graduated and we received the regular education as all the other aspirants in the regiment and throughout the Infantry School. This was the academy for future officers in Dresden until September 1934, with one exception.

During this time when the normal cadets trained at a camp proving ground, I was again sent with the other selected pilots for refresher training at Schleissheim. On October 1, 1934, I was promoted to *leutnant* and simultaneously eliminated, or "retired," from the army. I then joined the *Deutsche Luftfahrtverbände* officially, and in this organization I earned the title of *kettenführer*, or "section leader."

This organization that we called the "black Luftwaffe" was the camouflage for the future Luftwaffe, and I later became the chief instructor at the fighter school. In 1935, when Hitler terminated all the restrictions placed on Germany as stated in the Treaty of Versailles, and everything was in the open, we were officially designated the Fighter Pilots School, and it was then that we were again officially readmitted into the German armed forces, in this case the Luftwaffe. I was then officially reinstated as a *leutnant*.

I attended this school and flew the Arado and Heinkel types, and became quite proficient. This was where I also met and became lifelong friends with Günther Lützow, Günther Radusch, Hannes Trautloft, and many others. I also knew Adolf Galland and Dieter Hrabak as well from these early days. It was strange how we would all be thrown together later. While there, we were visited by Hermann Göring. This was when we were informed as to the unveiling of the Luftwaffe.

On April 1, 1936, I was assigned to JG.2 *Richthofen*, and I was assigned to the 5th *Staffel*, or 5/JG.2, located at Jüterbog-Damm. My primary job while there was to train the young new pilots who came to us from the fighter school. On April 20, 1936, I was promoted to *oberleutnant*. This was also Hitler's birthday, which was in fact the established date for all promotions. We held a memorial service on April 21, celebrating the day that Baron Manfred von Richthofen had been killed in 1918.

Since the squadron leader was given a command at the academy, I became the commanding officer of that squadron at the age of twenty-seven. Before the war began, this was normal at my age. During the war, we had squadron leaders who were younger than twenty-one, and *geschwaderkommodoren* younger than I was who were *majors*, or *oberstleutnante*.

Then, setting aside my duties a little, I was married to Marilies von Berchem in September, and she was Catholic. This created a strange environment for my father and I. I was later to learn that because I was married, I could not go to Spain with Lützow, Galland, Trautloft, and the others. Well, although I was unable to go to Spain, my son Klaus was born the next year on June 21, 1937, which was a great highlight in my life.

The Bf-110 [Me-110] was coming into production, and we in the Luftwaffe were going through a selection process for the pilots who would fly it. Since it was really Göring's pet project, the 110 had this elite stigma attached to it. During this selection process, I came to know Helmut Lent, who became a great friend and was an outstanding flier.

This was an interesting year, as I was one of a few pilots chosen to fly some airplanes to England, following a visit by the commander of the Royal Air Force. I was able to meet some outstanding British fliers, and made some friends that would actually serve me well after the war. I suppose that I was lucky that, even given my future leadership of the night fighters, my old friends held no grudges against me many years later.

I think that really shows the professionalism of the British, which I have always appreciated. One of the men I met was a Mr. [Charles G.] Grey, an editor of the journal *The Aeroplane*. He was a very interesting character, and this was a very innocuous meeting, at least until December 1939, but that comes later.

Later that year I became the adjutant to the group commander and was stationed at Döberitz, not far from Berlin. In 1938, a third group of JG.2 [III/JG.2] was stationed at Fürstenwalde to the east, and it was there that I became a squadron leader, holding the position but not the rank. Later in 1938, we were given a new name and refitted as 2. *Staffel* ZG.76, a heavy fighter squadron.

I had flown many hours in the Bf-108, which we called the *Taifun*, and then transitioned into the Bf-109, which I liked very much. We had all of these fighters at that time, although the 108 was a trainer. I found these early model 109s interesting since they had wooden propellers. This would of course change later, but it was still a novelty from the previous era. As a *staffelkapitän* I flew the 109 all the time, and logged many hours in it. I was definitely in love with that fighter. Then I began flying the Bf-110.

It must be said, as it is often forgotten, that the Heinkel Aircraft Company had produced the He-112, which was, in my opinion, a better fighter, since it had a wide landing gear and a tighter turn

Göring addressing the officers at the *Reichsluftfahrtministerium* in Berlin, October 7, 1940. Wolfgang Falck, second from the left, is to receive the Knight's Cross. Werner Streib is at the far end of the line. *Wolfgang Falck*

Wolfgang Falck receiving his Knight's Cross from Göring's adjutant, Bernd von Brauchitsch, son of the army chief of staff. *Wolfgang Falck*

Galland and Hitler in 1942, following the successful Operation Cerberus. Galland planned the air cover that helped the warships *Prinz Eugen*, *Scharnhorst*, and *Gneisenau* dash through the Channel back to Germany. *Raymond F. Toliver*

Generalleutnant Adolf Galland, after receiving promotion and being awarded the Diamonds decoration, February 19, 1942. *Adolf Galland*

Hans-Joachim Marseille (left) receives the German Cross in Gold from *Oberst* Eduard Neumann in 1942. *Eduard Neumann*

Hans-Joachim Marseille in 1942, after being awarded the Swords. *Raymond F. Toliver*

Oberst Eduard Neumann as *kommodore* of JG27 in Libya, 1942. *Eduard Neumann*

Hans-Joachim Marseille in September 1942, not long before his death. The strain of the war clearly shows on his face. *Raymond F. Toliver*

Hauptmann Werner Streib (left) and Wolfgang Falck, as Streib became the new *kommodore* of NJG.1. *Wolfgang Falck*

Dietrich Hrabak, CO of JG.52 (left), with Wolfram von Richthofen (right) in the Crimea, 1943. *Dietrich Hrabak*

Left to right: Dr. Max Otto, Reinhard Seler, Horst Adameit, Walter
Krupinski (shaking hands with Hitler), Erich Hartmann, and Walter
Mose. Krupinski received the Oak Leaves and Hartmann received the
Swords to their Knight's Crosses. *Walter Krupinski*

Oberleutnant Kurt Schulze (who
contributed the foreword to this book)
flew 103 missions, during which he
was credited with three victories. He
was once shot down at the Russian/
Finnish border but was rescued by
German mountain troops. After the
war, he spent two years as a POW in
France. He currently lives in Southern
California. *Kurt Schulze*

Galland's loyal wingman, Gerhard
Schöpfel, had forty-five victories and
was awarded the Knight's Cross.
Gerhard Schöpfel

Walter Krupinski in March 1945, when he joined Galland's JV.44. *Author's collection*

The Knight's Cross with Oak Leaves, Swords, and Diamonds. Only twenty-seven were awarded, ten to the Luftwaffe and nine to fighter pilots. *Author's collection*

General der Flieger Walter Krupinski after his last tactical flight in the F-15 Eagle, Luke AFB, Arizona, July 1976. *Walter Krupinski*

Adolf Galland (left) and Kurt Schulze, at Galland's birthday celebration in California. *Kurt Schulze*

Left to right: Eduard Neumann, Herman Boschet, and Walter Krupinski in 1998. *Author's collection*

Heinz Ewald, Walter Krupinski's wingman for over two hundred missions in JG.52. Krupinski credited Ewald with saving his life on many occasions. Strasbourg, France, 1998. *Author's collection*

Wolfgang Falck (left) and Hajo Herrmann in Geissenheim, Germany, October 4, 1999. *Author's collection*

radius, due to a larger wing surface. I also know that the He-112 was easier to fly, especially later in Russia, or even North Africa where there were not too many paved runways.

I am quite certain that politics played some role in this decision, but I think both fighters should have been produced. The 112 would have been a much better fighter for early pilots, who could then graduate to the 109. It just made sense to me, since the He-51 was outdated by that time, and was only good for dive bombing and ground attack missions. Perhaps one good thing about not having the 112 in large numbers was that it looked just like a Yak, and that may have caused problems later.

During this time, we had unified with Austria and taken the Sudetenland, and then all of Czechoslovakia. All of this activity increased the buildup of the military, especially the Luftwaffe, and the units were dispersed all over the east and south. We received our new planes, the Me-110C *Zerstörer*. [When Willy Messerschmitt obtained a majority share in the Bayerische Flugzeugwerke, the aircraft he designed were redesignated based on his name, starting with the Me-109E and the Me-110C.] From this point forward we no longer operated in single-engine fighters; now we had a rear gunner, two engines, and greater range. It was with this unit that I flew my first missions of World War II. The shortcomings of this aircraft were yet to be revealed to us, the very shortcomings as a day fighter that made it a wonderful night fighter.

After we occupied Czechoslovakia I was stationed at Pardubice. Each of us unit leaders took over the command of individual Czech fighter units, and I did feel compassion for them. There were many Sudeten Germans living in the area who were very supportive of us, even very helpful and welcoming. They saw us as liberators of sorts. This was when we began using the Me-110 twin-engine fighters in great earnest, learning everything about them, including blind flying. This experience would become critical later. It was during this time I chose the ladybug as our emblem for the unit. I also had pins made for the crews, as it was a very morale-lifting thing to do.

The night before, we had had our briefing, planning our mission, and this was all very exciting. We had spent the best part of August near the Oder River, in Silesia. Well, the next day, on September 1, 1939, we invaded Poland, and I flew early morning operations to Krakau in the south. We started early, before sunrise, and on this particular mission we escorted a bomber group, which flew a raid on an enemy air field, and we encountered no opposition. We had a few flak guns open up below, but without any results.

The only excitement was when I almost shot down a Stuka by accident, due to the red letter "E" that was painted on it, and we were looking for the red-and-white checker pattern on Polish aircraft. Later, due to this near event, the ruling throughout the Luftwaffe was that black letters would be used, and even later in the war, when even white would be used, but that was usually on Western Front aircraft from 1944 onward.

No Polish aircraft were to be seen this first day. During the next few days, I scored my first three victories, all of them obsolete Polish aircraft. After the Polish campaign was finished, we were transferred to the Western Front to protect Germany against possible French air raids, but we never had any. This was the start of what was called "the phony war."

The second mission was interesting, because we came upon a German reconnaissance aircraft, a Heinkel He-45 that started shooting at me! I guess everyone was a little nervous. I had a good mission on September 5, when I shot down a Polish two-seater. That was my last contact until a few days later [September 11], when I shot down a Polish-flown Fokker trimotor, and then I shot down a reconnaissance plane.

Soon afterward we relocated, and I was told that I had to go meet with Göring in Breslau, with my *staffel*. When we arrived I met with his nephew, who was an *oberleutnant*, and he took me to Göring's special train. This was when he handed me the Iron Cross Second Class, very unceremoniously, I might add. It was in a bag. I later learned that I was, in fact, the first Luftwaffe officer to receive that decoration. My *staffel* was going to fly escort for Göring's Ju-52, taking him to the front. He toured our air field and remarked about the unit, asked a few questions about the Me-110, and seemed to have a really good time. Then he was gone.

However, of great interest is the fact that it seemed Göring had only just left, when Hitler arrived aboard his Ju-52. He spoke with us very informally, asked about the war, our unit, and asked technical questions about the *Zerstörer*, and chatted almost as if we were all just comrades. I also had a chance to speak with Hans Baur, his personal pilot, who was an old Great War flier, and a record-setting Lufthansa airline pilot, and quite famous, and as fellow pilots we chatted. I have to say he was a very comfortable person to be with. Shortly after this we relocated back home, near Stuttgart.

On December 16, 1939, we received orders to relocate the unit to Jever on the North Sea, which is west of Wilhelmshaven, and by the next day we were established. We received new gear, all of it for flying over water, which was just extra rubbish to place into the aircraft. However, I could see the value in having an inflatable life raft, and a vest, just in case.

I was involved in a December 18 battle, now referred to as "the Battle of the German Bight" or "Bay," where the Royal Air Force tried to bomb German ships in the harbor at Wilhelmshaven with twenty-four [Vickers] Wellington bombers. I took the *staffel* on a routine patrol and familiarization flight, just to get used to the area. We had to be careful not to breach Danish airspace, so we followed our maps. I just happened to be marking my map when the radio came alive, stating that a British bomber force was en route. With my heading toward Helgoland and flying at about twelve thousand to thirteen thousand feet, we entered the airspace. I saw flak, and a plane was hit and going down, a Wellington bomber. I had to get closer to see anything more.

These fellows had been hit by flak pretty good, but I locked onto one Wellington and fired into him, killed his right engine, and he went into a slow spin toward the sea below. I then knew that we were at the extreme end of our mission as far as fuel was concerned, and we had to turn back, but I still wanted another kill, so I looked for another bomber. I attacked another, pretty far away, and then closed in for another pass. I got him, but I was also getting some defensive fire, killing my right engine.

Just when I thought the worst was over, I had thick smoke coming into the cockpit, so I opened the sliding windows to clear it out. I could breathe with the oxygen, but I could not see anything. "Okay," I thought, "I can make it on one engine, no real problem," and then the left engine locked up, and then I smelled fire, and then I learned firsthand that my remaining ammunition was on fire. All of this really started off a bad day, even with two more kills to my credit.

Well, I found out that all the glider training we had as early pilots paid off, since I was now flying a very heavy, smoking and burning powerless glider over the North Sea in winter. Then it dawned on me that I still had a long way to go to get home. I could see the ice below me, and the thought of freezing to death was what kept me in that cockpit as long as possible. I then thought about lightening the load, so to speak, so I began dumping my fuel. This would give me more time in the air, eating up distance until I could at best make dry land, or at worst hit more shallow water, close to shore where the sea rescue boys could get me. I was down to the treetops, and I mean I was probably touching branches, and I heard from my gunner [Alfred "Pauli"] Walz over the radio that we were going down. The best part was that I was not alone, and my boys knew where I was if I did go down.

Luckily, I made it to Wangerooge and touched down, a classic powerless, or "dead stick" landing. My faithful wingman flew on to Jever, refueled, dismissed his radioman and gunner, and came back. He picked me and Walz up. I should also mention that this place, Wangerooge, was where I was first introduced to the *Freya* radar system, very primitive at the time, but it was the beginning of the technology I would later become so familiar with.

Of the twenty-two bombers, we managed to shoot down twelve of them. Also on that mission was Johannes Steinhoff, then an *ober-leutnant* who would be promoted to *hauptmann* himself, leading a flight from IV/JG.2 in Me-109s. After this mission, we received some outstanding press, and our superiors in Berlin were pleased with the result.[5]

What followed this battle was a press conference, or more properly, a feeding frenzy. This was the first encounter between British and German aircraft, especially enemy bombers and our fighters, so this was big news. The Propaganda Ministry and even the world press were there. I was asked what I thought about the

British, my enemy, and I said that I admired them, that they were very brave. Steinhoff, *Oberst* Carl-August Schumacher, myself, and another pilot were ordered to Berlin.

This was the same time my unit joined JG.1. This was commanded by *Oberst* Schumacher, a really outstanding officer who was also on the mission in question. It was not long afterward that the same Mr. Grey, from *The Aeroplane*, wrote an article about me, remembering our meeting two years before. He was the first person to call me the "Happy Falcon," because of my good-natured humor, I suppose. He did not attack me as a "Nazi" or even as an enemy, but simply another flier just doing his job. We also flew many missions providing air cover for our navy, mostly destroyers and other ships, and we became very good friends with the navy men based at Wilhelmshaven.

In January 1940, I was promoted to *hauptmann* and made the commanding officer of I/ZG.76. While with this wing, I participated in the campaigns against Denmark and Norway, which commenced on April 9, 1940, flying the Me-110. These were pretty much ground attack and aerial umbrella missions, so there was not a lot of air combat for me at that time. Once, we encountered some [Bristol] Blenheims and I ordered an attack, but the weather was so cold the guns would not work, and all of the pilots had this problem.

I was very frustrated, but I tried many times warming the guns up, and finally managed to catch up to one of the bombers. I hit one, and he went down, and then I attacked another. That bomber just blew up, in a bright flash, and I was not too far away. It really shook me up, but I was undamaged. That was a very spectacular thing to see, and I was all alone. I thought my men had flown back due to weapons failures, but I found out they had continued following the formation also, just out of my sight. When I came in to land, I learned that I had not escaped unscathed, as a British gunner had hit my aileron, doing some good damage. Shortly after this I was awarded the Iron Cross First Class.

I was then reassigned to command a destroyer group in Düsseldorf, where I was to train a new group of young pilots. This was where

I first met Max-Hellmuth Ostermann, a wonderful young pilot who looked like he was twelve years old, but a fellow who could not handle the Me-110, so I sent him back to an Me-109 unit. I liked him very much, and I wish he had survived the war. He flew with JG.54, and while on the Eastern Front, shot down 102 enemy aircraft. He died in combat, but managed to receive the Swords. I still do not think he had even started shaving then.[6]

In March I was informed that we were going to invade Denmark, and our missions were bomber escort, as well as shooting down any enemy aircraft in the air, but not destroying aircraft on the ground. My flight plan took everything into account, including an early morning attack, low altitude, with the sun in the enemy's eyes. Getting the surprise was critical, as in every battle throughout time.

Well, we attacked the air field, but our orders were clear; we were ordered not to shoot up their aircraft, unless they violated the orders we issued and took off. We approached and the enemy planes were sitting there, running, and despite the leaflets dropped previously, telling the Danish air force to stand down, this one fellow was taking off, so following orders I shot him down just as he lifted off. The antiaircraft fire came up to greet us, and I was hit, then my right engine was shot out, so I radioed I was going to fly back to our new base at Barth. I knew the route and roads our army would take, so I just thought that if I flew along that route, and I did crash-land, I would be among friends.

I landed on the good left engine without any problem, with the exception of locating a bullet that had shredded the stick and lodged in my parachute. That was unnerving, so I dismissed it and then jumped into another Me-110, and while flying I saw one of my Me-110 crews on the ground, surrounded by Danish soldiers, so I landed and inquired. They were fine, and the Danes were not in any mood to fight, so I took off, once I confirmed that a rescue-and-repair team was on their way. I went on to Aalborg, thinking about how that parachute had stopped that bullet that had entered from underneath the fuselage, and probably saved my life.

We knew that we were going to fight British fighters soon. However, even if in the hands of an expert pilot, dogfighting against

Spitfires and Hurricanes [in an Me-110] was not recommended. The 110 had superior firepower, which could destroy any aircraft and at greater range than our enemies, but the lack of maneuverability and slow climb rate were sheer suicide. The diving rate was outstanding, and that was perhaps the saving grace of pilots flying the *Zerstörer*, including myself. I know that Hans-Joachim Jabs had scored day kills against British fighters in the Me-110, and he survived.

My later operations started on May 10 with the invasions of Holland, Belgium, and France, and also operations on the English Channel coast against the RAF. I could tell that the Me-110 was an excellent ground attack, and even a bomber attack fighter. It also had the range to be very effective, over two and a half times the range of the Me-109.

The invasion of Holland was a new experience, and we met a lot of flak on the way in, but we had no losses. Our *Fallschirmjäger* [paratroops] had landed earlier, taking key bridges and securing installations. We saw many Ju-52s shot down and burning, apparently troop transports hit by flak and attacked when they landed. During one of the missions, we encountered British destroyers, sailing to Holland from Britain, but when we flew over, they turned around, which I found interesting. Then we played with them a bit, and they fired at us but no harm was done, and we could do nothing to them. I learned later that these ships were supposed to rescue the Dutch royal family, so I guess we delayed that operation.

The invasion of France was more involved, but the great point of interest for me was Dunkirk, when we had the entire British army in Europe pinned against the sea, and then Hitler ordered the panzer divisions and their infantry to halt. I could not believe it as I flew over and saw the masses of men, and all the ships coming to get them. We had assumed that Hitler wanted the British to save face, abandon the war against us, and join us against the Soviet Union later. This was the theory, anyway.

This was where I first began to suffer losses to our Me-110s against the Spitfires and Hurricanes, and where we learned just how vulnerable they were. But it would take another two to three months of losses over England before the High Command saw that wisdom. The same would be said of the Stukas also, which were even easier targets. The only advantage was our heavy firepower in the nose, which could destroy any Allied aircraft. I never had the good fortune of shooting down a British fighter, but I did have a few experiences with them that I will never forget.

Once, I was flying over the Channel on an escort mission, when we were jumped by Spitfires. My flight was scattered and as I reported to the *geschwaderkommodore*, *Oberst* Huth, that we lost one crew killed, his Me-110 exploded—I saw this happen, and his fighter fell to earth in flames. Then I was hit from above and the right. The engines were still functional, but I had holes in the wings and fuselage. In fact, I had so many holes in the side of my aircraft I had in-flight air conditioning. The wind whistled in and cooled me off. The 110 was shaking as if it would fall apart.

Then I was hit again, so I inverted my fighter and tried to shake this man off of me, but it took both hands to move the stick and complete the half roll. It was about this point I looked at the altimeter, to see if bailing out was an option. Well, that was not working, since the instrument panel was shot away. Just then, I thought that this was one hell of a way to earn a paycheck!

Two Spitfires were still on my tail, and they were faster, and closing. I threw the machine down to the treetops, and I mean I was probably touching branches, and I heard from my gunner "Pauli" Walz behind me that they were still following, but seemed to be very reluctant to drop that low. Perhaps they were thinking that I was evading them into a flak trap or something, but I was certain that they could not get a good firing angle, not at high speed, and fighter pilots do not like low speed at low altitude.

Feeling a little better I climbed for more altitude, just in case we were forced to bail out, but then the two British fighters were still following, and when I reached almost three hundred meters, Walz called them out again, so back down into the trees for me. I was sweating like never before in my life. I was hoping Walz would be able to get a shot in, even if he did not hit them, just to scare them away. I was hugging the ground contours, crossed a road, and I really had to pull the nose up to avoid hitting a British soldier on a bicycle, believe that or not! I know I scared him because he fell off and hit the ground. Despite the grim circumstances, I laughed at the whole ordeal.

Well, I managed to shake off the Spitfires, and they probably broke contact due to being low on fuel, I will never know, but I was not complaining. Upon landing, I was informed that Kesselring had arrived to see his old friend Huth, and after climbing out I looked at Walz. He was white as well, and we were both drenched in sweat. I think I lost a couple of kilos in weight from the experience. Then I had to report to Kesselring, and Huth informed him of our pilot's and gunner's deaths.

We continued our patrols and a few minor support missions, and each flight became more dangerous. We were losing 110s and crews at an alarming rate due to the British fighters. This was when I knew that we were flying an inferior aircraft, inferior as far as dogfighting went. It took almost twice as long to train a destroyer pilot as it did a single engine pilot. I could get new fighters. It was waiting for the pilots to qualify in Destroyer School that crippled us operationally. We even had a few bomber pilots move in to handle some of the flying operations, since they had twin-engine and instrumentation experience.

I first began thinking about the night fighter idea after we relocated to Aalborg in northern Denmark. We could actually hear the British bombers passing overhead on their way to their targets. But it was at Deelen, Holland, that I made my decision. Every evening the RAF bombers flew over us on their way to bomb Germany, and us as well on their return trip. They would bomb our air field or machine gun our aircraft during low-level attacks, and here we were, the fighter pilots sitting in a trench!

As you may imagine, this was a very demoralizing situation for us. I thought, "If the RAF can fly at night, why couldn't we?" I then checked out three other crews, including Werner Streib, Radusch, and Their, as well as myself, about the possibility of flying the Me-110 at night, and the initial results were positive. Ironically, it was Streib who thought the entire plan was illogical, since he later became the first night fighter ace and a top-scoring pilot. Up until his death in 1986, I always reminded him of this.

Right before all of this started, the *Luftflotte* 2 commander, *Generaloberst* [later *Generalfeldmarschall*] Albert Kesselring came to see us. He was an extremely likeable man, very friendly, very intelligent, and seemed to know the answers to the questions he asked, just to see what our responses would be. He was well aware of us, and I was surprised that he even inquired as to the status of the night fighting method. I was unaware that anyone else was even aware of it. We discussed this and many other things.

I told him that it was possible to fight the British at night, but there would be necessary modifications implemented before this was feasible, including making the necessary arrangements with the local antiaircraft battery commanders regarding searchlights and later, the only radar station, which was located not far from us.[7] He listened very carefully, and he understood all of what I was saying, which gave me hope. I also became an even more than interested expert on radars and searchlights, as well as holding night flying navigation classes.

One night, or very early in the morning, the RAF returned from a mission into Germany, and as usual dropped a few bombs on our air field. I ordered the flight to take off with four planes to intercept. We were totally unprepared, but we four crews lifted off anyway. We did not even have runway lights. Three of us saw an enemy bomber and I attacked, but it disappeared into the fog just over the sea. Radusch actually took some enemy fire, but landed safely. I wrote that report up, and after I collected a few similar reports, I began to build my case.

However, from this we learned that it was possible to fly at night with a certain amount of organization, aircraft modifications, such as exhaust dampeners and new instruments with special illumination, as well as special ammunition for use at night to reduce muzzle flash, which would not blind us. Then we knew that we could fight the bombers. My group commander asked me to write a report about the incident, including all of my proposals for such missions.

I did the report about the mission, and I believe that this particular report was more or less the only one read by Göring and possibly even Hitler. I was called in to meet with

Generalfeldmarschall Erhard Milch, who flew to Aalborg, and was quite interested in my plans. We had a very long chat, and he asked me many questions, and I liked the discussion, and the man. I saw some promise in him, but after the meeting I did not really think much about it. Two years later, in January 1942, Galland told me that he knew Göring read it, and that Milch had discussed the night fighter operations in detail with Göring, and even mentioned my report. This report was the birth of the *Nachtjagdflieger*.[8]

Well, the birthday of the *Nachtjagdfliegerdienst* was actually on June 26, 1940, when I was made *kommodore* of the new outfit. This was after I received a call from Ernst Udet, asking me to come to Berlin. I still had part of my wing stationed in France on the north Channel coast, just west of Le Havre, and it was just before the beginning of the Battle of Britain, then we were ordered back to Germany, due to the bombing raids.

All of a sudden I received special orders from Kesselring back to Düsseldorf in order to fly against the British bombers at night. The RAF was attacking the Ruhrgebiet, Cologne, and so forth. I was very angry about the order because we had no experience; the crews did not possess the necessary knowledge to accomplish this task, and we did not have all the necessary equipment, all of which I had expressly requested in my report. I had not even received the special night ammunition I had ordered, which was tested and proven to be quite effective.

Ironically, I had just been assigned back to Düsseldorf with the *geschwader* in another memorandum, this one from Milch, which was way above my immediate chain of command. I was then informed that we were ordered to start night flying operations against the British bombers at night, and I protested. I pointed out, in very clear terms, the various reasons why such missions at that time were nothing more than suicide missions, as we were still unprepared. I was only two months beyond writing a proposal, so nothing had been established that met my criteria. I was still learning what was needed! Udet understood, and I learned that he had an ulterior motive.

We flew several night missions, which were very dangerous, given the lack of proper ammunition, the necessity for landing lights on the airstrip, and even establishing proper radio and telephone networks, wired on a separate system in case a bombing raid destroyed a radio tower or a telephone exchange. I also did not have enough experienced pilots for such missions, as many were replacements. We flew anyway, and on more than one occasion we came back shot up with nothing to show for our efforts.

Well, orders were orders. Upon my arrival, I ordered two Ju-88 medium bombers to Berlin-Schönefeld to take part in some tests, but I did not know what this was about at first. Udet informed me that our industry had developed some instruments, which could locate targets with distance and altitude, and this was why my crews were sent there. I met the civilian engineers, and they showed me to the station, called *Würzburg-Geräte* (WG).[9] But that was still in the near future.

There was a desk for me and another desk where another man sat, and he had a map, which was painted on a glass disk showing the present position of one of the Ju-88s, which was playing the "enemy." This was picked up by *Würzburg-Geräte*. The same controller guided the other Ju-88 to the target in order to come up from behind him. This type of flying took a lot of awareness, instrumentation, and natural cognitive ability. It was very exhausting, even if only for a couple of hours, and mentally demanding.

I watched this procedure three times. I saw the problem; these engineers were not pilots, and they gave the night fighter the present position to the target, which made the fighter fly a "*Hundekurve*," and the fighter had problems arriving in the right position. I asked the people if I could take over the directional guidance by radio, and I had no problem finding the heading of the target, and I gave the night fighter the correct orders to locate the bird, and it worked.[10]

The engineers were quite surprised that I guided the fighter to the target so quickly. I was deeply impressed and convinced that this was the way of the future for night fighting. I called Udet and gave him the full report, complete with my assignment and opinions. Udet reacted immediately and positively, and he asked me to arrange for two Fiesler *Storch* aircraft, and to mark off a night fighting maneuver area.

Udet correctly believed that if it worked at high speed and high altitude, it should work at lower speeds and altitudes. Udet came in and he took off in a *Storch* with a radio, and I flew the other one without any radio communications. I was the target and Udet was the fighter. If he located me and came in from behind, he would fire a signal rocket. I would then disappear and he would do it again. So, we flew at night without any position lights and he "killed" me twice. After landing, everyone was happy and this assured continued development. Afterward I reported to Kammhuber, and he then authorized the next step, the *Würzburg-Reise* and onboard radar. I then returned to my unit. That was when I was ordered by Göring in a telephone call to form *Nachtjagdgeschwader* (night fighter wing, or NJG) 1.

Udet and I had long talks about all of this, and I wrote down all of my points. He assured me that Milch wanted all of the details, with specific requirements, and I would receive what I needed. I gave him the list and said that I would write the formal report, which stated the following requirements:

1. Dimming switches for the cockpit instruments, including the gunsight, to reduce glare, with blackout curtains to eliminate side lighting, giving the night fighter away on dark nights.
2. Low-flash exploding ammunition and night tracer.
3. Landing light markers, specifically designed for approach path viewing, covered until the landing approach, and then uncovered to show the runways. This included special direct high-beam searchlights for the air fields.
4. All pilots having passed blind flying instrumentation in the 110, and also passed the handling and flight characteristics examinations, including blind landing and blind navigation.
5. Staggered, overlapping flights and attacks, coordinated between various units, based upon radar and ground control observation. The two-and-a-half-hour flying time of the Me-110 was sufficient to successfully engage

enemy bombers, both inbound and then outward bound, with overlapping attacks on a continuous basis. This also required basing the units along the well-traveled air corridors, minimizing the time to intercept, and allowing for more time to engage.

6. Better radios, and a consistent and effective radio communications network, so that all fighters could stay in radio contact, coordinated by the ground controllers, without overloading the channels, thus rendering communications ineffective. I also stated that special radios, with linguists, be established, listening to the RAF channels. Much intelligence could be gathered by listening to the enemy.

7. Establish very clear zones of responsibility, dividing up the flak and fighter zones, to avoid friendly fire situations. This would also increase the lethality of the overlapping defenses, which was what the Kammhuber Line became.

These were just a few of my demands, if the higher powers wanted to successfully address the night bombing issue. Udet looked approvingly, and he liked the tactic. This was when Udet said something very important to me, something that I never forgot: "Falck, remember that Göring's star rises and falls upon the Luftwaffe's success. Failure is not something he will accept, because his career depends upon it. Hitler is also looking at him, so the pressure is immense. You are now the next great feather in his cap. If you fail, we all fail, and I can assure you that is not a position to be in."

"Well," I thought, "me and my big mouth." I had started all of this as an idea, and it had snowballed into a major political issue at the highest level! Two days later, after arriving back in Düsseldorf on June 25, 1940, I was then summoned to Wassenaar in Holland to meet with Göring and *General* [Friedrich] Christiansen.

I must mention that there were many very important people in this meeting, all of whom I was unaware would be attending, so you could say I was ambushed! Senior generals such as [Gustav]

Kastner[-Kirdorf], [Bruno] Lörzer, Udet, [Wolfgang] Martini, Kesselring, Schmidt, and, of course, Göring, were all seated, and a few others who I cannot remember and did not know. Göring started the meeting, long winded as usual, and mentioned the issue at hand: British bombers attacking Germany. This was when he openly announced the creation of the night fighter wings. He ordered me to establish the first night fighter group, which I did with the help of Johannes Steinhoff, and it became NJG.1. He then made me *kommodore* on the spot, which was a first, since every other *kommodore* was a World War I veteran and a senior officer, all above the rank of *oberst*. I was only a *hauptmann*. When he mentioned this fact, there were no grunts of discontent, no eyebrows raised. I assumed from that response they were already aware of his decision.

Göring gave me a long list of orders, and he finally asked me what, if anything, I needed, or if I had any questions. Naturally, being me, I did. I stated that under no circumstances should the night fighters be placed under subordinate control of antiaircraft artillery commanders. This made no sense for many reasons, all of which I outlined in front of these high-ranking officers, so I was a little nervous. Then I remembered what Udet had said, and I found the strength to take a chance. I also stated that I needed all of my required materials as given to Udet, and written in my report for Milch.

I then suggested that the searchlight batteries be placed under my command and control. That area of responsibility was under the command of *Oberstleutnant* [Sebastian] Fichtner, and Göring would not allow that. He did say that he would order that the two of us work together, coordinating our efforts. I then requested my own radar expert, the very competent *Oberleutnant* [Georg] Teske, but Göring said that was impossible. Then I mentioned *Leutnant* Erich Bode in Denmark, who had given me my first crash course in radar, and Göring agreed to have him assigned to me.

I was then told to drive back to Düsseldorf and relieve two of my senior officers, and appoint their replacements. This was unheard of, and I asked for a letter signed by Göring, giving me such authority. He had one drafted, which he signed, and from that point I was answerable only to him. This was also quite unique. Then after a couple of hours the meeting broke up.

Then Udet came to me and pinched my arm in boyish excitement. "Wolf, I told you, your ideas went to the top. Now it is all up to you." As he left, Kesselring came to me, and he stated clearly that he had reservations about the entire affair, but that he trusted that if anyone could pull this thing off, it would be me. That made me feel better. I was then informed that my daughter Irmgard, named after my sister, had been born, so it was a great day all around. I was allowed home leave for a few days as a result, and it felt good to see my family again.

I returned to my base before going to Fürstenwalde to see the family, and I was with Johannes Steinhoff, my old friend. I called for Steinhoff to meet with me to receive his orders, as his new commanding officer, and I was very upset that he was very late and had not called me. I was pacing like an expectant father. I thought that the very man I was going to trust with my unit could not even make a meeting on time, and that I would have to make an example out of him, firing him, and thus ruining his career.

Then I heard a report that a Blenheim had been shot down nearby, and the news did not really have an impact on me. Then, within the hour, Steinhoff walked in, still in flight gear, and apologized for being late. He stated that he was flying in to see me when he came across a Blenheim and shot it down, hence being late. He and I then jumped into my staff car and drove to the crash site, where the dead crewmen were still strapped in. Steinhoff stood there and said, "Poor bastards," and I nodded. There is the exhilaration of the kill, but then, being pilots, we rarely see the end results. I said a silent prayer for them. Brave men, very sad, but it was war.

Then I saw the human side of "Macky" Steinhoff. There were many onlookers gawking at the crash and the bodies of the dead airmen. One of the men went up and kicked the lifeless body of a dead man, and Steinhoff, for the first time that I ever saw, and never really after that, exploded. He jumped at the person, screaming at him to be respectful, that these were soldiers, men who died such a noble death. I was also outraged, and we both dressed that idiot down for his actions. The rest of the crowd got the message.

I placed him in temporary command while I was gone. I then had to inform Fichtner that his unit was now under my command, he was being relieved, and as you may imagine, this meeting did not go well. He demanded to know under what authority a junior officer had to issue such a court-martial-worthy offense. I told him, "The *Reichsmarschall's* orders, sir, not mine," and I produced the letter signed by Göring. He was still enraged, and I was afraid that he was going to be a constant thorn in my side.

One night we had bombers reported crossing the North Sea coast, and at this time we did not have onboard aerial radars. In fact, we did not even have ground control to air radar and communication set up. On top of this, on the night in question, we had almost zero visibility with sporadic thunderstorms and heavy rain.

Fichtner, the nonflier, ordered me to send my men up anyway, and not being a pilot, I forgave this idiocy. So, in the spirit of détente, I offered to send him up with one of my best pilots to see the weather for himself. Naturally, and as I expected he declined the offer, but he kept his mouth shut regarding my future decisions on flight operations. In time, our relationship developed into a friendlier one. This may have been more due to the fact that I received calls from Kammhuber, Kesselring, and Göring on a regular basis, and that kind of clout could not be ignored.

Steinhoff was a mastermind, organizational genius, and an excellent pilot. More important, he was a great friend, extremely honest, and very dedicated to his work. He became one of my best friends until his death a few years ago. I loved and respected him very much, and more important as well, I could trust him with my life, and in air combat that is not a small thing. I cannot say that there were many people I ever had that much trust in.

On July 19, 1940, I was called to see Göring again, and he promoted me to *major* and I was the first official *geschwaderkommodore* of the new generation, and the youngest at that time. Soon Mölders, Lützow, Trautloft, and Galland all became *kommodoren*, so the new generation was taking over. That was as it should have been, in my opinion. I always believed that men commanding pilots should be flying combat with their men, leading by example. Men sitting in chairs, issuing orders, should have the firsthand experience to justify those orders. This was what I called "white knuckle command."

I highly respected the World War I pilots in command, as these were real heroes in every sense of the word, but I also understood that with the modern war and ever-increasing technology, they were, for the most part, completely out of their depth. Some of them understood this and worked within their limitations, while others refused to accept that they were unprepared for this new age. It would be almost the same as giving a medieval monk a computer and expecting him to be competent with minimal instruction.

It should be said that on July 20, 1940, Werner Streib of 2/NJG.2 accomplished what we had been working on. He scored the first confirmed night kill, which was a British Whitley bomber. By October he had ten confirmed kills. I received his after action report for the first mission, and I requested all of the reports from all the units be sent to me. Soon I had massive amounts of paperwork coming in, most of it worthless from an operational perspective, but all of it worth quite a bit regarding the lessons learned from each flight.

I requested all of the unit reports, which were normally overall summaries of actions, combining all of the after action reports into the unit diary. Yes, I wanted those copies, but I also wanted each and every individual pilot's reports, right down to the smallest detail. This included rounds fired, weather, altitude, speed, radio contacts, any kills made, all contacts, damage reports, fuel use reports, flying times. I wanted it all. I had to know what I was working with, and most important, what was not working so well that could be improved.

Once I was able to read their after action reports, see the ground control reports, then, if possible, after speaking with the pilots to learn from them each specific detail, I could develop a better picture of what was developing and then take corrective action if necessary. This was important, since we were literally flying through uncharted terrain. Every success, every shortcoming, every maneuver, anything that could be improved upon was approached accordingly.

Once I collected the reports, I wrote my own, and when Göring received Streib's report, he was ecstatic. He called me on July 22 and thanked me. I told him that Streib was the one to thank, as he had managed to prove the concept. Later, upon my recommendation, Göring personally authorized and awarded Streib his Knight's Cross. Streib, the banker before becoming a pilot, finished the war with sixty-seven night kills and one day victory, and he was a stellar personality. I was also proud to not only recommend him but also see him receive the Oak Leaves later.[11]

I found out from Udet, who heard firsthand from Kesselring, that Göring had personally sung my praises to Hitler regarding the night fighters. According to Udet, and this was later confirmed by Kesselring himself to me, Hitler asked if Göring thought the expense was worthwhile and if he saw any future in it. Göring replied "Yes," and Hitler gave one of his rare smiles, and then said, "Very well, this is between you and Falck."

It is well known that Germany had the toughest air defenses in the war. I know this firsthand and [Josef] Kammhuber was the reason why, so that was why it was called the Kammhuber Line. He was a great believer in flak, creating twenty-mile-wide defensive belts that grew stronger as they fell back deeper into German territory. The entire Reich was broken up into specific grid squares, each with its own flak and fighter zones, searchlights, ground control, and telephone and radio centers. Soon we received even more advanced radar guided artillery, which made the 105mm and 88mm guns even more effective. We also had radar-controlled searchlights, which really made a difference.

Initially the searchlights would pick up the incoming bombers, often heard by the ground observers, and also picked up on our ground-to-air radar. Oftentimes a smaller raid would hit the radar sites, knocking them out before the main strike came. Many times these strikes would be made by Pathfinder aircraft, and the "master of ceremonies" who would fly ahead, drop flares and a few bombs, marking the target easily for the main force following behind.

Then there were the special raids hitting the radar locations, as they could home in on the emissions that emanated from the radars. This was a British tactic to blind us electronically. The searchlights then joined or even replaced the radar. This was why I requested a redundant system, as a backup in case we lost these critical intelligence gathering areas.

The Kammhuber Line was the first layer in a very complex defense network. It started in France along the Channel coast, Belgium, Holland, and Denmark, all starting at the North Sea approach in a sort of irregular circular pattern; then, like the ripples in a lake when a stone is thrown, it grew outward and expanded. The defensive belts went from Norway to the border with Switzerland, and all the way from France to Poland, later in the war.

Also, in 1943, the line extended to Italy as well, all the way to the Gustav Line under Kesselring, when Hitler ordered guns of the heavy 88mm and 105mm type transferred to that theater of operations. I would have to say that the Kammhuber Line was one of the best concepts and actions undertaken by the Reich Defense Department and the Luftwaffe.[12] That was until Hitler took away our flak guns. This decision placed even more pressure upon me and the newer *Wilde Sau* units, but at least it left fewer flak guns to shoot us down as well.

Not long after this I received another wing, which became NJG.2. I very soon had crews fresh from destroyer school as well as a flood of volunteers and complete groups, which we converted to night fighting.[13] Since I was the "Old Man" and the inventor of this idea, the men named me the "Father of the Night Fighters," a nickname that has followed me ever since. That is my primary nickname, among a few others, perhaps less flattering!

As you know, several books have been written about that over the years. With this new position, I was fortunately able to requisition what I needed, and this helped tremendously in organizing and deploying new units. I could bypass normal channels, unlike the day fighter force, as Kammhuber used his authority to push through everything with a quick pace after the start of 1941. By 1942 we really wanted for nothing, but by 1943 we were hard pressed to get newer and replacement equipment. Getting new pilots as the war progressed was a different story altogether.

After this inaugural scenario was successful, and the force officially established, Göring awarded me the *Ritterkreuz* officially on October 1, 1940, for my service, but I arrived on October 7, and was there to also see Werner Streib receive his Knight's Cross as well, and *Major* Bernd von Brauchitsch, son of the army chief of staff and a good friend of mine as well as Göring's adjutant, placed the medal around my neck.[14]

Afterward we had lunch, and I sat next to Milch. The one discussion that came to my mind was the rule that the families of men who died with less than ten years' service received no pension, and I asked him if that could be changed. I was promised that he would look into it, and he kept his word. Those of us at the table were also informed that those of us so decorated would receive estates in the east on top of our pensions when the war was over. I thought that kind of odd, but I did not say anything.[15]

During this time of building up the night fighters, my request to include Ju-88 and Do-17 medium bombers within the night fighter community was scrutinized, and once again I had a meeting with Göring, and this time Dietrich Peltz and Kammhuber were there. Having twin-engine fighters used for night fighting was one thing, but requesting bombers for such missions raised eyebrows. Then I had a message to fly to Cologne to meet with Kammhuber.

I flew in bad weather to get there, diverted to Münster, where I managed to land without fuel and unable to locate the runway. Well, despite standing on the brakes and reversing the throttle, I crashed head-on into a Ju-88, which was quite embarrassing. Following this event, I arrived, and I discussed the current developments with the aircraft types, modifications I had requested, and the rather slow delivery of all the items I had requested. I told him bluntly that I could not be expected to perform my job properly if I did not have the required radars, planes, and trained crews. Göring understood, and he said that he would have a chat with Milch and Lörzer about the problems. I told him, above all, that I needed those medium bombers, and more Me-110s.

Then I had another meeting not long afterward with Göring in Berlin, due to my previous meeting with Kammhuber, and Milch and Peltz were there, in which I explained my rationale, such as longer ranges for those aircraft, further extending air-to-air contact and shadowing missions. I also developed the concept of an airborne control aircraft, a tracking plane with a pilot and a radio operator, who could relay information from the aircraft in flight to the respective zone ground control commanders. I knew that this method would also free up the radio channels, allowing the most critical data to be streamlined.

I then explained to Göring that the bomber and reconnaissance pilots were already instrument qualified, many had bad-weather flying experience, and they could be trained on aerial gunnery. The medium bombers would also allow for an extra crewman, working as a radar operator, freeing the gunner to do his job and also handle air-to-ground communications. These issues had to be addressed.

I also explained that using these aircraft made logistical sense, as we could use the older versions being replaced by newer models for bomber service, thus saving on aircraft production. I also stated that if these bombers could be retrofitted at the factories for night fighting, it would save us a great deal of time. Göring listened, and he was absolutely fascinated, and Peltz looked at me, and I could tell that he saw the logic, but that I was treading into his waters. Well, the meeting was over, or so I thought, when the room was called to attention. Then Hitler walked in, with a couple of officers, including *Generaloberst* Alfred Jodl.

Well, he walked in, waved his hand, took his seat and simply said, "Continue." I had stopped in midsentence and was going back to one of my points when Hitler interrupted me. "Falck, how much will all of these planes cost?" I was stunned at the question because I did not have an answer. Budgetary concerns were not part of my operational repertoire, so I simply said, "My *Führer*, I really have no idea, my apologies."

Hitler leaned forward with his elbows on the large oak table, and he looked at me, then at Göring. "Well, I do happen to know. I ordered a study on this plan of yours, from top to bottom. I could outfit three panzer divisions for the cost of your radars and fighters, not to mention Kammhuber wanting more flak guns. However, I am also interested in this using of bombers idea. Tell me more."

So I did, and after I was finished, about twenty minutes later, Hitler nodded to Göring and said, "Make this work," and then he stood, we went to attention, and he left without any ceremony. Once the door closed behind him, Göring came up to me and punched my arm and said: "You see? Even the *Führer* sees the value in this concept. Now, Falck, the rest is up to you." I left that meeting feeling pretty powerful, I have to admit.

Then Milch walked up to me and said, "Falck, be careful what you wish for." I was not quite sure how to take that comment.

Being back in Düsseldorf I had a lot of planning to do. I also came to know the *gauleiter* [political district commander] who was a former pilot himself. I found him to be the most enthusiastic and easiest person ever to work with, a very friendly character. I had to develop good working relationships with all of these *gauleiter* throughout Germany. Their cooperation was critical to my success, although some were much less willing to work with me than others.

Due to this fact, always I carried that wrinkled and crumbling letter signed by Göring with me everywhere I went. Once I had the Knight's Cross around my neck, and became a rather well-known quantity, at least by name alone, I received a lot less "flak" from these people, so to speak.

I had worked out my plan from top to bottom. I created two parts to my fighter force, the short-range interceptors and the long-range interceptors. These two units were organized as such based upon which aircraft were flown by each unit, such as the medium bombers converted to night fighting, spending more time in the air. These were the planes that actually followed bombers back to England from their bases in northern France, Holland, and Denmark.

Some of these bombers were special aircraft, fitted with additional internal fuel tanks, turning them into flying fuel cells, and no armament. They carried a pilot, copilot, and a radio/radarman, no gunner. These were strictly observation aircraft, to monitor enemy formations. They were to stay out of direct sight and have no contact with the enemy. I preferred the Do-17 for these missions, as it was fast and was a reliable aircraft.

Sometimes, when we detected enemy bombers taking off from their bases, I would have commanders send a few of these long-range night fighters into British airspace, to hit them at the beginning. I returned to Deelen, Holland, and got cracking on these missions and training. The Me-110 units handled the regions within their sectors, attacking inbound and outward-bound bombers that slipped through the long-range fighters. I knew as an airman that we were not just going to make a material impact upon the enemy; the psychological impact would also be tremendous.

I also began a test program using forward mounted searchlights in the nose of a Do-17. This proved a failure, since rear gunners would just shoot out the light, and the beam showed every gunner in the enemy bombers where the attacking fighter was, giving a clear direction in which to fire. After that failure, I thought about other things that we could do.

I was very interested in the new infrared searchlights that were developed, and we tried them out. They were primitive by today's standards, but they did work. You could actually find the enemy in the dark, and once the radar located the enemy, you could shut it off, lessening the chance of being detected, and use the infrared alone, which picked up the heat signature.

Unfortunately it was a fragile assembly, was only good to about three hundred to five hundred meters, and often just the vibration of the engines worked parts of it loose. Then they were mounted in specially designed rubber mounts, under the nose, dampening the vibration effect, and they worked better. We just did not have enough of these.

Among the many other tests, Kammhuber ordered me to conduct a study on the use of overlapping radars, both ground to air, and the feasibility of using the newer air-to-air radar as well, so that our fighters could locate the enemy in the air more precisely. I took this task to heart, and I called upon every expert within these respective fields throughout the Reich, and Kammhuber rubber-stamped every request. Upon completion of these experiments, we had installed *Freya* long-range and *Würzburg* direct contact from fighter-to-bomber location radar systems.

The year 1941 was to prove challenging, to say the least, as my mother died in February, and my father conducted the service, and she was buried in Bremen. I was also given a lecturing tour, speaking to youth groups, explaining to them about the Luftwaffe, the night fighters, and my experiences, and so forth. This was a public relations tour, nothing more really. I guess the entire program was designed to get the young men prepared for military service, and get them excited about a possible future in the Luftwaffe.

The summer started very well for us, that is until we heard about the invasion of the Soviet Union. This was not good news for us, especially me. I knew what that meant. I also thought about the fact that if it was hard to get what I needed before June 22, 1941, how much more difficult would it be to get my things from that point forward?

I also paid several visits to the flight schools, as I became the self-appointed carnival pitchman of sorts for my night fighters. We needed volunteers, badly, but I would only take volunteers, and the best need only apply. These were heady times, and I rather enjoyed the respite, but I did miss the unit. I personally reviewed many of the applications for the night fighters, as flight students completed primary and often secondary training.

After one of these lectures, I returned to Deelen. I had learned that we had lost a couple of fighters and crews in accidents, not even in combat. The landing lights I had ordered had been delivered, but they were nowhere to be found, and the electrical system had not been updated, per my orders. I also learned from the local deputy commander that a flak officer had decided to use some of my lights to supplement his flak perimeter. His defense was that "they were just laying there in crates, so we used them." He had no reason to, so I sent my ground crews over to rip them up and have them wired on my field. I could not believe it.

Well, this guy found out "his" lights were missing and he was incensed, and he stormed over to my base. Being an *oberstleutnant* himself, and knowing the rank of the base commander, he was probably under the illusion that he could pull rank and confiscate my lights again. When he came in, my adjutant told me I had a visitor. I walked in, and this guy was fuming. Then he saw my Knight's Cross, and then, as prearranged, my adjutant popped his head in and said, "*Herr Major, Reichsmarschall* Göring on the line for you, sir." I told the flak commander to please wait.

I walked out of the room and then closed the door. I placed my finger to my lips, and my young man tried not to laugh. I began talking as if I was on the phone with Göring, knowing he could hear me from my office. "Yes, *Reichsmarschall,* I did receive the lights and equipment, but I have not received the electrical upgrades as promised by *Generalfeldmarschall* Milch." I was trying not to laugh!

After about four minutes of this charade, I handed the phone to my man and walked back into the room. "Now, *Herr Oberstleutnant,* what may I do for you?" He looked as if I had just dropped a dung heap on him. I knew why he was there, but now he was in the position of demanding the return of items his men had stolen, that were issued to me from both the Luftwaffe supreme commander and expedited by the Luftwaffe commander in chief. His response was a simple apology, that there was some kind of mistake, and then he left. We had an excellent working relationship from that point forward!

To make things worse, that very same evening the phone rang and my adjutant said it was Kammhuber. I took the phone, and he told me that there was a massive RAF raid heading our way, and that he wanted everything in the air. We had not received any reports of incoming bombers. Making matters worse, I had mostly new crews, fresh from school, and my spare parts had not arrived. Half my planes needed engine parts, many experienced pilots were on leave, several fighters needed tires and cables. Maintenance was necessary, so therefore spare parts were needed. I did not even have my complete fuel and lubricant allotment yet.

I also did not have the required ammunition, and much of the ammunition we did have was old, exposed to weather long before I received it, and many rounds failed to fire and the guns became jammed. I also did not have replacement bulbs for the instrument panels, and my landing lights were just being placed along the runway. On top of all of that, our monthly fuel delivery was over a week late.

Kammhuber wanted no excuses; he wanted the fighters up to engage the enemy that he said was reported inbound. Well, following orders we went up and saw nothing resembling an enemy plane, and the ground radar controllers were just as perplexed. We did manage to lose a few fighters due to mechanical failures, crash-landing, one crew bailed out, some landed in fields, one hit the North Sea. It was a disaster, and I was waiting for the other shoe to drop.

However, despite this episode, things were not all bad. We were steadily scoring kills, and we had our one hundredth night victory on April 26, 1941. While modest when compared to some of the day fighter units, we were proud. We had been in existence unofficially for a year at that time, active as a designated unit for ten months, and had to beg, borrow, or acquisition everything we had. I was quite proud. By 1943 we were very well established.

We were both responsible for the defense of Germany both night and day, and it was a job full of problems. In August 1943 I asked Galland, who was general of fighters, to give me a command somewhere at the front; I could not take Hitler and Göring anymore. He understood completely, but he told me that not even he could cut me orders. This had to come from Milch, that I was "hot property."

Not long after this [April 26, 1941] I was ordered to Hamburg for another meeting, so I took off from Deelen in my Me-110. Kammhuber wanted complete updates on all aspects of the operations, and Martini was there to address my communications concerns. I learned about the new transmission and receiver units we were getting soon. These were more powerful, working on a narrower bandwidth, and also much lighter by half in weight, which was always good news.

I also received a briefing on the new radar systems for the fighters. These were the advanced airborne radars, such as the early *Morgenstern*, *Flensburg*, and advanced SN-2 [Lichtenstein] sets. We were also going to receive new devices to detect enemy bombers from their exhaust emissions, the early *Naxos* detection system, and so forth. This was all very technical, even over my head, but I had the experts to work out the details. These guys were just brilliant.

On my return flight to Deelen, I was informed over the radio that an unknown aircraft was flying in my area at the same altitude, so I was vectored to the location. I could not see it, and I opened the throttles, but could not catch it, either. When I landed, I saw the plane in question; a Spitfire had landed on the airstrip after its pilot, Peter Tomlinson, had an engine failure.

It was not often that one was able to have a drink and speak with the enemy, especially a Spitfire pilot, so I invited him to the officers' club. Fraternization was greatly discouraged, but nearly all of us fighter pilots abandoned that taboo. I had met with downed British bomber crews on several occasions, and I had a great time with them. I even remained in contact with a few of them long after the war.

He and I spoke at length, and I found him a very likable person. We connected again after the war, as he was living in South Africa. We went to visit him, and he came to Saint Ulrich and visited us. We became great friends until he died. It was interesting to speak with an old enemy, down on his luck, or perhaps lucky since he survived the war.

I suppose I should mention the events of November 1941. Udet had committed suicide, which shocked the entire nation, not to mention the fighter community. The official story was that he had died testing a new aircraft, which everyone knew was a lie. I was called to attend his funeral, and as a man I admired, truly a friend, I went. Mölders was ordered to attend also, and he flew from his base in the Ukraine. His He-111 crashed in bad weather, and no sooner did we bury Udet, we were burying this great man also, and he was the first recipient of the Diamonds. It was a very somber mood indeed, and we were freezing, it was so cold.

At Mölders' funeral, I was in the honor guard with Galland, Schalk, Lützow, and others. This was when Göring appointed Galland *general der jagdflieger*, and Galland's best friend and competitor was barely cold. He was later promoted to *generalleutnant*, and I guess the rest is well-chronicled history. Galland did make great contributions and changes to the fighter arm. We all benefitted from his genius and experience. However, I sometimes think that the war may have been over sooner had a less-able man been in charge. I guess we will never know.

Then the worst thing imaginable happened; the Japanese bombed Pearl Harbor, and we were also at war with America. There was not a single officer I knew who truly believed that we could win the war now. It was just going to be impossible, and many of us openly discussed what we thought Hitler would do to negotiate a peace. Of course, these discussions were done in private and only amongst trusted fellow officers. I knew that it would only be a matter of time before we began fighting American aircraft as well.

I would have to say that 1942 was the apex of our night fighting success. This was before the British began developing effective countermeasures, as well as night fighters of their own. But we also had an almost unlimited budget, great men, and a new line of aircraft, as I saw the Me-210 and 410 as the next generation of short-range night fighters. In addition, I had perfected the aerial component to the Kammhuber Line, and successes were mounting. This success continued through 1943, and I was pleased.

In January, I visited the Heinkel works and spoke with Professor [Ernst] Heinkel personally, as he was developing the He-219 twin-engine fighter. He was of the opinion that it would be a good night fighter, so Kammhuber asked that I accompany him and look at it. We flew to Rostock, which was one of the worst places to be during the later British bombings. We were both very impressed with the fighter, but due to delays from Milch's office, and other factors, we were late getting them, and we did not really get enough to staff all of the units fully.

Right after the launching of Operation Cerberus, which was Galland's planning for the air umbrella over the *Prinz Eugen*, *Scharnhorst, and Gneisenau,* a superb operation by any standard, I received orders regarding a similar operation. We were to fly cover for the *Prinz Eugen and Admiral Scheer*, which were to leave Wilhelmshaven and go to Norway. The Royal Navy ruled the North Sea, so this was definitely a mission of great importance. The mission was a great success, although we lost two Me-110s, and we never learned what happened to them.

In June [1942] I was ordered to report to Galland as a member of his staff. I reported and was told to fly to Vinitza in the Ukraine, which was where Göring's staff was located. From there I went to Crete, where I was to organize an aerial escort for our transport and supply ships to North Africa. The most interesting part of this operation was that I had no specific orders, no plans, and when we landed in Heraklion, we had no base.

My radioman Walz asked what we were supposed to do, and at just that time, British bombers appeared, heading at low altitude right for the air field. I told Walz to get off and run, and we were just out of the blast radius when the bombs fell, and one blew up my Me-110. I was pretty damned angry. We also lost our suitcases, uniforms, personal items, everything went up.

We were taken care of by the local garrison, and Kesselring arrived in his Do-17, and we spoke. He agreed that the entire mission was a waste, and although I could not fly back with him, he would send the bomber back for Walz and I. I went on some sightseeing tours at Knossos, and just relaxed until the next day, when his plane arrived for Walz and I.

I arrived back at Deelen two days later, and after a few organizational issues, was ordered to join Kammhuber in Venice for a meeting in mid-July. We were to meet with Italian general Bielo, who was in charge of the Italian night fighters, a pretty pathetic group. We were supposed to serve as advisors, but what they needed was a complete reorganization program. I could not believe that they were even considered operational, although their hearts were in it, their experience and expertise were somewhat lacking, to put it mildly. Well, at least the hotel was nice, very first rate.

We left on July 18, and I was asked to submit a report. That was perhaps some of the most entertaining reading the Air Ministry ever received. In fact, I was told by one of the staff officers that when Milch read the six-page report, they could hear him laughing all the way down the corridor. I guess he enjoyed it. However, the report was very unflattering, and the result prompted a visit from our ally to see an effective night fighter operation.

The following month I was visited by General Bielo at the air field at Echterdingen. We gave him the complete tour, from the aircraft, men, radar apparatus, and I explained the air network, while Kammhuber explained the ground defenses that enhanced the defensive positions stretching across Europe, to include the Kammhuber Line with the flak batteries and fighters working in conjunction. I could see that he was quite impressed, and to his credit he asked dozens of questions, all technical or tactical in nature, and his adjutant took notes.

In August I met again with Jeschonnek and Milch, and we had many discussions, but the most important part was our relationship with the navy. We had a spy ship, a steamer in the North Sea, packed with all of the necessary radar and communications equipment, and it worked as a floating early warning system and controller platform. I had also worked with Deutsche Bahn, and we had a special train, fitted with special railcars. One contained radio communications gear, one for the pilots' sleeping quarters, a library, and a galley for preparing meals.

I had assigned [*Oberleutnant* Heinrich Prince zu Sayn-] Wittgenstein as the first commander of the "Dark Night Train," and they were operating out of Russia at first. I had special orders issued for another such train for the west, hence my meeting with [Hans] Jeschonnek and Milch. I had to travel from the Black Sea to Finland, then Norway, and through the Balkans. These inspections were also to look at any major gaps in the defense network, and we had quite a few, to be honest. I visited every major city and town, and covered the entire Eastern Front. I spoke with all of the pilots, and gathered their reports and recommendations.

These trips were good for another reason; I was able to reunite with many old friends, such as the *kommodoren* I had spent time with a decade earlier when we were all just young fresh student pilots, especially Trautloft, Hrabak, and Lützow. I was able to meet some of the outstanding day fighter aces, speak with them, and learn of their hardships. The men in North Russia, and especially the men in Finland and Norway, suffered miserably.

This was when I also first met Robert *Ritter* von Greim, who was highly respected throughout the Luftwaffe. We stayed up late after dinner, and he presented a fine red wine, one of my weaknesses, and I learned much from this meeting. Greim knew that the war was lost in the east, he said so in so many words.

Greim had no faith in Hitler and had never joined the party, and he hated Göring, thought of Milch as a lackey; Jodl was an idiot and Göbbels was a crippled hanger-on, and he said flatly that Himmler was psychotic, and that [Martin] Bormann was someone who needed a sense of self-importance. He hated them all. I realized that I was in the presence of a man who saw the future, and knew the past. I left that visit with a deep sense of foreboding for my country. I trusted Greim's instincts, and I respected his insights.

I finished the tour, and I sent my report to Jeschonnek, including the recommendation that all the medium bombers be retrofitted as night fighters, at least the Ju-88 and Do-17 models, as newer models came on line to the front. He called me in for a meeting a few days later, and we discussed it in great detail. He agreed with my recommendations, and issued the appropriate paperwork, giving me authorization to do what I needed.

We had also increased the numbers of all of our radar units, both ground-to-air and air-to-air units in the fighters, and the entire network grew even more, from the North Sea to the Adriatic Sea and northern Mediterranean Sea. When the British developed their radar detection systems, we developed devices to home in on their detection beams. Then they created a disruption method, which we countered, and so on.

The British also introduced "window," also called "chaff," which they first used over Hamburg and were nothing more than half-meter long strips of tin and aluminum dropped from the bombers to disrupt the onboard radars in the night fighters. The first few times it worked, but then a few of our pilots figured out how to beat that method. It also interfered with the radar-guided AA guns and searchlights, which had to go to manual operation.

The pilots learned quickly that when the screen went snowy, they just focused upon the darker shadows, which were the bombers, barely visible through the visual static. This technique was not new to us, since we had discovered this tactic when the navy developed the first versions of our radars, so we knew how to counter this problem.

I also knew that there would be greater losses of planes and pilots, thus a greater demand placed upon the training schools, and as such, the inevitable drain of aircraft and crews for the night fighters. At that point I became depressed, and for the first time began doubting that we would win the war, but I kept those thoughts to myself.

I only flew occasionally for about three years to remain current, and after my promotion to *oberstleutnant* on January 1, 1943, I was transferred to the General Staff where I became 1A, which is chief of operations in the staff of Air Fleet Reich at Wannsee, west of Berlin. In fact, Galland's office was right down the hall from me, so we had many personal moments, and I learned a lot about the political intrigues from him. We often had to visit Göring at the East Prussian HQ he had. Galland and I spent many hours with him on his private train, which he called "*Amerika*."

We heard about Stalingrad over the radio. It was unbelievable, as the magnitude of this disaster was not lost upon us. We knew that we could not win the war at that point, not with North Africa being overrun. It was only a matter of time, just as Greim had foreseen. I was then ordered to create a control center in Bucharest, Romania, by Kammhuber. This was to enhance the day fighter defenses of the Ploesti oil fields, which were our greatest strategic production of petroleum. I inspected that facility and was very impressed with all of the organization.

This was when I began working with *Generaloberst* Alexander Löhr, whose HQ was in Belgrade. He was a completely different type from what I was used to, well educated, and he understood the science behind my project. He gave me complete and unquestioned support. He and I boarded a Ju-52 to meet with Marshal Ion Antonescu, the Romanian leader. We discussed the air defenses and other matters, and when we were finished, Löhr returned to Belgrade.

I also had many opportunities to meet with the German ambassador to Romania, Rolf *Freiherr* von Killinger, a man with whom I had absolutely nothing in common. Ironically, I was awarded the Bulgarian Commander's Cross, and Kammhuber received a similar award from King Boris. We also received the *Virtutea Aeronautica*, which was a high honor.

There were many interesting people I interacted with, and my adjutant was *Major* Douglas Pitcairn, a successful pilot from the Russian Front and a real character.[16] Then, while traveling to Rome for a meeting with Kammhuber, I heard that we had lost Africa.

Sicily followed in two months, and the news only grew worse. Then I was invited to meet the pope, but of course I had to decline. That would not have gone over well with my superiors.

Not long after this trip I was again called to Karinhall to meet with Göring, where I was to give a detailed briefing on the status of the night fighters. In attendance was a lot of brass, all of the names I have mentioned before, and this meeting was an evaluation of my forces, and whether or not Göring was going to continue funding the night fighters. I was not too surprised, as the momentum of the night bombing had increased, especially after the thousand bomber raids started.

I impressed upon Göring that we had inflicted an average of 7 to 10 percent casualties per mission. I did not count those aircraft knocked down by flak, just my night fighters. The *Wilde Sau* also had their own records when they came into the picture, which I kept separate from my files. This meant that on a great night we could knock down seven to ten out of a hundred bombers, sometimes even more, which was rare, but it had been achieved. The ratio was an actual average; combining all components in the night defenses was between 10 to 18 percent, which was very solid.

Then he suddenly broke up the meeting, took Lörzer out with him, leaving Kammhuber and I sitting there, confused. A few minutes later he came back with Lörzer, and I knew that he had taken some medication, a stimulant of some kind. I had heard about his drug addiction, but I suppose this was the first time I ever saw it firsthand. Then Göring gave me a friendly order; he wanted a special unit of my night fighters equipped to chase and shoot down the RAF Mosquitoes that flew not only as bombers, but also worked as the master of ceremonies, and later as night fighters. They were much faster than any of our fighters.

Göring also said that he gave Galland the same order. Both of us were to have specialized single-engine fighters, whose only mission was to catch these intruders. I understood what he was saying, and I completely agreed with him, and I told him so. However, I pointed out all of the problems with that request, and without getting too technical, as he tended to yawn a lot when anyone did, I put it in the simplest terms I could. We just did not have any fighters fast enough to chase down the Mosquitoes, unless we were lucky enough to catch one.

This was when he told me that he had ordered a German version, also made of wood, which he also called the *Moskito*, and this would be his answer to the British "wooden wonder." I then asked him how long would it take to get this new fighter on line, and he said that he had spoken to Professors Willi Messerschmitt and Ernst Heinkel, and both were to create designs for his approval. He thought about six months before the first prototype would be ready. Well, I just nodded my head, wondering where he thought he would have the time or the trees to make his new weapon. It was my time to yawn at that point, and Kammhuber, sitting next to me, just touched his foot to mine, as if to say, "Just humor him."

One of the most unique events to occur, in which I was somewhat involved, was in June 1943, when Hajo Herrmann entered the picture. He was a bomber pilot, an outstanding airman on all accounts, and he had an idea. He wanted to create a night fighter unit that used day fighters, using searchlights to switch the blacked-out cities into brilliantly illuminated locations to hunt British bombers. I know that he was in discussions with Galland, because Dolfo called me, and I spoke with him about the method. At first I was skeptical, but Hajo had some great ideas.

I recalled my own experience flying at night, without any specialized equipment, nothing at all, just as Herrmann wanted to do. However, his plan was different. He would fly the faster Me-109s and Fw-190s, using the brightly lit cities to illuminate the bombers from below, while his pilots flew above them. This way they would be silhouetted against any clouds, their shadows easy to see. Once they were caught by radar, and then tracked by searchlights, the day fighters would be able to get them on visual contact, no onboard radar being needed. This meant less cost to the program, but a higher loss ratio for day fighters and even pilots.

My concern was not about the practicality of such a program; I knew that they would have successes, but I was worried about the attrition rate we may suffer, due to the fact that night flying is dangerous enough without being in battle. But, since his pilots would all be instrument qualified, some even former bomber or reconnaissance pilots, I had no objections.

Göring was even very excited, and I think he was wondering if I would have any objections about sharing the night fighter role. I assured him that I would enjoy any and all assistance, once the logistics and tactics were worked out. I did not want to have just another night fighter operation going on, with aircraft in the sky without any command and control. It was crowded enough with the RAF up there. I wanted to have both methods, and all units, working together to be the most effective.

I knew how difficult it would be to get the proper relationship established between Herrmann and the flak units. I had my own stories, and he had his. Well, we met and discussed this. I was very impressed by his concept as he detailed it. I knew that he was going to have a lot of trouble convincing the flak gunners to not fire upward into enemy bomber formations, until the orders were given. I also knew that the *gauleiter* were going to be hard to convince that lighting their cities under bombardment was a sound idea.

I made a few calls, and gave Herrmann some contacts, and he had a meeting with Jeschonnek, Milch, and even Göring on the matter, and he finally received the assistance he needed. He was fortunate that we in the night fighters already had a good, established relationship with all parties concerned. I suggested that he meet with Kammhuber, and that managed to seal the deal, so to speak.

Herrmann, who is still a great friend to this day, managed to get his single-seat fighters in the air, and they did have some great success. Unfortunately, later in 1944 his JG.300 was increased into additional units, such as JG.301 and 302, and then they became day fighter units in 1944 with the Home Defense. I saw the merits of his method, especially from a psychological standpoint. Once we worked out a method of overlapping belts and zones of responsibility, the RAF began feeling the triple hammer blows of both fighter groups and flak.

The way it worked was quite simple. My radar-guided night fighters would engage the enemy outside the target zones, on the outer periphery of the grids. Then Herrmann's *Zahme Sau* [Tame

Boar], using twin-engine and even single-engine fighters would shadow the formations, usually flying in the stream formation. They provided accurate plots for direction, altitude, speed, and other critical details. These were sent via radio to the ground controller. They plotted the enemy and our units, and kept all informed.

This started in July 1943, when I was promoted to *oberst*; Jeschonnek committed suicide in August and *General* Günther Korten replaced him. This was not an easy relationship, as Korten ordered the night fighters to also actively engage the American daylight raids. This was not really feasible for a number of reasons. Pitting Me-110s against Thunderbolts, Mustangs, Lightnings, and Spitfires was already proven to be a flawed concept. Then, in September, the Allies invaded Italy.

Once the bombers passed through the radar-guided fighters, they would be engaged by the flak units, and then on prearranged signals, the flak would stop firing, and the *Wilde Sau* using the lights from below would then attack the survivors. Due to their short range, they usually carried drop tanks and could engage for almost two hours. The twin-engine fighters could land and refuel, and then catch the enemy bombers on the way out. Sometimes the *Wilde Sau* units scattered throughout the Kammhuber Line had time to rearm and refuel, then engage the enemy again as they left the target area.

I can only imagine what those poor RAF boys were enduring in their minds, with three to six waves of fighters hitting them, on top of the flak. Some of our twin-engine fighters would follow them into British airspace, shooting them down when they thought they were safe. Well, by late 1943, and especially in 1944, the tables were turned, because the British began sending their own night fighters into our airspace to engage our night fighters. We lost quite a few great pilots that way. This was when we had to change our methods, especially in using the runway lights, which were a dead giveaway to enemy planes hunting us down.

The successes of the *Wilde Sau* brought Herrmann the Oak Leaves and Swords, as well as a position on the General Staff. It also almost got him killed when he was hit by our own flak once, and he was blown out of his fighter at very high altitude. It also brought an order from Göring for him to stop flying, which was an order all of us dreaded. Interestingly enough, although not without precedent, Herrmann did not obey, and he still flew. Herrmann actually scored nine kills as a *Wilde Sau* pilot, on top of his great record of sinking seventy thousand or so tons of shipping. He led an interesting group of volunteers, as they were all volunteers. He was, as I said, a great aviator, and a very brave man.

During this time, I was informed by Galland that a rumor I had heard was in fact true, that Himmler wanted to create his own elite SS air force. He did not think that the Luftwaffe, or even the *Wehrmacht* in total for that matter, was exhibiting enough National Socialist zeal. I could not believe that, and Galland just laughed it off, but then he grew serious. Himmler was not one to challenge. Fortunately, this infantile suggestion later died its own death, and we were the better for it.

In choosing the night fighter pilots later in the war, I did the same as I had in the beginning; I visited the destroyer school. There I created a report for the standards for the foundation of the night fighters, and several pilots came forward. We gave volunteer notifications later. Also from the battle units, and later even from the fighter units, came the best men, including Hajo Herrmann and the Wild Boars to take their shot.

Such men as Prince Heinrich von zu Sayn-Wittgenstein, Prince Egmont zur Lippe-Weissenfeld, Helmut Lent, Werner Streib, Paul Zorner, Hans-Joachim Jabs, and Heinz-Wolfgang Schnauffer, and the others, were simply the best at conventional night fighting. It was their success and the propaganda that followed that lured young recruits from flight schools into the night fighter program, more so I believe than my personal lectures and visits.

Our night fighter force was impressive, working through intelligence, radar and flak commands; we had our intercept monitors and search reporting service with radar for all of them. We even used coast watchers who used acoustic listening devices to pick up any noise of incoming aircraft. There was never, at any time, any mention of the high-frequency war, it was all too new. That was when I was transferred to the *Luftwaffenbefehlshaber Mitte* in Berlin, and became more or less an administrator.

From this position, I finally had access to all of the intelligence, ours and the enemy data. This newfound wealth of information taught me a lot. It taught me just how little real, valuable intelligence we were being given at the front. I could plot the enemy coming in from their bases, our spotters kept track of their direction, while the shadow fighters monitored their speed and altitude. All of these factors were on a glass wall map, where lights indicated the positions of friend and foe alike. We could listen to their transmissions, knew their codes and call signs, and could usually determine their targets half of the time.

We were also constantly improving the science and technology. The way it worked was like this: the ground radar would pick up the British bombers coming in over the North Sea and give their location, speed, and later, with better radar, their altitude every fifty miles. We could take off, vector at the coordinates that we received en route, and the onboard radar operator would then cut his radar on, which would help us find the enemy in pitch darkness.

Once a bomber was picked up, the radar operator guided the pilot in and the attack was made visually. Later, the radar operator would shut the scope off, as the British had detectors that would pick up the beam, and then home in on the source, and this would guide their own night fighters into vectoring positions against our night fighters. It was really quite exciting, but very dangerous.[17]

The Kammhuber Line was one of the best actions undertaken by the *Reichsverteidigungs-dienst* (Reich Defense Service) and the Luftwaffe. The night fighters complemented the overall defense network, although we were later to become the most important component, and were expected to destroy the lion's share of enemy bombers. As the war progressed, we learned from our early mistakes.

Also, you must remember that there were many continuous upgrades to all of the systems, to include creating better jamming devices to prevent the enemy from detecting us, and then also jamming our radars, or even sending deceptive signals to throw off our fighters and ground control centers. I would say that there were perhaps more scientists and specialists working within the night fighter technology area than in any other part of the military program.[18]

I had all of this equipment that was to be moved, and could fall into Soviet hands. I ordered those items that could not be taken with us to be destroyed immediately, and then the personnel evacuated. I valued the people over the technology, which was state of the art for that time. Today, there is no difference between night and day fighter aircraft anymore. They see each other via radar and thermal imagery; they can engage each other without a pilot seeing his target. Because of the new technologies, you cannot compare the aerial warfare of today with the primitive methods we used in the Second World War, which was the same difference as our war versus the Great War.

We had managed to build up our ground-control intercept relays into a formidable defensive network, complementing the Kammhuber Line. The greatest feat I had to contend with was working through the various personalities and egos within the various military districts. Trying to coordinate these military commanders, especially the flak artillery unit commanders, was a primary job all on its own. I was finally able to get a lot of these things done, especially when Kammhuber and Göring began making telephone calls on my behalf. Göring may not have been good for very much, but he did have a way of removing obstacles from my path.

The men became better, the technology as well, and the aircraft became more specialized and capable of performing the tasks required, and our ability to cooperate with the ground defense, which was always a great problem in the beginning, began to work itself out. We knew that we had the right program with which to inflict heavy damage against the British. All we had to do was hope that Göring and others in Berlin kept their hands out of it and let us do our jobs. Inevitably, this was not to be the case. [19]

We also had a great amount of support from Hitler, and especially Göring, with regard to resources, at least until 1943 or 1944. We were able to develop our ground-to-air, and also air-to-air radar systems, especially the upgraded *Lichtenstein*, to include *Himmelbett* supplementing *Wotan* from the early days, *Freya* and WG, among others. [20]

For me, and Germany, 1944 was a watershed year, and so many things happened, and none of them good. We were losing the air war on both fronts where the day fighters were outnumbered, and we night fighters were also being outmanned. On July 20, I had just finished a full day's paperwork at my Wannsee office when the phone rang. I thought it was Galland, calling me back about a report he had sent to me. It was not Galland.

This was when I learned that Stauffenberg had tried to kill Hitler. I was in shock to be honest, as I had met and spoken with Stauffenberg the previous week, regarding the Operation Valkyrie plans for the military defense of Berlin, should there be any repeat of the 1918–1919 revolution. All the senior leaders from all branches of the military were briefed on this plan. The assassination attempt not only concerned me from a professional standpoint, Stauffenberg was my wife's cousin. I first met him in 1936. I liked him very much.

He epitomized the German officer; he was good looking, very devoted to his family, and a devout Catholic. He was well educated and well spoken. I wondered about my wife, my family, and even myself. I had no idea just how deep the Gestapo would go, but if I knew them at all, no one would be safe. I knew my father-in-law was anti-Nazi throughout, and as an *oberst* from the Great War, and the officer in charge who ordered the army to shoot Hitler and the rest during the 1923 *Putsch*, I knew his days were numbered— hence the connection that disturbed me.

Well, Berlin was sealed off, I was given my orders to handle things, and I answered to *Generaloberst* Hans Stumpff, who was at that time my immediate boss, and he placed me in charge of all of Berlin. I was in my room, with my pistol, prepared to do what I had to, but I was not going to join the great many who had already been arrested, and subsequently shot. As history shows, those shot were the lucky ones.

By 1944 I was having my own problems with Hitler and Göring, and I needed an escape. I spoke to Galland about this problem. Galland understood my plight, as he was having his own problems with them, and he was well aware of my connection to Stauffenberg, and I was concerned that my old acquaintance *General* [Werner] Kreipe was not my ally. This fear was later dispelled. Well, Galland did me a great service, and in September 1944, I became Fighter Pilot Leader-Balkans, which included Greece, Romania, Bulgaria, and Yugoslavia, and I returned on a few occasions to observe my empire.

While there, I received reports about the Stauffenberg family being arrested, the children taken away, and the events that occurred at Plötzensee Prison. It was medieval to say the least. I called my wife as often as I could, just to see if the family was doing well. I just never knew when Himmler and his henchmen would continue their roundups. I am certain that Galland saved my life. At least if I died it would not be at the hands of the SS or Gestapo. The one bright light was that Pitcairn was still there, so I had a smiling face to greet me.

The radar systems in Greece to the Peloponnesus were within my "empire" as well. I was initially situated at Pancevo, near Belgrade, on this second Balkan assignment, and this meant that I was responsible for the defense of these countries night and day against hostile air raids. Most of these raids were conducted by American day bombers, mostly B-24 types, and a few B-17s, which were increasing after the Allies took Sicily and then invaded Italy.

This job was important but it did not last long. Later, in October 1944, we corrected our positions, because all these fighter units were withdrawn to the Home Defense Force of Germany proper over a period of time, and all during this short period we had constant trouble with partisans and the Russians.

As the situation deteriorated, I had all female Reich workers sent home by train, as this was not a place where they needed to be. To get to the train they had to cross the Danube River. Well, some vehicles were not so lucky, one struck a mine, drowning all the women onboard. Some of my girls came back, after having climbed out of the river. They decided that they would stay and fight, so we trained them on the weapons.

In Pancevo, because we did not have enough regular soldiers, all of the support staff were hastily trained on the infantry weapons we had, and I had helped establish defensive perimeters. We also had established foot and reconnaissance patrols to locate and report on any enemy activity. The women were the last line of defense, and as appalling as this was to me professionally, and personally, it made perfect sense logically. However, I then ordered them to try and get out again, and this time they called from Vienna. They were safe! My heart felt much better for them.

We had several engagements when the partisans attacked, and this lasted for several days. Some of these partisans wore German uniforms, which was a real problem. I flew a *Storch* to try and locate a band of them after we received somewhat reliable information that they were going to attack us. Once I saw anything of interest, I would radio to the ground troops, who would be waiting in ambush.

On this plane with me was a *major* with a machine gun, just in case we did come across anything. Well, we saw some, but this *major* only fired one shot and did not know how to operate the weapon. He was not a combat officer. I was furious, so I flew low again and fired my pistol out the window as I passed overhead. This gave the German soldiers and the civilians we recruited the idea of where they were.

As I came in to land, there was a small hill between the Germans and partisans, and neither could see the other, but they were headed into each other. The *Storch* landed in the wet mud, and tipped over forward, and we were upside down hanging by our straps. The soldiers got to us and broke us out, and soon afterward we captured about thirty or so partisans. I handed them over to the army commandant.

I had the reports coming in from all up and down the Eastern Front. Romania switched sides and joined the Allies, and then Bulgaria also defected from the Axis. As the war closed in on us we retreated towards Vienna, and thus ended my command of the Balkans. I received last-minute calls and a few radio messages from my subordinates all over the Balkans, following my orders to retreat. Most were encircled, and these calls were farewells. I never heard from any of these men again, their fates not too hard to understand. My empire had all but dissolved, and I had jaundice.

I had my faithful Me-110 blown up, as there was no fuel anyway, and I joined my collective troop in vehicles on the drive out of hell. After a while we came across a tank, and we breathed easier when it turned out to be German. Well, we all then crossed the Tamis River, and no sooner had the bridge been blown, we saw Soviet tanks on the opposite bank where we had been. That was close to be sure.

That was the first time in my life, as a nonsmoker, I asked for a cigarette, and I had more than one.

We reached Vienna, and the SS Home Guard was stopping all persons coming in from the east. They were going to take me and my staff and form a small unit to work with them. The highest rank was an undecorated, and obviously inexperienced *unterscharführer*, and I told him in no uncertain terms that I had my own orders, and to basically mind his own business.

I know that my decorations and rank were intimidating to him, so we were given a guide through the city. This was when I ran into my old commanding officer, *Generalmajor* [Albrecht] von Massow. He was the flight center and training commander, and when he asked me if I wanted a job, I said "yes." That month through November was quite eye opening for many reasons.

I was in a state of shock when I saw just how cavalier these people were operating, and I could not understand why. The Russians had crossed the Oder River, and it was only a matter weeks, if we were lucky, before they hit Berlin. East Prussia was under threat. Then I heard some of the radio broadcasts coming out of the Propaganda Ministry, promising that the new weapons were going to the front, and that our brave armies had stopped or crushed another enemy division here, or a battalion there.

I looked at these other staff types, and the civilians, who just had no idea. I then suggested that all the staff and workers be trained on infantry weapons, because they would need them. You would have thought that I had just suggested that we celebrate May Day. They were not comprehending the reality of it all.

In December, Hitler launched his offensive in the west, which proved to be just another futile effort, and Operation *Bodenplatte* on New Year's Day was another disaster, and they just seemed to mount. Then on January 19, 1945, there was the Fighters' Revolt, and it only really took that name after the war, by the way. I think that Galland, Trautloft, and Steinhoff can provide more information on that.

This was when Galland lost his job, and that fact probably saved his life. Afterward I had a call from Lützow, just as he was leaving for Italy, to where he had been banished. He asked me to have his adjutant bring a few things before he left. I had known that man for a decade, and I admired him. I also felt sorry for him and the others.

The last few months of the war were a trying time for me personally, and after a fright, my older sister Ilsa and her family managed to get out of East Prussia, but my father, who was with them, did not escape. He has not been heard from since. I also called upon old friends, and managed to organize a few air evacuations of civilians and friends of mine who were in danger.

I personally flew one of the twin-engine supply planes, and loaded up some people. We had to get them out, especially the women and children. We had all heard of what was happening to the women and young girls who were captured by the enemy. Then there was the bombing of Dresden. I ended up riding a train to the south, to attend a crazy school for no good reason, and I was ironically with *Generalmajor* Schumacher, whom I had known for years, when we heard the radio broadcast from Hitler.

This was Easter Sunday, and he was ordering the final resistance, all civilians and disbanded military to create groups, called *Wehrwolf*, to target the advancing Allies on all fronts. I was then ordered to organize the resistance movement. Well, I asked this school leader if I could borrow his car and driver, as I had to have clearance from my Luftwaffe superior Kreipe to take on another task, non-Luftwaffe related. Believe it or not, he actually gave me his car, with the promise that I would send it back if I could not do the job, or come back with it if I could.

This was good, because Kreipe was in Bavaria as was my family. As I was leaving, this commandant threatened to "find me" if I failed to fulfill my national duty. I thought this odd, since I had spent over a decade serving my country, and this clown was not even in the military, but I believe one of the SA old guard. Well, I found Kreipe, and since he had no use for me, he told me to go home and be with my family. This was great, and all I had to do was check back on a daily basis in case a job surfaced.

I then did receive orders to go to Munich and join von Greim's staff, so I did. Munich was in chaos as a coup was underway, Greim was ordered by Hitler to Berlin, and Göring had been fired. On

April 26, Hanna Reitsch flew him into Berlin, where he received his new orders, and was shot in the process. Grievously wounded, and now a *generalfeldmarschall*, he flew out of Berlin as the Russians were crawling through the streets.

While Greim was on his odyssey, I was meeting with Trautloft, hoping that he may know something about my new job. He did not, so I went to see the *kommandant* at Bad Aibling, who thought I was supposed to inform him of my top secret assignment. I was stunned, because I thought he was the man to tell me my duties. I ended up with old friends, where we learned that Hitler was dead. The family, all anti-Nazis from the start, broke out the best champagne and liquor, as they had been saving it for years for such an event.

The Americans came and I surrendered, but there is a good story here. I had bumped into a sergeant and a lieutenant, and I addressed the officer and identified myself. The officer was very professional and understanding. They took me into custody, and I joined some other officers, including Hungarians of all things, and one was a general, the other a colonel, I believe.

The next day the Hungarians were taken away, and I was outside. There were some concentration camp prisoners that were walking by, as a camp had existed nearby. The soldier guarding me handed his rifle to one of these men, and told him to shoot me. He just handed the rifle back and plodded along. I can say that I had never felt such a feeling of relief. Soon there were well over a thousand of us POWs marching off to an uncertain future. We entered the horse racing track—guarded only by a few tanks and troops, as there was no fence—joining fifteen thousand others.

There were no toilet facilities, washing areas, nothing. There were no barracks, no beds, just the ground. If we were lucky you got to lay on grass, otherwise the dirt track was your bed. We were given nothing to eat or drink for quite a few days. Soon afterward I was called in by an American captain and told I was the camp commander, as I was the senior ranking officer.

I found out that all but senior officers, unless they were SS, SA, Gestapo, or card-carrying NSDAP members, were given quick discharges. I was a colonel and staff officer, and all of us in field grade rank or above were held, pending further investigations. Within a few weeks, almost all of the prisoners had either been released or handed over for special treatment, pending war crimes trials.

Soon I was alone, and my two American captors, a captain and a lieutenant, were ordered to Austria. They drove me to Regensburg, which was the official discharge location for officers, or so I was told. Then we learned that no staff officers would be released from there, so we drove off again. Finally, my captors, feeling guilty, and understanding me and my situation, forged the proper paperwork and signed my release. Then they drove me to my family. They even fitted me with a civilian suit, and I dumped the uniform.

Later I rode a bicycle in my new clothes, with my fake discharge papers, through many American checkpoints, and had no problems. I wanted to see my sister and her family, just to see that all was well with them. The only problem I had was a checkpoint guard who stole my cigarette case I had been carrying for years, and my scarf. I missed that case, not because I really smoked, but because it had the Iron Cross First Class mounted on it, the one I managed to retrieve from the burned-out fighter on Crete. It also had names of my friends and each type of aircraft I had flown. It was more of a memento than anything else.

I confirmed that Irmgard and her family were fine, but Ilsa and her family did not make it at first. They were used as slave labor, until they were taken to Berlin, and then they managed to escape to the west. I tried here and there to find work to earn money, but after the war, no one dared hire a war criminal, as all of us were labeled. I tried to become a night guard in a factory to make enough money to survive, but I did not get that job. They did not dare employ me, even with all of my certificates, qualifications, and curriculum vitae. The next year in April I was tracked down, and ordered to report to the British garrison at Bielefeld. There was some question as to the legitimacy of my discharge, so I thought the jig was up.

But the British Army of the Rhine must have had certain information about me. They hired me as a "civil officer" in 1946 for a series of forty-seven stores not far from Bielefeld. I asked the *major*, "Do you know who I am?" and he answered "Yes," that he knew I had been a colonel in the air force and had the Knight's Cross.

226 THE GERMAN ACES SPEAK

He said that they were looking for people they could trust and were reliable. Germany had been partitioned under the Allied occupation, and the Americans and British wanted to get the German work force back into gear, to stabilize the economy. That was quite intelligent, simply due to the fact that the lack of work, high inflation, and the cost of living in Germany, rising after the First World War, were the reasons and methods by which the National Socialists came to power. The new enemy after the war was Communism, and a working, productive society was not very likely to start revolutions. So I became the boss of 145 German labor employees, and my boss was a Captain "R. E.," and after some time we became good friends. In the evenings I attended a school for tradesmen, and after some time, I passed the examination. I also took advanced English classes to improve in that language.

In 1948, I joined a German company, which was a branch of the medical and pharmaceutical industry, and after some further education I became a businessman. After that I changed over to a large printing-press company, which had started to produce playing cards. I started out as a lowly office employee, being promoted year after year until I finally became the manager of that company. Later, around 1954, we moved to Switzerland, where I obtained my private pilot's license. It was not that difficult, but it was forbidden in Germany at that time. Later, that was lifted and I flew again in Germany.

In 1961, a high-level employer with North American Aircraft Company in Los Angeles asked me during an international fighter pilots' meeting to join his company as a consultant in Germany. That was my chance to return to my old world. I liked my new career, especially when it came to reequipping the new German air force. The aircraft industry was something that I knew about, and I had all of the old contacts, and knew most of those working in the Defense Ministry.

In 1967, I was asked to work as a consultant to McDonnell Douglas. They courted me to leave North American, as they were also wanting to sell new military aircraft. I then became a consultant on an annual renewable basis, for a nice fee. I gave North American the contracted two weeks' notice. I really liked the fringe benefits as well. I was selling aircraft at airshows, basically. I was responsible for the German government buying the F-4 Phantom. So I was very busy in Bonn for the next twenty years working for MDC. I worked for them until I was seventy-five years old! It was a wonderful and most interesting time, and MDC in its policies towards its employees is, to say the very least, unique. I was also exposed to the corporate corruption, bribery, and other methods of doing business, things that I never participated in, and there were many investigations of all the companies involved. We were all cleared, but some others were less fortunate, as it should have been. Since my official retirement in 1986, I have been living here in Tyrol and I enjoy life in this beautiful countryside. This is the most beautiful part of Austria.

I had the great pleasure of knowing, commanding, and befriending the greatest pilots in history. And, on top of their bravery and skill, they were just really good men. They were real heroes, who knew the risks they were taking, and continued taking those risks without complaint. Even when completely exhausted, and even wounded, these fellows continued to climb back into the cockpit, for years on end. Yes, they were remarkable men.

When asked about the most memorable men I served with, I think of such characters as Prince Wittgenstein, who like Weissenfeld was a nobleman, yet not a National Socialist. He was typical of us pilots: simply apolitical. Collectively, we just did not care. Wittgenstein fought for Germany as had his family for five hundred years, and he was quite successful and a true gentleman, as were all of them. He was killed in the war during an attack on a bomber, as was Helmut Lent, who won the Diamonds with more than 100 victories, who died in an accident, along with Schnauffer, who had 121 victories and the Diamonds, who died in a traffic accident in France after the war, a tragic way to go.[21] Hans Jabs, a good friend of mine, finished the war with the Oak Leaves and 50 victories, but the best was definitely Schnauffer.

These were extraordinarily brave men. All of these men were under my command, and all were outstanding persons; full of idealism and first-rate hunters and great pilots. They were very distinguishable people, strong willed and very ambitious, but in a good sense. They were highly intelligent with immediate responses to crises, untiring and happiest when they were on flight operations. Each in his own way was a unique character, but all were very reliable, and I was proud to have known them.

Many dangers faced the night fighters, which the day fighters were fortunate not to have. We did not have to deal with enemy escort fighters until later in the war, as did the day fighter force, but we had the worry of our own flak, collision with our own planes, as well as the enemy bombers, the flares dropped by the British planes to blind us, which would also illuminate your plane, allowing the enemy gunners to shoot you down, the possibility of your onboard radar not working, leaving you blind, and flying across the sky locating black painted aircraft, it goes on. The fighting at night, I think, worked on the nerves more than fighting during the day; all of these unknowns would mentally wear you down.

My most interesting and dangerous missions were, of course, against the RAF. Later on, I was given the order by my boss that I was not to fly combat any longer because I was needed for the planning and development of the defense organization. I had seven confirmed victories, with a few more unconfirmed. Altogether I only flew ninety combat missions. This was not a great amount of time in the air, as I was given so many desk jobs and administrative duties.

I would say that the most memorable mission was perhaps the one with Steinhoff over Wilhelmshaven, in December 1939. That was really, at least in my opinion, the day that started the British on their path to a night bombing campaign against us. We shot down the majority of their Wellingtons, but that would later prove to boomerang back on us.[22]

From my first marriage, I have a son named Klaus, born in 1937, and today he manages a firm and the forests of his mother's lands in southern Bavaria. He has a daughter himself who is a manager of a large storehouse in Cologne. My daughter Irmgard, who was named after my sister, was born in 1940; she's married and lives in Munich and has two sons who are students at the University of Munich. [Eri,] my second wife, had two sons, both of whom I educated and prepared their careers.

One is a banker and married with a son and a daughter; the other was in the merchant marine and then served twenty years with Lufthansa as an instructor in their emergency division, and he also has a son and daughter. My third wife, Gisela, also has three sons; the eldest is a doctor in Hamburg. Her second son lives in Finland and is an artist, while the youngest owns his own company where he develops and constructs buildings, installations, and such all over the world for all kinds of fairs concerning German industry. None of them is married!

There is something interesting about Gisela; she is the widow of Hans "Assi" Hahn, a well-known fighter pilot during the Battle of Britain, and during the war, he achieved 108 victories and the Knight's Cross with Oak Leaves, but was shot down and captured over the Soviet Union in 1943, after making a forced landing. He spent over seven years in Russian labor camps until he was released. He wrote his autobiography titled *I Tell the Truth*. (I know that Erich Hartmann did not think much of his book, we discussed it a few times many years ago, and on that I have no comment, since I never experienced what they did.)

I first met Assi in 1937 when I joined JG.2 and we, including our wives, became good friends. Eri died of cancer in November 1982, and this was when I learned that Assi was also dying of cancer. Assi died in December 1982, five weeks after my second wife, and I was with him before he died. In late 1983 Gisela moved from Southern France, where she and Assi had their home, to Tyrol, and we started a life together. My second wife, Eri, and I built the home in Saint Ulrich where I now live with Gisela. I still wake in the morning and look at my mountain as I have breakfast.

Regarding my advice to young people, be grateful that we are living in relative peace; that you have a home and do not suffer from hunger. Take over the responsibility for your family and your country, be tolerant of everyone, stay honest and busy, and look forward to what you intend do with your life. Always have a target, and make sure that what you are fighting for is worthwhile. Life is short!

Appendix

German Pilots Who Scored Victories in World War II and the Spanish Civil War (not a complete listing).

Name	Victories	Units
Hartmann, Erich	352	JG.52
Barkhorn, Gerhard	301	JG.52, 6; JV.44
Rall, Günther	275	JG.52, 11, 300
Kittel, Otto	267	JG.54
Nowotny, Walter (Austria)	258	JG.54, 7, 101; Kdo Nowotny
Batz, Wilhelm	237	JG.52
Rudorffer, Erich	222 (Possibly 2 more)	JG.2, 54, 7
Bär, Heinrich	221	JG.51, 77, 1, 3; EJG.2; JV.44
Graf, Hermann	212	JG.52, 50, 11
Weissenberger, Theodor	208	JG.5, 7
Ehrler, Heinrich	208	JG.77, 5, 7
Schuck, Walter	206	JG.5, 7
Philipp, Hans	206	JG.76, 53, 54, 1
Hafner, Anton	204	JG.51
Lipfert, Helmuth	203	JG.52, 53
Krupinski, Walter	197	JG.52, 5, 11, 26; JV.44
Hackl, Anton	192	JG.77, 11, 26, 300
Stotz, Maximillian (Austria)	189	JG.54
Brendel, Joachim	189	JG.51
Kirschner, Joachim	188	JG.3, 27, 53
Steinhoff, Johannes	178	JG.52, 77, 7, 2, 26; JV.44
Josten, Günther	178	JG.51
Schack, Günther	174	JG.51, 3
Reinert, Ernst-Wilhelm	174	JG.77, 27, 7
Schmidt, Heinz	173	JG.52

Lang, Emil	173	JG.52, 54, 26
Brändle, Kurt	172	JG.53, 3
Ademeit, Horst	166	JG.54
Wilcke, Wolf-Dietrich	162	JG.53, 3, 1
Sturm, Heinrich	158	JG.52
Marseille, Hans-Joachim	158	LG.2; JG.52, 27
Thyben, Gerhard	157	JG.3, 54
Düttmann, Peter	152	JG.52
Beisswenger, Hans	152	JG.54
Gollob, Gordon (Austria)	150	ZG.76; JG.3, 77
Tegtmeier, Fritz	146	JG.54, 7
Wolf, Albin	144	JG.54
Tanzer, Kurt	143	JG.51
Müller, Friedrich-Karl	140	JG.53, 3
Trenkel, Rudolf	138	JG.77, 52
Setz, Heinrich	138	JG.27, 77
Gratz, Karl (Austria)	138	JG.52, 2
Wolfrum, Walter	137	JG.52
Weber, Karl-Heinz	136	JG.51, 1
Fönnekold, Otto	136	JG.52
Müncheberg, Joachim	135	JG.26, 51, 77
Waldmann, Hans	134	JG.52, 3, 7
Wiese, Johannes	133	JG.52, 77
Schall, Franz (Austria)	133	JG.52, 7
Grislawski, Alfred	133	JG.52, 50, 1, 53
Ihlefeld, Herbert	132 (9 in Spain)	LG.2; JG.77, 52, 77, 52, 103, 25, 11, 1
Dickfeld, Adolf	132	JG.52, 2, 11
Clausen, Erwin	132	LG.2; JG.77, 11
Borchers, Adolf	132	JG.77, 51, 52
Lemke, Wilhelm	131	JG.3
Hoffmann, Gerhard	130	JG.52
Sterr, Heinrich	129	JG.54
Eisenach, Franz	129	ZG.76; JG.54, 1

Dahl, Walter	129	JG.3, 300; EJG.2
Dörr, Franz	128	JG.77, 5
Oesau, Walter	127 (10 in Spain)	JG.51, 3, 2, 1
Zwernemann, Josef	126	JG.52, 77, 11
Hrabak, Dietrich	125	JG.76, 54, 52
Ettel, Wolf-Udo	124	JG.3, 27
Tonne, Wolfgang	122	JG.53
Weiss, Robert (Austria)	121	JG.54, 26
Schnaufer, Heinz-Wolfgang	121 (all night kills)	NJG.1, 4
Marquardt, Heinz	121	JG.51
Leie, Erich	121	JG.2, 51, 77
Obleser, Friedrich	120	JG.52
Wernicke, Heinz	117	JG.54
Norz, Jakob	117	NJG.2; JG.1, 5
Birkner, Hans-Joachim	117	JG.5, 52
Beerenbrock, Franz-Josef	117	JG.51
Lambert, August	116	SchG.1; SG.2; JG.77
Mölders, Werner	115 (14 in Spain)	JG.51, 53
Schrör, Werner	114	JG.3, 27, 54
Crinius, Wilhelm	114	JG.52, 27
Lent, Helmuth	113	ZG.76; NJG.1, 2, 3
Korts, Berthold	113	JG.52
Dammers, Hans	113	JG.52
Bühligen, Kurt	112	JG.2
Woidich, Franz	110	JG.27, 52, 400
Ubben, Kurt	110	JG.77, 2
Lützow, Günther	110 (5 in Spain)	JG.3; JV.44
Seiler, Reinhard	109 (9 in Spain)	JG.54, 104
Vechtel, Bernard	108	JG.51
Hahn, Hans	108	JG.54, 2
Bitsch, Emil	108	JG.3
Lucas, Werner	106	JG.3
Bauer, Viktor	106	JG.51, 3
Sachsenberg, Heinz	104	JG.52; JV.44
Boremski, Eberhard von	104	JG.3; EJG.1
Grasser, Hartmann (Austria)	103	ZG.52, 2; JG.51, 1, 210

Galland, Adolf	103	JG.27, 26; JV.44
Wurmheller, Josef	102	JG.53, 2
Ostermann, Max-Helmuth	102	JG.54
Mayer, Egon	102	JG.2
Geisshardt, Friedrich	102	LG.2; JG.77, 26, 27
Freytag, Siegfried	102	JG.77, 7
Wernitz, Ulrich	101	JG.54
Priller, Josef	101	JG.51, 26
Miething, Rudolf	101	JG.52
Steinbatz, Leopold (Austria)	99	JG.52
Späte, Wolfgang	99	JG.54, 7, 400; JV.44
Schleef, Hans	99	JG.3, 5, 4
Dähne, Paul-Heinrich	99+	JG.52, 11, 1
Bartels, Heinrich	99	JG.5, 27, 51
Rödel, Gustav	98	JG.27, 21
Hannig, Horst	98	JG.54, 2
Schleinhege, Hermann	97	JG.3, 54
Rademacher, Rudolf	97	JG.54, 7, 1
Mertens, Helmuth	97	JG.3
Höfemeier, Heinrich	96	JG.51, 4
Eichel-Streiber, Dirthelm von	96	JG.51, 26, 77, 27; JV.44
Münster, Leopold	95	JG.3
Resch, Rudolf	94 (1 in Spain)	JG.77, 52, 51
Müller, Rudolf	94	JG.5
Klöpper, Heinrich	94	JG.51, 1
Döbele, Anton	94	JG.54
Schnell, Siegfried	93	JG.54, 2
Rossmann Edmund	93	JG.52
Bennemann, Helmuth	93	JG.52, 53
Romm, Oskar	92	JG.51, 3
Loos, Gerhard	92	JG.54
Resch, Anton	91	JG.52
Schentke, Georg	90	JG.3
Kemethmüller, Heinz	89	JG.3, 54, 26
Rüffler, Helmuth	88	JG.3, 51, 7

Wöhnert, Ulrich	86	JG.54
Wachowiak, Friedrich	86+	JG.52, 3
Mader, Anton	86	ZG.76; JG.2, 11, 77, 54
Köppen, Gerhard	86	JG.52
Jennewein, Josef (Austria)	86	JG.26, 51
Zellot, Walter	85	JG.53
Preinfalk, Alexander	85	JG.77, 51, 53
Quast, Werner	84	JG.52
Ewald, Heinz	84	JG.52
Wessling, Otto	83	JG.3
Sayn-Wittgenstein, Heinrich Prince zu	83	KG.51; NJG.2, 5, 100, 3
Missner, Helmuth	82	JG.52, 54
Hasse, Horst	82	JG.51, 3
Grünberg, Hans	82	JG.3, 52, 7 JV.44
Götz, Hans	82	JG.54
Darjes, Emil	82	JG.54
Wagner, Rudolf	81	JG.51
Philipp, Wilhelm	81	JG.26, 54
Nemitz, Willi	81	JG.52
Broch, Hugo	81	JG.54
Beyer, Franz	81	JG.3
Bachnick, Herbert	80	JG.52
Würfel, Otto	79	JG.51
Nordmann, Karl-Gottfried	78	JG.51
Lücke, Max-Hermann	78	JG.4, 51
Krafft, Heinrich	78	JG.51, 3
Ewald, Wolfgang	78 (1 in Spain)	JG.52, 3
Eder, Georg-Peter	78	JG.51, 2, 1, 26, 7; EJG.2
Ohlrogge, Walter	77	JG.3, 7; EJG Süd, 1
Meier, Johann-Hermann	77	JG.26, 52
Haiböck, Josef	77	JG.26, 52, 3
Bonin, Hubertus von	77 (4 in Spain)	JG.26, 54, 52
Thiel, Edwin	76	JG.52, 51
Teumer, Alfred	76	JG.54, 7

Mietusch, Klaus	76	JG.26
Mayerl, Maxmilian	76	JG.51; EJG.1
Kroschinski, Hans-Joachim	76	JG.54
Wandel, Joachim	75	JG.54
Semelka, Waldemar	75	JG.52
Röhring, Hans	75	JG.53
Neumann, Karl	75	JG.5, 7
Grollmus, Helmuth	75	JG.54
Fassong, Horst Günther von	75	JG.51, 11
Bunzek, Johannes	75	JG.52
Meltzer, Karl-Heinz	74	JG.52
Haas, Friedrich	74	JG.52
Geisser, Otto	74	JG.52, 51
Frielinghaus, Gustav	74	JG.3; EJG.1
Schultz, Otto	73	JG.51
Michalski, Gerhard	73	JG.53, 4
Lindner, Anton	73	JG.51
Herget, Wilhelm	73 (57 at night)	ZG.76; NJG.3, 1, 4; JV.44
Schnell, Karl-Heinz	72	JG.51, 53; JV.44
Mink, Wilhelm	72	JG.51; EJG.1
Glunz, Adolf	72	JG.52, 26, 7
Scheel, Günther	71	JG.54
Rollwage, Herbert	71+	JG.53, 106
Heckmann, Alfred	71	JG.3, 26; JV.44
Fuss, Hans	71	JG.3, 51
Richter, Rudolf	70	JG.54
Omert, Emil	70	JG.3, 2, 77
Linz, Rudolf	70	JG.5
Lemke, Siegfried	70	JG.2
Lange, Heinz	70	JG.26, 54, 51
Joppien, Hermann-Friedrich	70	JG.51
Hofmann, Karl	70	JG.52
Zweigart, Eugen-Ludwig	69	JG.54
Weismann, Ernst	69	JG.51

Köhler, Armin	69	JG.27, 77
Kalden, Peter	69	JG.51
Tange, Otto	68	JG.51
Süss, Ernst	68	JG.52, 50, 11
Strelow, Hans	68	JG.51
Streib, Werner	68	ZG.1; NJG.1
Ratzlaff, Kurt	68	JG.52
Maltzahn, Günther von	68	JG.53
Losigkeit, Fritz	68	JG.26, 1, 51, 77
Leppla, Richard	68	JG.51, 105, 6
Kaiser, Herbert	68	JG.77, 1; JV.44
Jung, Heinrich	68	JG.54
Huppertz, Herbert	68	JG.51, 5, 2
Höckner, Walter	68	JG.77, 26, 1, 4
Dombacher, Kurt	68	JG.5, 51
Burkhardt, Lutz-Wilhelm	68	JG.77, 1, 7
Strassl, Hubert	67	JG.51
Schiess, Franz	67	JG.53
Kageneck, Erbo Graff von	67	JG.1, 27
Hammerl, Karl	67	JG.52
Füllgrabe, Heinrich	67	JG.52, 11
Fuchs, Karl	67	JG.54
Findeisen, Herbert	67	JG.54
Dinger, Fritz	67	JG.53
Denk, Gustav	67	JG.52
Hoffmann, Reinhold	66	JG.54
Fleig, Erwin	66	JG.51, 54
Schoenert, Rudolf	65	NJG.5
Radusch, Günther	65 (1 in Spain, 63 night)	ZG.1; NJG.1, 2, 3, 5
Meurer, Manfred	65 (night)	NJG.1, 5
Kempf, Karl-Heinz	65	JG.54, 26
Grassmuck, Bertold	65	JG.52
Döbrich, Hans-Heinrich	65	JG.5
Schönert, Rudolf	64 (night)	NJG.1, 2, 3, 5, 6, 100, 10

Rökker, Heinz	64 (night)	NJG.2
Rockker, Heinz	64 (night)	NJG.2
Petermann, Viktor	64	JG.52, 7
Lindner, Walter	64	JG.52
Hermichen, Rolf	64	ZG.1, 76; SKG.210; JG.26, 11, 104
Harder, Jürgen	64	JG.53, 11
Gallowitsch, Berndt	64	JG.77, 51, 7; EJG.2
Welter, Kurt	63	JG.301, 300; NJG.10, 11, Kdo Welter
Staiger, Hermann	63	JG.51, 26, 1, 7
Schilling, Wilhelm	63	JG.54; EJG.1
Mammerl, Karl	63	JG.52
Homuth, Gerhard	63	JG.27, 54
Hoffmann, Heinrich	63	JG.51
Götz, Franz	63	JG.53, 26
Neumann, Helmuth	62	JG.5
Maase, Horst	62	JG.51
Hübner, Wilhelm	62	JG.51
Haase, Horst	62	JG.51, 3
Cordes, Heinz	62	JG.54
Rauch, Alfred	60	JG.51
Munz, Karl	60	JG.52, 7; EJG.2
Mors, August	60	JG.5
Kelter, Kurt	60	JG.54
Hrdlicka, Franz	60	JG.77, 2
Carganico, Horst	60	JG.77, 5
Bob, Hans-Ekkehard	60	JG.54, 3, 51; EJG.2; JV.44
Beutin, Gerhard	60	JG.54
Tangermann, Kurt	60	JG.54, 52, 7
Zorner, Paul	59 (night)	NJG.2, 3, 5, 100
Steffen, Karl	59	JG.52

Stahlschmidt, Hans-Arnold	59	JG.27
Michalek, Georg (Austria)	59	JG.54, 3, 108
Franke, Alfred	59	JG.53
Engfer, Siegfried	59	JG.3, 1
Eckerle, Franz	59	JG.54
Borchers, Walter	59	ZG.76; NJG.3, 5
Trautloft, Hannes	58 (5 in Spain)	JG.77, 51, 54
Schwaiger, Franz	58	JG.3
Rath, Gerhard	58 (night)	NJG.3, 2
Nehring, Adolf	58	JG.52
Jahnke, Walter	58	JG.52, 11, 7
Haberda, Helmut	58	JG.52
Friebel, Herbert	58	JG.53, 51
Freuwörth, Wilhelm	58	JG.52, 26
Forbig, Horst	58	JG.54
Buchner, Hermann	58	StG.1; SG.2, 154; JG.7
Brönnle, Herbert	58	JG.54, 53
Becker, Martin	58 (night)	NJG.3, 4, 6
Wolf, Hermann	57	JG.52, 11, 7; EJG2
Wagner, Edmund	57	JG.51
Seifert, Johannes	57	JG.26
Gittelmann, Heinrich	57	JG.51
Ebener, Kurt	57	JG.3, 11
Dittlmann, Heinrich	57	JG.51
Dahmer, Hugo	57	JG.26, 77, 5, 2
Bauer, Konrad	57	JG.51, 3, 300
Ahnert, Heinz-Wilhelm	57	JG.52
Wick, Helmuth	56	JG.2
Strüning, Heinz	56	ZG.26; NJG.2, 1
Seeger, Günther	56	JG.53, 2
Schumacher, Karl	56	JG.52
Schönfelder, Helmuth	56	JG.51
Kraft, Josef (Austria)	56 (night)	NJG.4, 5, 6, 1

Knappe, Kurt	56	JG.51, 2
Iskem, Eduard	56	JG.77, 200, 53
Holtz, Helmuth	56	JG.51
Hohagen, Erich	56	JG.51, 2, 27, 7; JV.44
Hackler, Heinrich	56	JG.77
Fransci, Gustav Eduard	56 (night)	KG.40; NJG.100
Ellendt, Hans	56	JG.52
Eberwein, Manfred	56	JG.52, 54
Tautscher, Gabriel	55	JG.51
Galland, Wilhelm-Ferdinand	55	JG.26
Frank, Hans-Dieter	55 (night)	ZG.1; NJG.1
Bareuther, Herbert	55	JG.51, 3
Vinke, Heinz	54 (night)	NJG.1
Simsch, Siegfried	54	JG.52, 1, 11
Reiff, Hans	54	JG.3
Puschmann, Herbert	54	JG.51
Ohlsten, Kurt	54	JG.54
Leber, Heinz	54	JG.51
Hauswirth, Wilhelm	54	JG.52
Geiger, August	54 (night)	NJG.1
Bendert, Karl-Heinz	54	JG.27; JGr.104
Badum, Johann	54	JG.77
Sommer, Adalbert	53	JG.52
Sattig, Karl	53	JG.54
Meimberg, Julius	53	JG.2, 53
Kientsch, Willi	53	JG.27
Heyer, Hans-Joachim	53	JG.54
Brunner, Albert	53	JG.5
Berres, Heinz-Edgar	53	JG.77
Wefers, Heinrich	52	JG.52, 54
Rupp, Friedrich	52	JG.54
Quarda, Sepp	52	JG.54
Pichler, Johann	52	JG.77
Pflanz, Rudolf	52	JG.2

Knocke, Heinz	52	JG.1
Hoffmann, Werner	52 (night)	ZG.52, 2 NJG.3, 5
Häfner, Ludwig	52	JG.3
Gross, Alfred	52	JG.54, 26
Ehlers, Hans	52	JG.3, 1
Drewes, Martin	52 (43 night)	ZG.76; NJG.5, 1; JV.44
Brill, Karl	52	JG.54, 7
Barten, Franz	52	JG.51, 53
Schulz, Otto	51	JG.27
Lippe-Weissenfeld, Egmont Prince zu	51 (night)	ZG.76; NJG.2, 1, 5
Greiner, Hermann	51	NJG.1
Dilling, Gustav	51	JG.3
Willius, Karl	50	JG.26, 51
Rübell, Günther	50	JG.51, 104
Lütje, Herbert	50	JG.2; NJG.1, 6
Lüddecke, Fritz	50	JG.51
Knittel, Emil	50	JG.54
Jabs, Hans Joachim	50 (28 night)	ZG.76; NJG.3, 1
Düllberg, Ernst	50	JG.3, 27, 76, 7
Toll, Günther	49	JG.52
Sterl, Andreas	49	JG.52
Stendel, Fritz	49	JG.51, 5
Quatet-Faslem, Klaus	49	JG.53, 3
Quante, Richard	49	JG.54
Müller, August	49	JG.51
Koller, Herbert	49	JG.54
Kollak Reinhald	49 (night)	ZG.1; NJG.1, 4
Ehrenberger, Rudolf	49	JG.53, 77
Arnold, Heinz	49	JG.5, 7
Zimmermann, Oskar	48	JG.51, 3
Vogt, Gerhard	48	JG.26
Stumpf, Werner	48	JG.53
Siegler, Peter	48	JG.54

Häger, Johannes	48	NJG.1
Beckh, Friedrich	48	JG.51, 52
Seidel, Georg	47	JG.51
Schmidt, Erich	47	JG.53
Müller, Xaver	47	JG.54
Kutscha, Herbert	47	ZG.76, 1; SKG.210; JG.3, 27, 11
Karch, Fritz	47	JG.2
Hübner, Ekhard	47	JG.3
Hannack, Günther	* 47	LG.2; JG.77, 27
Golinski, Heinz	47	JG.53
Drünkler, Ernst Georg	47	ZG.2; NJG.1, 5
Balthasar, Wilhelm	47 (6 in Spain)	JG.27, 3, 2, 1
Surau, Alfred	46	JG.3
Sturm, Alfred	46	JG.3
Semrau, Paul	46	NJG.2
Schulte, Franz	46	JG.77
Schnörrer, Karl "Quax"	46	JG.54, 7
Rammelt, Karl	46	JG.51
Laskowski, Erwin	46	JG.51, 11
Fink, Günther	46	JG.54
Daspelgruber, Franz	46	JG.3
Böwing-Treuding, Wolfgang	46	JG.51
Augenstein, Hans-Heinz	46 (night)	NJG.1
Zwesken, Rudi	45	JG.52, 300
Vinzent, Otto	45	JG.54
Theimann, Willi	45	JG.51
Stollnberger, Hans	45	LG.2; SG.1, 10
Schöpfel, Gerhard	45	JG.26, 54, 4, 6
Schmid, Johannes	45	JG.2, 26
Mai, Lothar	45	JG.51
Lechner, Alois	45 (night)	NJG.100, 2
Küken, Wilhelm	45	JG.51
Frank, Rudolf	45	NJG.3

Föhl, Heinz	45	JG.52
Wever, Walther	44	JG.51, 7
Steinmann, Wilhelm	44	JG.27, 2; JV.44
Reinhard, Hans-Günther	44	JG.54, 1
Moritz, Wilhelm	44	ZG.1; JG.77, 1, 51, 3, 4; EJG.1
Matoni, Walter	44	JG.27, 26, 2, 11
Knacke, Reinhold	44	ZG.1; NJG.1
Hofmann, Wilhelm	44	JG.26
Gildner, Paul	44	ZG.1; NJG.1
Frese, Hans	44	JG.3
Becker, Ludwig	44 (night)	NJG.1, 2
Stolte, Paul-August	43	JG.54, 1, 3
Pöhs, Josef	43	JG.54
Niese, Eberhard	43	JG.77, 4
Mütherich, Hubert	43	JG.77, 54, 51
Miksch, Alfred	43+	JG.3, 1
Goltzsch, Kurt	43	JG.2
Franzisket, Ludwig	43	ZG.1; JG.27, 26
Borris, Karl	43	JG.26
Schramm, Herbert	42	JG.53, 27
Schmidt, Rudolf	42	JG.77
Plücker, Karl-Heinz	42	JG.1, 52
Olejnik, Robert	42	JG.3, 1, 400; EJG.2
Klemm, Rudolf	42	JG.54, 26
Hannig, Norbert	42	JG.54, 7
Gabl, Josef	42	JG.51
Brocke, Jürgen	42	JG.77
Brandt, Walter	42	LG.2; JG.77, 3
Stechmann, Hans	41	JG.3
Schneider, Gerhard	41	JG.51
Reinhold, Gerhard	41	JG.5, 7
Redlich, Karl-Wolfgang	41 (4 in Spain)	JG.27
Fellerer, Leopold (Austria)	41 (night)	NJG.1, 2, 5, 6

Boos, Hans	41	JG.3, 51
Meister, Ludwig	41 (night)	NJG.1, 4
Baake, Werner	41 (night)	NJG.1
Stratznicky, Erwin	40	JG.77, 3
Steinhausen, Günther	40	JG.27
Segatz, Hermann	40	JG.26, 51, 5, 1
Seckel, Georg	40	JG.77, 200, 4
Schwarz, Günther	40	JG.51
Schütte, Josef	40	JG.3
Schmidt, Dietrich	40 (night)	NJG.1
Neuhoff, Hermann	40	JG.53
Lausch, Bernhard	40	JG.51
Klein, Alfons	40 (1 in Spain)	JG.52, 11
Huy, Wolf-Dietrich	40	JG.77
Husemann, Werner	40	JG.77
Hessel, Bernhard	40	JG.51
Heitkamp, Walter	40	JG.52
Hahnlein, Georg	40	JG.54
Haala, Sigurd	40	JG.54
Decker, Otto	40	JG.52
Busch, Rudolf	40	JG.51
Bremer, Peter	40	JG.54
Sochatzy, Kurt	39	JG.3
Sinner, Rudolf	39	JG.27
Seelmann, Georg	39	JG.51, 103
Saborowski, Rudolf	39	JG.3
Mayer, Hans-Karl	39 (8 in Spain)	JG.53, 26
Ludwig, Georg	39	JG.77
Lasse, Kurt	39	JG.77
Fuchs, Robert	39	JG.54
Ehle, Walter	39 (33 night)	ZG.1; NJG.1
Bonin, Eckhard-Wilhelm von	39 (night)	NJG.1, 102
Tratt, Eduard	38	ZG.1, 26, 2; ErprGr.210; SKG.210

Rüttger, Karl	38	JG.52
Rohwer, Detlef	38	JG.3, 1
Reibel, Ludwig	38	JG.53
Peissert, Herbert	38	JG.53
Marotzke, Horst	38	JG.77
Lüth, Detlef	38	JG.3, 1
Lübking, August	38	JG.5, 7
Loos, Walter	38	JG.3, 301, 300
Litjens, Stefan	38	JG.53
Koall, Gerhard	38	JG.3, 54
Gerth, Werner	38	JG.53, 3, 300, 400
Dortenmann, Hans	38	JG.54, 26
Domeratzky, Otto	38	LG.2; SG.1, 2
Dirtenmann, Hans	38	JG.26, 54
Börngen, Ernst	38	JG.27
Baumann, Helmuth	38	JG.51
Zander, Friedrich	37	JG.54, 1
Walter, Albert	37+	JG.51
Volke, Maximilian	37	JG.77
Rühl, Franz	37	JG.3
Ransmayer, Hans	37	JG.54
Radener, Waldemar	37	JG.26, 300
Neumann, Klaus H.	37	JG.51, 3, 7; JV.44
Leesmann, Karl-Heinz	37	JG.52, 1
Hagedorn, Franz	37	JG.53
Gleissner, Hans	37	JG.52
Bahr, Günther	37	ZG.1; SKG.210; NJG.4, 6
Zink, Füllberk	36	JG.26
Zibler, Emil	36	JG.3
Widowitz, Wulf-Dietrich	36	JG.5
Weik, Hans	36	JG.3; EJG2
Wehnelt, Herbert	36	JG.2, 51
Stöber, Kurt	36	JG.54
Sawallisch, Erwin	36 (3 in Spain)	JG.77, 27

Rolly, Horst	36	JG.5, 400
Nordmann, Jörgen	36+	JG.52
Löhr, Ernst-Heinz	36	JG.3
Körner, Friedrich	36	JG.27
Kornatz, Hans	36	JG.52, 53
Keil, Georg	36	JG.11, 2
Förner, Friedrich	36	JG.27
Ernst, Wolfgang	36	JG.77, 53
Bergmann, Helmuth	36	NJG.4, 1
Beier, Wilhelm	36	NJG.1, 2, 3
Walther, Horst	35	JG.51
Ulbrich,	35+	JG.51
Stolle, Bruno	35	JG.51, 2, 11
Söffing, Waldemar	35	JG.26
Schöpper, Hans-Wilhelm	35	JG.77, 4
Rieckhoff, August	35	JG.52
Piffer, Anton-Rudolf	35	JG.1
Meyer, Rudi	35	JG.51
Mazurek, Marian	35	JG.53
Luy, August	35	JG.5
Lehner, Alfred	35	JG.5, 7
Kühlein, Elias	35	JG.51, 7
Helmer, Robert	35	JG.77
Heinzeller, Josef	35	LG2; JG.3, 2, 54
Hamer, Joachim	35	JG.51
Einsiedel, Heinrich Graf von	35	JG.3
Bringmann, Arnold	35	JG.3
Bretnütz, Heinz	35 (2 in Spain)	JG.53
Bertram, Günther	35 (night)	KG.4; NJG.100
Wettstein, Helmuth	34	JG.54
Taubenberger, Hans	34	JG.51
Stengel, Walter	34	JG.51
Specht, Günther	34	ZG.26; JG.11
Scholz, Günther	34 (1 in Spain)	JG.54, 5
Schmitz, Günther	34	JG.77

Schlick, Horst	34	JG.77, 7
Naumann, Johannes	34	JG.26, 6, 7
Modrow, Ernst-Wilhelm	34	NJG.1
Klemenz, Otto-Karl	34	JG.52
Kennel, Karl	34	ZG.26, 2; SG.1, 2
Johnen, Wilhelm	34 (night)	NJG.1, 5, 6
Husemann, Werner	34 (night)	NJG.1, 3
Hissbach, Heinz-Horst	34 (night)	NJG.2
Heilmann, Wilhelm	34	JG.54
Hahn, Hans von	34	JG.53, 3, 1, 5
Greisert, Karl-Heinz	34 (1 in Spain)	JG.3
Füreder, Georg	34	JG.54, 11
Färber, Leonard	34	JG.52
Baumgartner, Wilhelm	34	JG.77
Bascilla, Erwin	34	JG.52, 77, 301
Weidlich, Bruno	33	JG.77
Schmetzer, Reinhold	33	JG.186, 77, 4
Schlüter, Harro	33	JG.3
Scherflink, Karl-Heinz	33 (night)	NJG.1
Müller, Siegfried	33	JG.54, 26
Leykauf, Erwin	33	JG.54, 26, 7
Kurz, Günther	33	JG.52
Krahnke, Wolfgang	33+	JG.51
Kossatz, Günther	33+	JG.51
Kociok, Josef	33	ZG.76; SKG.210; NJG.1
Knoke, Heinz	33	JG.1, 11
Hadeball, Heinz-Martin	33 (night)	NJG.1, 4, 6, 10
Fischer, Karl-Reinhardt	33	JG.54
Eberle, Fritz	33	JG.51, 1, 4
Dettke, Alfred	33	JG.54
Cech, Franz	33	JG.3
Beyer, Heinz	33	JG.5
Sofling, Waldemar	33	JG.26
Wolter, Robert	32	JG.77

Wiegand, Günther	32	JG.26
Schuster, Hermann	32	JG.3
Rabiega, Josef	32	JG.52
Prager, Hans	32	JG.54, 26
Neuböck, Ludwig	32	JG.52
Machold, Werner	32	JG.2
Lange, Helmut	32	JG.51
Kalb, Johann	32	JG.52
Hohenberg, Werner	32	JG.52
Hessen, Ernst	32	(Unknown)
Heck, Walter	32	JG.54
Hacker, Joachim	32	JG.51
Glöckner, Rudolf	32	JG.5
Furch, Ralph	32	JG.51
Frey, Hugo	32	LG.2; JG.11, 1
Brand, Richard	32+	JG.51
Belser, Helmuth	32	JG.53
Zick, Siegfried	31	JG.11
Weiss, Franz	31	JG.5
Vögl, Ferdinand	31	JG.27
Sprick, Gustav	31	JG.26
Seidl, Alfred	31	JG.53, 3, 7
Schwienteck, Georg	31	JG.52
Schulz, Hans-Gottfried	31	JG.51
Schmude, Karl-Heinz	31	JG.54, 7
Rauch, Hubert	31 (night)	NJG.1, 4
Meindl, Franz	31	JG.51, 11
Lieres und Wilkau, Karl von	31	JG.27
Lautenschlager, Gerhard	31	JG.54
Geyer, Horst	31	JG.51; EKDo.262
Friedrich, Erich	31+	JG.77
Eyrich, Waldemar	31	JG.3
Crump, Peter	31	JG.54, 26
Bretschneider, Klaus	31+	JG.53, 300
Bachmann, Friedrich-Wilhelm	31	JG.52

Aubrecht, Hermann	31	JG.51
Aloe, Herbert	31	JG.54
Stratmann, Willi	30	JG.2
Seyffardt, Fritz	30	SG.1, 2, 151, 152
Schumann, August-Wilhelm	30 (4 in Spain)	JG.52
Schumacher, Werner	30	JG.5
Schneider, Hans-Werner	30	JG.52
Schmitt, Norbert	30	ZG.1; SG.2, 10
Schäuble, Karl	30	JG.3
Pfränger, Willi	30	JG.5
Pfahler, Hans	30+	JG.51
Müller, Hans	30 (night)	NJG.10
Müller, Friedrich-Karl "Nase"	30 (night)	JG.300; NJG.10, 11
Möller, Hans	30+	JG.53
Merkle, Hans-Jörg	30	JG.52
Lippert, Wolfgang	30 (5 in Spain)	JG.53, 27
Leickhardt, Hans	30 (night)	NJG.1, 5
Langer, Karl Heinz	30	JG.3
Koch, Harry	30	JG.26, 2
Heimann, Friedrich	30	JG.51
Heilmann, Friedrich	30	JG.51
Haller, Günther	30	JG.54
Grossfuss, Detlef	30	JG.2
Friedrich, Gerhard	30 (night)	NJG.1, 4, 6
Ferger, Heinz	30 (night)	NJG.2, 3
Ebersberger, Kurt	30	JG.26
Dörffel, Georg	30	LG.2; SG.1, 2
Doppler, Alwin	30	JG.11
Brückmann, Fritz	30	JG.52
Brandt, Paul	30	JG.54
Blazytko, Franz	30	JG.27
Berger, Horst	30	JG.5
Bartz, Erich	30	JG.51
Wohlers, Heinrich	29 (night)	NJG.1, 4, 6
Szameitat, Paul	29 (night)	NJG.1, 5, 3

Stadeck, Karl	29+	JG.51
Sigmund, Rudolf	29 (night)	NJG.1, 3
Schröder, Eduard	29	JG.53; NJG.3
Rippert, Horst	29	JG.27
Meyer, Otto	29 (8 in Spain)	JG.2, 26, 27
Meier, ?	29+	JG.51
Matuschka, Siegfried Graf von	29	JG.54
Leiste, Hermann	29	JG.54
Klemenz, Otto-Karl	29 (night)	NJG.1, 5
Kirchmayr, Rüdiger von	29	JG.1, 11; JV.44
Grosse, Egon	29	JG.51
Gromotka, Fritz	29	JG.27
Dörnbrack, Werner	29	LG2; SG.2, 4
Diergaardt, Rolf	29	JG.3
Altendorf, Rudolf	29 (night)	NJG.3, 4, 5
Woitke, Erich	28 (4 in Spain)	JG.3, 52, 77, 27, 1
Wischnewski, Hermann	28	JG.300
Stigler Franz	28	JG.27; JV.44
Schob, Herbert	28 (6 in Spain)	LG1; ZG.76, 26
Schmied, Hans	28 (night)	NJG.3, 100
Pingel, Rolf	28 (6 in Spain)	JG.26, 53
Pfüller, Helmuth	28+	JG.51
Palm, Albert	28+	JG.77, 4
Lüty, Gerhard	28	JG.52
Lau, Fritz	28 (night)	NJG.1
Kriegel, Gerhard	28	JG.54
Krause, Hans	28	NJG.101, 3, 4
König, Hans-Heinrich	28 (night)	ZG.76; NJG.3; JG.11
Jung, Erich	28 (night)	NJG.2
Hunerfeld, Udo	28	JG.54
Heinecke, Hans-Joachim	28	JG.27, 53
Heesen, Ernst	28	JG.3, 1
Grumme, Ernst-Dietrich	28	JG.51, 301
Galubinski, Hans	28	JG.53

Burk, Alfred	28	JG.52, 27
Bucholz, Max	28	JG.3, 1, 5; NJG.101
Bock, Eberhard	28	JG.3, 1, 27
Benning, Anton	28	JG.106, 300, 301, 302
Linke, Lothar	28 (23 night)	ZG.76; NJG.1, 2
Walz, Albrecht	27	JG.53
Unterleichtner, Ossi	27	JG.27, 54
Tismar, Werner	27	JG.77
Tietzen, Horst	27 (7 in Spain)	JG.51
Thierfelder, Werner	27	ZG.26; EKdo.262
Spenner, Manfred	27	JG.52, 53, 4
Schade, Kurt	27	JG.52
Russ, Otto	27	JG.53
Reschke, Willi	27	JG.300, 301, 302
Puls, Werner	27	JG.52
Proske, Gerhard	27	JG.54
Petzchler, Horst	27	JG.51, 3
Mayer, Wilhelm	27	JG.26
Maximowitz, Willi	27	JG.3
Löffler, Kurt	27	JG.51
Kortlepel, Erwin	27+	JG.3
Kolbow, Hans	27	JG.51
Kiworra, Hermann	27	JG.52
Horwick, Anton	27 (night)	NJG.2, 7
Grimm, Heinz	27 (night)	NJG.1, 2
Gerecke, Rudolf	27	JG.54
Fözö, Josef	27 (3 in Spain)	JG.51, 108
Clade, Emil	27	JG.27
Brechtl, Josef	27	JG.54
Bleckmann, Karl	27	SG.1, 2
Zoufahl, Franz-Josef	26	JG.51
Wurzer, Heinrich	26	JG.302
Werfft (Wessely), Peter	26	JG.27

Weber, Karl-Heinz	26	JG.51
Stehle, Fritz	26	ZG.76; JG.7
Schnellmann, Wolfgang	26	JG.27
Schellmann, Wolfgang	26 (12 in Spain)	JG.77, 2, 27
Remmer, Hans	26	JG.27
Pützkuhl, Josef	26 (night)	NJG.100, 5
Pausinger, Paul	26	JG.54
Paashaus, Karl	26	JG.53
Meyn, Wilhelm	26	SG.3
Maisch, ?	26 (night)	NJG.100
Koch, Raimund	26	JG.3
Knauth, Hans	26	JG.51
Hammer, Alfred	26	JG.53
Fureder, Georg	26	JG.54
Dahn, Friedrich	26	JG.5
Wald, Harry	25	JG.51, 3
Tichy, Ekkehard	25	JG.55, 3
Streichan	25	JG.54
Stedtfeld, Günther	25	JG.51, 7
Schulte, Helmuth	25 (night)	NJG.5
Schlitzer, Gottfried	25	JG.51
Salwender, Florian	25	JG.77, 5
Meckel, Helmuth	25	JG.3, 77
Lignitz, Arnold	25	JG.51, 54
Kuhn, Alfred	25 (night)	NJG.7
Kray, Ferdinand	25+	JG.51, 302
Krakowitzer, Friedrich	25	JG.51
Köster, Alfons	25 (night)	NJG.1, 2, 3
Kiel, Johannes	25	ZG.26, 76
Hördt, Helmuth	25	JG.51
Göbert, Helmut	25	JG.77
Förster, Richard	25	JG.77, 1
Förster, Gerhard	25	JG.51
Emberger, Alfred	25	JG.52
Brinkhaus, Franz	25 (night)	NJG.2, 3

Briegleb, Walter	25 (night)	NJG.2, 3
Böttner, Karl-Heinz	25	JG.77
Böttcher, Herbert	25	JG.77
Bellof, Ludwig	25 (night)	NJG.?
Walter, Horst	25	JG.51
Bach, Otto	25	JG.1
Albrecht, Egon	25	ZG.1, 76; SKG.210; JG.76
Adolph, Walter	25 (1 in Spain)	JG.1, 27, 26
Woltersdorf, Helmuth	24 (night)	NJG.1
Wenneckers, Hans-Gerd	24	JG.1, 11
Baten, Gerhard	24	JG.52
Theme, Hans	24	JG.52
Strohecker, Karl	24 (night)	NJG.100
Spoden, Peter	24 (night)	NJG.5, 6
Scheer, Claus	24 (night)	NJG.100
Krahl, Karl- Heinz	24	JG.2, 3
Keller, Hannes	24	JG.51
Kaldrack, Rolf	24 (3 in Spain)	ZG.76, 1; SKG.210
Hoppe, Helmuth	24	JG.26
Hirschfeld, Ernst-Erich	24	JG.300, 54
Hartrampf, Horst	24+	JG.54
Giese, Wilhelm	24	JG.3
Dahms, Helmuth	24 (night)	NJG.100
Büttner, Erich	24+	JG.51, 7
Baum, Heinz	24	JG.3
Baten, Kurt	24	JG.52, 1, 7
Babenz, Emil	24	JG.53, 26
Wünsch, Karl	23	JG.27
Viedebantt, Helmuth	23	ZG.1, 76; SKG.210, 10
Unger, Willy	23	JG.3, 7
Thimming, Wolfgang	23 (night)	NJG.1, 2, 4
Sternberg, Horst	23	JG.26

Schumacher, Leo	23	ZG.76; JG.1; JV.44
Schneider, Bernhard	23	JG.27
Schaus, Jakob	23 (night)	NJG.4
Schadowski, Hans	23 (night)	NJG.3
Sannemann, Heinrich	23	JG.3
Renzow, Hans-Werner	23	JG.77
Reitmeyer, Ernst	23 (night)	NJG.5
Raupach, Richard	23	JG.54, 7
Prestele, Ignatz	23 (4 in Spain)	JG.53, 2
Peters, Erhard	23 (night)	NJG.3, 4
Patuschka, Horst	23 (night)	NJG.2
Nielinger, Rudolf	23	JG.51
Müller, Fritz R.G.	23	JG.53, 7
Macher, Helmuth	23	JG.53
Leschert, Heinrich	23	JG.53
Leonhard, Karl	23	JG.53, 11
Landt, Günther	23	JG.53
Kutenberger, Alfred	23	JG.52
Krüger, Alfred	23	JG.52
Koch, Herbert	23 (night)	NJG.3
Keller, Lothar	23 (3 in Spain)	JG.3
Kamp, Hans-Karl	23	ZG.76; NJG.4; JG.300
Heinze, Helmuth	23	JG.51
Gren, Kurt	23	JG.51, 3
Göbel, Siegfried	23	JG.53
Gilhaus, Franz	23	JG.52
Fuchs, Robert	23	JG.51
Dühn, Ewald	23	JG.52
Döring, Arnold	23 (night)	KG.53; JG.300, 2; NJG.2, 3
Dohse, Hartwig	23	JG.3
Bussmann, Rolf	23 (night)	NJG.1, 2, 5
Barte, Walter	23 (night)	NJG.1, 3
Autenrieth, Hans	23 (night)	NJG.1, 4

Wintergerst, Eugen	22	JG.77, 1
Vogel, Michael	22	JG.3
Steffens, Hans-Joachim	22	JG.51
Simon, Friedrich	22	JG.51
Schultz, Ernts-Albrecht	22	JG.53
Schaschke, Gerhard	22	ZG.76
Richter, Hans	22	JG.27
Meyer, Eduard	22	ZG.26
Mayer, Otto	22	JG.27
Louis, Joachim	22	JG.53
Leube, Hermann	22 (night)	NJG.3
Laube, Ernst	22	JG.77, 3, 27, 4
Kühl, Helmuth	22	JG.53
Klager, Ernst	22	JG.53
Heller, Richard	22	ZG.76; JG.10
Heeg, Friedrich	22	JG.52
Harder, Harro	22 (11 in Spain)	JG.53
Gärtner, Arthur	22	JG.54
Erhardt, Peter	22 (night)	NJG.5
Eckard Reinhold	22 (night)	ZG.76; NJG.1, 3
Dassow, Rudolf	22	ZG.1, 76; JG.6
Busse, Heinz	22	JG.51
Buschmann, Hubert	22	JG.3
Bertram, Otto	22 (1 in Spain)	JG.2
Beese, Arthur	22	JG.26
Zimmer, Herbert	21	JG.3
Wolf, Robert	21 (night)	NJG.5
Wold, Robert	21 (night)	NJG.5
Winkler, Max	21	JG.27
Werra, Franz von	21	JG.3, 53
Wegmann, Günther	21	ZG.26; EKdo.262; JG.7
Walther, Rudolf	21	JG.52
Villing, Martin	21	JG.5
Sturm, Gustav	21	JG.27, 51, 7

Steis, Heinrich	21	JG.27
Schumann, Heinz	21	JG.51, 2 SKG.10
Schrade, Hans	21	JG.54
Schauder, Paul	21	JG.26
Ruppert, Kurt	21	JG.26
Ritzenberger, Karl	21	JG.52
Reuter, Horst	21	JG.27
Pichon-Kalau von Hofe, Werner	21	JG.54, 51
Müller, Erich	21+	JG.77, 7
Lorentzen, Friedrich	21	JG.3
Klante, Helmuth	21	JG.5
Kijewski, Herbert	21	JG.3, 1
Kaiser, Theodor	21	JG.3
Humer, Alfred	21	JG.3
Hopf, Werner	21 (night)	NJG.5
Hofrath, Kurt	21	JG.3
Förster, Josef	21 (night)	NJG.2, 3
Ebert, Adolf	21	JG.77
Dippel, Georg	21	JG.26
Budde, Alfred	21	JG.54
Bielefeld, Werner	21	JG.51
Becker, Paul	21	JG.27
Altner, Herbert	21 (night)	NJG.5, 11
Ziehm, Helmuth	20	JG.51
Wirtz, Ludwig	20 (night)	NJG.1, 2
Wiesmahr, Gustav	20+	JG.52
Westphal, Hans-Jürgen	20	JG.51, 26, 53
Udet, Hans	20	JG.26
Tritsch, Willi	20	LG2; SchG.1; SG.151, 152
Treuberg, Eberhard von	20	JG.52, 3
Tonne, Günther	20	ZG.76, 1; SKG.210, 10
Tetzner, Hans	20	JG.77, 5

Tammen, Heinrich	20	JG.52
Spiess, Wilhelm	20	ZG.26
Söthe, Fritz	20 (night)	NJG.4
Sommer, Gerhard	20	JG.11, 1
Senoner, Kurt	20+	JG.51
Schwarz, Gerhard	20	JG.51
Schulze, Kurt	20	JG.5
Schnoor, Emil-Rudolf	20	JG.1
Schneider, Walter	20	JG.26
Schneider, Gottfried	20 (night)	NJG.2
Schicketanz, Otto	20	JG.52
Scheyda, Erich	20	JG.26
Schalk, Paul	20	JG.5
Roth, Willi	20	JG.26
Richter, Ernst	20	JG.54
Pohl, Ottokar	20+	JG.77
Munzert, Hermann	20	JG.53
Munsche, Karlheinz	20+	JG.2
Munderloh, Georg	20	JG.54
Menge, Robert	20 (4 in Spain)	JG.26
Meissner, Hans	20 (night)	NJG.3
Mappatsch, Hans-Joachim	20	JG.54
Liebelt, Fritz	20	JG.51
Lehmann, Alfred	20	JG.52
Kosse, Wolfgang	20+	JG.26, 5, 1, 3
Köhne, Walter	20	JG.52, 1, 11
Klassen, Ferdinand	20	JG.52
Klaffenbach, Hans	20	JG.4
Kaiser, Adolf	20 (night)	NJG.1, 2, 100
Jung, Harald	20	JG.51
Hübner, Gerhard	20	JG.52
Hübl, Rudolf	20	JG.1
Heym, Günther	20+	JG.51
Hegener, Wilhelm	20	JG.51
Heckmann, Günther	20	JG.51, 1, 7

Happatsch, Hans-Joachim	20	JG.54
Hammel, Kurt	20	JG.5, 27, 77
Hahn, Franz	20	JG.51, 4
Gref, Hans	20 (night)	NJG.100
Gosemann, Heinz	20	JG.3
Goralski, ?	20	JG.77
Förg, Rasso	20	JG.3
Flecks, Reinhard	20	JG.1
Finkler, Paul	20	JG.54
Engleder, Rudolf	20	JG.1, 7
Engel, Wilhelm	20 (night)	NJG.1, 4, 6
Ebert, Walter	20	JG.2
Eberhardt, Paul	20	JG.52
Dreyer, Willi	20+	JG.53
Davier, Heino von	20	JG.52
Brinkmann, ?	20 (night)	NJG.3
Bolz, Helmuth-Felix	20 (3 in Spain)	JG.2
Berschwinger, Hans	20 (night)	NJG.1, 2
Baudach, Helmuth	20	JG.2, 7; EKdo.262
Artner, Rudolf	20	JG.5
Stritzel, Fritz	19	JG.2
Dippel, Hans	19	JG.26
Sommer, Hermann	19 (night)	NJG.2, 102
Schott, Georg "Hurr"	19 (3 in Spain)	LG.2; JG.1
Schmidt, Winfried	19	JG.3
Schellwat, Fritz	19 (night)	NJG.1
Rossiwall, Theodor	19 (2 in Spain)	ZG.76, 26; NJG.4, 1
Reischer, Peter	19	JG.26
Reif, Emil	19	JG.51
Pritzl, Otto	19	JG.51, 3, 7
Ney, Berthold	19 (night)	NJG.2, 3
Myrrhe, Lothar	19	JG.3
Mix, Erich	19 (+11 WWI)	JG.1, 2, 53
Lüer, Friedrich	19	JG.54

Lüchau, Karl-Heinz	19	JG.54, 11
Kasten, Dietrich	19	JG.53
Kalkum, Adolf	19	JG.53
Gruber, Otto	19	JG.3
Gassner, Anton	19	JG.52
Gantz, Benno	19	JG.51
Gammel, Fritz	19	JG.53
Funcke, Hans	19	JG.52
Claussen, Hans	19	JG.54
Christl, Georg	19	ZG.26; JG.10
Berg, Heinz-Otto	19	JG.52, 77
Wenzel, Werner	18	JG.3, 7
Weinitschke, Dietrich	18	JG.5
Wehmeyer, Alfred	18	ZG.26
Täschner, Rudolf	18	JG.53
Strakeljahn, Friedrich-Wilhelm	18	JG.77, 5; SG.4
Schnorr, Willi	18	JG.54, 11, 7
Scheufele, Ernst	18	JG.5, 4
Schenck, Wolfgang	18	SG.2; ZG.1; SKG.210, KG.51
Scharf, Ludwig	18	JG.5
Schäfer, Hans	18	JG.3
Roisch, Kurt	18	JG.3
Rapp, Werner	18 (night)	NJG.1, 5
Potzel, Arno	18	JG.77
Peterburs, Hans	18+	ZG.1, 76; SKG.210, 10; SG.4
Papendick, Heinz	18	JG.3
Nabrich, Josef	18 (night)	NJG.1
Müller, Erwin	18	JG.77, 7
Mudin, Alexander	18	JG.51
Mrotzeck, Fritz	18	JG.3
Meyer, Walter	18	JG.54, 26
May, Heinrich	18	JG.3
Lüdtke, Horst	18	JG.3

Kühdorf, Karl	18	JG.77
Köhne, Hermann	18	JG.1
Kloss, Werner	18	JG.3
Klipgen, Rolf	18	JG.53
Iffland, Hans	18	JG.3
Hörschelmann, Jürgen	18	JG.3
Holler, Kurt	18 (night)	NJG.2, 3, 4
Heizmann, Otto	18	JG.11
Haugk, Helmuth	18	ZG.76, 26
Hartmann, Karl-Wilhelm	18	JG.52
Gerlitz, Erich	18	JG.51, 27, 53, 5
Gerhards, Günther	18	JG.52
Gentzel, Hannes	18	JG.102; ZG.2
Fries, Otto H.	18 (night)	NJG.1
Franz, Richard	18	JG.3, 11
Fränzl, Herbert	18	JG.11, 52
Ensslen, Wilhelm	18 (9 in Spain)	JG.52
Eckhoff, Max	18	JG.2
Ebeling, Heinz	18	JG.26
Düding, Rudi	18 (night)	NJG.100
Drdla, Hubert	18	JG.3, 7
Dietrich, Klaus	18	JG.51
Deicke, Joachim	18	JG.77
Claus, Georg	18	JG.53, 51
Bülow-Bothkamp, Hilmer von	18 (+6 WWI)	JG.77, 2; NJG.101, 105
Breves, Adolf	18 (night)	NJG.1
Braunshirn, Georg	18 (5 in Spain)	JG.54
Brandis, Felix-Maria	18	JG.5
Bösch, Oskar	18	JG.3
Biederbrick, Helmuth	18	JG.54, 1
Beckmann, Helmuth	18	JG.27
Bahnsen, Jens	18	JG.27, 53
Asper, Roloff	18	JG.54
Ziemer, Heinz	17	JG.11

Wüst, Josef	17+	JG.3, 52
Winter, Rudolf	17	JG.300
Weniger, Rupert	17	JG.53
Venth, Heinz	17	JG.51
Ulenberg, Horst	17	JG.26
Smola, Rudolf	17	SG.2, 151
Schneeweis, Wolfgang	17 (night)	NJG.101
Schmidt, Ludwig	17 (night)	NJG.6
Schlüter, Herbert	17	JG.300, 7
Raum, Hans	17 (night)	NJG.3
Quack, Wilhelm	17	JG.54
Puchberger, Friedrich	17	JG.52
Pitzl, Eduard	17	JG.52, 53
Nägele, Franz	17	JG.77
Müller, Siegfried	17	JG.51, 3, 7
Mischke, Helmut	17+	SG.4
Lohoff, Helmuth	17	JG.51
Kutz, Walter	17	JG.3
Krüger, Horst-Benno	17	JG.2
Krais, Uwe	17	JG.3
Kettner, ?	17+	JG.52
Johannes, Bernhard	17	SG.2, 10
Jenne, Peter	17	ZG.1, 26; JG.300
Hagenah, Walter	17	JG.3, 11, 7
Haase, Ernst	17	JG.302
Grothues, Klaus	17	JG.300
Gerth, Peter	17	JG.51
Gärtner, Franz	17	JG.53
Galland, Paul	17	JG.26
Blechschmidt, Joachim	17	ZG.1
Berg, Rudolf	17	JG.3
Wuenschelmeyer, Karl	16	JG.26
Werner, Otto	16	JG.77
Venjakob, Otto	16	JG.54
Suschko.Leo	16	JG.3

Stöwer, Heinz	16	JG.11
Steinicke, Karl-Heinz	16	JG.3
Starke, Heinrich	16	SG.1, 2, 77, 10, 151
Springer, Ferdinand-Herbert	16	JG.3
Scheer, Friedrich	16	JG.53
Säwert, Heinz	16 (night)	NJG.5, 6
Rupp, Bruno	16 (night)	NJG.3
Rogall, Hubertus	16	JG.77
Paczia, Erich	16	JG.53
Niederreichholz, Kurt	16	JG.1
Niederhöfer, Hans	16	JG.27
Müller, Alfred	16	JG.27
Morlock, Willi	16 (night)	NJG.1
Meyer, Conny	16	JG.26
Mahlkuch, Hans	16	JG.77
Kunz, Josef	16	JG.5
Krämer, Gerd	16	JG.51
Köker, Burchard	16	JG.77
Kendler, Franz	16	JG.52
Keil, Josef	16	JG.3, 301
Heitmann, Hans	16	JG.26
Heiser, Helmut	16	JG.300, 7
Hartwein, Hans-Dieter	16	JG.5
Hackbarth, Georg	16+	JG.51, 1
Gransow, Burkhard	16	JG.77
Gräf, Kurt	16	JG.3
Goetze, Manfred	16	SG.77, 10
Göbel, Richard	16	JG.52, 53
Fischer, Arno	16	JG.52, 53
Fengler, Georg	16 (night)	NJG.1, 4
Ermisch, Heinz	16	JG.52, 300
Dreisbach, Heinrich	16	JG.5
Demuth, Karl-Emil	16	JG.1
Brönner, Hugo	16	JG.51

Böker, Burchard	16	JG.77
Blaurock, Friedrich	16	JG.77
Beth, Arthur	16	JG.5
Bergmann, Götz	16+	JG.51
Berger, Ludwig	16	JG.77
Ahrensmeyer, Elmar	16	JG.51
Ziegenhagen, Helmut	15	JG.54, 11
Wübke, Waldemar	15	JG.54, 101; JV.44
Worlitzsch, Joachim	15	JG.53
Wollmann, David	15	JG.5
Winkler, Ernst	15	JG.3, 1
Wimmers, Oskar	15	JG.11
Thomas, Erich	15	JG.53
Swoboda, Hubert	15	JG.1
Staege, Hermann	15	LG.2; JG.2, 53
Simon, Erich	15 (night)	NJG.3
Sieg, Heinz	15	JG.53
Sengschmitt, Fritz	15	ZG.76, 26
Schöw, Werner	15	JG.53
Schindler, Gerhard	15	JG.52, 27
Schiffer, Johannes	15	JG.3, 1
Schalk, Johannes	15	ZG.26; NJG.3
Rüping, Karl-Emil	15	JG.3
Rolland, Heinz	15 (night)	NJG.1
Riedel, Hans	15	JG.77
Raimann, Gerhard	15	JG.54
Radlauer, Heinz	15	JG.51
Prinz, Werner	15	JG.51
Penschke, Fritz	15	JG.52
Patzak, Rudolf	15	JG.54
Ohly, Hans	15	JG.53, 3
Neumayer, Johannes	15	JG.27
Neuhaus, Josef	15	ZG.26; JG.7
Müller, Hans	15 (night)	NJG.3
Matzak, Kurt	15 (night)	NJG.1

Markhoff, Hans	15	JG.52
Lotzmann, Manfred	15	JG.52
Liedke, Kurt	15	JG.53
Leicher, Otto	15	JG.52
Kürter, Heinz	15	JG.52
Kraft, Georg	15 (night)	NJG.1
Kraft, Erwin	15	JG.54, 11
Konter, Helmut	15 (night)	NJG.100
Koch, Hans-Günther	15	JG.51
Keller, Otto	15 (night)	NJG.5
Jung, Hans-Ulrich	15	JG.3
Hier, Paul	15	JG.54, 76
Guhl, Hermann	15	LG.2; JG.26
Gerstmayer, Lorenz	15	JG.51
Fladrich, Kurt	15 (night)	NJG.4
Fischer, Siegfried	15	StG.1; SG.1
Fernsebner, Josef	15	JG.52
Engst, Hubert	15	JG.300
Dudeck, Heinz	15	JG.77, 27
Drühe, Herbert	15	JG.11
Dreesmann, Rudolf	15+	JG.51, 301
Dobislav, Max	15	JG.1, 27
Diesing, Ulrich	15	ZG.1
Conter, Helmuth	15 (night)	NJG.100
Baumann, Lothar	15	JG.77
Augustin, Jakob	15+	JG.2
Adelhütte, Hans	15 (night)	KG.3; NJG.3
Zuzic, Herwig	14	JG.77, 1
Wunder, Oskar	14	JG.52
Witzel, Hans	14	JG.26
Werth, Johann	14	NJG.2
Wagner, Gerhard	14 (night)	NJG.5
Tham, Gustav	14 (night)	NJG.5, 10
Telge, Wilhelm	14 (night)	NJG.1
Stoll, Jakob	14	JG.53

Spott, Johann	14	JG.53
Simross, Herbert	14 (night)	NJG.100
Seiz, Walter	14	JG.53
Schrangl, Hans	14	JG.11, 7
Schöfbeck, Erich	14	JG.27
Schmoller-Haldy, Hans	14	JG.54
Schliedermann, Hans-Joachim	14	JG.27
Salffner, Gustav	14	JG.300
Reich, Günther	14	JG.3
Raich, Alfons	14	JG.3
Pöske, Ernst	14	JG.3
Ottnad, Alexander	14	JG.27
Nebel, Karl-Heinz	14	JG.51
Möller, Klaus	14 (night)	NJG.3
Maurer, Ottmar	14	JG.51
Lücke, Walter	14	JG.77
Lubich, Ivo von	14+	JG.51, 2
Lohberg, ?	14	JG.52
Lass, Hans	14	JG.27
Küpper, Heinz	14	JG.3, 1
Kronschnabel, Josef	14	JG.53
Köberich, Günther	14 (night)	NJG.3
Klug, Franz	14	JG.51
Kischnick, Helmuth	14	JG.5
Keller, Franz	14	JG.11
Kehrle, Josef	14	JG.1
Hutter, Georg	14	JG.1
Hondt, Erich	14	JG.1, 11; JV.44
Hommes, Heinz	14	JG.53
Hohmeyer, Herbert	14+	JG.52
Hener, Rudolf	14	JG.3, 7
Griese, Heinrich	14 (night)	NJG.1, 4, 6
Glöcker, Helmuth	14+	JG.51
Gäth, Wilhelm	14	JG.26
Fitschen, Wilhelm	14	JG.77

Fiedler, Reinhold	14	JG.5
Faust, Karl	14	JG.3
Espenlaub, Albert	14	JG.27
Ehrhardt, Otto	14	JG.3
Dormann, Wilhelm	14 (night)	NJG.1; JG.300
Dehrmann, Herbert	14	JG.3
Culemann, Hans-Gunnar	14	JG.27
Bussert, Joachim	14+	JG.51
Breukel, Wendelin	14 (night)	NJG.2, 4
Braune, Erhard	14	JG.27
Blume, Walter	14	JG.26, 27
Birk, Heinz	14	JG.5
Bär, Ernst	14	JG.77
Barann, Leo-Lothar	14	JG.11
Baagoe, Sophus	14	ZG.26
Altendorf, Heinz	14	JG.53
Wille, Gerhard	13+	JG.51
Wiggers, Ernst	13	JG.51
Wickop, Fritz Dietrich	13	JG.1
Traphan, Rudolf	13	JG.3
Timme, Horst	13+	JG.52
Suhr, Helmut	13	JG.301
Soukup, Herbert	13	JG.53
Schwaneberg, Siegfried	13+	JG.51
Schuecking, Norbert	13	JG.11
Schild, Heinrich	13	JG.26
Schemel, Joachim	13	JG.77
Schade, Hans	13	JG.53
Roller, Robert	13	JG.3
Röhrich, Kurt	13	JG.3
Peltz, Werner	13	JG.52
Niederhagen, Kurt	13	JG.77
Neumann, Eduard	13 (2 in Spain)	JG.27, 26
Mohn, Günther	13	JG.3
Michno, Erich	13	JG.52

Meyer-Arend, Robert	13	JG.3
Mangelsdorf, Rudolf	13 (night)	NJG.2, 3
Loos, Kurt	13 (night)	ZG.2; NJG.1, 5
Lennartz, Helmuth EKdo.262	13	JG.11, 7;
Krainik, Erich	13	JG.27
Kothmann, Willi	13+	JG.27
Koslowski, Eduard	13	JG.53, 26
Kley, Erwin	13	JG.2
Keller, Friedrich	13	JG.27
Kelch, Günther	13	JG.26
Karlowski, Hans	13 (night)	NJG.1, 2
Kaiser, Emil	13	JG.27
Jürgens, Helmuth	13	JG.51
Jürgens, Hans	13	JG.27
Jung, Hans	13	JG.3
Jung, Detlef	13	JG.54
Jauer, Erich	13	JG.26
Helstrick, Heinz	13	JG.5
Heinze, Ernst-Günther	13	JG.53
Halstrick, Heinz	13	JG.5
Hahn, Hans	13 (night)	NJG.2
Groth, Erich	13	ZG.2, 76
Grabmann, Walter	13 (7 in Spain)	LG1; ZG.76; JG.26
Gossow, Heinz	13	KG.33; JG.300, 301, 7
Gleuwitz, Gerhard	13	JG.52
Gerhardt, Werner	13	JG.2, 1, 26
Geise, Otto	13	JG.11
Gayko, Werner	13	JG.5
Förster, Hermann	13	JG.27
Focke, Wulf	13	JG.77
Florian, Ernst	13	JG.1
Fintscher, Hugo	13 (night)	NJG.2, 3
Feyerlein, Hans	13	JG.53

Ellenrieder, Xaver	13	JG.26
Eberth, Alfred	13	JG.11
Dressmann, Rudolf	13	JG.51
Broo, Karl	13	JG.53
Braasch, Kurt	13	JG.53
Bohatsch, Walter	13	JG.3, 7
Bockl, Alfred	13	JG.26
Böckel, Albert	13	JG.26, 7
Bochmann, Horst	13	JG.77
Bauhuber, Helmuth	13	JG.51
Bartosch, Hieronymus	13	JG.51
Zink, Dieter	12	JG.3
Zilken, Helmut	12	JG.54
Wirth, Otto	12	JG.3
Wienhusen, Franz	12	JG.77, 5, 4
Wellhausen, Jürgen	12	JG.300
Wehrhagen, Wolfgang	12	JG.77
Tornow, Heinz	12 (2 in Spain)	JG.51
Teige, Waldemar	12 (night)	KG.53; NJG.6; NJSch.Lft.1
Szardenings, Rudolf	12 (night)	NJG.3
Strobel, Ludwig	12	JG.51
Steinmuller, Friedrich	12	JG.53
Steiner, Franz	12	JG.11; JV.44
Stefanink, Karl	12	JG.77
Stange, Willi	12	JG.3
Spreckels, Robert	12	JG.11, 1
Sieckenius, Hans	12	JG.51
Schulz, Albert	12 (night)	NJG.2, 3
Schöppler, Anton	12	JG.5, 7
Schmidt, Johannes	12	JG.26
Schlauch, Otto	12	JG.52
Scheidt, Hermann	12	JG.51
Schawaller, Heinz	12	JG.51
Schäfer, Hans	12 (night)	NJG.2, 3

Schade, Eberhard	12	JG.27
Saynisch, Walter	12	JG.27
Rudschinat, Siegfried	12	JG.11
Rost, Wolfgang	12	JG.5
Rössner, Hans	12	JG.77
Rosenberg, Heinrich	12+	JG.27
Reuter, Heinz	12 (night)	NJG.2, 3
Perl, Gustav	12	JG.53
Perle, Helmuth	12 (night)	NJG.2
Ott, Siegfried	12	JG.77
Ney, Siegfried	12 (night)	NJG.1
Neu, Wolfgang	12	JG.26
Nairz, Max	12	JG.53
Nacke, Heinz	12	ZG.76; NJG.3, 101
Morr, Hans	12	KG.40; ZG.1; JG.53
Mecke, Erhardt	12	JG.5
Matern, Karl-Heinz	12	ZG.1, 76; SKG.210
Manz, Wilhelm	12	JG.3, 53
Lutter, Johannes	12	ZG.1, 76, 2; SKG.210, 10; SG.4
Löfgen, Richard	12	JG.300
Laufs, Peter	12 (night)	KG.30; NJG.2
Kunz, Franz	12	JG.53, 26
Krenz, Herbert	12	JG.27
Krause, Gerhard	12	JG.53
Kiefner, Georg	12	JG.26; JV.44
Keppler, Gerhard	12	JG.27
Kapp, Karl-Heinz	12	JG.27
Jaekel, Egbert	12	SG.2
Hornig, Gerhard	12	JG.77
Hocke, Rudolf	12	JG.53
Hillenbrux, Werner	12 (night)	NJG.1
Hiebl, Georg	12	JG.11

Hein, Kurt	12	JG.26
Heilig, Bruno	12 (night)	NJG.2
Haninger, Rudolf	12	JG.1
Hachfeld, Wilhelm	12	LG.2; JG.51; ZG.2
Haberland, Karl	12	JG.2
Günther, Alfred	12	JG.26
Greth, Rudolf	12	JG.54
Gransow, Günther	12	JG.51
Gomann, Heinz	12	JG.26, 7
Glaubig, Gotthard	12	JG.3
Funk, Waldemar	12	JG.51
Funk, Karl-Heinz	12+	JG.51
Fritz, Hans	12	JG.3
Florian, Otto	12	JG.3
Fischer, August	12 (night)	NJG.1, 5, 100
Fenske, Walter	12 (night)	NJG.1, 2
Engling, Egon	12 (night)	NJG.2, 3
Dobrath, Walter	12	JG.1
Diekwisch, Erwin-Peter	12	StG.1; SG.5, KG.200
Degner, Franz	12	JG.5
Degener, Karl	12	JG.6, 7
Bunje, Helmut	12	NJG.6
Budke, Wilhelm	12	JG.53
Brenner, Heinz	12	JG.3
Braukmann, ?	12+	LG.2; JG.77
Brandt, Fritz	12 (night)	NJG.2, 3
Bergmann, Karl	12	JG.3
Beckh, Gerhard	12	JG.51
Beck, Gerhard	12	JG.51
Bauer, Ludwig	12	JG.27
Bär, Hans	12 (night)	NJG.3, 5
Bälz, Kuno	12	JG.3, 51
Alf, Rudolf	12	JG.2, 7
Aistleitner, Johann	12	JG.26

Adam, Hans	12	JG.51
Zschäbitz, ?	11+	JG.52
Yung, Fritz	11	JG.301
Walter, Albert	11 (night)	NJG.4, 6
Vollet, Hans	11	JG.5
Vivroux, Gerhard	11	JG.3
Todt, Hans	11	JG.301, 7
Tingerding, Hermann	11	JG.27
Tangerding, Hermann	11	JG.27
Stockmann, Gerhard	11	JG.53
Steinicke, Heinz	11+	JG.51
Springer, Herbert	11	JG.3
Sommerhoff, Hubert	11	JG.53
Seidel, Heinz	11	JG.302
Schwartz, Erich	11	JG.26
Schumann, Walter	11	JG.77
Schröter, Fritz	11	JG.2; SKG.10; SG.5, 4
Schneider, Hans	11	JG.5
Schneider, August	11	JG.5
Schmid, Rudolf	11	JG.11
Schleef, Erwin	11	JG.54
Scheiter, Wilhelm	11	JG.27
Scheib, Wilhelm	11	JG.77
Schaller, Wolf	11	JG.53
Rose, Helmut	11	JG.53, 3
Riehl, Erwin	11	JG.77
Preussger, Helmut	11	JG.54
Potthast, Friedrich	11 (night)	NJG.1
Pölz, Hubert (Austria)	11+	StG.2, 3; SG.151
Pfeiffer, Karl-Georg	11 (night)	NJG.1
Niebelschutz, Wolfgang von	11 (night)	NJG.2, 4, 5
Neuerburg, Erwin	11	JG.51, 3
Müller, Robert	11	JG.5
Milius, Walter	11 (night)	NJG.1, 3

Mildner, Wilhelm	11+	JG.51
Meyer, Willi	11 (1 In Spain)	JG.77
Meier, Erwin	11	JG.53
Löschenkohl, Ferdinand	11	JG.3, 7
Löffler, Hannes	11	JG.27
Liebolt, Erwin	11	JG.26
Leibold, Erwin	11	JG.26
Laun, Hans	11	JG.1
Lacha, Martin	11	JG.1
Kurpiers, Rudolf	11	JG.5; ZG.26
Krah, Heinz	11	JG.52
Knüppel, Herwig	11 (8 in Spain)	JG.26
Kittler, Herbert	11	JG.77
Kirchner, Horst	11	JG.51, 302
Kaiser, Josef	11	JG.5
Jank, Wolfgang	11 (night)	NJG.5, 100
Hülshoff, Karl	11 (night)	NJG.2
Hoffmann, Reinhold	11	JG.3
Hoffmann, Friedrich	11	JG.27
Hermann, Hans	11+	JG.54
Hermann, Hans	11	JG.3
Henseler, Wilhelm	11 (night)	NJG.1
Heiner, Englbert	11 (night)	KG.27; NJG.6; NJSch.Lft.4
Heidenreich, Hans	11	JG.51, 7
Haupt, Benedikt	11	JG.51
Hartl, Andreas	11	JG.302
Hammel, Kurt	11	JG.26
Halfmann, Johann	11	JG.54
Günther, Paul	11	SG.2, 77, 10
Günther, Joachim	11	JG.26
Greb, ?	11	JG.77
Girnth, Heinz	11	JG.53
Gabler, Kurt	11	JG.300
Fuchs, Heinz	11	JG.1

Flügge, Karl-Heinz	11	JG.51
Felser, Walter	11	JG.5
Feiser, Walter	11	JG.5
Fahrenberger, Hans	11	JG.27
Dadd, ?	11	JG.52
Buchholz, Fritz von	11 (night)	NJG.1
Brutzer, Arthur	11	JG.77
Brandes, Heinz-Helmuth	11	ZG.1; JG.11
Bönsch, Herbert	11 (night)	NJG.2
Bongart, Peter	11	JG.7
Bolm, Ulrich	11	JG.11
Bittkau, Helmut	11	JG.51
Bernhardt, Max	11+	JG.51
Bergmeier, ?	11	JG.52
Benkendorf, ?	11	JG.3
Bauer, Herbert (Austria)	11 (+51 TD)	StG.2; SG.103, 2
Bartling, Günther	11	JG.54
Bachhuber, Frindolin	11	JG.54
Altnorthoff, Ernst-Georg	11	JG.27
Ahrens, Peter	11	JG.26
Zeis, Alfred	10	JG.53
Zechlin, Ernst	10 (night)	NJG.2, 5
Wunderlich, Horst	10	JG.51
Wöhrle, Heinrich	10	JG.53
Windish, Fähnrich Walter	10	JG.52, 7
Willmann, ?	10	JG.3
Willinger, Franz	10	JG.51; EKdo Rechlin
Wiesinger, Wilhelm	10	JG.27
Weinmann, Emil	10 (night)	NJG.6, 102
Wehren, Joachim von	10	JG.77
Wandam, Siegfried	10 (night)	NJG.1, 5
Vogel, Helmut	10	JG.53
Vogel, ?	10	JG.77
Victor, Ludvig	10+ (night)	NJG.6

Unzeitig, Robert	10	JG.26
Tschiersch, Martin	10 (night)	NJG.2
Tonn, Wolfgang	10 (night)	NJG.1
Tödt, Hans	10	JG.301
Tober, Friedrich	10 (night)	NJG.3, 4
Thomas, Helmuth	10	JG.52
Theiss, Hans	10	JG.300, 7
Ter Steegen, Herbert	10 (night)	NJG.5
Stückler, Alfred	10	JG.27
Strasen, Gerhard	10 J	JG.77, 26, 4
Stienhaus, Walter	10	JG.3
Steindl, Peter-Paul	10	JG.26
Speidel, Werner	10 (night)	NJG.3
Spanke, Theo	10	JG.54
Siekmann, ?	10	JG.77
Setzepfandt, Karl-Günther	10	JG.3
Seifert, Werner	10	JG.3
Schwanecke, Günther	10	JG.77, 5
Schulze, Alfred	10	JG.27
Schmid, Karl	10	JG.51
Schmelzinger, Emil	10	JG.11, 77
Schick, Walter	10	JG.51
Scherer, Walter	10	ZG.26
Scherer, Kurt	10	JG.4
Schäfer, Rolf-Dieter	10+	JG.52
Ruschen, Helmuth	10	JG.51
Rudloff, Hans-Werner von	10	JG.52
Rohlfing, Walter	10 (night)	NJG.3
Richter, Rudolf	10	ZG.2
Reschke, Heinz	10 (night)	NJG.6
Rentsch, Wolfgang	10	JG.3, 7
Recker, Walter	10	JG.53
Rathke, Waldemar	10 (night)	NJG.100
Rachner, Hans	10	JG.3
Pufahl, Wilfried	10	JG.53

Portz, Robert	10	JG.52
Pilz, ?	10	JG.52
Pierer, Hans	10	JG.52
Pazelt, Helmuth	10	JG.51
Patzelt, Helmuth	10	JG.51
Pancritius, Hans	10	JG.1, 11
Oloff, Heinz	10 (night)	NJG.1
Oberheide, Heinz	10 (night)	NJG.3
Müller, Wilhelm	10	JG.26, 7
Müller, Hermann	10	JG.27, 7
Möckel, Wolfram	10 (night)	NJG.3
Misch, Heinz	10 (night)	NJG.2, 3
Meister, Dieter	10+	KG.40; ZG..1; JG.2
Mangold, Egon	10 (night)	NJG.100, 200
Lüddecke, Robert	10 (night)	NJG.2
Leuchs, Rolf	10 (night)	NJG.6
Launer, Richard	10 (night)	NJG.1, 4, 6
Laube, Martin	10	JG.53
Langer, Hans	10+	JG.51, 7
Landsenbacher, ?	10	JG.7
Külp, Franz	10	JG.27, 7
Kromer, Alfred	10	JG.54
Krause, Bodo	10	JG.77
Krahforst, Josef	10 (night)	NJG.4
Köpcke, Manfred	10+	JG.52, 51, 4
Klein, Hans	10	JG.52
Klaiber, ?	10 (night)	NJG.5, 100
Kerkhoff, Ernst	10	JG.52
Kaufmann, Johannes	10	JG.4
Kastenhuber, Hans	10	JG.11, 52
Kaross, Eberhard	10	JG.2; NJG.100
Kärchner	10	JG.77
Kammer, Kurt	10	JG.51
Juhls, Erich	10	JG.53

Jarsch, Lothar	10 (night)	NJG.2
Jakobi, Alfred	10	JG.5
Hosnedl, Siegmund	10	JG.53
Horn, ?	10+	JG.51
Honnefeller, Günther	10	SG.77, 10
Holzinger, Franz	10	JG.54, 7
Holtfreter, Günther	10 (night)	NJG.3
Hiller, Otto	10 (night)	NJG.5
Havenstein, Klaus	10 (night)	NJG.3
Hausschild, Hans	10 (night)	NJG.100
Hartmann, Ludwig	10+	JG.2
Hanstein, Helmut	10	JG.3
Handrick, Gothardt	10 (5 in Spain)	JG.26, 77
Hammer, Kurt	10	JG.51
Hahne, Wolfgang	10	JG.52
Hackstein, Heinz	10	JG.11
Guttmann, Gerhard	10	JG.26
Gruber, Viktor	10	JG.27
Grothe, Otto	10	JG.54
Gross, Artur	10	JG.302; NJG.4, 6
Greiner, Arbert	10	JG.52, 11, 7
Göbel, Hubert	10+	JG.301, 7; EKdo.262
Glitz, Willi	10 (night)	NJG.3
Gienanth, Hans-Eugen	10 (night)	NJG.1
Gendelmeyer, Wolfgang	10	JG.3
Gehring, Erich	10	JG.53
Fries, Heinz de	10 (night)	NJG.100
Framm, Gerd	10	JG.27
Fischer, Alfred	10	JG.3
Finster, Lenz	10 (night)	NJG.1
Fest, Wilhelm	10	JG.11
Fensch, Fritjof	10 (night)	NJG.4
Fels, Konrad	10	JG.77
Fassner, Franz	10	JG.52

Esser, Hans	10	JG.77
Engel, Walter	10 (night)	KG.3; NJG.1, 5
Eickmeier, Bruno	10 (night)	NJG.1
Eichhoff, ?	10+	JG.2
Ehrenberg, Ernst	10	JG.52
Dieterle Manfred	10	JG.300
Cohrs, Werner	10	JG.52
Buschmann, Franz	10 (night)	NJG.1, 3
Bürschgens, Josef	10	JG.26
Burggraf, Wilhelm	10	JG.301
Buchheit, Ludwig	10	JG.52
Bubel, Eduard	10	JG.11
Bos, Heinrich	10	JG.54
Bonow, Kurt	10 (night)	NJG.5, 10
Böhm-Tettelbach, Karl	10	ZG.26
Boddem, Peter	10 (all in Spain)	J.88
Blömertz, Günther	10	JG.26
Bleymüller, Alexander	10	JG.53
Beulich, Erich	10	JG.5
Bertram, Karl-Friedrich	10	JG.3
Berndt, Paul	10	JG.54, 11
Beck, Rudolf	10	JG.51
Beck, Kurt	10	JG.26
Bänsch, Karl-Heinz	10+	JG.2
Balfanz, Wilfred	10	JG.51, 53
Anlauf, Robert	10+	JG.52
Angres, Heinz	10	JG.3
Adams, Hans	10	JG.51
Zirngibl, Josef	9	JG.26
Witzel, Karl	9	JG.27
Witt, Hermann	9	JG.53
Winterfeldt, Alexander von	9 (+4 in WWI)	JG.2, 77
Wiegand, Heinfried	9	JG.5
Wennecke, ?	9	JG.1
Weihs, Hans-Dieter	9	JG.7

Weber, Joachim	9	ZG.26; EKdo.262; Kdo Nowotny; JG.7
Völker, Heinz	9 (night)	NJG.2
Vockelmann, Karl	9	JG.53
Tweitmeyer, Johann	9	JG.77
Trübenbach, Hans	9	JG.52
Tischtau, Manfred	9 (night)	NJG.5
Thielen, Werner	9	JG.54
Szuggar, Willi	9 (5 in Spain)	JG.52, 26
Stroinigg, Hans	9	JG.51
Stenglein, Hans	9	JG.27
Steddin, Werner	9	JG.77
Stebner, Theodor	9	JG.51, 5
Stakeljahn, ?	9	JG.5; SG.4
Stahlberg, Erwin	9	JG.3, 300, 7
Sonner, Michael	9+	JG.51
Slomski, Alexander	9	JG.51
Seewald, Karl-Ludwig	9	JG.3
Schulwitz, Gerhard	9	JG.26
Schratter, Robert	9 (night)	NJG.5
Schön, Walter	9 (night)	NJG.1
Scholze, Heinz	9	JG.52
Schneider, Hugo	9	JG.27
Schmidt, Rudolf	9	JG.53
Schmidt, Karl	9	JG.51
Schmale, Willi	9 (night)	NJG.1, 3
Schlegel, Rolf	9	JG.53
Scheider, Hugo	9	JG.27
Scharl, Alfred	9	JG.53
Schanz, Georg	9	JG.27
Schalk, Paul	9	JG.11
Schäfer, Ernst	9	JG.300, 302
Sauer, Kurt	9	JG.53
Ruge, Wilhelm	9	JG.53

Rüdel, Hans-Ulrich	9	StG.3, 2; SG.2
Rohlfs, ?	9	JG.77
Rentz, ?	9	JG.11
Rathofer, Fritz	9	JG.1
Quaritsch, Karl-Heinz	9	JG.53
Ponec, Karl-Heinz	9	JG.3
Polak, Heinz	9	JG.53
Pissarski, Georg	9	JG.3
Philipp, Rudorf	9	JG.27
Petermann, Werner	9	JG.77
Pelinka, Hans	9	JG.51
Otten, Karl-Heinz	9	JG.52
Ohl, Wolfgang	9	JG.51
Oberländer, Horst	9	JG.5
Müller, Rudolf	9	JG.53
Müller, Hans-Volkmar	9	JG.53
Moycis, Rudolf	9	JG.27
Mölders, Victor	9	ZG.1; NJG.1; JG.51
Moldenhauer, Harald	9	KG.2; JG.3, 1
Messmer, Paul	9	JG.51
Meschke, Heinz	9	JG.77
Mendl, Arthur	9	JG.5
Meien, Ulrich von	9 (night)	NJG.100, 200, 5
Makrocki, Wilhelm	9	ZG.76; JG.26
Lingnau, Erich	9	JG.51
Licht, Albrecht	9	JG.54
Leuschel, Rudolf	9	JG.26
Kutzner, Otto	9	NJG.2, 3
Kunze, Bernhard	9	JG.1
Kunert, Hans	9	JG.53
Krug, Heinz	9	JG.26
Köster, Peter	9+	EJG.2; JG.7; JV.44
Koppe, Heinz	9 (night)	NJG.2, 3
Kohl, Hermann	9	JG.51

Kohl, ?	9	JG.3
Koch, Erwin	9	JG.51, 1
Kaiser, Franz	9	JG.53
Kahl, Heinz	9	JG.1
Jenisch, Kurt	9	JG.27
Ilk, Iro	9	LG.1; JG.300
Holstein, Hermann	9	JG.53
Hoffer-Sulmthan, Herbert	9	SG.1, 77, 10; JG.400
Hess, Günther	9	JG.53
Herzog, Gerhard	9 (night)	NJG.1
Hermann, Kurt	9 (night)	NJG.2
Hermann, Hajo	9 (night, Wilde Sau)	KG.4, 30; JG.300
Hepe, Hans-Jürgen	9 (1 in Spain)	JG53; J.88
Hellenberger, Willi	9	JG.51
Heldt, Alfred	9 (night)	NJG.3
Heisel, ?	9	JG.52, 11
Heidel, Alfred	9	JG.27
Haugk, Werner	9	ZG.77, 76
Harbort, Rudolf	9	JG.7
Hanke, Heinz	9	JG.1
Hallenberger, Willi	9	JG.51
Günther, Erwin	9	JG.52
Gruber, Friedmann	9	JG.11
Greiner, Willi	9	JG.302, 301
Gerken, Heinz	9+	JG.51
Gasthaus, Willi	9	JG.51
Gaissmayer, Anton	9	JG.300, 302
Frenzel, Harald	9	JG.3
Frädrich, Gerhard	9+	JG.54
Fritze, Rudolf	9	JG.52
Fricke, Erich	9	JG.54
Fluder, Emmerich (Austria)	9	JG.27
Fedgenhäuer, Martin	9	JG.3
Falkensamer, Egon	9	JG.51, 11

English, Irving	9	JG.77
Engelhard, Werner	9	JG.77
Elstermann, Willi	9 (night)	NJG.3; JG.6
Elbracht, Heinz	9	JG.5
Dörre, Edgar	9	JG.26
Dobrick, Erich	9	JG.11
Denzel, Robert	9 (night)	NJG.1
Damoser, Rudolf	9	JG.54
Christof, Ernst	9	JG.26
Buzzi, Bruno	9	JG.5
Büschen, Wilhelm	9	JG.6, 7; ZG.26
Bruhn, Heinrich	9	JG.54
Böhner, Otto	9	JG.53
Bley, Paul	9+	EKdo.262, Kdo Nowotny
Birkenstock, Hans-Jörg	9 (night)	NJG.1, 4, 6
Below, Friedrich	9	JG.53
Beckmann, Erich	9	JG.53
Becker, Karl	9	JG.11
Barnikel, Friedrich	9	JG.52
Amon, Georg	9	JG.53
Ziller, Horst	8	JG.27
Wulff, Ulrich	8 (night)	NJG.5
Wittke, Paul	8	JG.27
Wiegand, Kurt	8	JG.300
Widmaier, Viktor	8	JG.11
Werthner, Hans	8 (night)	NJG.2, 3
Werner, Lothar	8	JG.2
Weise, Reinhard	8	JG.3
Wassermann, Erich	8	JG.27
Warrelmann, Alfred	8 (night)	LG.1; NJG.3
Walterscheid, Clemens	8+	JG.2
Wallner, Otto	8+	JG.51
Vorhauer, Hans von	8	JG.1
Vacano, Martin von	8	JG.53

Tschirk, ?	8	JG.11
Torfer, Josef	8	JG.27
Thüroff, Heinrich	8	JG.53
Tetteroo, Gerd	8	JG.51
Terry, Ernst	8 (2 in Spain)	JG.51
Strassner, Johannes	8 (night)	NJG.2
Stock, Hermann	8 (night)	NJG.3
Stephan, Herbert	8	JG.302
Stark, Günther	8+	JG.4
Sliwa, Leo	8	JG.77
Skreba, Willi	8	JG.77
Seuss, Wilhelm	8 (night)	NJG.4, 5
Seeler, Karl-Heinz	8	JG.300, 302, 7
Schulte, Hans-Georg	8	JG.53
Schubert, Hans	8	JG.1
Schmidt, Gottfried	8	JG.26
Schmidt, Friedrich-Wilhelm	8	JG.3
Schlosstein, Karl-Friedtich	8	JG.77, 5
Schlichting, Joachim	8 (5 in Spain)	JG.27
Schirra, Helmuth	8	JG.3
Schellner, Heinz-Walter	8	JG.302
Schaedle, Gerd	8	JG.3
Rysavy, Martin	8	JG.26
Rosenberg, Helmut	8	JG.77
Ring, Bodo	8	JG.27
Riha, Alfred	8	JG.3
Rettberg, Ralph von	8	ZG.26, 2
Renberg, Ralph von	8	ZG.26, 2
Rasper, Hans	8 (night)	NJG.1, 101
Preu, Karlheinz	8	JG.53
Painczyk, Roman	8	JG.77
Niklas, Helmuth	8 (night)	NJG.1, 3
Nelte, Werner	8	JG.54
Muras, Rudolf	8	JG.27
Müller, Hans	8	JG.301

Müller-Haagen, Rainer	8	JG.Süd, 200
Monska, Otto	8	JG.27
Möckel, Wilhelm	8	JG.77
Missfeld, Johannes	8	JG.51
Migge, Günther	8 (night)	JG.300; NJG.10
Michaels, Herbert	8	JG.3
Methfessel, Werner	8	LG.1
Messerschmidt, Alfred	8	JG.51
Merbeler, Johann	8	JG.51
May, Friedrich	8	JG.2
Mayer, Leander	8+	JG.51
Marx, ?	8	JG.51
Martens, Hans-Herbert	8+	JG.51
Manz, Walter	8	JG.53
Maertens, Hans-Herbert	8+	JG.51, 3
Maack, Ernst	8	JG.27, 11
Lühr, ?	8	JG.77
Löber, Gerhard	8	JG.51
Lipcsey, Adalbert von	8	JG.27
Lesch, Heinrich	8	JG.5
Langemann, Werner	8	JG.53, 11
Lange, Friedrich	8	JG.26
Langanke, Gustav-Adolf	8	JG.27
Kuthe, Wolfgang	8 (night)	NJG.1
Kuhlmann, Erich	8 (4 in Spain)	JG.53
Kroker, Eberhard	8	JG.302
Krenzke, Erich	8	JG.27
Kirnbauer, Herbert	8	JG.52
Kilian, Jürgen	8	JG.77
Keitel, Hans-Karl	8	JG.51
Keinath, Alfred	8	JG.77
Kaiser, Erich	8	JG.1
Just, Gottfried	8	JG.1
John, Heinz	8	JG.51
John, Hans-Dieter	8	JG.51

Johne, Helmut	8	JG.51
Johannsen, Hans	8	JG.26
Job, Alois	8	JG.1, 11
Jensen, Heinrich	8	JG.51
Jahn, Ferdinand	8	JG.77
Jäckel, Ernst	8	JG.26
Hübsch, Anton	8	StG.2; SG.2
Hosmann, Karl	8	JG.77
Hofmann, Hermann	8	JG.26
Helber, Rolf	8+	JG.51; JG.Süd
Heidrich, Hans	8+	JG.53, 51
Hänsel, Helmuth	8	JG.77
Hallenberger, W.	8	JG.303
Hackl, Ernst	8	JG.27
Graziadei, Norbert	8	JG.300
Graf, Egon	8	JG.3
Gorlach, Gerhard	8	JG.54
Glass, Hans-Joachim	8	JG.77
Gerhard, Dieter	8	JG.1, 52
Führmann, Heinz	8	JG.54, 7
Friese, Helmuth	8	JG.52
Frentzel-Beyme, Karl	8	JG.54
Franz, Günther	8 (night)	NJG.1, 3, 6
Frank, Heinz	8	LG.2; SG.1, 2, 151
Frankenberger, Heinrich	8 ·	JG.53
Förster, Paul	8 (night)	NJG.1
Flindt, Rudolf	8	JG.77
Fehre, ?	8	JG.300
Falck, Wolfgang	8 (night)	ZG.76; NJG.1
Ertel, ?	8	JG.77
Errer, Heinz	8	JG.51
Engler, Günther	8	JG.3, 7
Ebhardt, Rolf	8	NJG.1
Eberle, Karl	8	JG.77
Dobnig, Josef	8	JG.53, 51

Busch, Erwin	8	JG.26
Burggraf, Albert	8	JG.53
Buhl, Adolf Johann	8 (1 in Spain)	LG.2
Buddenhagen, Horst	8	JG.3
Brunner, Josef	8 (night)	NJG.1, 6
Brunke, Helmuth	8+	JG.51
Brock, Friedrich	8	JG.54
Bierwirth, Heinrich	8	JG.26
Beyer, Horst	8	JG.3
Beyer, Georg	8	JG.26
Berger, Hans	8	JG.1
Bellstedt, Alfred	8+	KG.40; ZG.1; JG.2
Behrens, Robert	8 (night)	NJG.100
Bär, Fritz	8	JG.51
Arnold, Walter	8	JG.27
Andersen, Lorenz	8	JG.5
Zinkenbach, Igor	7	JG.27
Zimmermann, ?	7	JG.52
Zeller, Joachim	7	JG.26, 7
Zeddies, Karl-Ludwig	7	JG.51
Willenbrink, Egbert	7	JG.53
Wieland, Edmund	7	JG.27
Wiegand, Werner	7	JG.51
Wenninger, Eberhard	7+	JG.51
Weihe, Hermann	7 (night)	NJG.100
Weber, Willi	7	JG.51
Vogt, Heinz	7	JG.77
Villforth, ?	7 (night)	NJG.2
Uiberacker, Friedrich von	7	JG.26
Tiedmann, Helmut	7	JG.3
Thun, Rudolf E.	7 (night)	NJG.5, 6
Taube, Fritz	7 (all in jet)	JG.7
Stumpf, Armin	7	JG.77
Ströbele, Georg	7	JG.3

Steins, Bruno	7	JG.52
Staroste, Gerhard	7	JG.77
Stammberger, Otto	7	JG.26
Stahl, Hermann	7	JG.77
Spies, Walter	7	JG.53, 1, 11, 27
Selle, Erich von	7	JG.26
Schröder, Ernst	7	JG.300
Schreiber, Alfred	7	SG.26; EKdo.262; Kdo Nowotny; JG.7
Schöpper, Erich	7	JG.3
Schmitz, Wolfgang	7	JG.27
Schmidt, Karl-Heinz	7	JG.3
Schmid, Otto	7	JG.1
Schmeidler, Hans	7	JG.77
Scheffel, Rudolf	7	ZG.1; JG.26
Schausten, Reinhard	7	JG.51
Schauenberg, Karl	7	JG.300
Sauber, Robert	7	JG.51
Rusack, Karl-Heinz	7	JG.300
Rudolph, Heinrich	7	JG.11
Rochel, Kurt	7 (6 in Spain)	Unknown
Richter, ?	7+	JG.54
Reiter, Theo	7	JG.53
Reiser, Robert	7	JG.3
Reiser, Hans	7	JG.3
Reinartz, Fridolin	7	JG.3
Reiche, ?	7	JG.302, 301
Rauhaus, Rudolf	7	JG.1
Rathenow, Johannes	7	JG.1
Prues, Walter	7 (night)	NJG.1
Pritzwitz, von	7	JG.77
Preiss, Ewald	7	JG.300
Pieper, Ulrich	7	JG.77
Pfeiffer, Ernst	7	JG.7

Pfeffer, Alfred	7	JG.11
Opalke, Horst	7	JG.3
Notemann, Helmuth	7	JG.53
Nolting, Erhard	7	JG.3
Niedermayr, Max	7	JG.77
Neuner, Herbert	7	JG.1
Munding, Karl	7	JG.5
Müller, Robert	7	JG.2, 1
Müller, Kurt	7	ZG.2
Müller, Gustl	7+	JG.51
Mühleise, Eduard	7	JG.77
Mischkot, Bruno	7	JG.26, 3, 2; EJG2
Mihlan, Heinz	7	SG.4; JG.51
Metzler, Fritz	7	JG.52
Mentnich, Karl	7	JG.27
Meissner, Hans	7	JG.1
Martin, Max	7	JG.26
Margstein, Walter	7	JG.53
Marburg, Gerhard	7	JG.3
Mang, Paul	7	JG.53
Malsch, Franz	7+	JG.4
Lüpke, Hans-Joachim	7	JG.1
Lüdtke, Heinz	7	JG.3
Lüdicke, Manfred	7	JG.77
Loose, Fritz	7 (all in jet)	JG.7
Lindemann, Theodor	7	JG.26, 77
Lennhoff, Rudi	7	JG.11
Laub, Karl	7	JG.26
Langmann, Günther	7	JG.51
Kuhn, Adalbert	7	JG.3
Kropf, Willi	7	JG.301
Kräuter, Wilhelm	7	JG.1
Kolb, Karl	7 (1 in Spain)	JG.53
Koch, Gerhard	7	JG.301
Kiesling, Walter	7 (night)	NJG.3

Keidel, Wilhelm	7 (2 in Spain)	JG.52
Kaufmann, Werner	7	JG.53
Kaufhold, Karl	7	JG.54
Karsten, Kurt	7 (night)	NJG.4, 6
Kapp-Herr, Hermann von	7	JG.3
Kaminski, Herbert	7	ZG.26, 76; JG.53
Kabus, Karl-Heinz	7	JG.11
Kabisch, Helmut	7	JG.52
Jüppner, Hans	7	JG.11
Josten, Reinhard	7	JG.51
Jochim, Berthold	7	JG.11
Jeworrek, Heinz	7	JG.3
Jenschko, Alfred	7	JG.77
Jansen, Josef	7	JG.27
Illner, Johann	7	JG.51
Humburg, Heinrich	7+	JG.26, 7
Hübner, Werner	7	JG.51
Horten, Walter	7	JG.26
Horstmann, Herbert	7	JG.77
Holl, Walter	7	JG.26
Hipper, Heinz	7	JG.53
Hillgruber, Walter	7	JG.27
Hiller, Karl	7	JG.11
Hentschel, Erwin	7	SG.2
Henrici, Eberhard	7	JG.26
Henning, Horst	7	KG.77; NJG.3
Henkemeier, Hans-Leopold	7	JG.54
Helm, Albert	7	JG.3
Helm, ?	7 (night)	NJG.3
Hecker, Karl-Dieter	7	JG.3
Hartigs, Hans	7	JG.26
Haese, Fritz	7+	JG.51
Güthenke, Hans-Georg	7	JG.11
Grzymalla, Gerhard	7	JG.26
Grünlinger, Walter	7	JG.26

Grübling, Josef	7	JG.77
Grosser, Heinz	7	JG.11, 77
Gräf, Fritz	7 (night)	NJG.4
Gramlich, Benno	7 (night)	NJG.3, 10
Gottuck, Hans	7	JG.300, 7
Goetze, Kurt	7	JG.11
Gmelin, Knud	7	KG.40; ZG.1
Giesecke, Herbert	7+ (night)	NJG.3
Geyer, Norbert	7	JG.3
Geisen, Walter	7	JG.5
Gehrels, Fritz	7	JG.51
Gassel, Erich	7	JG.77
Führing, Karl	7	JG.51
Fühlinger, Walter	7	JG.26
Fleischhacker, Heinz	7	JG.51
Esser, Wilhelm	7	JG.53
Ernst, Erich	7	JG.53
Erler, Albert	7	JG.4
Erhardt, Matthäus	7	JG.300
Emler, Kurt	7	JG.302
Eichhorn, Günther	7	JG.5
Ehrig, Friedrich	7	JG.7
Ehlen, Karl-Heinz	7	JG.26
Ederer, Josef	7	JG.53
Ebbighausen, Karl	7 (3 in Spain)	JG.26
Eberspächer, Helmuth	7	SKG.10, KG.51; NSG.20
Eberhardt, Kraft	7 (all in Spain)	J.88
Dimter, Willi	7 (night)	NJG.1
Diepgen, Hans-Joachim	7	JG.54
Delakowicz, Richard	7 (night)	NJG.4
Decker, Franz	7	JG.52
Dau, Arthur	7	JG.51
Dahmen, Hans	7	JG.300
Clerico, Max	7	JG.54

Clässen, Johann	7	JG.3
Büttner, Herbert	7	JG.77
Burda, Johannes	7	JG.3
Burath, Eberhard	7	JG.51, 1
Bülow, Günther Rudell von	7+	JG.2
Buhrow, Ernst	7	JG.77
Brunner, Willi	7	JG.5
Brucki, Edmund	7	JG.3
Bromen, Wilhelm	7	StG.2; SG.151, 9
Brandl, Josef	7	JG.27
Bornholt, Wilhelm	7	JG.3
Bockemeyer, Rolf	7 (night)	NJG.1, 5
Birnstill, Franz	7	JG.3
Bietmann, Ludwig	7 (night)	NJG.1
Biermann, Herbert	7	JG.11
Bell, Kurt	7	JG.54
Bellinghausen, Theodor	7 (night)	NJG.100
Becker, Karl-Heinz	7 (night)	NJG.11
Bauer, Martin	7 (night)	NJG.1, 7
Bauer, Johann	7	JG.3
Bahr, Hans-Joachim	7	JG.5
Arnoldy, Hans-Jakob	7	JG.77
Amend, Hermann	7	JG.5
Ambs, Alfred	7+	JG.7
Adam, Heiz-Günther	7	JG.26
Zilling, Günther	6	JG.54
Ziegenfuss, Kurt	6	JG.51, 1
Zacher, Hans	6	JG.51
Würtz, Wilhelm	6	JG.26
Wolf, Hermann	6	JG.53
Wolff, Lothar	6+	KG.40; ZG.1; JG.4
Wojnar, Harald	6+	JG.52, 3
Wilke, Hermann	6	JG.27
Wilcke, Hermann	6	JG.27

Wiest, Heinz	6	JG.51
Wielebinski, Paul	6	JG.3
Wessel, Albert	6	JG.77
Weiroster, Gottfried	6	JG.11
Wegner, Fritz	6	JG.1, 7
Völlkopt, Karl-Heinz	6 (night)	NJG.1
Vandeveerd, Heinrich	6	JG.26, 27
Trowal, Franz	6	JG.77
Trabert, Willi	6	JG.27
Tabbat, Adolf	6+	JG.26
Suwelack, Gerhard	6	JG.27, 7
Strack, Oskar	6	JG.52
Stiegler, Helmuth	6	JG.1
Stickel, Heinz	6	JG.51
Stephan, Willi	6	JG.52, 27
Stendel, Günther	6	JG.52
Stellfeld, Robert	6	JG.1
Stahl, Fritz	6	ZG.26
Sprenger, Gerhard	6	JG.3
Sommavilla, Erich	6	JG.53
Smiatik, Horst	6	JG.52
Sculte, Horst	6	JG.11
Schwerdtner, Heinrich von	6	JG.53
Schulze, Horst	6	JG.11
Schulz, Egon	6	JG.3
Schröder, Georg	6+	JG.2
Schreiber, Otto	6	JG.52
Scholz, Hans-Joachim	6	JG.3
Schnabel, Heinz	6	JG.3
Schmied, Hermann	6	JG.3
Schmidt, Heinz	6	JG.27
Schmidt, Fritz	6	JG.77
Schiller, Georg	6	JG.3
Schiebeler, Kurt	6	JG.54, 400, 7
Ryll, Hartmut	6	JG.77, 400

Runge, Johannes	6	JG.54
Ritschel, Frany	6	JG.11
Riepe, Ernst	6	JG.27
Ressel, Heinz	6	JG.3
Reinwald, ?	6	JG.3
Reinbrecht, Ekke-Eberhard	6	LG, 2; JG.77
Rahner, Erich	6	JG.51
Raab, H.	6	JG.3
Quatember	6	LG.2
Preisler, Bela	6	JG.5
Pöttgen, Rainer	6	JG.27
Ostrowitzki, Bruno	6	JG.3
Osterkamp, Theodor	6 (+32 WWI)	JG.51
Osswald, Heinrich	6	JG.77
Niemayer, Otto	6	JG.77
Neuberger, Alfred	6	JG.11
Necesany, Kurt	6	KG.40; ZG.1
Müller, Herbert	6	JG.301, 7
Müller, Hans	6	JG.5
Müller, ?	6	JG.51
Mittermaier, Alfons	6	JG.51
Maurer, Walter	6 (1 in Spain)	KG.6
Marschhausen, Günther	6	JG.77
Mannchen, Alfred	6	JG.27, 77, 11
Malm, Willibald	6	JG.26
Mackenstedt, Wilhelm	6	JG.26
Lülwes, Heinz	6	JG.51
Lüder, Rudolf	6	JG.5
Lüdecke, Friedrich	6	JG.5
Lösch, Waldo	6	JG.3
Lorenz, Wilhelm	6	JG.11
Lindenschmid, Albert	6	JG.1
Lilienhoff, Rolf von	6	JG.5
Licha, Ludwig	6	JG.77
Leonardy, Bernhard	6	JG.52

Lehmann, Hans	6	JG.1
Kürbiss, Werner	6	JG.51
Küll, Gustav	6 (2 in Spain)	JG.51
Kühnel, Hans	6	JG.3
Kruse, Fritz	6 (night)	NJG.1
Krieger, Walter	6	JG.51
Kraft, Erwin	6	JG.51
Köstler, Oskar	6 (night)	NJG.1
Kopperschläger, Heinrich	6	JG.53
Koch, Robert	6	JG.77
Koal, Fritz	6	JG.27
Kniewasser, Hermann	6	JG.3
Knier, Leopold	6	JG.27
Knichel, Karl	6	JG.53
Klötzer, Walter	6	JG.27
Klein, Willi	6	JG.53
Kirsch, Hermann	6	JG.53
Kinzinger, Adolf	6	JG.54
Kiesel, Wolfgang	6	JG.51
Kickert, Rolf	6+	JG.51
Keune, Helmut	6	JG.3
Kehl, Fietrich	6	JG.26
Kath, Otto	6	JG.51, 54
Kastermüller, Simon	6	JG.53
Kadlcik, ?	6 (night)	NJG.4
Jessen, Heinrich	6	JG.26
Janson, Lothar von	6 (1 in Spain)	JG.53
Jänke, Erwin	6+	JG.51
Jäger, ?	6	JG.3
Hubatsch, Herbert	6 (night)	NJG.1, 5, 6
Horstmann, Hermann	6	KG.40; ZG.1
Horn, Gustav	6	JG.77
Höhnisch, Heinrich	6	JG.53
Höhn, Georg	6	JG.5
Höger, Hans	6	JG.77

Hillmann, Fritz	6 (3 in Spain)	JG.53
Hilleke, Otto-Heinrich	6	JG.26
Hien, Willibald	6 (4 in Spain)	JG.53
Heuer, Robert	6	JG.51, 3, 7
Herzog, Helmuth	6	JG.51
Herkenhoff, Heinz	6	JG.53
Helms, Bodo	6	JG.5
Hausmann, Richard	6	JG.54
Hanneck, Gottfried	6+ (night)	NJG.1
Hahn, Otto	6	JG.77
Habspiel, Willi	6	JG.52
Günther, Ernst	6	JG.27
Gumprecht, Herbert	6	JG.2
Grüber, Heinz	6	JG.53
Gräb, Herbert	6	ZG.1
Graf, Alois	6	JG.51
Gottlob, Heinz	6	JG.26
Görbing, Kurt	6	JG.77
Göhmann, Fritz	6	JG.53
Gloerfeld, Wolfgang	6	JG.11
Germeroth, Rudolf	6	JG.3
Gärtner, Josef	6	JG.26
Gaedicke, Alfred	6	JG.11
Fresia, Heinz	6	ZG.76
Freitag, Hermann	6	JG.3
Födisch, Lothar	6	JG.300
Fischer, Max-Bruno	6	JG.3
Faltin, Kurt	6	JG.1
Fahlbusch, Helmut	6	ZG.76
Ertmann, Horst	6	JG.1
Emmerich, Peter	6+	JG.51
Eickhoff, Heinrich	6	JG.27
Dürkop, Otto	6	JG.54
Drössler, Kurt	6	JG.5
Dreizehner, Gerhard	6	JG.11

Draeger, Paul	6+	JG.3
Dörr, Heinrich	6	JG.301
Desinger, Willi	6	JG.3
Clemens, Kurt	6	JG.3
Christmann, Herbert	6	JG.11
Busse, Lothar	6	JG.51
Büsgens, Günther	6	JG.52
Büsen, Franz	6	JG.27
Buschmann, Herbert	6	JG.51
Bülow, Hakon von	6	JG.54
Buchholz, Erich	6	JG.1
Brücher, Heinz	6+	JG.51
Brockerhoff, Wilhelm	6 (night)	NJG.3
Breitfeld, ?	6 (night)	NJG.5
Brauns, Wilhelm	6 (night)	NJG.2
Brandt, Kurt	6	JG.77
Böttge, Erwin	6 (all in jet)	JG.7
Bolte, Karl	6	JG.27
Boll, Hermann	6	JG.3
Bohm, Paul	6 (night)	NJG.2
Blum, Christoph	6	JG.301
Blaut, Heinrich	6	JG.3
Bischoff, Günther	6	JG.300, 7
Bilfinger, Fritz	6	JG.1
Berthel, Hans	6	JG.52
Benz, Siegfried	6	JG.26
Beissel, Egon Graf	6	JG.77
Beck, Albin	6	JG.3
Andel, Peter	6	JG.26
Albrecht, Heinz	6	JG.11
Zemper, Ulrich	5	JG.53
Zehart, Ottmar	5	JG.3
Wurm, Heinz	5	JG.1
Wulff, Hermann	5+	JG.51
Wöffen, Antonius	5	JG.27

Wittbold, Günther	5	JG.4
Wilff, Hermann	5	JG.51
Wigge, Winfried	5	JG.53
Wichmann, Helmut	5	JG.3
Westerhoff, Karl	5	JG.3
Weinzierl, Walter	5	JG.302
Wegener, Erich	5	JG.301
Wallrath, Karl-Heinz	5	JG.3
Wallner, Ernst	5 (night)	NJG.6
Walchhofer, Johann	5	JG.27
Wagner, Erich	5	JG.53
Vollbracht, Friedrich	5	LG.2
Volkmer, Fridolin	5	LG.2
Volkmann, Wilhelm-Erich	5	JG.3
Vogel, Dietrich	5	JG.77
Viebahn, Erich	5+	JG.51
Ursinius, Werner	5	JG.53
Umbach, Hans	5	JG.27
Troha, Egon (Austria)	5	JG.26, 27, 3
Tröger, Heinz	5	JG.1
Timm, Fritz	5	JG.1
Tiedemann, Henri	5	JG.11
Thörl, Hugo	5 (night)	NJG.4
Teegler, Werner	5	JG.3
Taubert, Helmuth	5	JG.77
Ströhlein, Fritz	5	JG.51
Stoffel, Siegfried	5	JG.1
Stockhowe, Ernst	5	JG.53
Stiebler, ?	5+	JG.52
Stepman, Willi	5	JG.27
Steinhilper, Ulrich	5	JG.52
Steinbach, ?	5	LG.2
Stangl, Anton	5	JG.54
Sommer, Botho	5	ZG.76
Schypek, Joachim	5	JG.54

Schütze, Hans-Georg	5 (night)	NJG.2
Schummer, Rudolf	5	JG.53
Schönrock, ?	5	JG.1
Schönfeldt, Heinz	5	JG.3
Schneider, Otto	5	JG.11
Schneider, ?	5	JG.77
Schmitz, ?	5	LG.2
Scheuchenpflug, Heinrich	5	JG.53
Scheuber, Helmuth	5	JG.51
Schenk, ?	5	JG.300
Schenkelberg, Alfred	5	JG.54
Scharfenberg, Rudolf	5	JG.300
Schacht, Arthur	5	JG.27
Sauder, ?	5	JG.51
Sarzio, Gustav	5 (night)	NJG.1
Saar, Oskar	5	JG.27
Rusche, Dieter	5	JG.302
Rühl, Heinrich	5	JG.53
Ruland, Georg	5	JG.54
Rott, Frank-Werner	5	JG.53, 27, 77
Rose, Werner	5	JG.3
Rohde, ?	5	JG.77
Roch, Eckard	5	JG.26
Rey, Günther	5	JG.54, 26
Reiher, Gerhard	5	JG.52, 3, 7
Reichenberger, Walter	5 (night)	NJG.2
Rathmann, Kurt	5	JG.52
Raneu, ?	5 (night)	NJG.100
Rabenstein, Walter	5	JG.27
Quasinowski, Ernst	5 (4 in Spain)	JG.52
Puttfarken, Dietrich	5	KG.51
Prigge, Rolf	5	JG.27, 7
Polster, Wolfgang	5	JG.26
Pohland, Heinz	5	LG.2
Plass, Joachim	5+ (night)	NJG.5

Pissot, Otto	5	JG.3
Pintsch, Rudolf	5	JG.3
Piel, Gerhard	5	JG.300
Philipp, Richard	5 (all in jet)	JG.7
Philipp, Eerhard	5	JG.77
Pflitsch, Siegfried	5	JG.51
Pejas, Oswald	5	JG.27
Pavenzinger, Georg	5	JG.51
Paulisch, Hans-Werner	5	JG.54
Patho, Wolfgang	5	JG.53
Patan, Robert	5	JG.27
Pankalla, Gerhard	5	JG.53
Opitz, Kurt	5	JG.53
Obst, Heinz	5	JG.3
Nonn, Walther	5	JG.77
Nitzsche, Hans	5	JG.27
Nitz, Horst	5	JG.2
Nächster, Fritz	5+	JG.51
Muschter, Fritz	5	JG.53
Müller, Wilhelm	5	JG.54, 26
Müller, Kurt	5	JG.26
Müller, Kurt	5 (3 in Spain)	Unknown
Müller, Hugo	5	JG.300, 102; SKdo Elbe
Müller, Helmut	5	V(Z)/LG.1
Müller-Dühne, Gerhard	5	JG.26
Moser, Werner	5	JG.1, 52
Möllerke, Kurt	5	JG.3
Moller, Eugen von	5	JG.27
Mikoleit, Hans	5	JG.51
Meyer, Erich	5	JG.301
Metz, Rudolf	5	JG.3
Metzner, Günther	5	JG.11
Mett, Gerhard	5	JG.301
Menge, ?	5	JG.77

Maul, ?	5	JG.5
Matzdorf, Adelmar	5	JG.3
Martin, Paul	5	JG.27
Martin, Kurt-Werner	5	JG.51
Malapert, Peter von	5	JG.54
Maetzke, Eberhardt	5	JG.1
Lutzka, Richard	5	JG.5
Lüders, Franz	5	JG.26
Lüdemann, Heinz	5	JG.77
Lüddecke, Fritz	5	JG.26
Lück, Heinz-Günther	5	JG.1
Loos, Gottfried	5	JG.3
Lomberg, Günther	5 (night)	NJG.6
Löffler, Oskar	5	JG.3
Lion, Karl-Hermann	5	SG.1, 101
Lindelaub, Friedrich	5	JG.26
Liesendahl, Frank	5	JG.53, 2
Liedtke, Karl-Friedrich	5	JG.77
Leisebein, Manfred	5	JG.52
Lehn, Walter	5	JG.51
Lehmann, Georg	5	JG.1, 27
Lange, Gerhard	5	JG.6
Landry, Hans-Herbert	5	JG.3
Lamprecht, Bernhard	5	JG.53
Kutzera, Karl-Heinz	5	JG.1
Küttner, Siegfried	5	JG.3
Kurz, Hans	5 (night)	NJG.2
Kuhrke, Siegfried	5	ZG.26
Kuhn, Walter	5	JG.52
Krug, Willi	5	JG.3
Kreil, Max	5	JG.301
Kratz, Benno	5 (night)	NJG.6
Kraft, Karl	5	JG.1, 7
Krafftschick, Rudolf	5	JG.27
Kowalski, Herbert	5	JG.27

Kotiza, Eugen	5	JG.26, 1
Kornatzki, Horst-Günther von	5	JG.3
Koplik, Franz	5	JG.1
Köpf, Thomas	5	JG.2
Koch, Karl-Heinz	5	JG.5
Knier, Leopold	5	JG.5
Knieling, Wolfgang	5 (night)	NJG.6
Klotz, Herbert	5	JG.11
Klötzer, Hartmut	5	JG.53
Kleun, Erich	5	JG.5
Klein, Hans	5	JG.77
Kleinert, Alfred	5	JG.53
Klein, Erich	5	JG.5
Kittelmann, Hans	5+	JG.51
Kirsten, Otto	5	JG.3
Kirchner, Günther	5	JG.1
Kirchhoff	5	JG.1
Keller, Erich	5	JG.4
Kayl, Gottfried	5	JG.53
Kampe, Karl	5	JG.27
Kälber, Fritz	5	JG.11
Kaiser, Josef	5	JG.27
Junck, Werner	5	JG.53
Jänke, Hans-Joachim	5	JG.1, 7
Jaksch, Julius	5	JG.3
Jacobs, Friedrich	5	JG.51
Hupfeld, Arndt-Richard	5	JG.53
Hoyer, Johannes	5+	JG.3
Houwald, Wolf-Heinrich von	5	JG.52
Houwald, Otto-Heinrich von	5 (all in Spain)	J.88
Höschen, Friedhelm	5+	JG.51, 302
Hoppe, Kurt	5	JG.27
Hopfer, Hans Walter	5+	JG.51
Hölscher, August	5	JG.301, 7
Holland, Albert	5	JG.11

Hölker, Walter	5 (night)	NJG.5
Hofmann, Julio	5	JG.53
Hinz, ?	5	JG.3
Hinkelmann, Joachim	5	JG.3
Hicke, Walter	5	JG.53
Heuser, Heinrich	5	JG.26
Herzig, Heinz	5	JG.51
Herterich, Werner	5	JG.77
Henz, Helmut	5	JG.77
Henning, Erich	5	JG.2
Heinrichs, Dietrich	5	JG.77
Heinig, Günther	5	JG.3
Heim, ?	5 (all in jet)	JG.7
Hegenauer, Bruno	5	JG.26, 53
Heckmann, Theo	5	JG.27
Heckmann, Hubert	5	JG.1, 7
Hayessen, Hans-Joachim	5	JG.27
Harms, Hans	5	JG.53
Hanshen, Ulrich	5	KG.40; ZG.1
Hanf, Gerhard	5	JG.77, 1
Haesler, Alfred	5 (night)	NJG.1, 4
Hachtel, August	5	JG.400
Haas, Otto	5	JG.27
Haase, Julius	5	JG.53
Gutermann, Willy	5	KG.40
Grübert, Hans	5	JG.54
Grimm, Josef	5	JG.27
Greissinger, Rolf	5	JG.52
Goy, Rudolf	5 (3 in Spain)	JG.53
Götz, Horst	5	JG.3
Gollasch, Erich	5 (night)	NJG.1
Giessubel, Vincenz	5 (night)	NJG.2, KG.40
Ghesla, Wilhelm	5	JG.53
Gerber-Schulz, Heinz	5	JG.77
Geissler, Max	5	JG.52

Geides, Georg	5	JG.52
Gehrke, Heinz	5	JG.26
Gawlick, Franz	5	JG.53
Gardiewski, Erberhard	5 (night)	NJG.1, 2
Führmann, Erich	5	JG.11
Fuchs, Kurt	5	JG.27
Fröschmann, Eramus	5	JG.53
Frölich, Hans-Jürgen	5	JG.26
Franzisket, Max	5	JG.5; ZG.1
Frank, ?	5	JG.11
Fraass, Helmuth	5	JG.53
Fleischmann, Georg	5	ZG.76
Fischer, Siegfried	5	JG.53
Federle, Josef	5 (night)	NJG.6
Fast, Hans-Joachim	5	JG.26
Esche, Willi	5	JG.301
Erichsen, Dieter	5 (night)	NJG.4, 6
Engau, Fritz	5 (night)	NJG.11; JG.11
Elsner, Rudi	5+	JG.51
Elles, Franz	5	JG.27
Eickhoff, Christian	5	JG.26, 2
Eichler, Kurt	5	JG.3
Ehmke, Otto	5	JG.3
Edmann, Johannes	5	JG.26
Dürr, Hermann	5	JG.301
Doyé, Hans	5	JG.27, 51
Dotze, Gottfried	5	JG.26
Döring, Werner	5	JG.27
Dirksen, Hans	5	JG.26
Dietze, Gottfried	5	JG.26
Cramon, Friedrich-Franz von	5	JG.3
Coester, Wolf-Dieter von	5	JG.52
Busenkell, Albert	5	JG.27
Burkel, Hans-Joachim	5	JG.27
Bugaj, Karl	5	JG.1

Buck, Rolf	5	JG.77
Buchholz, Horst	5	JG.51
Buchholz, Günther	5	JG.1
Brunner, Willi	5	JG.51
Bruhns, Erwin	5+	JG.51
Brandt, Josef	5	JG.3
Bozicek, Franz	5	JG.5
Borreck, Hans-Joachim	5	JG.26
Bornemann, Karl-Heinz	5	JG.54
Born, Karl	5	JG.1, 27
Born, Heinz	5	JG.11
Borchers, Hans-Jürgen	5	JG.3
Bohn, Kurt	5	JG.26
Bleyer, Paul	5+	JG.2
Bleck, Alfred	5	JG.54
Blech, Georg	5	JG.1
Birkigt, Heinz	5	JG.11
Birke, Gerhard	5	JG.26
Bindseil, Alfred	5	JG.1
Bilek, Alfred	5	JG.3
Beutelspacher, Ernst	5	SG.2, 1
Bertram, Ludwig	5	JG.11
Baumgarten, Erwin	5	JG.27
Bauer, Alfons	5	JG.51
Auth, Alois	5	JG.300
Aufhammer, Fritz	5	JG.301
Appel, Walter	5	JG.27
Angst, Paul	5	JG.3
Anders, Werner	5	JG.3
Achleitner, Franz (Austria)	5	JG.1, 3
Zerlett, Josef	4	JG.27
Willers, Dieter	4	JG.51
Wieland, Helmut	4+	JG.51
Werner, Georg	4	JG.51
Wemhöner Hans	4	JG.26

Vogel, Veit Dr.	4	JG.51
Steinke, Rolf	4	JG.51
Stein, Gernot	4	JG.27
Stauffert, Hans	4	JG.3
Spahn, Johann	4	JG.26
Schulze-Dickow, Fritz	4	ZG.26
Schulte-Blanck, Günther	4	JG.53
Schreiter, Fritz	4	JG.51
Schreiner, Franz	4	JG.27
Schnecker, Karl	4	JG.51
Schiffbauer, Robert	4	JG.26
Schiemert, Heinrich	4	JG.27
Schallmoser, Eduard	4+	JV.44
Roka, Franz	4	StG.2, 1
Rey, Günther	4	JG.26
Reinicke, Leonard	4	JG.301
Rebel, Alfred	4	JG.51
Pritzel, Otto	4	JG.302
Priebe, Ekkehard	4	JG.51
Plenzat, Kurt	4	StG.2; SG.2
Pitcairn, Douglas	4	JG.51
Otte, Walter	4	JG.26, 27
Niese, Alfred	4	JG.26
Meyer, Hermann	4	JG.26
Merz, ?	4	JG.26
Lindenberger, Alfred	4 (+12 WWI)	JG.300
Lessing, Hans	4	JG.51
Lenz, Anton	4	JG.51
Langelotz, Hubert	4	JG.302
Kremmer, Kurt	4	JG.27
Kranefeld, Kurt	4	JG.26
Kolbe, Harald	4	JG.51
Kirstein, Helmut	4	JG.51
Janke, Johannes	4	JG.51
Hopfer, Hans-Werner	4	JG.51

Hientzsch, Manfred	4	JG.27
Henrici, Oskar	4 (all in Spain)	J.88
Held, Albrecht	4	JG.26
Heitmann, Hans	4	JG.26
Heinrich, Kurt	4 (all in Spain)	J.88
Heck, Herbert	4	JG.26
Haase, Arthur	4	JG.51
Grimmling, Walter	4 (1 in Spain)	Unknown
Göttmann, Leonard	4	JG.3
Fritsch, Paul	4	JG.26
Franz, Wolfgang	4	JG.26
Flegel, Norbert	4 (all in Spain)	J.88
Fischer, Edmund	4	JG.26
Essl, Franz	4	JG.52
Eigenbauer, Josef	4	JG.51
Dylewski, Kurt Heinz	4	JG.26
Burghardt, Rolf	4	JG.302
Buddenbrock, Fritz-Joachim von	4	JG.27
Brustellin, H.-H.	4	JG.51
Bitter, Gerhard	4	JG.27
Besekau, Helmut	4	JG.51
Bernhard, Gerd	4	JG.302
Belz, Alfre	4	JG.27
Beeck, Fritz	4	JG.51
Baumbach, Hans-Joachim	4	JG.51
Andres, Werner	4	JG.27
Alt, Erich	4	JG.51
Zestermann, Alexander	3	JG.51
Zeisler, Gerhard	3	JG.301
Woldenga, Bernhard	3	JG.27
Wilhelm, Heinz	3	JG.51
Werner, Heinrich	3	JG.51
Weber, Hans-Joachim	3	JG.301
Verhoeven, Werner	3	JG.26

Ungar, Fritz	3	JG.26
Ufer, Helmut	3	JG.26
Telschow, Albrecht	3	JG.51
Sy, Siegfried	3	JG.26
Sulzgruber, Max	3	JG.301
Strobl, Helmut (Austria)	3	JG.27, 3
Striebel, Hermann	3	JG.51
Stoltmann, Herbert	3	JG.51
Steinberg, Günther	3	JG.26
Stange, Hermann	3 (all in Spain)	J.88
Staege, Wilhelm	3 (all in Spain)	J.88
Seufert, Bernhard	3 (all in Spain)	J.88
Sellin, Kurt	3	JG.51
Seidl, Norbert	3	JG.26
Seebeck, Karl	3	JG.26
Schwamb, Otto	3	JG.302
Schulz, Heinz	3	JG.26
Schulze, Martin	3	JG.301
Schulze, Kurt	3	JG.5, 51
Schultenkemper, Clemens	3	JG.27
Schubert, Gustav	3	StG.1
Schnell, Heinrich	3	JG.26
Scharein, Georg	3	JG.301
Sattler, Josef	3	JG.301, 302
Saalmann, Hans-Joachim	3	JG.51
Röbbers, Rudolf	3	JG.51
Ripke, Hermann	3	JG.26
Ries, Eduard	3	JG.302
Richter, Heinz	3	JG.26
Rezepka, Hans-Friedrich	3	JG.51
Reinhart, Emil	3	JG.51
Reimet, Fritz	3	JG.51
Rehfeld, Herbert	3	JG.27
Pointner, Anton	3	JG.27
Podewils, Heinrich	3	JG.5

Piske, Herbert	3		StG.77; SG.10
Orzegowski, Ernst	3		StG, 77; SG.10
Oeckel, Hans	3		JG.26
Nitschke, Horst	3		JG.27
Niess, Anton	3		JG.51
Neumann, Ludwig	3		JG.51
Münch, Heinz	3		JG.26
Müller, Wilhelm	3		JG.26
Müller, Rudi	3		JG.51
Meyn, Rudolf	3		JG.51
Meyer, Georg	3		JG.51
Merz, German	3		JG.302
Menzel, Franz	3		JG.301
Meixner, Rudolf	3		JG.51
Marz, ?	3	(all in Spain)	J.88
Lutz, Albert	3		JG.51
Leyerer, Hans	3		JG.51
Leisner, Otto	3		JG.7, 300
Lampferhof, Ernst	3		JG.26
Kupka, Ernst	3		JG.51
Kruska, Kurt	3		JG.26
Krüger, Fritz	3		JG.27
Kreplin, Peter	3		JG.51
Koch, Kurt	3		JG.51
Kizina, Horst	3		JG.27
Kierstein, Paul	3		JG.26
Kestel, Melchior	3		JG.26
Keller, ?	3		JG.51
Karl, Gerhard	3		JG.26
Kalitzki, Wilhelm	3		JG.26
Jung, Johannes	3		JG.27
Jäschke, Herbert	3		JG.302
Janssen, Günther	3		JG.51
Jäckel, Konrad	3		JG.26
Hutzler, Kurt	3		JG.27

Hübel, Kurt	3	JG.51
Horn, ?	3	JG.51
Höness, Guido	3 (all in Spain)	J.88
Hollmann, Paul	3	JG.51
Hoffmann, Heinz-Horst	3	JG.5
Hemmerling, Eduard	3	JG.51
Helmholtz, Gottfried	3	JG.26
Heinrich, Otto	3	StG.77; SKG.10
Hegenauer	3	JG.26
Hecker, Michael	3	JG.26
Haugil, Friedrich	3	JG.51
Hanusch, Fritz	3	JG.26
Hager, Viktor	3	JG.26
Hager, Robert	3	JG.26
Graf, Albin	3	JG.51
Gerlach, Hans-Joachim	3	JG.27
Georgi, ?	3	JG.26
Fronhöfer, Willy	3	JG.26
Fleischmann, ?	3 (all in Spain)	J.88
Fink, Walter	3	JG.27
Fährmann, Gottfried	3 (all in jet)	JV.44
Epphard, Herbert	3	JG.51
Engfer, Hans	3	JG.301
Emanuel, ?	3	JG.301
Eichinger, Leopold	3	JG.26
Ehrig, Hans-Jürgen	3 (1 in Spain)	J.88; JG.51
Eberz, Bernahard	3	JG.26
Droste, ?	3 (all in Spain)	J.88
Dreifke, Wolfgang	3	JG.27
Donner, Konrad von	3	JG.26
Dietsche, Karl-Heinz	3	JG.302
Dieckmann, Fritz	3	JG.302
Diecke, Rudolf	3	JG.302
Delor, Rudolf	3	JG.26
Dardun, Walter	3	JG.51

Dachmann, Willi	3	JG.26
Corinth, Gerhard	3	JG.26
Clemens, Hans	3	JG.51
Brunotte, Erich	3	JG.51
Brügelmann Helmut	3	JG.26
Braunschweiger, Heinz	3 (all in Spain)	J.88
Bossler, Rudolf	3	JG.51
Bode, Erich	3	JG.26
Birk, Leonhard	3	JG.51
Biedermann, Erwin	3	JG.26
Berlinska, W.ilhelm	3	JG.302
Bausch, ?	3	JG.302
Baumgartner, ?	3	JG.51
Baumann, Heinrich	3	JG.51
Bauer, Josef	3 (all in Spain)	J.88
Baasch, Dieter	3	JG.5
Ayerle, Hermann	3	JG.26
Awe, Fritz	3 (all in Spain)	J.88
Awe, ?	3	JG.234
Wyrich, Heinz	2	JG.26
Wosnitza, Alois	2	StG.77; SG.102, 103, 10
Wodarczyk, Heinz	2	JG.26
Wilms, ?	2	JG.26
Wenzel, Kurt-Erich	2	JG.26
Weige, Walter	2	JG.51
Walter, Gerhard	2	JG.302
Voss, Werner	2	JG.302
Vollbracht, Friedrich	2	ZG.2
Tippe, Ehrhard	2	JG.26
Tietze, ?	2	JG.51
Thiel, Albert	2	JG.51
Terry, ?	2	JG.234
Teilken, Heinrich	2	JG.26
Stutt, Rudolf	2	JG.26

Strumpell, Hennig	2 (both in Spain)	J.88
Streuff, Paul	2	JG.302
Streit, Hermann	2	JG.51
Strehl, Hans	2	JG.51
Stoll, ?	2	JG.26
Stangen, Helmut	2	JG.51
Stahl, Hermann	2	JG.51
Sicking, Oskar	2	JG.51
Seifert, Herbert	2	JG.301
Schwentick, Horst	2	JG.26
Schwan, Werner	2	JG.26
Schuch, ?	2	JG.301
Schrader, Karl-Hermann	2	JG.26
Scholz, Walter	2	JG.26
Schmidtke, Kurt	2	JG.26
Schlögl, Leopold	2	JG.26
Schiling, Franz	2	JG.26
Schieffer, Karl	2	JG.26
Scheu, Hans	2	JG.26
Scheller, Walter	2	JG.301
Scheidt, Erhardt	2	JG.26
Ruppert, Hans	2	JG.26
Rosen, Adolf	2	JG.51
Ritz, Otto	2	SG.9
Richter, Josef	2	JG.26
Richter, Horst	2	JG.26
Rempel, Edgar	2 (both in Spain)	J.88
Rehahn, Paul	2 (both in Spain)	J.88
Rappl, Georg	2	JG.51
Ramthun, Friedrich	2	JG.26
Rahardt, Heinz	2	JG.26
Ragotzi, Hans	2	JG.26
Prenzel, Horst	2	JG.301
Poferl, Anton	2	JG.51
Planer, Herbert	2	JG.52

Pietruschka, Werner	2	JG.26
Pflüger, Hans	2	JG.51
Ossenkopp, Karl-Heinz	2	JG.26
Oglodek, Josef	2	JG.51
Oemler, Gerhard	2	JG.26
Noller, Wilhelm	2	StG.2; SG.10
Nink, Wilhelm	2	JG.26
Nachtigall, Kurt	2	JG.302
Müller, ?	2	JG.234
Müller, ?	2 (both in Spain)	J.88
Möller, Fritz	2	JG.51
Mölders, Alexander	2	JG.51
Meyer, Erich	2	JG.51
Meiss, Heinz	2	JG.26
Maetzke, ?	2	JG.26
Lönnecker, Heinrich	2+	JG.300, 7
Lojewski, Alfred von	2 (both in Spain)	J.88
Lohmann, Heinrich	2	JG.51
Lixfeld, Paul	2	JG.300
Lissack, Gerhard	2	JG.26
Lindner, Erich	2	JG.26
Limpert, Paul	2	JG.51
Lewens, Richard	2+	JG.51, 302
Leitz, Emil	2	JG.26
Lau, Kurt	2	StG.1, 2; SG.103
Lastowski, Jörg	2	JG.51
Lage, Heinz zur	2	JG.51
Kruse, Ottomar	2	JG.26
Kretschmer, H.	2	JG.301
Körver, Alfred	2	JG.302
Konze, Herbert	2	JG.51
Kolbe, Günter	2	JG.302
Kohler, Erich	2	JG.26
Knoop, ?	2	JG.51
Klotz, Friedrich	2	JG.51

Klems, Heinz	2	JG.26
Klein, Heinz	2	JG.27
Klein, Erich	2	JG.26
Klaus, Johann	2	StG.1; SG.1
Kirchmeier, Hans	2	JG.5
Kindler, Franz	2	JG.51
Keller, Paul	2	JG.26
Kaiser, Helmut	2	JG.26
Kahse, Werner	2	JG.26
Kabis, Walter	2	JG.51
Jutzenka, Konrad von	2	JG.26
Just, Gerhard	2	JG.26
Jung Robert	2	JG.300
Joswig, Wilhelm	2	StG.1, 77, 2; SG.2
Jochem, Edmund	2	JG.51
Janda, Ernst	2	JG.26
Höhn, Erich	2	JG.51
Honsberg, Werner	2	StG.77; SG.77, 151
Hofmann, ?	2	JG.26
Hoffmann, Johannes	2	JG.26
Hiller, Franz	2	JG.26
Hilgendorff, Viktor	2	JG.26
Herpetz, Willi	2	JG.51
Herbster, Heinrich	2	JG.26
Heinz, Karl	2	JG.51
Heinemann, Ernst	2	JG.26
Heilmann, Karl	2	JG.51
Harder, Hans-Joachim	2	JG.26
Hanke, Erwin	2	JG.26
Hainisch, Herbert	2	JG.51
Hahne, Ernst	2	JG.26
Haferrkorn, Gottfried	2	JG.26
Hafer, Ludwig	2	JG.26
Gromoll, Manfred	2	JG.301

Grimm, ?	2	JG.26
Grebe, Ulrich	2	JG.26
Grawatsch, Harald	2	JG.26
Gräve, Alfons	2	JG.26
Gramberg, ?	2+	JG.300
Gossmann, Georg	2	JG.51
Glaser, Otto	2	JG.26
Glaass, ?	2	JG.301
Gilsa, Albrecht von	2	JG.51
Geiselhardt, Otto	2	JG.51
Gauss, Horst	2	JG.26
Freund, ?	2 (both in Spain)	J.88
Fischer, Werner	2	JG.26
Fischer, Ernst	2	JG.301
Fick, Albert	2	JG.51
Felk, Heinz	2	JG.51
Falkner, Gerhard	2	JG.26
Erbskorn, Hans	2	JG.26
Eierstock, Bartholomäus	2	JG.26
Eichstätt, Kurt	2	JG.26
Ehret, Karl-Heinz	2	JG.26
Ebel, Fritz	2	JG.301
Dumkow, Karl-Heinz	2	JG.51
Dittmar, Alfred	2	JG.51
Diemand, Alexius	2	JG.51
Dhein, Heinz	2	JG.51
Delfs, Rudolf	2	JG.51
Czwilinsky, Paul	2	JG.26
Cordes, Udo	2	KG.3; SG.2
Cadenbach, Wilhelm	2	JG.26
Buttke, Werner	2	JG.51
Busch, Hans	2	JG.51
Buder, Ernst	2	JG.51
Buckert, Erich	2	JG.26
Brucks, Helmuth	2	JG.26

Brucks, Helmut	2 (both in Spain)	J.88
Brinkmann, Fritz	2	JG.301
Brenner, Helmut	2	JG.302
Braxator, Horst	2	JG.27
Bracke, Walter	2	JG.51
Böwer, Herbert	2	JG.301
Bothmer, Dietrich von	2 (both in Spain)	J.88
Bolduan, Fritz	2	JG.302
Blohm, Peter	2	JG.26
Bildau, Kurt	2	JG.51
Bieger, Ernst	2	JG.26
Bieber, Rudolf	2	JG.26
Bergermann, Hans	2	JG.51
Belz, Alfred	2	JG.5
Beise, Güqther	2	JG.51
Beer, Heinrich	2	JG.26
Baumann, Josef	2	JG.26
Bauer, Eberhard	2	JG.5
Bärmoser, Max	2	JG.51
Bamberg, Karl-Heinz	2	JG.302
Bach, August	2	JG.51
Axthelm, Erwin	2	JG.27
Auffhammer, Fritz	2	JG.301
Alven, Heinrich von	2	JG.301
Ahrens, Werner	2	JG.27
Adam, Bernhard	2	JG.26
Zubaiko, Edwin	1	JG.26
Zimmermann, Hans	1	JG.26
Zimmerman, Heinrich	1	JG.51
Zeschke, Karl-Heinz	1	JG.26
Zarm, Hans	1	JG.301
Wurff, Rudolf	1	JG.301
Wolfsberger, Josef	1	JG.302
Wolf, Heinz	1	JG.26
Wölfert, Hans	1	JG.26

Witt, Herbert	1	JG.27
Witt, Gerhard	1	JG.301
Witt, ?	1	JG.51
Wirth, Helmut	1	JG.26
Windemuth, Heinrich	1 (Spain)	J.88
Wiese, Fritz	1	JG.51
Wiegeshoff, Jonny	1	JG.301
Wick, Ernst	1	JG.302
Weyrich, Rudolf	1	JG.26
Werner, Paul	1	JG.301
Wernecke, Horst	1	JG.302
Wendt, Kuno	1	JG.26
Weinreich, Helmut	1	JG.301
Weigmann, ?	1	JG.26
Weidenbeck, Gerhard	1+	JG.300
Weide, Herbert	1	JG.26
Wegner, Erich	1	JG.301
Weber, Gottfried	1	JG.26
Weber, ?	1	JG.51
Watermann, Theodor	1	JG.51
Walz, Kurt	1	JG.51
Walter, Hans-Georg	1	JG.26
Waliczek, ?	1	JG.51
Waibel, Jakob	1	JG.51
Voigt, Heinz	1	JG.26
Vetter, Karl	1	JG.302
Vavken, Kurt	1	JG.26
Ussmann, Julius	1	JG.51
Unger, Rudolf	1 (Spain)	J.88
Unger, Karl	1	JG.301
Uloth, Theodor von	1	JG.51
Ullrich, Walter	1	JG.26
Türwächter, I.	1	JG.51
Triebnig, Otto	1	JG.26
Treibnau, ?	1	JG.51

Toldrian, Walter	1	JG.301
Thran, Hans	1	JG.26
Thost, Paul	1	JG.26
Thom, Walter	1	JG.26
Tetzner, Horst	1	JG.51
Talkenberg, Manfred	1	JG.26
Stumpf, Walter	1	JG.26
Stubbe, Karl	1	JG.51
Straub, ?	1	JG.26
Stoy, Heinz	1	JG.51
Stolz, Otto	1	JG.51
Stolz, Erwin	1	JG.26
Stoller, Hans-Joachim	1	JG.26
Stocker, Wolfgang	1	JG.51
Stein, Wolf-Dietmar	1	JG.26
Steindl, Paul	1	JG.26
Steigenberger, Otto	1	JG.51
Steidel, Erich	1	JG.302
Stechbart, Manfred	1	JG.27
Staschen, Arno	1	JG.26
Stark, Alfred	1 (Spain)	J.88
Stangenberg, Ernst	1	JG.51
Standtke, ?	1	JG.51
Stahnke, Kurt	1	JG.26
Stahl, Hermann	1	JG.301
Spenst, Karl	1+	JG.300
Spanka, ?	1+	JG.300
Soiderer, Fridolin	1	JG.51
Sigmund, Leo	1 (Spain)	J.88
Siemer, Hermann	1	JG.51
Siegfahr, Robert	1	JG.301
Seyd, Günther	1	JG.26
Senft, I.	1	JG.51
Seifert, Gerhard	1	JG.26
Seelmann, ?	1	JG.51

Seehars, I.	1	JG.51
Schweikart, Wilhelm	1	JG.51
Schwarz, Paul	1	JG.26
Schulz, Max	1 (Spain)	J.88
Schramm, Werner	1	JG.26
Scholz, ?	1	JG.51
Schölta, Erich	1	JG.302
Schneider, Erich	1	JG.26
Schmitz, Wilfried	1+	JG.300
Schmidt, ?	1	JG.51
Schmidt, ?	1	JG.26
Schlothauser, I.	1	JG.51
Schlenker, Erich	1	JG.26
Schinabeck, Ignaz	1	JG.26
Schick, Karl	1+	JG.300
Schick, Erich	1	JG.26
Scheurer, ?	1	JG.51
Schenk, Willi	1	JG.51
Schenk, Heinz	1	JG.26
Schenk, Friedrich-Wilhelm	1	JG.300, 7
Schellknecht, Bernhard	1	JG.26
Schauff, Josef	1	JG.26
Scharwächter, Gustav	1	JG.5
Scharf, Alfred	1	JG.26
Schäfer, Siegfried	1+	JG.300
Sauter, ?	1	JG.301
Sandoz, Hans	1	JG.26
Sander, Hans-Walter	1	JG.26
Salomon, Heinz	1	JG.26
Saalfeld, Enzio	1	JG.51
Russ, Karl	1	JG.26
Ruopp, Albert	1+	JG.300
Rullkötter, W.	1+	JG.300
Rudolph, ?	1+	JG.300
Rübsam, F.	1+	JG.300

Rubensdorffer, Walter	1 (Spain)	J.88
Roth, Günther	1	JG.51
Rössner, Raimund	1	JG.26
Ropers, Heinz	1	JG.302
Roos, Ludwig	1	JG.26
Rohrmann, Friedrich	1	JG.26
Rödhammer, W.	1	JG.302
Rienth, Karl	1	JG.301
Richter, Günter	1	JG.302
Reuter, Heinrich	1	JG.302
Reuter, Erich	1	JG.302
Resech, ?	1	JG.302
Reittinger, Friedrich	1	JG.51
Reisinger, Karl	1	JG.51
Regenauer, Hans-Werner	1	JG.26
Reents, Siebelt	1 (Spain)	J.88
Rave, Bernd	1+	JG.300
Przybil, Leo	1	JG.26
Prymm, Roland	1	JG.26
Pritze, Hans	1	JG.26
Priebe, Eckehardt	1	JG.26
Priebe, Eckehardt	1 (Spain)	J.88
Pomaska, Alfred	1	JG.26
Pöllinger, Hans	1	JG.5
Plazer, Gerhard von	1	JG.26
Piwowarski, ?	1	JG.51
Pittmann, Helmut	1	JG.26
Pipke, ?	1+	JG.300
Philipp, Kurt	1	JG.5
Pfeiffer, Günther	1	JG.26
Petersen, Ortwin	1	JG.26
Paul, Arthur	1	JG.26
Patz, Werner	1	JG.26
Patzke, Günther	1	JG.26
Palm, Werner	1	JG.26

Palm, Werner	1 (Spain)	J.88
Otto, Gottfried	1	JG.26
Oetteking, ?	1	JG.26
Oesterheld, ?	1	JG.51
Obst, Paul	1	JG.51
Obée, Wolfgang	1	JG.51
Nüsken, Rudolf	1	JG.51
Noske, ?	1+	JG.300
Nischik, Ernst	1	JG.26
Nirminger, Hans	1 (Spain)	J.88
Nirminger, ?	1	JG.234
Nevack, Heinz	1	JG.302
Neumann, Erdmann	1	JG.26
Neider, Alfred	1	JG.51
Müller, ?	1+	JG.300
Mratzek, Ernst	1 (Spain)	J.88
Motsch, ?	1	JG.51
Mössner, Werner	1	JG.26
Mittag, Wilhelm	1	JG.26
Mitscher, Paul	1	JG.51
Minz, Werner	1	JG.5
Michel, ?	1	JG.51
Michalski, Werner	1	JG.26
Michaelis, R.	1	JG.301
Meyer, Otto	1	JG.26
Meyer, ?	1	JG.51
Meyer, ?	1	JG.26
Meurer, Wendelin	1	JG.51
Metz, Karl-Heinz	1 (Spain)	J.88
Mess, ?	1	JG.302
Mertschat, Arnold	1	JG.51
Mebus, ?	1+	JG.300
Maul, Helmut	1	JG.51
Matthes, Günther	1	JG.51
Marre, Gerhard	1	JG.51

Marischka, Hans	1	JG.26
Maier, Hans	1	JG.51
Maier, ?	1	JG.51
Maier, ?	1+	JG.300
Maeser, Günter	1	JG.302
Luycke, ?	1	JG.51
Lutz, Martin	1 (Spain)	J.88
Lühs, Walter	1	JG.26
Lövenich, H.	1+	JG.300
Loschinski, Gerhard	1	JG.26
Lork, Heinz	1	JG.5
Lorberg, Helmut	1	JG.26
Lonzius, ?	1+	JG.300
Lohrer, ?	1 (Spain)	J.88
Löffler, Josef	1	JG.301
Lindingen, Rudolf	1	JG.51
Lenz.Josef	1	JG.27
Lenz, Alfred	1	JG.51
Lenz, Adolf	1	JG.5
Leeb, Gerhard	1	JG.301
Ledl, Georg	1	JG.51
Leder, Josef	1	JG.26
Leder, Joachim	1	JG.26
Laufhütte, Diethelm	1	JG.27
Laufer, Wilhelm	1	JG.51
Laubenheimer, F.	1	JG.301
Lange, Helmut	1	JG.26
Landgraf, Werner	1	JG.51
Lambio, ?	1+	JG.300
Laborenz, Jakob	1	JG.302
Kuring, Heinz-Günter	1+	JG.300
Kurcharsowski, ?	1	JG.301
Kunze, Klaus	1	JG.26
Kummerow, Helmut	1	JG.51
Kummer, ?	1	JG.301

Kugler, Walter	1	JG.302
Kugler, Hermann	1	JG.27
Krusen, Bruno	1	JG.26
Kruse, Fritz	1	JG.51
Kröll, Theodor	1	JG.51
Kroeck, Hubert	1 (Spain)	J.88
Krista, Adolf	1	JG.301
Krieg, Heinz	1	JG.26
Krah, ?	1	JG.51
Kraft, ?	1+	JG.300
Koslowski, Wilhelm	1	JG.51
Korte, Werner	1	JG.26
Korte, Otto	1	JG.51
Körber, Herbert	1	JG.27
Kopp, Walter	1	JG.26
Konrad, Siegfried	1	JG.26
König, Fritz	1	JG.5
Konig, ?	1 (Spain)	J.88
Koller, Ludwig	1	JG.302
Kolb, ?	1	JG.26
Köhn, ?	1	JG.26
Kohlert, Rudolf	1	JG.51
Köhler, Otto	1+	JG.300
Köhler, ?	1+	JG.300
Koch, ?	1+	JG.300
Knittel, Werner	1	JG.51
Kloimüller, Herfried	1	JG.51
Klein, ?	1	JG.26
Kleemann, Günther	1	JG.26
Klärner, Adolf	1	JG.302
Klammer, ?	1	JG.302
Kiening, ?	1 (Spain)	J.88
Kiehling, Ernst	1	JG.301
Ketzer, Albrecht	1	JG.51
Kern, Heinz	1	JG.5

Kemmerling, ?	1+	JG.302
Kattlum, Heinz	1	JG.51
Karcher, ?	1	JG.26
Kalbus, Edwin	1	JG.26
Jüngling, Richard	1	JG.302
John, Franz	1	JG.51
Jentch, Paul	1	JG.26
Jenner, Anton	1	JG.26
Jecko, Rudolf	1	JG.51
Janke, ?	1	JG.302
Jakobi, Klaus	1	JG.301
Jäger, Franz	1	JG.51
Jaacks, Egbert	1	JG.302
Izquierd, ?	1+	JG.300
Ippoldt, Herbert	1	JG.301
Ibold, Walter	1	JG.300
Iberle, Rudolf	1	JG.26
Hundsdörfer, Wolfgang	1+	JG.300
Hummel, Otto	1	JG.26
Hörnig, Franz	1	JG.26
Hornatscheck, Heinrich	1	JG.26
Hormann, Kurt	1 (Spain)	J.88
Horch, Otto	1	JG.26
Hopp, Hans	1	JG.51
Holtey, Hubertus von	1	JG.26
Holbein, Erich	1	JG.51
Högel, ?	1	JG.26
Hoffmann, A.	1	JG.301
Hofen, Kurt	1	JG.26
Hocker, Ernst-Otto	1	JG.7, 301
Hirsch, Alfred	1	JG.51
Hilliger, Dieter	1	JG.26
Hiller, Alfred	1	JG.301
Heyne, Hans-Rudolf	1	JG.51
Heyarts, Josef	1	JG.26

Heuser, Helmut	1	JG.26
Herzog, Gerhard	1 (Spain)	J.88
Herzog, Gerhard	1	JG.26
Herre, Herbert	1	JG.302
Henschel, Günther	1	JG.51
Hennersdorf	1+	JG.300
Hennemann, Martin	1	JG.26
Hengst, ?	1+	JG.300
Heitmann, ?	1	JG.26
Heinrichs, Robert	1	JG.26
Heinrich, Manfred	1	JG.51
Hein, Hans	1	JG.51
Hein, Hans	1	JG.26
Heinemann, Hans	1	JG.26
Heine, ?	1	JG.51
Heindke, Siegfried	1	JG.26
Heilmayer, Franz	1 (Spain)	J.88
Heidorn, Werner	1	JG.51
Hefter, Ekkehard	1 (Spain)	J.88
Heerdegen, L.	1	JG.302
Haus, Willi	1	JG.5
Harold, Albrecht	1	JG.51
Harheim, Walter	1	JG.51
Hardt, Kurt	1	JG.51
Hänsel, ?	1+	JG.300
Hansberg, Otto	1	JG.26
Hannermann, Karl	1	JG.26
Hampel, ?	1+	JG.300
Halupczek, Gerhard	1 (Spain)	J.88
Hakenjos, ?	1+	JG.300
Hähnel, Joachim	1	JG.301
Hagedorn, A.	1	JG.301
Günther, Heinz	1	JG.301
Günther, Alfred	1	JG.26
Gschwind, ?	1	JG.51

Gruel, Siegfried	1	JG.26
Groth, Max	1	JG.26
Gross, Helmuth	1	JG.26
Greim, Helmut	1	JG.26
Grätz, ?	1	JG.301
Granabetter, Georg	1	JG.26
Grams, Willi	1	JG.26
Grad, Hermann	1	JG.26
Grabe, Horst	1	JG.51
Göring, Peter	1	JG.26
Goltzsche, ?	1	JG.51
Golja, ?	1+	JG.300
Godecke, Willi	1 (Spain)	J.88
Gocksch, Walter	1	JG.26
Gniffke, Fritz	1	JG.302
Glass, ?	1	JG.302
Gilsa, Kurt von	1 (Spain)	J.88
Gerlach, Heinz	1	JG.302
Genth, Karl-Georg	1	JG.26
Gassen, Gottfried	1	JG.51
Gamringer, Johann	1 (Spain)	J.88
Gäbler, Johann	1	JG.51
Fuchs, Heinrich	1	JG.51
Fröb, Karl	1	JG.26
Fritsch, Artur	1	JG.26
Fries, ?	1	JG.302
Freiberger, Anton	1	JG.26
Freckmann, ?	1	JG.301
Frank, Hans-Hermann	1	JG.51
Franke, Moritz	1	JG.51
Fölze, Heinz	1	JG.52
Föhl, Heinz	1	JG.51
Fischer, Karl	1	JG.27
Fischer, Hans	1	JG.26
Fischer, Klaus	1 (Spain)	J.88

Finke, Karl	1	JG.26
Findeisen, Helmut	1	JG.26
Feierabend, ?	1	JG.51
Fahnert, Friedrich-Wilhelm	1	JG.26
Fahldieck, Erwin	1	JG.5
Erdniss, Wilhelm	1	JG.51
Endriss, Max	1	JG.51
Ehses, Helmut	1	JG.51
Ehrlinger, ?	1	JG.5
Edhofer, Heinz	1	StG.2; SG.2
Eder, Max	1	JG.5
Eberhard, Günther	1	JG.51
Düsing, Wilhelm	1	JG.26
Dünkel, Fritz	1	JG.51
Driebe, Rudi	1	JG.301
Draheim, Manfred	1	JG.26
Dohms, Fred	1+	JG.300
Diestel, ?	1+	JG.300
Dienst, Werner	1	JG.302
Daig, Erwin	1	JG.27
Dähne, Kurt	1	JG.26
Czerny, Engelbert	1	JG.27
Czypionka, Jorg	1	10.NJG-11
Claar, Karl	1	JG.26
Christinnecke, Hans	1	JG.26
Chemnitzer, Max	1	JG.26
Carnier, Gerhard von	1	JG.51
Butterweck, Friedrich	1	JG.26
Büthe, ?	1+	JG.300
Busch, Max	1	JG.26
Burmeister, Fritz	1	JG.26
Burmeister, Erich	1	JG.51
Burkhardt, Alfred	1	JG.26
Burckhardt, Gottfried	1	JG.26
Buethe, ?	1+	JG.300

Budde, Heinz	1	JG.26
Brunn, Klaus von	1	JG.5
Brucker, Heinrich	1 (Spain)	J.88
Breuers, Hans	1	JG.302
Brenner, Peter	1	JG.301
Bremer, Herbert	1	JG.26
Bremer, ?	1+	JG.300
Braun, Ernst	1	JG.26
Brandt, Hans	1	JG.27
Bosch, ?	1+	JG.300
Bonack, Herbert	1	JG.27
Böhm, ?	1	JG.26
Boer, ?	1	JG.26
Boer, ?	1 (Spain)	J.88
Böcker, Heinrich	1	JG.26
Bluder, Hans	1	JG.26
Bloenertz, Günther	1	JG.26
Blickle, Wilhelm	1	JG.26
Blicke, Walter	1	JG.301
Birkner, Heinz	1	JG.26
Bertels, Konrad	1	JG.26
Berliner, Julius	1	JG.301
Benzinger, Adolf	1	JG.51
Benz, Georg	1	JG.51
Behrendt, Albert	1	JG.51
Beckert, Otto	1	JG.26
Becker, Kurt	1	JG.302
Barthel, Alfred	1	JG.26
Bartels, Heinz-Wilhelm	1	JG.26
Balka, Wilhelm von	1	JG.51
Backhaus, Hans	1	JG.26
Asmus, Erich	1	JG.26
Arnold, Ernst	1	JG.27
Angermann, Günther	1	JG.302
Angerer, Erwin	1	JG.5

Andreaus, Franz	1	JG.51
Altmann, Leberecht	1	JG.26, 1
Albert, Gerhard	1	JG.27
Ackermann, Dieter	1	JG.27

Note: names are presented in reverse alphabetical order as in the German achives.

Notes

Introduction

1. Telford Taylor, *Sword and Swastika*, (New York: Simon and Schuster, 1952), 364.

German Military Ranks, Medals, and Service

1. On Galland and the other legion men, see Samuel W. Mitcham Jr., *Men of the Luftwaffe* (Novato, CA: Presidio Press, 1988), 33–53.

2. See Colin D. Heaton and Anne-Marie Lewis, *Night Fighters: Luftwaffe and RAF Air Combat over Europe 1939-1945* (Annapolis, MD: Naval Institute Press, 2008), 21.

The Count: Walter Krupinski

1. Heaton, "The Count: *Luftwaffe* Ace Walter Krupinski," *Military History*, vol. 15, no. 2 (June 1998): 62–68.

2. Heaton, "Interview: *Luftwaffe* Eagle Johannes Steinhoff," *World War II*, vol. 13, no. 1 (May 1998): 28–34, 74. Also Heaton, "Luftwaffe Wing Leader," *Military History*, vol. 20, no. 6 (February 2004): 42–48.

3. Ihlefeld scored 9 kills in Spain as a sergeant, and finished World War II as a colonel with 132 confirmed victories and the Knight's Cross, Oak Leaves and Swords, and was a commander of JG.52. Samuel W. Mitcham Jr., *Eagles of the Third Reich: The Men Who Made the Luftwaffe* (Novato, CA: Presidio Press, 1997), erroneously states that Ihlefeld scored 123 kills.

4. See Heaton, "*Luftwaffe* Wing Leader," *Military History*, (February 2004): 42–48; Heaton, "Interview: *Luftwaffe* Ace Günther Rall Remembers," *World War II*, vol. 9, no. 6 (March 1995): 34–40, 77–78; Heaton, "*Luftwaffe* Eagle Johannes Steinhoff"; see also Helmut Lipfert and Werner Girbig, *The War Diary of Helmut Lipfert: JG.52 on the Russian Front 1943-1945* (Atglen, PA: Schiffer Publishing, Ltd., 1993), in total.

5. Jon Guttman, "Air War's Greatest Aces," *World War II* (February 1998): p. 26–28.

6. See Heaton, "Erich Hartmann's Last Interview," *World War II*. vol. 17, no. 3. (September 2002): 30–42, 85, for Hartmann's perspective.

7. Guttman, "Air War's Greatest Aces," p. 26.

8. Mitcham, *Eagles of the Third Reich*, 216–17.

9. One may read all the previous published interviews with the German case regarding their winter experiences. See bibliography.

10. Heaton, "The Count," 62–68; also Heaton, "Erich Hartmann's Last Interview," 30–42, 85.

11. See also Rall's experience in Heaton, "Luftwaffe Ace Günther Rall Remembers," 34–40, 77–78; Hartmann's experience in Heaton, "Erich Hartmann's Last Interview," 30–42, 85.

12. Heaton, "Erich Hartmann's Last Interview," 30–42, 85.

13. See Heaton, "Luftwaffe Ace Günther Rall Remembers," 34–40, 77–78 (Rall's perceptions).

14. Raymond F. Toliver and Trevor J. Constable, *The Blonde Knight of Germany* (New York: McGraw-Hill Professional, 1986), and there are also various older and even newer publication dates. It is very worthwhile reading.

15. See Heaton, "Erich Hartmann's Last Interview," 30–42, 85.

16. Heaton, "Interview: General Jimmy Doolittle," *Military History* (February 2004): 42–48.

17. See also Rall's experience with hot-shot Soviet pilot in Heaton, "Luftwaffe Ace Günther Rall Remembers," 34–40, 77–78.

18. See also Heaton, "The Count," 62–68.

19. See Guttman, "Air War's Greatest Aces," 28.

20. See Johannes Steinhoff, *The Final Hours: The Luftwaffe Plot Against Göring* (Washington, DC: Potomac Books, 2005), in total. This is one of several autobiographies that Steinhoff wrote chronicling the war and the men he served with, and it is extraordinary reading.

21. Heaton, "Luftwaffe Ace Adolf Galland's Last Interview," World War II. (January 1997): 46–52. See also Robert Forsythe, *JV-44: The Galland Circus* (UK: Classic Publications, 1996), in total; also John Foreman and Harvey, *The Messerschmitt Combat Diary Me.262* (UK: Air Research Publications, 1995), 217–77.

22. Foreman and Harvey, *Messerschmitt Combat Diary*, 85.

23. Ibid., 225–27.

24. Ibid., 247–48.

25. Ibid., 249.

26. On April 20, 1945, Ewald received the Knight's Cross, with Helmut Lipfert receiving the Oak Leaves from Hitler. This was also Hitler's birthday.

27. Foreman and Harvey, *Messerschmitt Combat Diary*, 254.

28. Harold Faber, ed., *Luftwaffe: A History* (New York: Times Books, 1977), 45–47.

29. On Eder with JV.44, see Foreman and Harvey, *Messerschmitt Combat Diary*, 203, 303.

General of the Fighters: Adolf Galland

1. Heaton, "Luftwaffe Ace Adolf Galland's Last Interview," 46–52.

2. Eduard von Schleich was known as the "Black Knight" on both sides of the Western Front in World War I, and in World War II he scored thirty-five kills, received the *Pour le Mérite* (Blue Max), and was knighted by Kaiser Wilhelm II. He died in 1947.

3. Richthofen died of a cerebral hemorrhage on July 12, 1945.

4. Edward Jablonski, *Terror from the Sky: Air War Vol. 1* (New York: Doubleday & Co., 1972), 15.

5. Cajus Bekker, *The Luftwaffe War Diaries* (New York: Da Capo Press, 1974), 28.

6. See Jablonski, *Terror from the Sky*, 44, for the details as he wrote them.

7. Schleich, like Theo Osterkamp (thirty-two kills and the *Pour le Mérite*, as well as the Knight's Cross in World War II with six kills), was in his fifties flying with, and against, men half his age.

8. Schöpfel also discussed this with author Colin Heaton in 1999 and again in 2000, and found it quite amusing that Hitler's friends started bailing out even that early in the war. See also Martin Gilbert, *The Holocaust: A History of the Jews of Europe During the Second World War* (New York: Henry Holt & Company, LLC, 1985), 152. Also Jablonski, *Terror from the Sky*, 146. Many rumors persisted as to what Hess's actual intentions were. Colin Heaton's interviews with certain insiders, such as Hitler's personal pilot, *Generalleutnant* Hans Bour, provide interesting possibilities. It was known sometime afterward that he had tried to meet with the Duke of Hamilton, whom he had met at the Berlin Olympics in 1936, and was trying to establish a separate peace with Britain. Tried at Nuremberg with Göring and many others, Hess was the last occupant at Berlin's Spandau Military Prison the time of his death on August 17, 1987, a death which is still controversial.

9. Colonel Edward R. "Buddy" Haydon had a similar experience in January 1945 while on a strafing mission. See Heaton, "The Man Who Downed Nowotny: Interview with Col. Edward R. Haydon," *Aviation History* (September 2002): 22–28. Haydon's full interview will appear in a subsequent Allied edition of this series.

10. Jablonski, *Terror from the Sky*, 96–106.

11. Ibid., 107.

12. Ibid., 122. This was the famous meeting in The Hague on September 3, 1940, where Göring decided to appease Hitler's fury over the Berlin bombing. That was what began the German campaign of bombing British cities.

13. Jablonski, *Terror from the Sky*, 136.

14. Ibid., 165–66.

15. Heaton and Lewis, *Night Fighters*, 9.

16. On his death, see Mitcham, *Men of the Luftwaffe*, 146.

17. Heaton, "Luftwaffe Ace Adolf Galland's Last Interview," 46–52. The actual date of this first meeting was January 28, 1942. See also Norman Cameron and R.H. Stevens (trans.), *Hitler's Table Talk 1941–1944: His Private Conversations* (New York: Enigma Books, 2000), 260.

18. On Martini and his function, see Heaton and Lewis, *Night Fighters*, 85–86; see also Mitcham, *Eagles of the Third Reich*, 27, 201, 325. On Dietrich Peltz, see Heaton and Lewis, *Night Fighters*, 31, 77; and Mitcham, *Eagles of the Third Reich*, 212, 231–32, 294. On Erhard Milch and his Jewish past being covered up by Göring and Hitler, see Bryan Mark Rigg, *Hitler's Jewish Soldiers: The Untold Story of Nazi Racial Laws and the Men of Jewish Descent in the German Military* (Lawrence, KS: University Press of Kansas, 2002), 29–30, 139–40, 177–78, 193, 201, 231, 257–59, 288. On his mother, ibid., 30. On Galland's being investigated for possibly being Jewish, 366 n.150.

19. Rigg, *Hitler's Jewish Soldiers*, 19, 30, 39, 76, 82, 93.

20. Heaton and Lewis, *Night Fighters*, 21. Mitcham, *Men of the Luftwaffe*, 198–200.

21. Mitcham, *Men of the Luftwaffe*, 197–201. See also Toliver and Constable, *Fighter Aces of the Luftwaffe*, 153–65. This section discusses Falck's career in a truncated form. See also Heaton, "Luftwaffe's Father of the Night Fighters," 42–48.

22. Mitcham, *Men of the Luftwaffe*, 197–201.

23. Jablonski, p. 11.

24. See Heaton and Lewis, Night Fighters, p. 21 on Milch.

25. Ibid, p. 77.

26. Rigg traces this fact in Hitler's Jewish Soldiers in total.

27. See Rigg, p. 39. See also Steinhoff interview, where both sources name the pilots in question, all of whom were awarded the Knight's Cross: Hauptmann Siegfried Simsch (95 victories), *Oberleutnant* Oskar "Ossi" Romm (92) and *Feldwebel* Rudolf Schmidt (51).

28. See Heaton, "Interview: *Luftwaffe* Ace Günther Rall Remembers," in total. Rall provided his own perspectives on both Hitler and Göring.

29. Heaton and Lewis, *Night Fighters*, 139. See also Heaton, *German Anti-Partisan Warfare in Europe, 1939–1945* (Atglen, PA: Schiffer Publishing, Ltd., 2001), for more details regarding Göring's deep involvement in the Holocaust. For more, see also Heaton, *Occupation and Insurgency: A Selective Examination of The Hague and Geneva Conventions on the*

Eastern Front, 1939–1945 (New York: Algora Publishing, 2008), 17, 25, 68, 76, 87, 92, 149, 153, 186, 218. On Göring's active participation regarding mass murder through starvation, see Mark Mazower, Inside Hitler's Greece: The Experience of Occupation 1941–44 (New Haven, CT: Yale University Press, 1997), 9, 31.

30. On the aftermath of Stalingrad, see Alfred Price, *Luftwaffe* (New York: Ballantine Books, Inc., 1969), 83–87.

31. Mitcham, *Men of the Luftwaffe*, 176.

32. Ibid., 231. Author Colin Heaton had the privilege of speaking with Peltz as well as Hajo Herrmann together in 1990 with Jeffrey L. Ethell. Peltz remembered this meeting quite clearly during his interview, along with Hajo Herrmann. Also present during this meeting were RAF aces John Cunningham and (night fighter ace) W. Dennis David, Desmond Hughes, Brian Kingcome, and *Luftwaffe* fighter pilot Ulrich Steinhilper.

33. Marseille was killed on September 30, 1942.

34. Mitcham, *Men of the Luftwaffe*, 212.

35. Heaton and Lewis, *Night Fighters*, 8.

36. Heaton, Occupation and Insurgency, as previously noted; see also Richard Z. Chesnoff, *Pack of Thieves: How Hitler and Europe Plundered the Jews and Committed the Greatest Theft in History* (New York: Anchor Books, 1999), in total, on the Third Reich's theft of Europe's great art collections.

37. For more on this tenuous relationship between Jeschonnek and Göring, see Faber, *Luftwaffe: A History*, 78–93.

38. Heaton and Lewis, *Night Fighters*, 8.

39. See Albert Speer, *Inside the Third Reich* (New York: The Macmillan Co., 1970), 289.

40. Ibid., 377. Speer wrote about this in his memoirs, thus corroborating Galland's recollection.

41. Ibid., 290.

42. See James H. Doolittle and Carrol V. Glines, *I Could Never be So Lucky Again* (Atglen, PA: Schiffer Publishing, Ltd.), 396, on German losses of pilots according to Galland.

43. Speer, *Inside the Third Reich*, 518–19. Speer recounts the date as August 10, 1944. See also Ian Kershaw, Hitler: 1936-1945 *Nemesis* (New York: W.W. Norton & Co., 2000), 732.

44. This was the March 4, 1944, Berlin raid, involving 500 heavy bombers with 770 fighters. The next raid was March 6, when the United States lost 69 bombers and 11 fighters, while the *Luftwaffe* lost 66 fighters. See Robert Forsyth, *JV-44: The Galland Circus* (UK: Classic Publications, 1996), 25.

45. On the copper mine located at Bor, Hungary, which was the largest such mine under Nazi control, see Gilbert, *The Holocaust*, 532, 733. There is little doubt Speer knew of these events, where the majority of these workers were sent to Mauthausen and murdered either in the death camp or worked to death at Bor proper.

46. Speer, *Inside the Third Reich*, 518.

47. See Heaton, "Jimmy Doolittle and the Emergence of American Air Power," World War II, vol. 18, no. 1 (May 2003): 47–52, 78. This is the second part of a two-part interview in subsequent editions.

48. Ibid. April 1944 cost Galland 489 fighter pilots and aircraft, with only 396 replacement pilots, and these were not the fully trained men of yesteryear. One of these was 102 victory ace Egon Mayer, KIA March 2, 1944, who almost killed USAAF ace Robert S. Johnson in 1943. See Heaton, "Interview: Zemke Wolfpack Ace Robert S. Johnson," Military History, vol. 13, no. 3 (August 1996): 27–32.

49. Author Colin Heaton met with Klopfer in 1985; Klopfer died in 1987. Klopfer was the last surviving member of the Wannsee Conference held in January 1942, where the Final Solution was finalized with Heydrich presiding. Of interest on this subject is the HBO film *Conspiracy* starring Kenneth Branaugh (Reinhard Heydrich) and Stanley Tucci (Adolf Eichmann). This drama was based upon the only surviving transcript of the meeting, maintained by Undersecretary of State Martin Luther.

50. Foreman and Harvey, *Messerschmitt Combat Diary*, 41. He was killed on July 18, 1944.

51. The last version of the Focke-Wulf was the Ta-152 high-altitude interceptor, flown by JG.302, which along with JG.301, was an expansion from the original JG.300 created as the *Wilde Sau* by Hajo Hermann.

52. Foreman and Harvey, *Messerschmitt Combat Diary*, 29–30.

53. Faber, *Luftwaffe: A History*, 182.

54. Foreman and Harvey, *Messerschmitt Combat Diary*, 30–32. See also Faber, *Luftwaffe: A History*, 178–79.

55. Ibid., 38. The actual date was May 29, 1944, and also present were Generals Korten, Bodenschanz, and *Oberst* Petersen.

56. Ibid., 50–53.

57. Werner Held, *German Fighter Ace Walter Nowotny: An Illustrated Biography* (Atglen, PA: Schiffer Publishing, Ltd, 2006), in total. Thierfelder died on July 7, 1944.

58. Nowotny had 255 confirmed kills on the Eastern Front. Every claim he made was verified, and he had another 32 probable kills that he only claimed as damaged.

59. Forman and Harvey, *Messerschmitt Combat Diary*, 63.

60. Interestingly enough, Nowotny's brother Rudolf corresponded with author Colin Heaton for several years, giving personal data and photos regarding his brother. Rudolf Nowotny was an infantry lieutenant who spent many years in Soviet captivity. Walter Krupinski knew him, and placed Heaton and Nowotny in contact with each other.

61. See Heaton, "Erich Hartmann's Last Interview," 22–28.

62. For a great first-person narrative, see Hans-Ulrich Rüdel, Stuka Pilot (New York: Bantam, 1974) in total. Rüdel also violated the no flying order, as did some others, such as Herman Graf.

63. See Foreman and Harvey, *Messerschmitt Combat Diary*. 63. See Held, *German Fighter Ace Walter Nowotny*, 143, and the actual date was September 26, 1944, when "Nowi" took over operational command. Eder confirmed this during his interview, which is forthcoming in the next volume in this series, *The Me-262 Stormbird*.

64. Ibid., 58–59, on some of Eder's victims. Eder would finish the war with thirty-six confirmed bomber kills, and another twenty-four probable kills in the jet.

65. In Held, *German Fighter Ace Walter Nowotny*, 149, he states that the operational strength was thirty jets. Eder also stated around thirty, but both sources may not have been counting damaged, spare parts or replacement aircraft.

66. Foreman and Harvey, *Messerschmitt Combat Diary*, 90–91. According to these authors, Franz Schall, G. Wegmann, Nowotny, F. Buttner, and Helmut Baudach took off in jets following the Fw-190Ds, which, under the command of *Oberleutnant* Hans Dortenmann, engaged the escort fighters to carve a path for the jets. Schall and Nowotny caught the bombers as they were leaving their target over Merseberg. Dortenmann managed to shoot down the P-47 flown by Lt. Charles C. McKelvey, which had already been hit by Schall's 30mm cannon. Schall also shot down the Thunderbolt flown by Lt. William L. Hoffert, who bailed out. Both Americans were from the 359th Fighter Group. According to these authors (p. 93), they state that Lt. R. W. Stevens of the 364th Fighter Group killed Nowotny. It is possible that Stevens shot out Nowotny's engine, but Galland's, Eder's, Haydon's, and Capt. Ernst Fiebelkorn's (20th Fighter Group) eyewitness accounts all seem to stand firm. Mustang pilot Lt. Anthony Maurice of the 361st Fighter Group claimed a kill also, although he was not near Achmer. This event was what had forced Helmut Baudach to bail out after suffering severe damage to his jet, courtesy of Maurice.

67. Ibid., 93. See also Held, *German Fighter Ace Walter Nowotny*, 151.

68. Foreman and Harvey, *Messerschmitt Combat Diary*, 63. The authors believe that Haydon and Fiebelkorn were chasing Schall's abandoned

jet, which continued to fly damaged after he bailed out, until it crashed. However, Haydon pursued only one jet, and he clearly saw the pilot in the 262 that he engaged as he himself lost airspeed when he cut the throttle to avoid a collision. Hayden closed to within less than one hundred feet of Nowotny yet he never fired his guns and described what and who he saw in the cockpit. His account matches those of Galland and Eder. See Heaton, "The Man Who Downed Nowotny," interview with Col. Edward R. Haydon, Aviation History, vol. 13, no. 1 (September 2002): 22–28. Haydon actually picked Nowotny's photo out of a line up of twenty German aces, and his memory was vivid. His description of Nowotny's facial expression was one of pure shock.

69. This data, following Jeff Ethell's discussion with Galland in 1982, and the series of interviews with Colin Heaton, assisted in creating a good picture of the events. This data enabled aviation artist Keith Ferris to paint the event in his classic print, *Nowotny's Final Encounter*. According to Held, a witness at Epe stated the fighter blew up above the ground, and then crashed. Haydon did not see this, as he had passed over the fighter as it stalled out, trailing fire and smoke. Haydon did see the smoke that arose from the crash, but not the impact. Eder corroborated Galland's version that no one at the air field could observe the impact, due to the trees. Held states that Schnörrer, along with the others, found Nowotny's parachute in the trees near the crash, and Nowotny's body was found nearby, as if he had managed to bail out, but too low to survive the jump. This was most likely Franz Schall's parachute. Galland's and Eder's versions are vastly different from Held. However, there is no doubt that his remains were in the wreckage, as Galland sent the pieces of his Diamonds to his family, as corroborated by his brother Rudolf Nowotny. Henceforth, the mystery as to what actually happened to Nowotny should be resolved.

70. Eder's interview in full will be presented in the next volume of this series, *The Me-262 Stormbird*.

71. See Held, *German Fighter Ace Walter Nowotny*, 153; Heaton, "Luftwaffe Eagle Johannes Steinhoff," 43.

72. See also the Steinhoff and Neumann interviews. This meeting is also chronicled in Steinhoff's *Final Hours*, 65–70.

73. This was Waffen SS *Gruppenführer* Felix Steiner, the creator and first commander of the 5th Waffen SS Division "*Wiking*," the first pan-European foreign volunteer (*Freiwilligen*) SS unit. Actually, Steiner was not involved in the bomb plot of July 20, 1944. However, it is quite possible that Steiner would have been a willing participant in replacing Hitler, according to SS *Brigadeführer* Otto Kumm and SS *Obergruppenführer* Karl Wolff, both interviewed by Heaton.

74. See Steinhoff, *Final Hours*, 77–82, and Steinhoff's and Trautloft's interviews in forthcoming volumes.

75. Greim held the *Pour le Mérite*, and was knighted by Kaiser Wilhelm II during World War I.

76. Price, *German Air Force Bombers of World War I*, 144–47.

77. Steinhoff related all of these facts in even more detail, and makes quite interesting reading. See also the following Neumann interview on this event.

78. Steinhoff's interview will be included in next volume of this series, *The Me-262 Stormbird*. See also Heaton, "Luftwaffe Eagle Johannes Steinhoff," 28–34, 74.

79. Faber, *Luftwaffe: A History*, 45–47.

80. As stated previously in the introduction, there has never been a documented case of a German fighter pilot deliberately shooting an Allied airman in his parachute. However, this practice was not beyond the realm of possibility for British and American pilots, who knew that a jet pilot had bailed out. It was a quiet acceptance in the USAAF, since it was believed that jet pilots were premium, highly trained pilots, and could not be allowed to return to the air. General Curtis LeMay, USAF, actually admitted this in his interview in 1985, although it was not written doctrine. General James H. Doolittle also acknowledged that it occurred, but it was not an order, only a "strong suggestion" in the respective fighter units. Brigadier General Robin Olds, USAF, also stated that this was not an unknown factor among American pilots.

81. Sachsenberg commanded the Fw-190D unit that protected the jets as they returned to the air field during those missions.

Mentor to Many: Eduard Neumann

1. For a very good overview of Marseille, see Toliver and Constable, *Fighter Aces of the Luftwaffe*, 101–15.

2. See Heaton, "Luftwaffe Eagle Johannes Steinhoff," in total. Steinhoff was Marseille's first squadron leader, and he fired him.

3. Rödel finished the war as an *oberst* with ninety-eight kills and the Oak Leaves to his Knight's Cross.

4. This mission was actually flown by a combined Australian and New Zealand fighter force, but the Germans did not differentiate between the various Commonwealth units.

5. A Lufbery circle, also called the "wheel," was a defensive measure where fighters would follow each other in a circle for protection. The theory was that any enemy engaging a fighter would be attacked by the fighter right behind. Marseille proved that this was not always a successful tactic, and he scored many kills in this fashion. This was the June 3, 1942, mission against a South African unit.

6. Only Joachim Muncheberg received the same award. Even Field Marshal Erwin Rommel only received the medal in the silver version. See Toliver and Constable, *Fighter Aces of the Luftwaffe*, 103.

7. *Signal* was the German military magazine, similar to the U.S. military's *Stars and Stripes*, and ran features, articles, and photograph sections heralding Germany's heroes during the war.

8. This call was placed by Rommel on September 28, two days before Marseille's death.

9. See Toliver and Constable, *Fighter Aces of the Luftwaffe*, 108–12.

10. *Leutnant* Hans Arnold Stahlschmidt was originally listed as missing in action, but later confirmed killed over El Alamein on September 5, 1942. He had fifty-nine victories and the Knight's Cross. Marseille was supposed to fly the mission, but a medical exam prevented this, and Stahlschmidt flew in his place. Marseille never recovered from the guilt.

11. This was Marseille's 382nd combat sortie. Given his 158 confirmed kills, that was an average ratio of 2.41 kills per mission. Had he flown 1,100 to 1,400 missions, as some of the other aces did, he could have theoretically scored 400 to 580 kills.

12. According to available records, the two pilots possibly with him as he bailed out were Pöttgen and Schlang, with the others mentioned possibly in the flight, such as Schrör, but not with Marseille on visual contact. Schrör stated that he lost visual on Marseille as he was several hundred feet above him, and could not see down. He did hear the activity on the radio.

13. This was Operation Torch, November 8, 1942.

14. See Heaton, "Colonel Hajo Herrmann: Master of the Wild Boars," interview with *Luftwaffe* Colonel Hajo Herrmann, World War II, vol. 15, no. 2. (July 2000): 30–36, 78–80.

15. See Mitcham, *Eagles of the Third Reich*, 262.

16. The pyramid-shaped monument is located at where Marseille was buried at Sidi Abd Rahman, near El Alamein. See Toliver and Constable, *Fighter Aces of the Luftwaffe*, 115.

Father of the Night Fighters: Wolfgang Falck

1. A good book on this subject, including the economy and the *Putsch*, is Konrad Heiden, *Der Fuehrer: Hitler's Rise to Powerpp*, trans. by Ralph Manheim (Boston: Houghton Mifflin Co., 1944), 199–202.

2. Ibid., 563–76.

3. Ibid., 699–702.

4. For more on Tukhachevsky (among many others), and his genius being squandered, see Heaton, *German Anti-Partisan Warfare in Europe*.

5. See Heaton and Lewis, *Night Fighters*, 16. See also Bekker, *The Luftwaffe War Diaries*, 74–76.

6. Ostermann was killed in action on August 9, 1942.

7. Heaton and Lewis, *Night Fighters*, 19–20.

8. Ibid., 20.

9. On the unit dispositions, see Bekker, *The Luftwaffe War Diaries*, 206-8.

10. On this topic, see Heaton and Lewis, *Night Fighters*, in total, and Herbert Malloy Mason Jr., *Duel for the Sky* (New York: Grosset & Dunlap, Inc. Publishers), 65–74.

11. See also Heaton and Lewis, *Night Fighters*, 17.

12. Ibid., 26–7.

13. The Destroyer School was the advanced fighter program that transitioned basic fighter pilots into the Me-110 twin-engine *Zerstörer*, where instrumentation, blind flying, and ground attack were also emphasized.

14. Heaton and Lewis, *Night Fighters*, 21.

15. This plan was actually to have all Oak Leaves recipients, and above, granted estates in the occupied east, once the Soviet Union was subdued, and the Slavic populations would serve in a modern form of medieval serfdom. The higher the decoration, the choicer the real estate that would be offered.

16. Pitcairn flew with Trautloft in JG.54 and finished the war with fourteen kills.

17. Heaton and Lewis, *Night Fighters*, 25.

18. Mason, *Duel for the Sky*, 72.

19. Ibid.

20. For great details on these devices and their use, see Heaton and Lewis, *Night Fighters*, in total. This book has segments of many of these collected interviews with men from the United States, United Kingdom, and German forces.

21. On Wittgenstein's death, see Price, *Luftwaffe*, 130. His radar operator, *Feldwebel* Ostheimer survived by bailing out as the aircraft fell apart.

22. Heaton and Lewis, *Night Fighters*, 16.

Bibliography

Primary Sources

Bundesarchiv/Militärarchiv (collectively at Koblenz, Freiburg, and Berlin-Lichterfelde)

Doc. N 179-*Literischer Nachwass vom Generfeldmarschall Erhard Milch.*

Doc. RH 2/2196-Air Organization and Service Office (Luftamt)

Doc. RH 2/2197-Air Organization Office, Various Studies and Evaluations.

Doc. RH 2/2200-Weapons Office Rearmament Program and Development.

Doc. RH 2/2206-Weapons Office Report on Foreign Equipment.

Doc. RH 2/2273-Air Organization Office Reports.

Doc. RH 2/2291-Weapons Office, German Training Programs in the Soviet Union.

Doc. RH 2/2299-Air Organization Office, Various Studies and Reports.

Personal letters, data, information, and documents from Hannes Trautloft, Erich Hartmann, Adolf Galland, Johannes Steinhoff, Eduard Neumann, Wolfgang Falck, Georg-Peter Eder, Walter Krupinski, Dietrich A. Hrabak, Herbert Ihlefeld, Hermann Graf, Erich Rudorffer, Edward R. "Buddy" Haydon, Robert S. Johnson, Raymond F. Toliver, Kurt Schulze, Ursula Steinhoff Bird, Günther Rall, Hajo Herrmann, Gustav Rödel, Werner Schrör, William F. Reid, Hans-Joachim Jabs, James H. Doolittle, Walther Dahl, and Rudolf Nowotny.

Much of this was possible with the research and interviews conducted by the late Jeffrey L. Ethell, who supplied these materials in 1990. In addition, the data and contacts supplied by Kurt Schulze and Jon Guttman over the years, in conjunction with Raymond F. Toliver are also noted.

Secondary Sources

Baird, William, ed. *17th Bomb Group.* Paducah, KY: Turner Publishing, 1995.

Bekker, Cajus. *The Luftwaffe War Diaries: The German Air Force in World War II.* New York: Da Capo Press, 1994.

Cameron, Norman, and R. H. Stevens, trans. *Hitler's Table Talk, 1941–1944: His Private Conversations.* New York: Enigma Books, 2000.

Chesnoff, Richard. *Pack of Thieves: How Hitler and Europe Plundered the Jews and Committed the Greatest Theft in History.* New York: Anchor Books, 1999.

Cooney, Patrick. "Dambusters Raid on the Ruhr," *World War II* 14, no. 1 (May 1999): 42–48.

Corum, James S., and Richerd R. Muller. *The Luftwaffe's Way of War: German Air Force Doctrine, 1911–1945*. Baltimore, MD: Nautical and Aviation Pubishing, 1998.

Corum, James S. *The Luftwaffe: Creating the Operational Air War, 1918–1940*. Lawrence: University of Kansas Press, 1997.

———. *The Roots of Blitzkrieg: Hans von Seeckt and German Military Reform*. Lawrence: University of Kansas Press, 1994.

———. *Wolfram von Richthofen: Master of the German Air War*. Lawrence: University of Kansas Press, 2008.

Doolittle, James H., and Carrol V. Glines, *I Could Never be So Lucky Again*. Atglen, PA: Schiffer, 2000.

Faber, Harold, ed. *Luftwaffe: A History*. New York: Times Books, 1977.

Foreman, John, and S. E. Harvey. *The Messerschmitt Combat Diary Me.262*. UK: Air Research Publications, 1995.

Forsythe, Robert. *JV-44: The Galland Circus*. UK: Classic Publications, 1996.

Forsythe, Robert, and Jerry Scutts. *Battle Over Bavaria: The B-26 Marauder versus the German Jets, April 1945*. UK: Classic Publications, 1999.

Galland, Adolf. *The First and the Last: The German Fighter Force in World War II*. London: Methuen, 1955.

Gilbert, Martin. *The Holocaust: A History of the Jews of Europe During the Second World War*. New York: Henry Holt, 1985.

Guttman, Jon. "Air War's Greatest Aces," *World War II*, vol. 11, no. 6. (February 1997): 22–36.

Hayward, Joel S. A. *Stopped at Stalingrad: The Luftwaffe and Hitler's Defeat in the East, 1942–1943*. Lawrence, KS: University Press of Kansas, 1998.

Heaton, Colin D., and Anne-Marie Lewis. *Night Fighters: Luftwaffe and RAF Air Combat over Europe, 1939–1945*. Annapolis, MD: U.S. Naval Institute Press, 2008.

Heaton, Colin D. "Colonel Hajo Herrmann: Master of the Wild Boars: Interview with Luftwaffe Col. Hajo Herrmann." *World War II*, vol 15, no. 2 (July 2000): 30–36, 78–80.

———. "The Count: Luftwaffe Ace Walter Krupinski: Interview with Luftwaffe Ace Lt. Gen. Walter Krupinski." *Military History*, vol. 15, no. 2 (June 1998): 62–68.

———. "Erich Hartmann's Last Interview." *World War II*, vol. 17, no. 3. (September 2002): 30–42, 85.

————. *German Anti-Partisan Warfare in Europe, 1939–45*. Introduction by Russell F. Weigley. Atglen, PA: Schiffer, 2001.

————. "Interview: General Jimmy Doolittle: The Man Behind the Legend." Pt. 1. *World War II*, vol. 13, no. 3 (March 2003): 30–42.

————. "Interview: Luftwaffe Ace Günther Rall Remembers." *World War II*, vol. 9, no. 6 (March 1995): 34–40, 77–78.

————. "Jimmy Doolittle and the Emergence of American Air Power: Interview with Gen. James H. Doolittle." Pt. 2. *World War II*, vol. 18, no. 1 (May 2003): 46–52, 78.

————. "Luftwaffe Ace Adolf Galland's Last Interview: Interview with General of the Fighters Adolf Galland." *World War* II, vol. 11, no. 5 (January 1997): 46–52.

————. "Luftwaffe Eagle Johannes Steinhoff: Interview with Major General Steinhoff." *World War II*, vol. 13, no. 1 (May 1998): 28–34, 74.

————. "Luftwaffe's Father of the Night Fighters: Interview with Luftwaffe ace Col. Wolfgang Falck." *Military History*, vol. 16, no. 6. (February 2000): 42–48.

————. "Luftwaffe Wing Leader: Interview with Lt. Gen. Dietrich Hrabak." *Military History*, vol. 20, no. 6 (February 2004): 42–48.

————. "The Man Who Downed Nowotny: Interview with Col. Edward R. Haydon." *Aviation History*, vol. 13, no. 1 (September 2002): 22–28.

————.*Occupation and Insurgency: A Selective Examination of The Hague and Geneva Conventions on the Eastern Front, 1939–1945*. New York: Algora, 2008.

————. "Zemke Wolfpack Ace: Interview with Col. Robert S. Johnson." *Military History*, vol. 13, no. 3 (August 1996): 26–32.

Heiden, Konrad. *Der Fuehrer: Hitler's Rise to Power*. Translated by Ralph Manheim. Boston: Houghton Mifflin, 1944.

Held, Werner. *German Fighter Ace Walter Nowotny: An Illustrated Biography*. Atglen, PA: Schiffer, 2006.

Jablonski, Edward. *Terror from the Sky: Air War*. Vol. 1. New York: Doubleday, 1971.

Kershaw, Ian. *Hitler: 1936–1945 Nemesis*. New York: W. W. Norton, 2000.

Killen, John. *A History of the Luftwaffe*. Garden City, NY: Doubleday, 1968. Reprint.

Lipfert, Helmut, and Werner Girbig. *The War Diary of Helmut Lipfert: JG 52 on the Russian Front, 1943–1945*. Atglen, PA: Schiffer, 1993.

Linkowitz, Jerome. *Their Finest Hours: Narratives of the RAF and Luftwaffe in World War II*. Ames: Iowa State University Press, 1989.

The Luftwaffe. Editors at Time-Life Books. Alexandria, VA: Time-Life, 1982.

Macksey, Jenneth. *Kesselring: The Making of the Luftwaffe.* New York: D. McKay, 1978.

Mason, Herbert Malloy Jr. *Duel for the Sky: Fighter Planes and Fighting Pilots of World War II.* New York: Grosset and Dunlap, 1970.

———. *The Rise of the Luftwaffe: Forging the Secret German Air Weapon, 1918–1940.* New York: Dial Press, 1973.

Mark Mazower. *Inside Hitler's Greece: The Experience of Occupation, 1941–44.* New Haven, CT: Yale University Press, 1997.

Mayer, S. L., and Masami Tokoi. *Der Adler: The Official Nazi Luftwaffe Magazine.* New York: T. Y. Crowell, 1977.

Mitcham, Samuel W. Jr. *Eagles of the Third Reich: The Men Who Made the Luftwaffe.* Novato, CA: Presidio Press, 1997.

———. *Men of the Luftwaffe.* Novato, CA: Presidio Press, 1988.

Mombeek, Eric. *Luftwaffe: A Pictorial History.* UK: Crowood Press, 1997.

Murray, Williamson. *Strategy for Defeat: The Luftwaffe, 1933-1945.* Maxwell AFB, AL: Air University Press, 1983.

Price, Alfred. *German Air Force Bombers of World War I.* Garden City, NY: Doubleday, 1968.

———. *Luftwaffe: Birth, Life and Death of an Air Force.* New York: Ballantine Books, 1969.

Proctor, Raymond L. *Hitler's Luftwaffe in the Spanish Civil War.* Westport, CT: Greenwood Press, 1983.

Rigg, Bryan Mark. *Hitler's Jewish Soldiers: The Untold Story of Nazi Racial Laws and the Men of Jewish Descent in the German Military.* Lawrence, KS: University Press of Kansas, 2002.

Rüdel, Hans-Ulrich. *Stuka Pilot.* New York: Bantam, 1974.

Speer, Albert. *Inside the Third Reich.* New York: Macmillan, 1970.

Steinhoff, Johannes. *Final Hours: The Luftwaffe Plot Against Göring.* Washington, DC: Potomac Books, 2005.

Tannehill, Victor C. *First TACAF: First Tactical Air Force in World War II.* Arvada, CO: Boomerang, 1998.

Taylor, Telford. *Sword and Swastika.* New York: Simon and Schuster, 1952.

Toliver, Raymond F., and Trevor J. Constable. *The Blonde Knight of Germany.* New York: McGraw-Hill Professional, 1986.

———. *Fighter Aces of the Luftwaffe.* Atglen, PA: Schiffer, 1996.

———. *Fighter General: The Life of Adolf Galland.* Zephyr Cove, NV: AmPress, 1990.

Index